GREAT BRITISH
WINE ACCESSORIES
1550-1900

The Brothers Clarke with Other Gentlemen Taking Wine
Gawen Hamilton, 1697–1737

GREAT BRITISH WINE ACCESSORIES

1550 ~ 1900

Robin Butler

BROWN & BROWN BOOKS
www.brownandbrown.co.uk

To Carol my wife, and my best friend

Great British Wine Accessories 1550–1900

Published by:
Brown & Brown Books
Borley Mill Studio, Borley,
Sudbury, Suffolk, CO10 7AB
www.brownandbrown.co.uk

This edition © Brown & Brown 2009
Edited images © Brown & Brown 2009
Text © Robin Butler

All rights reserved. No part of this publication may be reproduced or utilised in any form or by any means, electronic or mechanical, including photocopying or by any information storage and retrieval system, or transmitted, recorded or otherwise, without permission of the publisher.

A CIP record of this book is available from the British Library

ISBN 978-0-9563498-0-4

To order this book as a gift or incentive contact Brown & Brown on 01787 881157

Designed and edited by Rupert Brown

Production by Oli Brown

Text edited by Noël Riley

Picture compilation and research by Robin Butler

Printed by Colchester Print Group, Norfolk

Contents

1	Bottles	12
2	Bin labels	26
3	Corkscrews	40
4	Tasters	66
5	Wine coolers, cellarets and cisterns	74
6	Wine funnels	110
7	Decanters and carafes	124
8	Wine jugs	152
9	Wine labels	178
10	Coasters and decanter trolleys	194
11	Glasses, goblets and cups	222
12	Miscellaneous	248
13	Fakes and problems	270
	Glossary	280
	Select Bibliography	281
	Acknowledgements	282
	Index	284

A magnificent wine goblet with a bucket bowl on a double series opaque twist stem. The magnificence is manifested in the decoration of the enamelled royal coat of arms in colour on one side, and the Prince of Wales' feathers on the reverse. The decoration was done by the brother and sister William and Mary Beilby of Newcastle-upon-Tyne and it celebrates the birth of George Augustus Frederick, Prince of Wales (who became King George IV in 1820) on 12th August 1762. There are others like this, now dispersed in museums around the world. It dates from 1762/3 and at 8¾in/22.3cm, is a very large goblet.

Foreword by Hugh Johnson

I have two favourite drinking glasses; one that I use on special evenings to sip port, a lustrous cup like a lily-flowered tulip on a baluster stem containing what looks like a tear, the other a little pale blue vase-like thing, weighing no more than a light bulb, that I use in summer for light German wine.

The first was made in England at the turn of the 18th century, in the period when my house (and much of its furniture) was built, a period of great style and self-confidence in everything English. The second was made in Syria in the first or second century after Christ in one of the factories that mass-produced glass for the growing Roman Empire.

Scores, maybe hundreds, of lips have drunk from my glasses. They have tasted wines now forgotten and heard conversations now impossible to understand. To me they represent a cultural continuity that I rejoice to continue; the enjoyment of wine and the traditions and accoutrements that surround it. I feel a fellowship with all the men and women who have toasted each other, refreshed themselves and felt the humanising glow of wine warming their hearts.

I have always collected glasses and decanters, and curious corkscrews and coasters, coolers and candlesticks: everything that belongs in the reach and sight of a man enjoying his wine. They are benevolent objects; merriment clings to them. In most cases their design is practical, often elegant, sometimes whimsical. Like any wine lover I have some marked ideas about what works best.

Many years ago I was briefly in charge of what was then André Simon's Wine & Food Society. Members used to ask head office where they could get good wine glasses, fashioned after the president's advice of thin clear glass, cupping inwards to protect the bouquet, at modest cost. I soon discovered that no one made such a thing (this was the 1960s) and set about designing one. With the help of the Marquess of Queensberry, Professor of Glass and Ceramics at the Royal College of Art, I drew up a simple egg-shaped bowl on a shortish stem. He arranged to have it mass produced by Ravenshead Crystal, in what was little better than milk bottle glass, but of remarkably fine gauge. The technical difficulty, I remember, was to arrive at a thin and even edge. Cheap glasses are finished under a sort of overhead grill that fractionally melts the rim, leaving a tell-tale ridge not very agreeable on the lips. Ravenshead managed to finish them with no inelegant bulge. We sold them at a very reasonable price as The Connoisseur Glass. I wish they were still in production.

My frustration with the wine glasses and decanters available to the general public only grew as I met more and more wine lovers – to the point where I started a company to make and market classic designs. I scoured the antiques market for ideal models that I could reproduce or adapt and brought together in one suite the glass shapes refined by tradition in the classic wine regions: Champagne, Burgundy and Bordeaux, Jerez and the Douro. I opened a shop at number 67 St James's Street in London and started selling in America and the Far East. This is when I came across an authority who had thought of all these things and studied them exhaustively: Robin Butler.

Robin's first book was published in 1986. There was nothing like it: a dealer/connoisseur's account of the evidence of how our ancestors enjoyed their wine and the beautiful and ingenious things they used to make the most of it.

There is a lot to be learned from implements (and wine glasses and decanters are certainly implements). The thing that surprised and rather shocked me, I remember, was the clear evidence that our modern manner of appreciating wine, starting with its colour (no change there) and dwelling on its nose or bouquet (there's a term that needs updating) before sipping was not the way things were done. To inhale the scent of wine you need a glass with a bowl much bigger than the quantity of wine it contains. Such things were never made. Mainly, I suppose, because thin glass was difficult to make, expensive and fragile, the bowls of glasses were invariably made small. Venetian glasses were thin, but never, for some reason, bowl-shaped. When Ravenscroft came along and reinvented glass by adding lead, drinkers still demanded one-swallow wine glasses. The deep lustre of 17th and 18th century metal is a joy to admire and handle, but it took 200 years more development to arrive at the modern wine glass

I use a decanter almost every day and a corkscrew, it seems, almost every hour. These aesthetics and the practicalities of such familiar friends are perpetually fascinating. But so are the puzzles: what exactly is the function of this little silver tap, and what on earth did anyone use this for?

Wine-drinking paraphernalia is essentially the preoccupation of the leisured classes. In Britain, over a period of 300 years or so, these confident and often pampered people were setting the course for all the exporting wine regions of the world. Claret (or 'Newe French Claret' as it was called) was launched in London in Samuel Pepys's day. Port was invented as a claret substitute when Johnny Frenchman was being unfriendly. Champagne was made possible by stronger bottle glass developed in England, and sherry was developed from the old English favourite, sack, in competition to port.

In this period of expansion and ever widening choice Britain invented the wine merchant, too. Other countries (particularly wine-producing ones) often ask why we have (or had) so many grand old merchants. There were, after all, knowledgeable specialists in almost every county town. The answer was a culture of wine that existed nowhere else.

Robin Butler's new book is a wonderful guide and compendium to the fascinating physical evidence of all this that lies around us today, still as useful (much of it) and beautiful (some of it) as ever. The objects themselves are fascinating – and increasingly valuable. The explanations and anecdotes that surround them, and sometimes the identities of their makers and their original owners, all add up to a rich and vivid chapter of our social history.

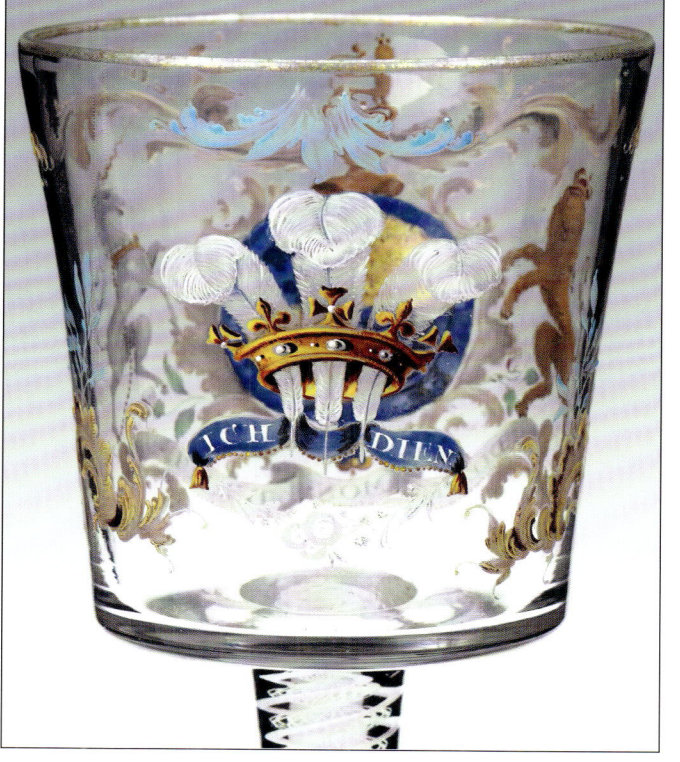

Introduction

In 1976, I began collecting objects used in the storage, serving and consumption of wine for a selling exhibition I decided to stage at my shop 18 months later in July 1978. I soon found that the subject of wine accessories made in previous centuries is a very broad one. If the tools and equipment used in the vineyard and on the premises of a vintner are taken into consideration, it becomes broader still. An overview of this latter aspect of wine accessories was undertaken in my original book published in 1986, *The Book of Wine Antiques*, but is not repeated here. In my 1978 exhibition, *The Philoenic Antiquary*, I did have examples of barrel dipsticks marked with calibrations peculiar to the wine trade, and hydrometers to measure alcohol level. I even had a 'boot and flogger'– a stool with a receptacle to hold a bottle (the boot), and a flat mallet (the flogger): a bottle was placed in the boot, and the cork driven home with the flogger. These and many other tools were used by wine merchants and those in the coopering and bottling businesses. While they may be of interest to a small number of collectors, they are of little or no concern to the man or woman who enjoys a glass of wine, and it is this last consideration which has determined their omission here.

The author with his 1978 exhibition in Devon.

Because the subject of old wine accessories is such an enormous one, indeed, much larger than most would imagine, it has been decided that this work will concentrate solely on things of interest to two groups – those with an interest in drinking wine and those who collect or have an interest in wine-related accessories. It has been further decided to restrict the coverage to pieces made in Britain before 1900. As Ireland was part of Great Britain for many years before 1900, glass and silver made there is included, as are a few objects made in remote countries for the British market.

It may be noticed that the word 'antique' appears very little and this is intentional. It is a word that has changed its meaning quite considerably and over a very long period. In the 18th century for example, antique meant Græco-Roman while in the 1950s and 1960s it referred to pieces made before 1830. This is because in 1930, a law concerning the export of antiques and works of art was passed exempting articles over 100 years old from import duty, but rather than making an exemption for things over 100 years old, the date was fixed at 1830. This dateline existed for several decades, so that 'antique' actually meant pre-1830 during that period. Many people in Britain held to that definition for a long while afterwards. Today, the word 'antique' is bandied about on television programmes and in the media generally, to an extent that has blurred the difference between something over 100 years old (many people's perception of its meaning), and a 'collectable'. 'Antique' is a word not much used in academic circles and by fewer and fewer whose business is buying and selling at the upper reaches of the antiques trade.

In *The Book of Wine Antiques* a chapter was given over to the history of wine. Since then, Hugh Johnson has written *The Story of Wine* which is a comprehensive account, and a very enjoyable read, so that chapter has been omitted, too. During the past 25 years many books have been written on specific sub-divisions of the subject of wine accessories made in previous centuries. These include books on bottles, wine labels, corkscrews (many of those) and drinking glasses. These can also be found in the bibliography. This book is not an attempt to compete with these monographs; rather, it is an illustrated overview of the whole subject. It is hoped that experts in and collectors of wine labels and corkscrews, for example, will find the occasional nugget of information which is fresh to them, or that this book will help them place their chosen subject in context. At a time when some collectors of corkscrews pay particular attention to those that were advertising material and made between World Wars I and II, giving little if any attention to all other corkscrews, then it is pertinent to give the longer perspective not only of corkscrews, but of their part in the progression of wine from the bottle in the cellar to the glass in the hand and the expectation of enjoyment through the skill of the winemaker and the later maturation of the wine.

It is a great sadness that the only museum in Britain given over to wine accessories was closed in 2002. Harveys Wine Museum was a delightful asset not only for the inhabitants of Bristol, but for the thousands of people from all over the world who visited it. The museum housed a remarkable group of collections, from superb wine labels to drinking glasses and bottles to tools of the vintner's trade. Many objects in the museum would have featured as illustrations here, but they have been dispersed all over the world. Its sale was a crass decision by a profit-driven multi-national company. The irony was that the proceeds of the sale were barely sufficient to pay the salary and bonus of a senior board member for a single year. Perhaps in the future some other organisation or company will assemble objects with a British wine connection for public display.

In recent times there has been a small number of exhibitions of wine accessories, accompanied by booklets or catalogues. The first was the loan exhibition of *Drinking Vessels, Books, Documents etc.* held at Vintners'

Hall for 10 days in June and July 1933. W.&A. Gilbey's exhibition in the summer of 1957 was entitled *The Compleat Imbiber*. My selling exhibition, *The Philoenic Antiquary*, took place in Devon in July 1978 and was followed by the superlative exhibition at the Goldsmiths' Company, entitled *The Goldsmith & the Grape* in July 1983. A vintage year for exhibitions of relevance to this subject came in 1985. First, Delomosne & Son had an exhibition entitled *The Baluster Family of Drinking Glasses* in May, followed a month or two later by *100 British Glasses* by Asprey & Co. Then there was Brian Beet and Jeanette Hayhurst's *Champagne Antiques* in November 1985 and the Duke of Buccleuch and Queensberry's *Drinking Treasures* held at Drumlanrig Castle in 1989 and the following year at his house, Bowhill. *A Celebration of Wine* at Dreweatt Neate's Auction rooms took place in November 1998. There was then quite a time lapse before Delomosne had another exhibition of *English Wine Glasses with Facet Stems* in 2005 followed by *The Seton Veitch Collection of Early English Drinking Glasses* the following year. In 2007 the Victoria & Albert Museum put on a small display entitled *The Art of Drinking* which was accompanied by an erudite book of essays by museum curatorial staff, and in 2008 Butler's Antiques and B. Silverman joined forces to show *Vintiques*. Finally, it must be mentioned that there are several wine museums around the world, but most of them are primarily given over to the history of local vine cultivation with little consideration of drinking artifacts. However, the Cooper Hewitt Museum in New York City did have an exhibition entitled *Wine: Celebration and Ceremony* in the Summer of 1985.

The general subject of antiques or, as academics prefer to call it, the decorative arts, is normally studied by material. Thus there are experts in furniture, silver, glass and so on. The joy of wine-related accessories is that the subject crosses many boundaries of conventional study, and even delves into the world of corkscrews which was never previously pigeon-holed; it is a subject on its own. It is inevitable in a work of this size, that comprehensive consideration of each aspect of such a subject cannot be given. However, within the space available, a degree of emphasis will be given to fields which have not been the subject of recent monographs over those that have.

In recent years, supermarkets and multiple-outlet wine merchants have brought inexpensive wine into an ever-increasing number of households. Wine shops run by individual vintners exercising their knowledge and taste have proved successful over many years, in some cases over generations, and we should be thankful that they are still numerous. They offer wine from around the world, and from the inexpensive – a friend of mine insists it is spelt *plonque* – to the finest and rarest wines. In short, the wine trade is flourishing. While the majority of wine drinkers may pour wine straight from the bottle into a glass and often without even the need for a corkscrew, there is a growing number who realise that decanting a wine is usually beneficial to its taste – particularly if it is red. What is not realised is that decanting can improve many white wines, too. Indeed many young wines, and most supermarket wines are young, are improved by being decanted. And once a decanter is used, then a funnel and coaster seem to be if not essential then at least desirable. The line of reasoning could be expanded...

It may be argued that decanting is pretentious, but surely if a wine is worth buying, then it is worth making the most of its flavours and of its appeal to anyone who may be sharing it. Decanting does just that. A brief anecdote may be in order here. Recently I had a three-bottle decanter (since sold), and before four friends arrived for supper (it was not a smart dinner party), I decanted three bottles of fairly inexpensive Chilean red wine of a recent vintage into it. At the table, while I was serving the casserole, I asked one of our friends if he would pour the wine, and handed him the large decanter. His reaction was one of pleasant surprise, if not amazement at its size, and although no questions were asked about what was in the decanter, it was perfectly clear that our friends felt it was something rather good. Nothing further was said about the wine, but I am sure they all thought it was finer than it was. All thanks to the decanter.

If a couple are entertaining at home and one partner has given much thought, not to mention considerable time, to preparing a meal, is it not reasonable that the other should take trouble to source complementary wines and present them with equal care and consideration?

My enjoyment of the numerous antique accessories for the wine enthusiast has always been rooted in practicality. While plain undecorated decanters have traditionally been favoured by wine *aficionados*, those with cut decoration allow refracted light to glisten through the wine, and can be equally satisfying to use. To see a dinner table well laid, with decanters in coasters or a trolley, is to set one's expectations and appetite alive for the dinner to follow.

I have only one misgiving about the use of antique wine accessories – wine glasses. It is only in recent years that a careful study has been made of the influence of wine glass shape and capacity on the nose and palate of wine. It is undeniable that drinking a good wine from an 18th century glass or goblet can add a certain something to the enjoyment, but it has nothing to do with the enhancement of bouquet and taste. In appreciating the full potential of a fine wine, modern glasses with their multiplicity of shapes and sizes are, if not essential, then at least desirable. It is not a whim that dictates that burgundy glasses are larger and more bulbous than claret glasses, nor that white wine glasses are smaller than red. While the degree to which some companies make glasses specifically for numerous wines made from different grape varieties and from different regions is questionable, the principle of having glasses of varying sizes and shapes to suit the wine is established beyond doubt.

It is worth considering here why 18th century wine glasses are so small compared with modern ones; it is not because people drank less. During much of the 18th century, wine glasses were not put on the table but were kept by servants on a side table, and later in the century, after its invention, the sideboard. During dinner, drinking wine was restricted to occasions when a toast was given. When that occurred, a footman would bring a glass fully charged to each diner, and the contents of the glass were taken in a single draught. The glass would then be taken by the footman to be re-charged for the next toast, and so on. If a different wine was used, the footman would rinse the glass in the dining room for re-use. It was because a single draught is not large that wine glasses reflected this social habit.

At the end of the dinner and after the ladies had withdrawn (to the withdrawing room), the servants were dismissed from the dining room, and gentlemen would gather to drink and indulge in conversation which would, or may have been, deemed unsuitable for mixed company – politics, business and bawdy talk. It was at this point that the serious drinking started, and larger glasses that today we call goblets were used. In winter or if it were cold and the household had one, the gentlemen would sit around a horseshoe-shaped table near the fire (see Chapter 12). Such a table, made specifically for the purpose, usually had a trolley or double coaster that would circulate wine around its inside edge, from one gentleman to the next. In one Cambridge college there is such a table with the added refinement of a mechanical embellishment which allows the double coaster to return to the right-hand end so that each drinker is served in turn, and the port is always passed to the left. For houses in which no such table existed, the dining table was used. During dinner, the table would always be covered with a white tablecloth until after the ladies left the room. The servants would then clear the table of its cloth, and any other

A group of British naval officers taking wine and punch. Mid-late 18th century

items that were no longer to be used, and bring the decanters and trolley or coasters for the gentlemen to continue their drinking; they were then dismissed from duty for the day. Again, goblets were used and the host would dispense wine, usually port, madeira or sweet sherry, from a dumb waiter. This was a piece of furniture invented at about the same time as binning, and the introduction of decanters and wine labels, in the 1730s. The dumb waiter consisted of two or three circular trays of graduated sizes, separated by turned elements which allowed the trays to rotate. The whole piece was set on a tripod base. Irish examples were sometimes fitted with built-in coasters.

In some British houses, where the host was particularly generous, it was the custom for gentlemen to remain at the table until all the decanters were emptied. It made for long absences before the gentlemen re-joined the ladies – when and if they were capable of doing so – and much was written about this unsociable habit which continental Europeans could not understand. The custom persisted well into the 20th century. For several centuries before the need for sobriety by those driving cars, and the perceived need for gentlemen to work hard at a job, there were many clubs and societies where men met and where drinking to excess was rife.

Even after World War II many clubs existed, mainly in cities, where men would go to drink champagne, hock or sherry after their day in the office, return home to change into a dinner or smoking jacket for dinner with their wives, and return to their club for the remainder of the evening to play billiards or cards and to take port and brandy. These men were often senior in the companies which they either owned or for which they worked (if work is the appropriate word). Their day was simple. They would arrive at their offices, often driven by a chauffeur, at ten in the morning, dictate a few letters and conduct meetings with clients and colleagues before going for a 'working' lunch. They would return to the office at about 4 pm to sign their letters before going to the club where they knew they would be seeing others who had done much the same. It was a cosy, hedonistic and thoroughly selfish existence. By the 1960s, such traditions were beginning to be considered unsuitable, and business was demanding much more of its captains than drinking the equivalent of two or three bottles of wine a day. The routine had died by the 1980s with the advent of the American work ethic. It is remarkable that it continued as long as it did.

The drinking habits of the English gentleman, whoever he is or might have been, did not start or end with the gentleman's club, but his habits had one very fortunate effect. It fuelled the success of the British wine merchant, enabling him to remain dominant in the world market as he continues to do today. For while individuals may not drink as they used to 50 or more years ago, there are many times more men and women who now drink wine. This has been brought about by supermarkets and wine shop chains promoting and offering a wider selection, and the opening of new and cheaper sources of wine from Australasia, Eastern Europe, and more recently South America. The wine market is buoyant and the finest wines are now bought for investment, fuelling ever higher prices for the best, with many of the most expensive wines being traded internationally. These, we are told, are often served as demonstrations of prestige in the Far East, where how much it cost would appear to be more important than how it tastes.

The way wine has been consumed, whether at home, in a restaurant, club or an aeroplane, has varied over time. In the late 20th century there was a move away from formality extending from dress codes in the office to personal greetings, and from letter writing to family eating. As affluence spread, so home-based dinner parties tended to give way to eating with friends in restaurants and gastro-pubs or, if friends were to come to your home in the evening, they may have had kitchen suppers rather than dinner in the dining room. Kitchens became larger because they had to have space for eating, not merely preparing food.

With these developments in socialising with friends came the abandonment of the more formal trappings of the dinner party. The raw ingredients of food became more widely available, television celebrity chefs told everyone how to cook more imaginatively, and an awareness of gastronomy grew at an almost frightening pace. Where our grandparents had one mustard (it had to be Colman's made from powder) today there are hundreds of different flavours, infusions, strengths and sizes.

As with food, so wine sales in Britain have escalated at a great rate. Supermarkets have aisles-full of wine from across the globe, and there are several chains of wine stores from which to buy wine. For the more discerning, there are still wine merchants who cater for individuality, where one can ask for help and advice about laying wine down for consumption in two, five, ten or even 25 years' time. The choice has never been greater and Britain leads the world in the variety it offers to its citizens.

In the USA for example, while French and Chilean wine are available, they are not seen in such profusion as they are in Britain, and American liquor store shelves are dominated by home produce. Not only that, but they seem to be fixated on the utterances and point scoring of one man, Robert Parker, and by the writing in one magazine, *The Wine Spectator*. That Mr. Parker prefers high-alcohol wine with maximum fruit extraction has meant that wineries produce wine to score well by pandering to his taste and adjusting their vinification methods to that end. In an American liquor store many if not most wines carry the points rating adjacent to the price of each wine. The influence of scoring wine with points has had a substantial effect on wine from around the world, and not one which all wine lovers welcome.

Throughout this book I have illustrated many objects which are unique or have a greater or lesser degree of rarity. I am highly conscious that the word 'rare' can be, and is, over-used in the antiques trade generally. I have encountered numerous occasions when the word has been used with scant justification by dealers when promoting their stock. It has become debased. And yet when an object exists in extremely small numbers it is justified. I have tried, and probably failed, to use synonyms where I have felt that the degree of emphasis can be achieved with an alternative, but the simple fact remains that in trying to give as complete a picture as possible within the confines of these pages, I have found a large number of objects which are rare or even unique. However, by describing something as unique I would lay myself open to someone informing me that he has, or knows of, another or others. As a general rule, I have used 'rare' when to my knowledge these objects are very seldom seen outside museums. I have restricted 'very rare' to objects of which I know less than about five exist even in museums. Unique is just that – there is only one of them. Of course, most things over 100 years old are unique because they were hand made; even pairs of objects like candlesticks which were made from castings are fractionally different from one another. But here we are verging on the pedantic.

In describing their stock most dealers are given to hyperbole; perhaps it is only natural. But when I see a table described as 'highly important and rare' and going on to extol its perceived virtues in a string of superlatives, I cringe as I suspect most readers do. Just occasionally I have used 'fine' here, and I make no apology when I feel the object deserves such an adjective. I may even have used 'important', 'magnificent' or 'seminal' but I have reserved those epithets for really special pieces which I am delighted to have found as illustrations within these pages.

Many objects illustrated in this book are made of bullion metals. British silver, silver gilt and gold is normally struck with two or more hallmarks and a maker's mark which is more correctly called a sponsor's mark. The hallmarks allow for a date, and the city where the object was tested (assayed), to be known. The date can be 'read' from the date letter which is one element of the hallmarks. Date letters change annually but before 1975, not necessarily on 1st January. Different cities where silver was hallmarked changed their date letters on different days of the year. For the sake of brevity and greater clarity, the dates given in this book refer to the first year of that change. Thus a piece with a date letter used between 29th May 1784 and 28th May 1785 will be shown as 1784.

Traditionally, the weight of all bullion metal was given in troy ounces, although in recent years metric measure has also been used. In the trade in antiques, the traditional measure has tended to be retained. There are approximately 31.1 grams in a troy ounce. A troy ounce is more than an avoirdupois ounce (about 28.35 grams) which is the unit of weight used for culinary and other purposes. Here the weight of articles made of silver and silver gilt has been given in both troy ounces (oz) and grams (g) wherever possible.

The book owes a great deal to everyone who has let me reproduce images of pieces that either they have, or that have passed through their hands and of which they have images in their archive. Indeed almost everyone I have asked has been extremely cooperative and helpful. Some have lent me valuable large-format transparencies, while others have allowed me to take photographs or provided me with high resolution images. But whether they have let me have a single image or many, I wish to express my considerable thanks to them all. There is a section of acknowledgements later, where I give particular thanks to a few for giving me valuable information or letting me have more than a handful of images.

Of course, a book like this would be nothing without the skill and imagination of the designer and publisher. It has been a real joy to work with Rupert Brown and his son, Oli, who have turned my sometimes less-than-wonderful digital images and ramblings on the page into what you see. The care and attention to detail in the layout of each page and its harmony with the page opposite has been a revelation; if only all publishers took such trouble. The enthusiasm that they have shown as I have produced each chapter in the form of a compact disc and which they have metamorphosed into a tangible book, has spurred me on to each new chapter. Enthusiasm is infectious and they have infected me with the will to produce what I was capable of and probably a great deal more than I thought was possible. To work with a small family firm who discuss each stage of the production and have a dialogue to evolve the best way to present the complexities of a book such as this, has been an education as much as it has been a pleasure. Much of what you see is attributable to their considerable skill, dedication and support. I am also greatly indebted to the editor, Noël Riley, whose combined knowledge of grammar, syntax and style married to a deep understanding of the decorative arts has resulted in a much improved text.

Were it not for my family and in particular my wife, Carol, this book could never have been written. She has never complained when I have risen at very unsociable hours to start tapping at my keyboard, and throughout the time I have been writing she has given enormous support and encouragement; I am delighted to dedicate the book to her.

Bottles

Wine bottles are among the most collected of wine-related antiques. Bottle collecting is a niche subject which encompasses those for medicine, beer, soda water, and even milk. However, early wine bottles are the pinnacle of achievement in the world of bottle collecting. First made in Britain in the 1630s, wine bottles followed a well-known pattern of development of shape which effectively culminated with a design first made in the early 19th century and which has altered little ever since.

1/1 A small collection of seven bottles found in 2007 in the cellars at Elderslie, a large Scottish house near Glasgow. Four of the bottles are marked A·S above KINGS INCH, the other three are marked KINGS INCH and 1784 around the edge of the seal with A S in the middle. A S was Archibald Speirs, son of Alexander Speirs who built Elderslie on the site of King's Inch. Some bottles still have remains of the wine inside. In this image one bottle has been partially cleaned to show the seal. Note the differing sizes, the slightly bellied bases of hand blown bottles made before 1821 and the sealing wax to cover the corks.

Chapter 1   Bottles

Bottle glass for wine was necessarily dark in colour, and while natural ingredients meant that in practice the colour was in the olive green/brown area of the spectrum the shade could vary quite substantially. It is known in collecting circles as 'black glass' because at first sight it appears almost that dark. It was necessary for bottles to be heavy and of thick construction because wine was given to secondary (malolactic) fermentation in the bottle before modern vinification methods. Assuming a bottle was properly stoppered, the build-up of gas (carbon dioxide) from the secondary fermentation could generate considerable pressure. As a consequence, bottles exploding in cellars was a common occurrence in the 17th and 18th centuries, and there are references to this phenomenon.

Before considering the design of wine bottles, thought must be given to how they were used. Before the mid-18th century, wine was drunk soon after it was landed in Britain - the sooner the better. Wine at that time was generally very poorly made, frequently adulterated with unpleasant additives, and it soon turned to vinegar, so quick consumption was necessary. By the late 1730s bottles began to be made for the long-term storage of wine and vinification practices improved. The notion of drinking wine as soon as possible after it was landed gradually became less fashionable.

In the 17th, 18th and early 19th centuries, a vintner would sell his wine by the measure or by the barrel, not by the bottle. Barrels of different sizes had names, such as firkin, kilderkin, puncheon and hogshead. The firkin was a very small barrel usually used for beer or cider and, when filled, was often part of a farm labourer's wages.

Until 1821, bottles were free blown and therefore of variable capacity, so it was important to buy the wine by the measure.

A vintner's customer, who might be a gentleman, tavern, or institution, would first have his own bottles made. Some bottles had an identifying mark of the owner seal-impressed onto a disc of glass which was fused to the side of the bottle. These bottles are known (perhaps rather confusingly to non-collectors) as sealed bottles. The vintner would then fill the bottles for the customer with the wine they had bought. It was either taken away or kept for safe keeping with the vintner. There is an often-quoted entry in the diary of Samuel Pepys for October 23rd 1663, which reads '...*to Mr. Rawlinsons and saw some of my new bottles, made with my crest upon them, filled with wine, about five or six dozen*'.

Bottle seals were sometimes impressed with initials, a crest, or device, particularly the last if it belonged to an inn-keeper. In this case the seal might be a representation of the name of the inn or tavern - King's Head, Anchor or Three Tuns for example. Other seals were variously impressed with the name of the owner, with a date, where he lived, or his occupation, or any combination of these. Particularly sought are bottles with the name and date; anything extra is regarded as a bonus. An especially valuable example might read 'Jno. Dean, Attorney, 1727' or 'Saml. Jones, St. Albans, 1763'. The earliest seals in the 17th century were usually initials flanking a coat of arms or device.

The history of British wine bottles starts with the pattern known as the 'shaft and globe' which appeared in the 1630s. It had a roughly spherical body and long neck. The earliest had necks with almost parallel sides, but tapered necks soon developed. The proportions of the neck shortened as the century progressed, until by the 1690s, it was less than the height of the body: the shaft and globe had become an 'onion'. The onion remained until about 1715 when the bottle became taller again, but the proportions changed and the new form is known among collectors as the 'bladder' shape. The bladder was almost the natural shape for a bottle to be free-blown with one deeply exhaled breath, the size depending on the capacity of the blower's lungs.

1/2 A very early shaft and globe bottle with a seal. It was made about 1660 and the seal is impressed with the crest of the original owner. The same crests were often used by many families, so it is not possible to say to whom the bottle originally belonged. The bottle has clearly been excavated or dredged and the surface chemically cleaned.

◁ 1/3 An English shaft and globe wine bottle of about 1670 and standing 8in/21·3cm high. It is very unusual in that the seal has been formed by two separate dies, one for A and the other for C, and that the lump of glass used for the seal was obviously more molten than it should have been causing it to run.

▷ 1/4 A fine and rare shaft and globe bottle with an impressive seal. It reads OX and ON either side of a crown and above a complex cypher and the date 1678. It was made for Anne & William Morrell, licensees of the Crown Tavern in Oxford from 1660–1679. William Morrell became mayor elect of Oxford in 1677, but 'being sick of gout, Sir Sampson Whyte did office for him for that time.' He died in 1679 and Anne carried on alone until 1696. The Morrells had other dated bottles for '74 and '75, and Anne Morrell dated seals for 1683, 1685 and 1688 which are known. A careful study of the cypher will reveal all the letters of W A MORRELL, although there is only one R (but 2 Ls).

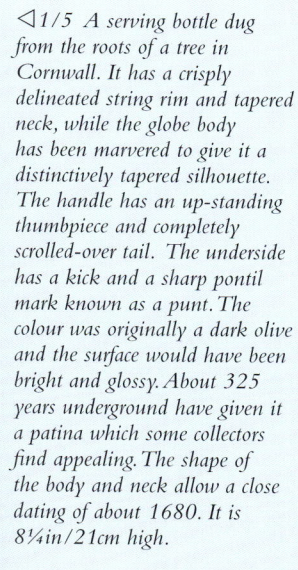

◁ 1/5 A serving bottle dug from the roots of a tree in Cornwall. It has a crisply delineated string rim and tapered neck, while the globe body has been marvered to give it a distinctively tapered silhouette. The handle has an up-standing thumbpiece and completely scrolled-over tail. The underside has a kick and a sharp pontil mark known as a punt. The colour was originally a dark olive and the surface would have been bright and glossy. About 325 years underground have given it a patina which some collectors find appealing. The shape of the body and neck allow a close dating of about 1680. It is 8¼in/21cm high.

▷ 1/6 An early 18th century serving bottle of onion form and of small (half-bottle) size. Note the thumb-piece to the handle, and the high kick to the base which can be seen through the body of the bottle. Stylistically it can be dated closely to about 1710–15. It is interesting to compare the high gloss finish of glass which has not been buried, to the excavated example (left) which was underground for over 300 years.

Chapter 1 Bottles

▷1/8 *A unique bottle dating from about 1715. It is diamond-point engraved all over with a fashionable lady and gentleman drinking a toast. Around the base of the neck is engraved* JOHN LITTLER 1739 *(the date is not visible from this angle). The remainder of the body is engraved with flowers and decorative scrolls. One might surmise that an amateur artist engraved the bottle to mark a celebration some 15–20 years after the bottle was first made.*

△1/7 *A sealed onion-shaped bottle of about 1700–1710 with a good gloss finish to the glass. The squat dumpy form is typical of the period, and the seal is attached at the shoulder. The seal is a crest of a fox statant (standing) on an heraldic wreath and beneath a baron's coronet – probably a rebus on the name of the armiger. Several families have a fox statant as their crest including, perhaps not surprisingly, those named Fox and Reynolds. In other versions of this bottle, the fox appears to be passant (with his foreleg raised), in which case the crest would be one of about 20 families, of which Pierpont is one.*

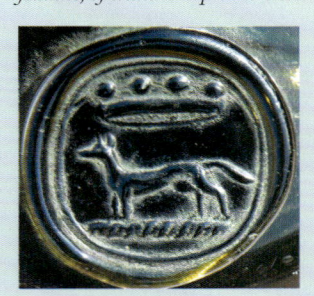

◁1/9 *This bladder shape of bottle developed from the onion and differs from it in being taller and often somewhat oval if viewed from the top. Note the bladed string rim which allowed the cork to be securely tied with string at a time when the fermentation of wine in the bottle with explosive results was commonplace. The seal, which reads* Io: COLLARD *(Io was a common shortened form of John) above the date 1725, is bright and clear and adds considerably to its collector appeal. Several John Collards are recorded as having lived in the south of England in the early 18th century.*

Around 1725, the bladder developed straighter, more upright sides. This was achieved by the bottle being 'marvered' during its making, that is, it was rolled on a flat steel surface to produce a more or less parallel-sided bottle, although it tended to be slightly wider at the base than at the shoulder. Such bottles are termed 'mallets' as their shape bears more than a passing resemblance to a stonemason's mallet. The mallet gradually became taller and developed into the cylindrical form which has persisted to the present day. However, while bottles were hand blown, the proportions were always variable, and they often developed a degree of sagging near the base (see 1/10, below).

Another aspect of the blown bottle was that it invariably had a kick. This was a deep depression on the underside of the bottle caused when the pontil rod was pushed in before removal. The extent of the kick can be quite considerable. While it reduced the volume it also increased the strength of the bottle, making it less liable to break under pressure. Modern champagne bottles have a pronounced kick for this reason.*

An interesting variation on the onion-shaped bottle had a handle, which suggests it was used at the table. Similarly, some mallet and early cylindrical bottles or those of octagonal section, had handles. All these forms are considered to be highly collectable and they are termed serving bottles.

Bottles made before the development of the mallet and cylindrical forms were stored in cellars on beds of sand. This allowed them to be kept on their sides, keeping the corks moist and thus being prevented from shrinking, which could have disastrous effects.

Mallets and cylinders caused a big change in storage techniques. From about 1730, cellars were divided into 'bins'. These were brick or stone compartments accommodating several dozen bottles, or the contents of a barrel, about three hundred bottles each. With their cylindrical shape, bottles were stored on their sides and, undisturbed, sediment would gather on the lowest side of the bottle. Gently handled, the wine could be decanted, allowing clear wine to be served. It was this development which allowed wine to mature for longer periods, and connoisseurship in wine to burgeon.

All bottles have a swelling just below the rim of the neck. Today, this serves to keep the capsule in place whether it is lead foil, plastic or, in a few instances, sealing wax. With champagne and other sparkling wines it forms a very necessary anchor for the wire cage to hold the cork in place. Before the 19th century, the shape of the swelling developed in a distinctive progression of sections, and it was used to tie the cork to the bottle.

In the world of wine, the hollow in the base of the bottle is called a 'punt'. It has the same derivation as pontil.

1/10 By the mid 1720s, the mallet form had evolved and this is a good example of the shape which bears a strong resemblance to a stonemason's mallet. Typically the mallet had sides which taper slightly outward toward the base. Like this, they are often asymmetrical being hand blown. The seal has a coat of arms and motto, but no date. The glass (also called the 'metal') is a dark olive green. The coat of arms on the seal, and the motto beneath – VIRTUTE NON SANGUINE (by virtue, not by blood) is possibly for Hayward-Curtis or Curtis-Hayward. It is 8in/20cm high. About 1725–40.

▷ *1/11 This is a transitional shape between a mallet and squat cylinder – a shape which lasted for much of the remainder of the 18th century. It is a paler shade of olive green than many, and the pronounced kick (sometimes called a punt) can be seen clearly as a cone in the base. I*H has not been identified. While the mallet shape could be stored on its side to keep the cork moist, this shape was the first capable of being binned, with bottles being stacked several high on top of one another. It is 8in/20cm high.*

Chapter 1   Bottles

△1/12 This large onion-shaped bottle probably holds about six to eight bottles and shows that it is difficult to date bottles entirely by shape. Bottles of this size and sometimes considerably larger, holding up to two or three dozen bottles are known, and the larger ones are called carboys. It is rare to see a sealed dated bottle of this size; it is 11¾in/30cm high.

△1/13 This large bottle or carboy was made in the second half of the 18th century, but because the shape was made over several decades it is impossible to date it precisely. The seal JEK is not previously recorded. It is 15in/38cm high and 11in/28cm diameter and probably holds about 7·5litres (10 bottles). Others are known with three to four times the capacity.

△1/14 Another transitional mallet or squat cylinder sealed bottle with a conical string rim collar in dark olive glass. The seal reads GLANRAUON 1749 the u having the value of a v. It is 7¼in/18.5cm high. Note the uneven shape and its having come to rest off-centre and sagging as the glass cooled.

△1/15 This is a fine octagonal bottle bearing the seal of Jnº Andrews and the date 1770. This bottle, or another just like it, has quite a history having been left in a will dated 1852 to George Francis Stuart at the Army & Navy Club. A John Andrews (1736–1809), who may have been the original owner, was a well-known historical writer who lived at Kennington, and on his death was referred to as an 'able historian, profound scholar and politician'.

△1/16 This bottle, dated 1789, is a rare magnum size being nearly 11in/28cm high. It can be noted that the shape had changed little in the previous 50 years, indeed it was to change little in the succeeding 30. The seal reads W. Oakeley 1789. It is interesting to see the lines made by the engraver when cutting the letters on the seal that made the impression. This is quite usual.

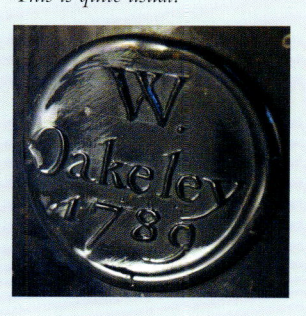

Chapter 1   Bottles

1/17 Although the date of this bottle is the same as the last one, it is an entirely new form, and bears a close resemblance to some modern champagne bottles and those made co-evally in France. Other bottles of this form are seen, although the cylinder of various proportions was more common. The seal reads G·H·H·SILLATON 1789 although Dumbrell records the first initial as C. It is 10¼in/26cm high.

1/18 A cylindrical wine bottle of about 1820. The seal has a script R beneath a ducal coronet, probably for the Duke of Rutland. Tall, narrow cylinder bottles very much along the pattern of today's Bordeaux bottles, although substantially heavier and darker, began to be made about 1760, becoming the standard pattern before the end of the century. The neck of this bottle and the fact that it is mould-blown suggest the date given. 10¾in/27·3 high.

1/19 Three squat cylinder sealed and dated bottles.
From left to right:
G·C 1796. SIR WILL STRICKLAND BAR^T around 1809, and E MOGRIDGE above 1806.
Note the lines to aid the engraver on the last bottle – a feature sometimes seen.
Bart is an abbreviation for Baronet, the lowest hereditary title in Britain.

Chapter 1 Bottles

△1/20 A unique half-size bottle with amateur decoration in gold paint depicting a two-masted ship within a laurel wreath and above the legend *Succeß to the John Blackwell*. The John Blackwell was presumably the name of the ship or her captain; if the ship, then she was possibly a privateer, privateering being a form of state-approved piracy in the 18th century.

△1/21 A narrow cylindrical sealed bottle made by Ricketts of Bristol, and impressed on the base
H. RICKETTS & CO
BRISTOL GLASS WORKS
The patent taken out by Henry Ricketts on 5th December 1821 was for a three-part mould which allowed bottles of standard capacity to be made for the first time, and which prepared the way for modern wine bottles. The mould mark at low shoulder level can be seen. The bottle seal reads WL over A. Some Ricketts bottles are marked W Leman Chard 1771 but are not that date. Leman was a brewer in Chard and the bottles probably commemorate the founding of the firm.

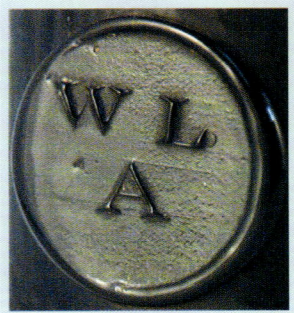

△1/22 An early 19th century bottle with a form of decoration ascribed to the Alloa glassworks in Scotland and which comprises knurled vertical applied ribs called rigarees or rigaree ribbons. Rigarees appear at about the same time as knurled mouldings on furniture. This bottle also has an applied seal for D·T above a Masonic set square and compasses. 11in/28cm high.

△1/23 A globular wine bottle of dark olive green glass with opaque white splashes and probably about magnum capacity. White-splashed glass of this type is usually called Nailsea, and some was made there (it is just south of Bristol), but it was also made elsewhere. The bottle dates from the opening years of the 19th century and is 9¼in/23·5cm high.

△1/24 A magnum bottle of shaft and globe form. It is crudely diamond-point engraved with a stippled effect. It depicts agricultural tools – a plough, harrow, sickle, spade, fork, scythe and rake beneath the legend WALTER GALBRAITH and the date 1834. This form of decoration is also traditionally held to be from Alloa in Scotland and is not particularly rare. It is 10in/25·4cm high.

1/25 An early example of a standard size and shape bottle by H. Ricketts & Co. Glassworks, Bristol and so moulded on the base. Note the impression on the shoulder of the bottle which reads IMPERIAL PATENT, a slightly earlier form than simply PATENT. The seal K beneath a crest and baron's coronet is for William Edwardes, 2nd Lord Kensington (1777–1852) or possibly his son, the 3rd Lord Kensington (1801–1872). The mould impression can be clearly seen at low shoulder level. The bottle dates from 1825–30, and represents the first standard size bottle which has been modified little since.

1/26 A pair of brown glass bottles stipple-engraved with the date, 1872, and on one, MERRY·CHRISTMAS and the other, HAPPY· NEW·YEAR Each is also engraved with a moon and stars, Prince-of-Wales feathers and a crown. In addition, one is engraved with flags, ships and a lighthouse, the other a harp, Stars and Stripes and the Union flags. They show a similarity of iconography and technique with scrimshaw.

The wine bottle manufacturing process received a major break-through when on 5th December 1821, Henry Ricketts of Bristol registered his patent for 'manufacturing Glass Bottles for Wine, Porter, Ale or Cyder'. Ricketts' glassworks produced countless bottles to a pattern which has remained the standard with few alterations. They were made in an iron mould, impressed PATENT around the neck and the join of the mould can usually be seen clearly. The name of the company is also seen impressed or raised on the underside. The advantage of Ricketts' patent was that bottle became a standard size, an advantage to both consumer and wine merchant alike.

Today, the standard bottle size is 75cl, but before relatively recent legislation, so-called standard bottle sizes varied from country to country and from district to district. Before Ricketts' invention, bottle sizes were even more variable. Early large bottles are often simply called carboys, and they could have a capacity of up to three or four dozen bottles. By the end of the 19th century, large bottles had names, but they were different in the champagne region from those in Bordeaux. Further to confuse, burgundy bottles can be given either form, but fortunately jeroboams of burgundy are not very often seen.

BOTTLE SIZES   100cl = 1Litre

Capacity	Bottle Equivalent	District	Name
37.5 cl.		All	Half-bottle
50 cl.	Some sweet wines		Jennie
75 cl		All	Bottle
150 cl.	2 bottles	All	Magnum
225 cl.	3 bottles	Bordeaux	Marie-Jeanne
300 cl.	4 bottles	Bordeaux	Double Magnum
		Champagne	Jeroboam
450 cl.	6 bottles	Bordeaux	Jeroboam
		Champagne	Rehoboam
6 Litres	8 bottles	Bordeaux	Imperial
		Champagne	Methuselah
9 litres	12 bottles	Champagne	Salmanazar
12 litres	16 bottles	Champagne	Balthazar
15 litres	20 bottles	Champagne	Nebuchadnezzar
18 litres	24 bottles	Champagne	Melchior
20 litres	28 bottles	Champagne	Solomon
27 litres	30 bottles	Champagne	Primat
30 litres	40 Bottles	Champagne	Melchizedek

Burgundy bottles are given the same names as champagne bottles but are not seen larger than methuselahs and only rarely seen at that size.

The Bordeaux imperial is often spelt in the French manner - impériale.

Bordeaux is not usually bottled in sizes larger than imperial, but larger formats are occasionally seen in the USA.

The Marie-Jeanne is rarely seen, but is also known as a tregnum, while in Scotland the same measure of port is called a tappit hen.

1/27 Since 1707, a British wine gallon is 231 cubic inches, while an imperial gallon is 277.42cu in. A wine half pint is therefore 14.4375cu in (236.48ml). It is because the United States adopted the wine gallon as their measure while Britain used the imperial gallon, that the US gallon is not the same as the UK gallon. This is an official wine half pint measure with the stamps around its top edge to signify that it has been tested for accuracy.

Postscript

Antique wine bottles have been the subject of avid collection in recent years, resulting in prices that would seem to many to have little bearing on their utility, craftsmanship or even visual appeal. Of course, this would not be the opinion of a bottle collector, but the reader can judge. There are dozens of bottle collectors' clubs in Britain, America and on mainland Europe. While their main concern is old medicine and beer bottles, early wine bottles of black glass are the most desirable, and by a considerable degree.

In mid-2008 a serving bottle of about 1680 was dug from the roots of a tree in Cornwall, and emerged intact. As a result of being buried, the surface was quite degraded; at least that is what many would say, but to others, it had acquired a desirable patination. It sold at auction for about £24,000. While many would find it hard to equate the price with, say, that of a fine mahogany wine cooler, a set of four silver coasters, or even a good motor car, the buyer felt value was added by it not having seen daylight for over 300 years, and its place of origin being known exactly. Added to that, the rarity of a bottle of that date and its having a handle which had survived undamaged (if the surface is discounted) all adds up to its being a very collectable item indeed, not to mention it being a world record price for a bottle.

The mind-set behind collectors of wine glasses, labels, or bottles are all different from one another and certainly from the rest of mankind, but they exist and they determine prices to a greater or lesser extent. They each have criteria which in their own chosen world is important to them, and this is expressed in the prices they are prepared to pay.

Bin labels

In 1861, when the Chancellor of the Exchequer, William Gladstone, reduced the tax on certain imported wines, the Single Bottle Act was also passed which allowed the sale of single bottles 'off licence'. It was the Single Bottle Act which caused the introduction of the printed paper label on wine bottles. Before this, wine could not be sold by the bottle legally and in Britain all bottles were unlabelled, although bottles with paper labels had already been in use in the USA and elsewhere for more than a decade.

Until the mid-19th century, vintners and wine merchants sold wine from the barrel and bottled it for the customer. The customer would keep those bottles in his cellar in a bin set aside for bottles from the same barrel. A label by the bin would indicate what wine was in it. They were very rarely specific, and merely read 'claret', 'sherry', or 'port' for example, in letters large enough to be read by the light of a candle, and almost always in upper case.

The earliest bin labels appear to be those made of lead with white-painted letters against the bare metal. They probably date from the years immediately following the introduction of the practice of binning in the 1730s. By the mid- to late-18th century, tin-glazed earthenware (delftware) labels appeared and a standard pattern and size developed. These had deep magenta or (less often seen) blue lettering on a white(ish) background, even to those with dark blue lettering had a very pale blue ground. Blue lettering is less common than magenta, and probably somewhat earlier in date.

PORT

BURGUNDY

Chapter 2 Bin Labels

Pottery labels were used from the late 18th century and subsequently followed the same pattern as the delftware models, that is a coat-hanger shape with squared corners, later having the upper corners rounded. These had black lettering against a more or less white ground, although very rare examples have been seen with blue lettering; an apparently unique set is known with copper lustre lettering in lower case. Almost all bin labels are about 5in/13cm wide and 3½in/9cm high, although exact measurements of individual labels may vary by as much as ¾in/2cm.

Lead-glazed labels were made in well-known factories such as Wedgwood, Coalport and Spode, many having the factory mark impressed on the back, although the impression is frequently light, and often all but illegible. In addition many labels, particularly those by Wedgwood, were made for the firm of Farrow & Jackson who made and bought-in to sell a huge variety of equipment for the wine, spirit and beer trades. This ranged from beer engines to champagne corking machines, and from corkscrews to refrigerators, which in the 1890s were made to resemble Georgian cabinets. Their impressed mark is also often seen, and sometimes in addition to the pottery mark. They had businesses both in London and Paris.

Bin labels were usually glazed and have a hole at the top so that they can be hung from a nail or hook in the wall of the cellar in, or by the bin. Some bin labels are left partially un-glazed or, in pottery terminology, in the biscuit. This was to allow a more accurate description of the bin contents to be pencilled on the unglazed portion. Thus a bin label may read 'claret' and pencilled above on the unglazed area may be 'Ch. Margaux 1874'. Some bin labels were left entirely in the biscuit, and had no factory-applied legend on them.

2/2 A very rare delftware bin number. Bin numbers are very seldom seen before the 19th century, but this must be dated about 1750, or even earlier from the style of the calligraphy and the material from which it is made. It measures 5in/12·6cm square.

▽2/3 A delftware bin label for PORT. These are among the earliest bin labels and are usually dated to the mid-18th century, but the dark blue lettering against a pale blue glaze is preferred to the more usually seen deep magenta lettering against an off-white glaze. Delftware is the British version of the tin-glazed earthenware popularised in the Dutch town of Delft.

2/4 Two delftware bin labels. The left hand label for MADEIRA is a deep magenta on a whitish background. The lettering is more than usually uneven, and the pigment has leached into the white glaze. The right hand label is unusual for a delftware label in having black lettering, also for having the number 3 in addition to HERMITAGE – a less frequently seen wine.

2/5 A bin label for sherry. This is an early example of a lead-glazed pottery label with the bin-shaped suspension hole and bold lettering reminiscent of that found on delftware labels. It was probably made in the late 18th century, but could be as late as 1860.

A seldom-seen form of bin label, considerably smaller than the standard five-inch model, is about 3–3½in/7·6–8·9cm wide but otherwise of similar appearance (see 2/15). This type was made to hang inside a cellaret or wine cooler before the wine was decanted. To this end, some cellarets and wine coolers were fitted with small hooks on which these labels would hang (see 5/39).

Bin labels are very difficult to date accurately because they were made to the same designs over a prolonged period. Labels that one might think should be dated to the early 19th century can be seen in Farrow and Jackson's catalogue of 1898. As utility objects they were not redesigned at frequent intervals, and the same design may have been used for upwards of 50 years. However, a few were made to different designs and shapes which allow a more confident and early dating to be made. While the prime need for bin labels was in the days before the bottle with a paper label, it is clear from the evidence that they were in production long afterwards.

2/6 The set of four small bin labels is of an unusual model, and apart from port these uncommon names. The cracks can be made invisible by an expert restorer, but the owner has chosen to keep them as they are. Bin labels were often cracked when taken from the nail in the cellar which in itself is not a friendly environment for pottery. The two lower labels, while not strictly for wine, are a very rare form. These are all early 19th century.

2/7 Six lead bin labels, the names of the wines being stamped out with a lettering tool (notice the similarity of the a s). The Vin de Grave is a rare name, and lead bin labels are equally rare. They are difficult to date, but were probably made in the second half of the 18th century. It is possible that these are stencils, but the softness of lead makes this unlikely as do the suspension holes.

Chapter 2 Bin Labels

Bin labels with wine names on them were intended for domestic use by the end user, but private customers were not the only people needing to know the contents of a bin. Wine merchants, and some gentlemen with large cellars, needed a different system to ascertain their holdings. This involved numbering each bin and keeping a cellar book to cross-reference every number with a wine. Such a system allowed a fuller description of each wine, and for the frequent change of bin contents.

2/8 Two 19th century bin labels of rounded coat hanger shape. The left hand one is unusual being for BROWN SHERRY or what today would be termed cream sherry. Sweet wines were very popular in early Victorian times. CHAMPAIGNE is a delightful mis-spelling sometimes seen on silver wine labels also. The brown sherry label probably predates the champaigne label by 20 years.

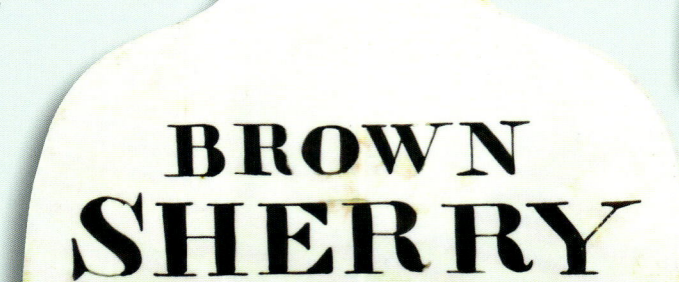

2/9 A very unusual bin label for Bronte. This bin label has very rare lettering in lustre purple/pink, suggesting a date of c1830. Marsala was first imported to Britain in 1773 by Woodhouse, and following Lord Nelson's ennoblement by the King of Naples in 1799 as Duke of Bronte, the firm re-named their marsala 'Bronte' because the great hero had ordered vast quantities for the Navy. Silver wine labels for Bronte are recorded from 1805–1847.

2/10 The left hand bin label was probably inspired by a French model with its brown lettering within a border, and its tent-like outline. It is an unusual label with an uncommon name.

2/11 The right hand label has taken a bin number blank and had CALCAVELA, a popular Portuguese white wine from the 1760s–1830s, enclosed in a very unusual scroll cartouche. Sophisticated embellishments are seldom seen in a cellar.

2/12 Four bin labels that may be from the same set. It is rare to find individual chateaux on bin labels, and just as rare to see the vintages, so these are exceptional. It was legal to sell wine by the (labelled) bottle from 1861. Note also the bin-shaped suspension holes which are usually considered an early feature but these are clearly post-1861. And was the householder not too worried which port house supplied the 1847 vintage in his cellar?

2/13 A set of four bin labels which one must presume Earle & Co of Chelmsford offered to their customers as a form of self publicity. Wine merchants' names are never usually seen on bin labels. They are of mid- to late-19th century date.

Chapter 2 Bin Labels

2/14 A bin label that was originally blank and left in the biscuit (unglazed). It has writing in pencil which reads '9 dozen Magnums of Champagne vintage 1868 from Tod [sic] Heatley 1874'. Todd Heatley were London wine merchants who in 1874 tried to off-load 3,400 cases of top-end 1865 vintage claret at Christie's when the market in Bordeaux wines crashed. The best classed growths fetched between £1·95 and £3 a dozen. Perhaps the champagne on this label was bought at the same auction.

▷ *2/15 Two bin labels for claret. The left hand one, dating from about 1830–70, is stamped WEDGWOOD on the reverse, and the upper section of it left unglazed, so that a more detailed description of the wine could be marked in pencil. The right hand label was designed to hang inside a wine cooler or cellaret and is later in date. (see 5/39 in Coolers).*

▷ *2/16 An enlarged detail showing the reverse of a bin label with the stamped maker's mark of WEDGWOOD, and the retailer's mark of FARROW & JACKSON LONDON & PARIS. Impressed or stamped marks are seldom as clear as this example.*

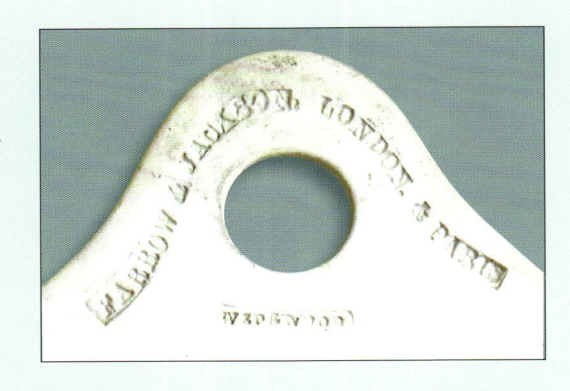

2/17 A bin label for port. It is a common variety with rounded shoulders, and of coat-hanger shape. Many labels of this model have an impressed mark of the factory in which they were made. This one was made by Copeland, and is similar to those marked Spode. The impressed marks are often poorly struck.

2/18–20 This bin label for SAUTERNE would not seem unduly rare, but close examination reveals the slight impression of SPODE above the middle E. The reverse of the label (below) which was originally the front, has had the legend VIN DAY painted over. Correctly the label should read VIN D'AY (Ay is a town in the Champagne region). The computer-enhanced image (right) clearly shows the lettering under the paint. Misspellings are very collectable.

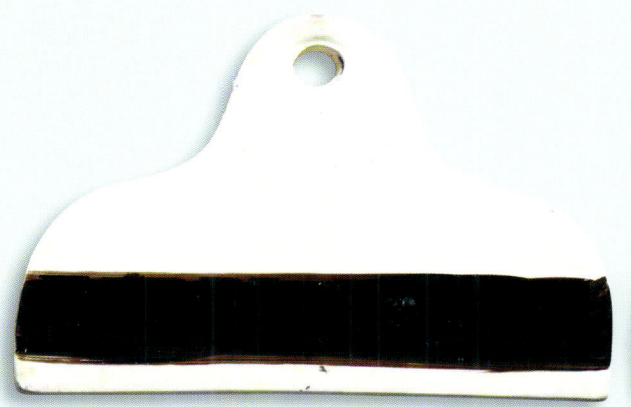

2/21 An unusual set of five labels painted on sheet tin or zinc, and an earlier one for BRANDY of coat-hanger shape. The set has suffered from having been in a damp cellar.

Chapter 2 Bin Labels

2/22 A large blank bin label almost 6in/15cm square. It is unusual to have blank labels finished with a glaze which makes it difficult to write on them.

Bin numbers appear to have been first used in the early 19th century, when they were of a similar pattern to those used for named wines. By about the mid-century, they developed into circular pottery labels of approximately 3in/7·5cm diameter, with large black numbers. Occasionally bin numbers with beaded edges are seen, and these are probably early examples. Farrow & Jackson's catalogue of 1898 offers half-size (1½in/4cm diameter) labels for 3s/15p a dozen, while the standard size bin numbers are 4s6d/22·5p a dozen. The smaller sizes are rarely seen.

In addition to the standard bin labels, there were many made in slate, lead or wood. Slate examples were professionally made and could be either painted or marked with chalk, while leaden ones were cut from sheet or cast to shape, with the lettering pierced, painted or chalked. Wooden bin labels appear to have been made by amateurs or estate carpenters and, being perishable, are rarely seen.

2/23 Four bin numbers with beaded edges. This pattern is not often seen, and they are probably an early form of circular bin number – perhaps c1850. They are 3in/7·5cm diameter.

2/24 One of a set of 20 wood bin labels from Kentwell Hall in Suffolk. It reads:
Claret
Vintage 1858
White & Co.
Chateau Lafite
The pottery bin labels from the same cellar all read Claret, Madeira, Sherry, Port or Hock – no interesting names. The wine merchants or shippers on the wood labels were variously White & Co., Devers of Yarmouth, Earle, Gardiners or Sikes. One label was for 'dinner sherry'. From the other labels it is clear that substantial amounts of wine was purchaesd in the 1850s and early '60s.

2/25 Another wooden bin label from the same set, for Hock Steinheimer 1856. The set was probably fashioned by the estate carpenter. One bin label is for a quarter pipe of 1863 port bottled in 1866 (the equivalent of 178 bottles). Another reads 'Claret, 1848 Vintage, White & Co, Bought 1866.' Clearly the owner liked mature wine.

36 Chapter 2 Bin Labels

COOKING.

◁ 2/26 Twenty from a set of bin numbers which probably went to 36. The fact that sets of numbers tend to be split among collectors, as well as some numbers being broken, results in complete sets being rare. No. 29 has probably been in a fire as the glaze is very crackled and the number has turned brown. These date from the late 19th century.

▷ 2/27 Six from a set of zinc bin labels. They are fitted with glass covers and cardboard writing surfaces which can be replaced. They exactly correspond with the labels in Farrow & Jackson's catalogue and would have been priced at 5s/(25p) per dozen in 1898.

▷ 2/28 A collection of 15 bin label hooks for driving into the wall of a cellar from which the bin labels or numbers could be suspended. Many bin labels were nailed or screwed to the wall and were broken in the process of installation or being changed.

◁ 2/28a While the wine was clearly not worth drinking, the man who commissioned this label felt it was worth having a label made for it.

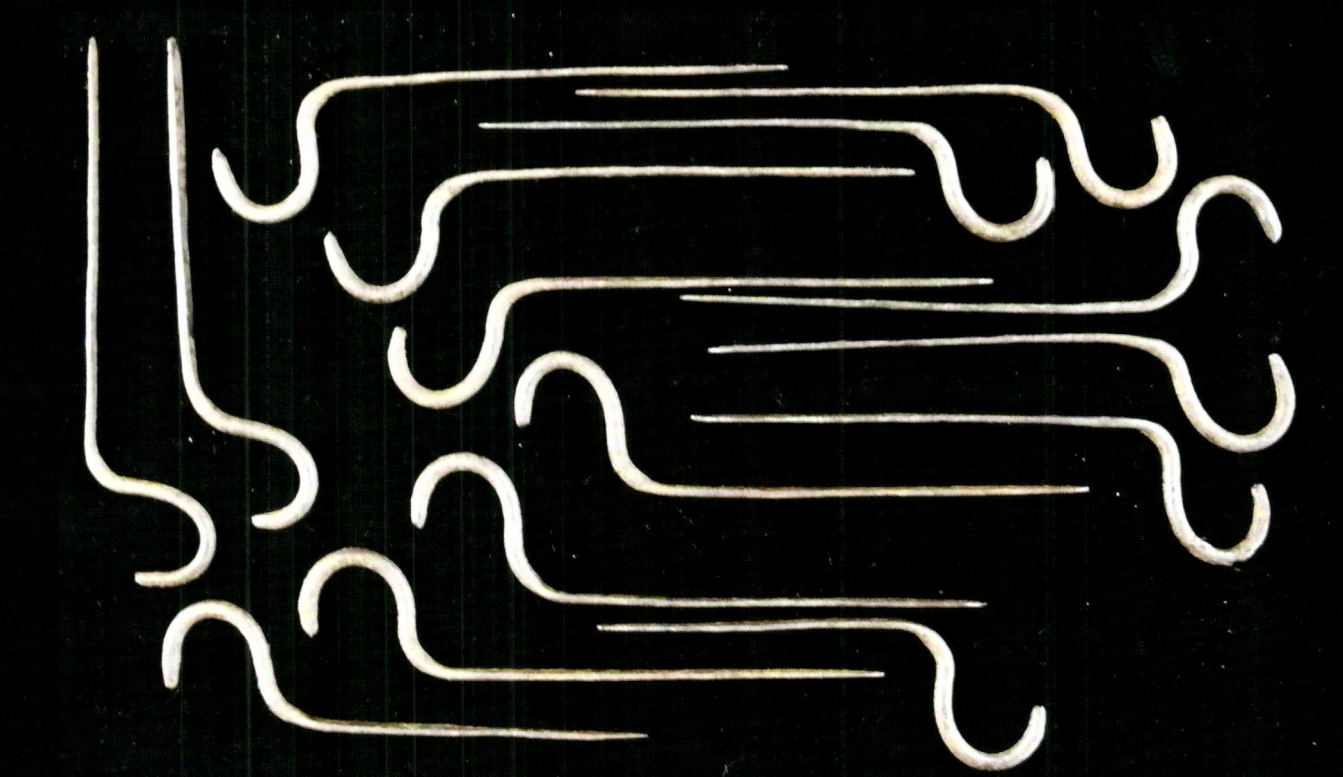

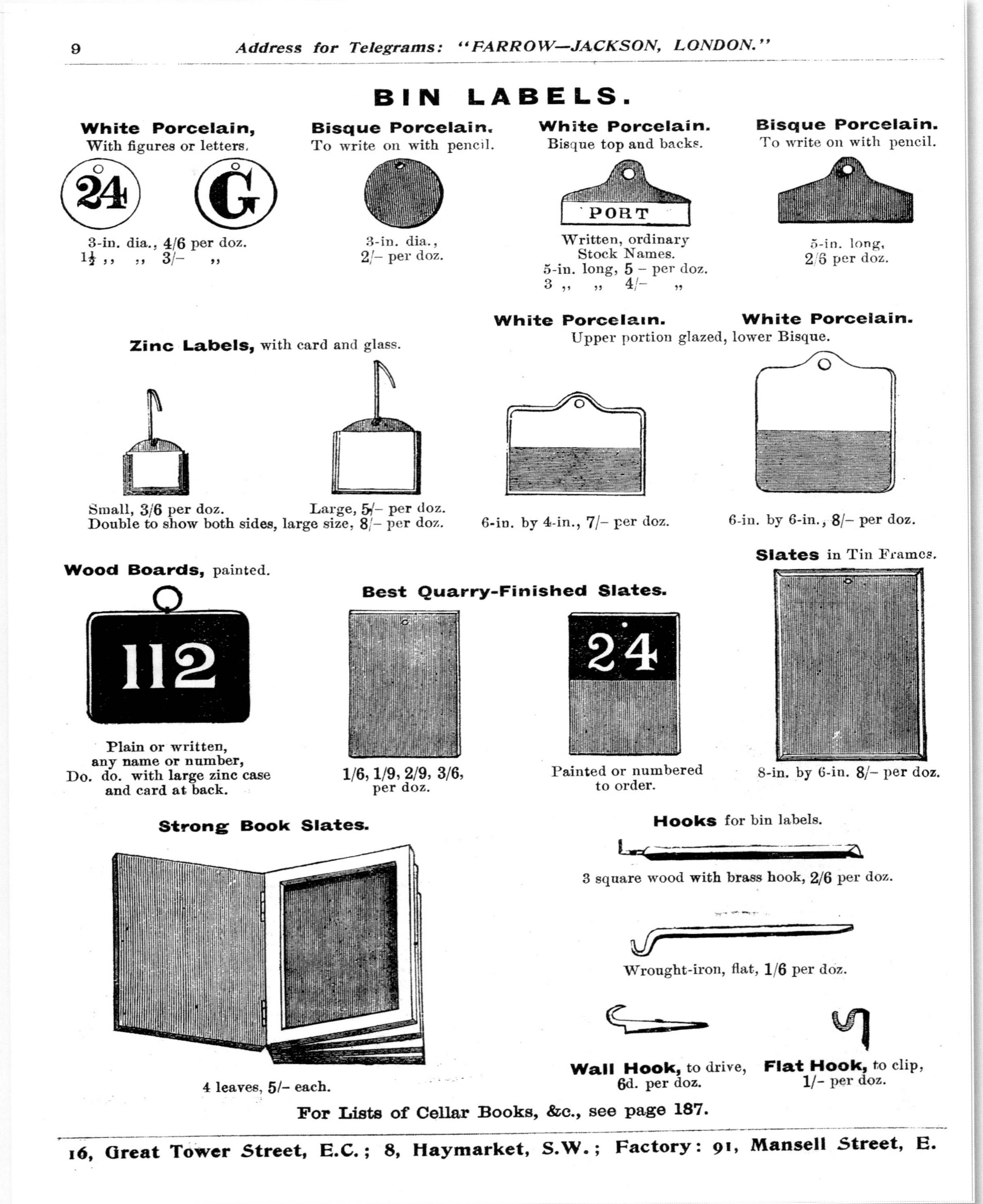

Chapter 2 Bin Labels

Address for Telegrams: "FARROW—JACKSON, LONDON."

BIN LABELS.

White Porcelain, With figures or letters.
3-in. dia., 4/6 per doz.
1½ ,, ,, 3/- ,,

Bisque Porcelain. To write on with pencil.
3-in. dia., 2/- per doz.

White Porcelain. Bisque top and backs.
Written, ordinary Stock Names.
5-in. long, 5/- per doz.
3 ,, ,, 4/- ,,

Bisque Porcelain. To write on with pencil.
5-in. long, 2/6 per doz.

Zinc Labels, with card and glass.
Small, 3/6 per doz. Large, 5/- per doz.
Double to show both sides, large size, 8/- per doz.

White Porcelain. Upper portion glazed, lower Bisque.
6-in. by 4-in., 7/- per doz.

White Porcelain.
6-in. by 6-in., 8/- per doz.

Wood Boards, painted.
Plain or written, any name or number,
Do. do. with large zinc case and card at back.

Best Quarry-Finished Slates.
1/6, 1/9, 2/9, 3/6, per doz.

Painted or numbered to order.

Slates in Tin Frames.
8-in. by 6-in. 8/- per doz.

Strong Book Slates.
4 leaves, 5/- each.

Hooks for bin labels.
3 square wood with brass hook, 2/6 per doz.

Wrought-iron, flat, 1/6 per doz.

Wall Hook, to drive, 6d. per doz. **Flat Hook,** to clip, 1/- per doz.

For Lists of Cellar Books, &c., see page 187.

16, Great Tower Street, E.C.; 8, Haymarket, S.W.; Factory: 91, Mansell Street, E.

◁ *2/29 A page from Farrow & Jackson's catalogue of 1898 showing bin labels and associated accessories with their prices and alternative sizes. Note the bin label hooks and zinc labels as well as coat-hanger shapes and the large blank label.*

▷ *2/30 Four from what clearly was a large set of slate labels. They were probably from a wine merchant's shop, but the possibility that they were made for domestic use cannot be ruled out. The style of lettering suggests very late 19th century or even early 20th century date.*

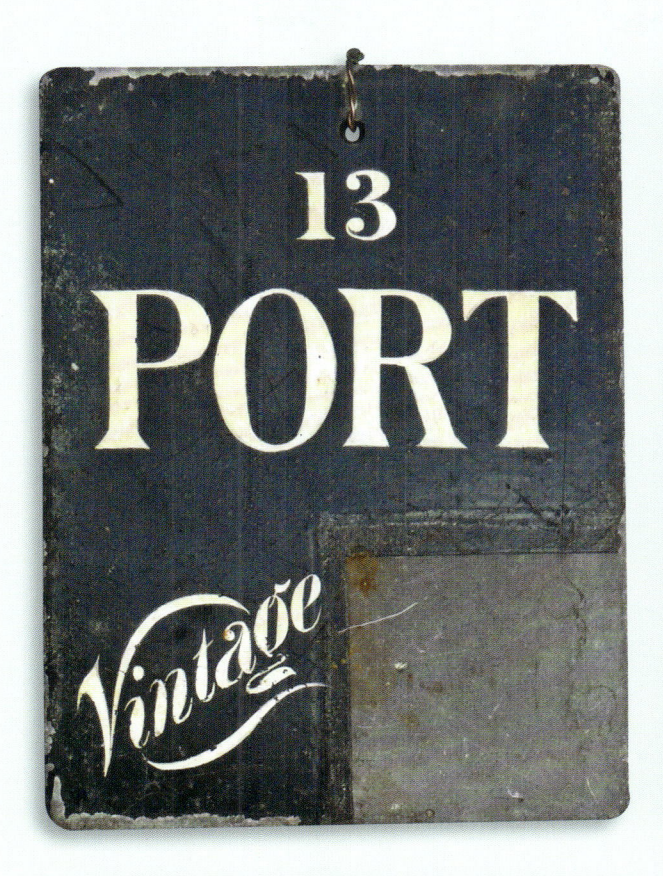

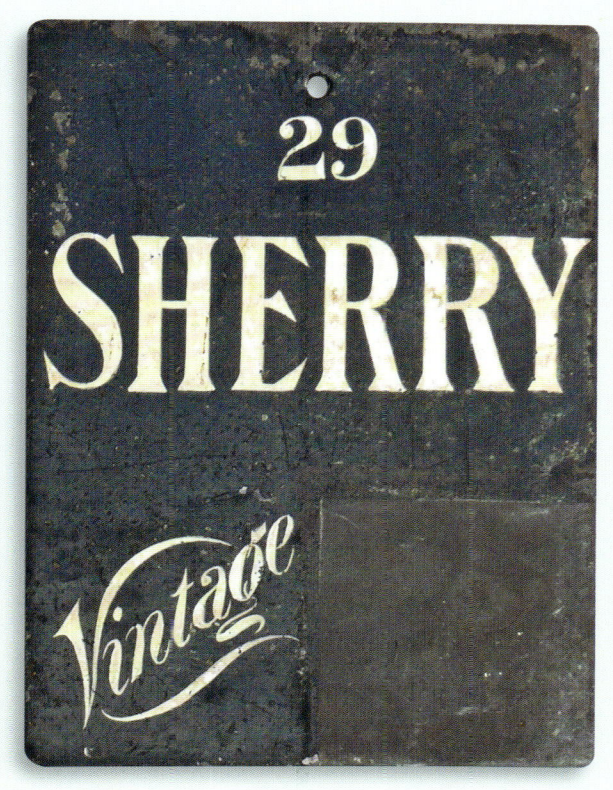

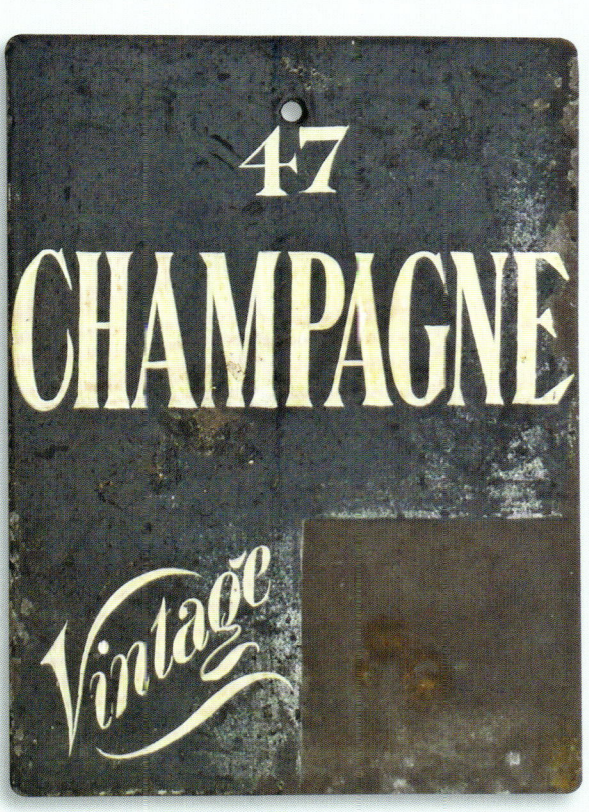

Corkscrews

Within the world of wine-related antiques, corkscrews are a subject quite unlike any other. While wine labels and funnels usually fall under the heading of silver, cellarets under furniture, and decanters under glass, corkscrews are in a category of their own. Indeed they were only considered collectables rather than antiques at least until the late 1970s, and some would say later than that.

The world has moved on, and now corkscrews are avidly sought by a veritable army of enthusiasts in many countries. There are numerous clubs and societies devoted (almost literally) to their history and collection, of which the chief is ICCA (the International Correspondence of Corkscrew Addicts). The ABCDE (the Association of British Corkscrew Devotees and Enthusiasts is another, while the CCCC (the Corkscrew Collectors' Club of Canada) is the largest worldwide organisation.

Almost the only sensible way to remove the barrier between wine in a bottle and those who want to drink it is to use a corkscrew. Making a better corkscrew has been the motive behind hundreds, if not thousands, of patents and registrations worldwide since the first one was taken out by the Reverend Samuel Henshall on 24th August 1795. Not all British patents will be mentioned here; that discussion would take a whole book and has been covered admirably elsewhere. What follows is a selection of the more innovative and collectable patents and a general picture of the corkscrew scene and its development.

3/1 *A fine miscellany of 18th and early 19th century simple and mechanical corkscrews*

Chapter 3 Corkscrews

First, it should be said that corkscrew history is a lot older than Henshall's patent, nor was he all that one would expect of a man of the cloth, but that is another story. Probably the earliest mention of a corkscrew is in the minutes of the Wardens of the Goldsmiths' Company on 19th August 1648 which records the seizure of a 'scowrer and worme' because it was substandard, that is, it was less than 92·5% pure silver. It is therefore clear that cork was first used to stopper a bottle before the 1650s. It appears that there are no surviving corkscrews made before the 1670s. This is hardly surprising as early corkscrews are small and relatively fragile.

However the Star Chamber Accounts of the Vintners' Company have an earlier mention of corks for bottles. In 1605 Edmund Tomlin, Butler to the Lords of the Star Chamber was being paid 13s4d/67p for 'bottles to bring the Lords' wine in'; 5s/20p for drinking glasses; and 2s6d/12½p for 'Corks to stop bottles'.

Before approaching the development of the corkscrew it is sensible to establish the names of its various parts. The business end is the worm or helix and it is joined to the handle by the shank which may be plain or decorated. The shank penetrates the handle if it is not made of the same material, and it is usually held at the top by a brass screw above which is a split ring called a suspension ring. Some corkscrews (Lund's London Rack for example) have a side handle, and mechanical corkscrews usually have a cage or barrel which slides over the neck of the bottle. Names are given to different types of helix as can be seen in 3/42 and 3/43. Before the end of the 19th century most corkscrews were fitted with a brush; this was to remove the debris from the pouring area once the capsule of wax had been removed.

Corkscrews were often part of travelling canteens of the 1680s and 90s together with cutlery, beakers, spice boxes, and other accessories suitable to a gentleman of taste on the move. Some have been parted from their case and its other accessories. The corkscrews in these canteens or *étuis* have silver handles with steel worms and they fold or separate into two parts to make them more compact, although by modern standards they are small when open. The most popular form of very early corkscrew did not fold but had a handle formed as a finger-ring with the worm enclosed in a screw-on sheath. A variant had a hollow handle which unscrewed to hold a nutmeg. It has been suggested that the sheath element was a pipe tamper but this is unlikely as some are seal-engraved with initials or a crest. A more logical explanation is that it was a seal for use when covering the cork with sealing wax and impressing the molten wax as a signal of ownership. It is also notable that the helixes of early corkscrews are quite short; it is not that they have lost some of the helix but that they were made that way.

3/2a A very early finger-ring corkscrew with a sheath. These were popular from about 1680–1710, and this being of brass or bronze is a rarity. The seal at the end has not been engraved, but it would have been used to seal the wax capsule of the bottle. Note the gradual taper of the helix, indicating it has not been shortened, and also the hand-made thread of the union between the sheath and the corkscrew.

▷ *3/2b A very early corkscrew type: the finger ring with sheath. It is marked with a maker's mark thus:*

The maker is not currently known but he entered his mark in 1688–9; of course it may have been made a few years later. It is in the running to be the earliest known corkscrew. This model continued to be made into the early 18th century, but probably not much after 1710.

▷ 3/4 When the component parts of this corkscrew are assembled, it is mace-shaped. The fact that it is tarnished enables the construction to be seen clearly; the sheath is made from sheet silver and seamed along its length. The sphere was made to hold a nutmeg used in the making of punch and other concocted drinks, and the grater encloses the helix in the sheath when assembled. Unmarked, it dates from around 1730, give or take 20 years.

△ 3/3 This is a very rare and early corkscrew. It has a steel helix and silver handle in the form of a flat ring surmounted by a pair of birds, and the helix is protected by a silver sheath. It commemorates a cock fight, clearly between two famous birds. The legend on one side reads:
'At Shrovftide Last
a Game there Last
by Bonny Red
and Lanthorn bred
Bonny Red in time of day
did Stovt dunn slay
Lanthorn att night
blue outt ye Light'.

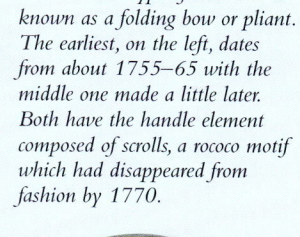

The 'y' of ye is not actually a y but thorn (pronounced th), being an ancient runic letter of the alphabet which fell into disuse in the late 17th century.
The reverse reads:
'Maintaind by Thomas Bostock Handed by TD'.
The style of the engraving and the content suggest a date somewhat before 1700, perhaps as early as 1680.

▽ 3/5 This type of corkscrew is known as a folding bow or pliant. The earliest, on the left, dates from about 1755–65 with the middle one made a little later. Both have the handle element composed of scrolls, a rococo motif which had disappeared from fashion by 1770.

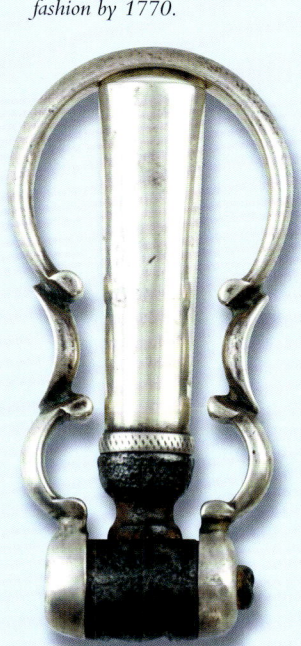

The right hand example dates from about 1800. Note the seal which was probably used for sealing the wax capsules on new bottles, although some say they are pipe tampers.

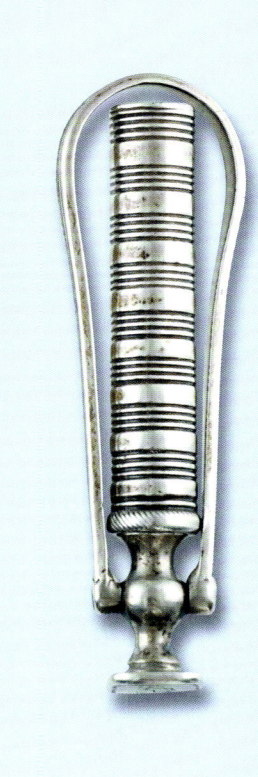

Chapter 3   Corkscrews

The idea that a wire helix can remove something tightly wedged in a cylinder was first considered by gunsmiths in the late 16th century when it was necessary to remove wadding from the barrel of a gun or pistol. In that case, the corkscrew-like double helix was attached to the end of a long wooden rod. It was not until the 17th century that wine bottles were stoppered with corks. It is said that, previously, slightly tapered wooden bungs wrapped in cloth impregnated with oil or wax were used as stoppers and projected from the bottle; they were extracted manually. It is probable that the earliest corks were similarly shaped, projected from the bottle, and were likewise removable without a corkscrew. It was the introduction of cylindrical corks driven completely into the neck of the bottle that prompted the invention of the corkscrew. The short worms of early corkscrews suggest that corks were also short. In the 18th century, corkscrews continued to be made so that they could be carried in a gentleman's pocket without damaging his coat. This was achieved by the sheath covering the helix or by the handle protecting it when folded.

Two particular corkscrew models were very popular for well over a century. One was the 'peg and worm', in which a bodkin-like piece of steel rested inside a helix

△3/6 *This is about as magnificent as corkscrews go. The sheath and handle are made of carnelian (red agate) and both are encased in gold cagework, a technique very popular in the mid-18th century for work of the highest quality. The cagework is in the rococo style with typical scrolls, flowers and cornucopiae in an asymmetrical arrangement. It dates from about 1760.*

△3/7 *An extraordinary pair of corkscrews possibly made by the same maker as the previous one. The handles and sheaths are grey striated agate (chalcedony) and are likewise embellished with gold cagework in the rococo style although with perhaps slightly less brio. The asymmetry is clearly shown – note the central decoration of the handle which is different on one side compared with the other, although they are the same when one is turned over. They are 3¾in/8·3cm long.*

with a short shank which had a hole at the end. When required for use, the bodkin was removed and inserted in the hole to form a T-shaped corkscrew (see 3/17). The other type had a sheath to cover the worm and, with a larger hole at the end of the shank, also became a T. It is likely that Henshall's application was a small development of an existing idea that had not been patented before as the wording of his patent is headed '... *a new method of constructing and improving corkscrews*'.

Few corkscrews survive from the 18th century, and many that do were made for the extraction of corks from perfume bottles These were small and the corkscrews were equally small – less than 3in/7·5cm) in any dimension – so they fall outside the scope of this book. They can, however, be seen in many corkscrew books: corkscrew *afficionados* are interested in all corkscrews and not only those used to open wine bottles. Although 18th century corkscrews are few in number, the quality of materials and workmanship far exceeds anything made in the machine age. In Britain as in France and elsewhere, the finest were wrought from gold and other luxurious materials, and fine examples are also seen in silver.

3/8 Another corkscrew almost certainly from the same workshop. Agate-handled gold-mounted corkscrews are extremely rare. They were also made in France but the proportions of French examples are different.

3/9 An amber-handled corkscrew with a silver sheath. The reeded decoration of the sheath suggests a date soon after 1800. Amber is the fossilised form of resin, and clearly this amber is less hard than some as the ribbed decoration of the barrel-shaped handle is quite abraded. Nevertheless, it is a rare collector's piece. 3½in/8·9cm long.

Chapter 3   Corkscrews

3/10 This is an Irish folding bow or harp corkscrew and the proportions and design are typically Irish. The handle is silver although not hallmarked, which is equally typical. However, it does have the maker's mark of Benjamin Slack who was a freeman of the Company of Goldsmiths of Dublin from 1766–1773. (see detail below).

3/11 Another Irish harp. This one is stamped SINGLETON on the inside of the handle (just visible). Robert Singleton is listed as a 'cutler and corkscrew maker' and several corkscrews by him are recorded. He was at Upper Blind Quay in Dublin in 1754, moved to Exchange Street in 1778 and Cork Hill from 1785–1794. The detail shows the owner's initials on the top of the handle.

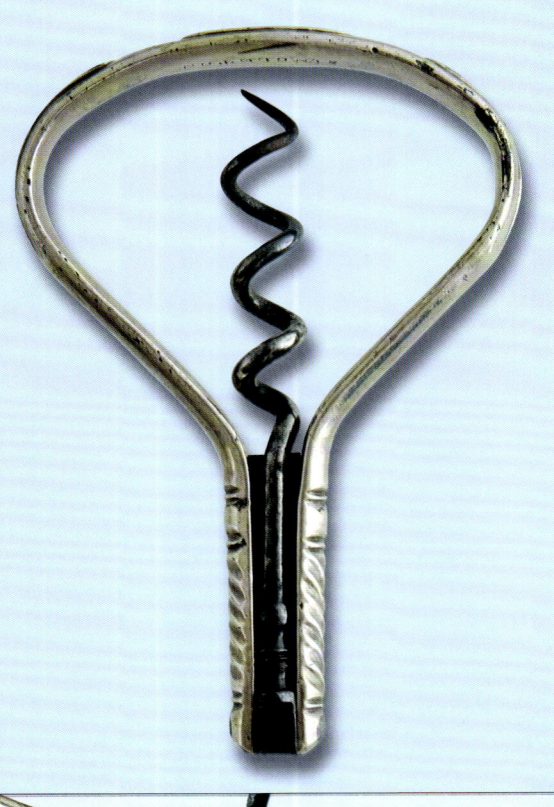

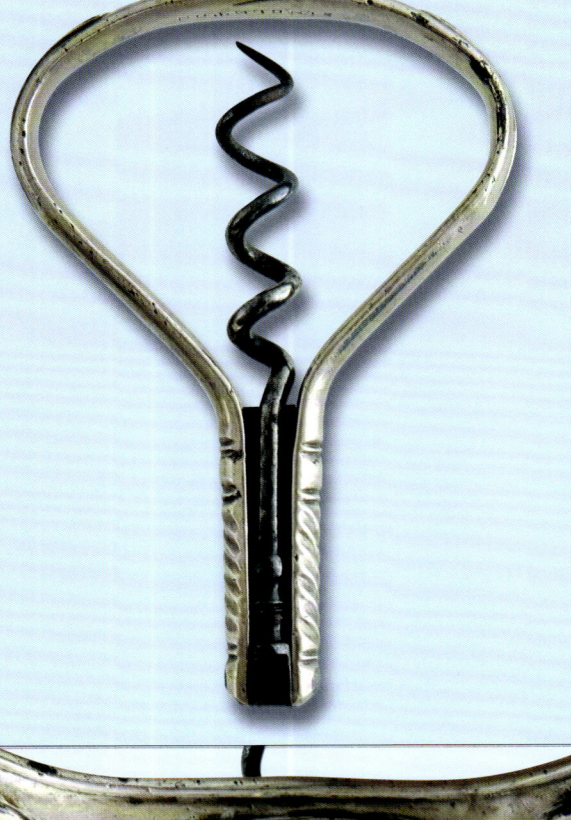

3/12 A frequently seen mechanical corkscrew is known as the Farrow & Jackson model, and in their 1898 catalogue it is simply given the title No. 1. The design is much older however, and this silver example is fully hallmarked, on the wing nut and on the frame, for 1798. The maker's mark is that of Robert Twyford of whom little is known. It looks as if the helix has been shortened to a small extent, which is something to be aware of in corkscrew collecting. In this instance the shortcoming is more than recompensed by the rarity of the model in silver and of this date. It is 6in/15·2cm long.

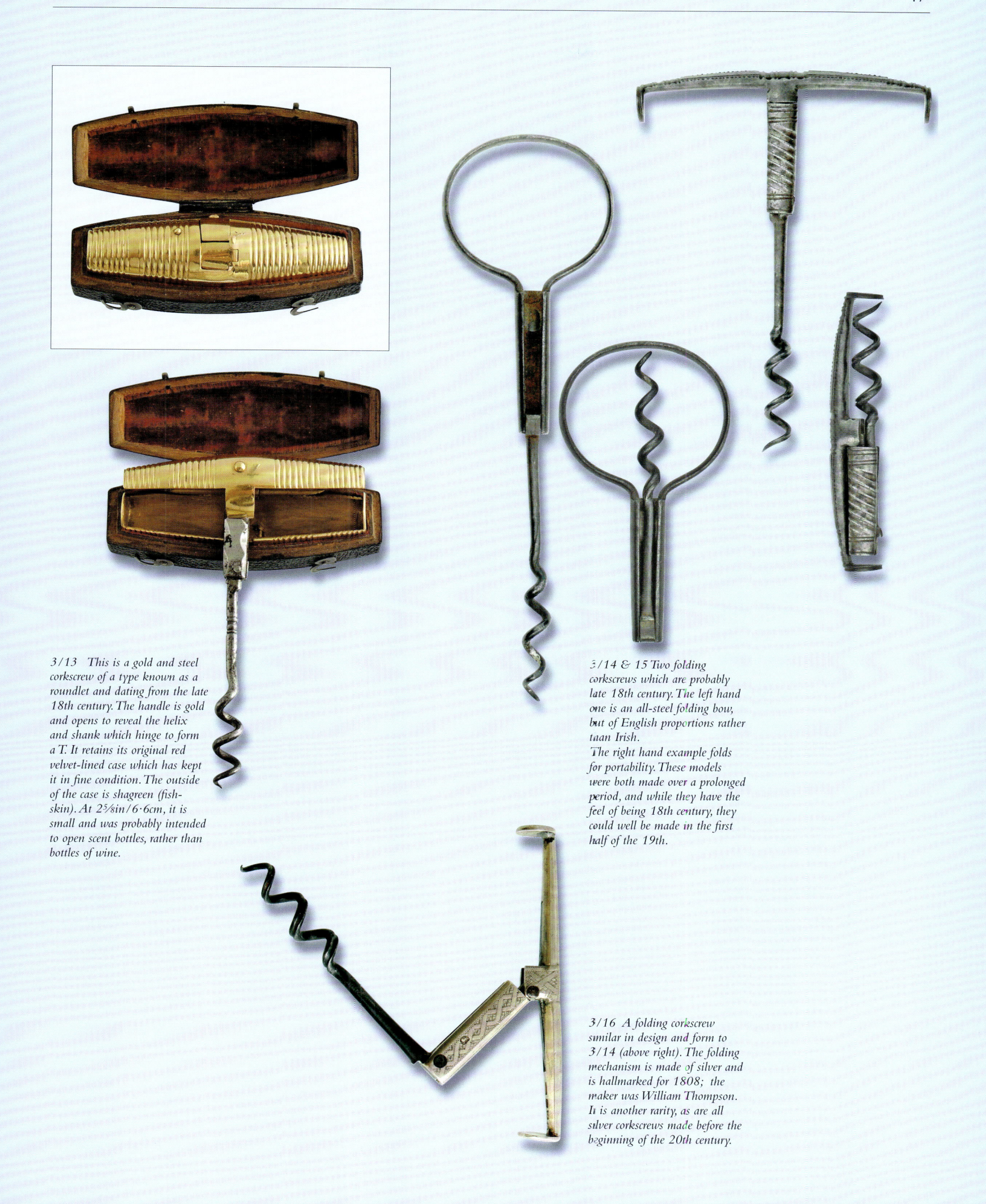

3/13 This is a gold and steel corkscrew of a type known as a roundlet and dating from the late 18th century. The handle is gold and opens to reveal the helix and shank which hinge to form a T. It retains its original red velvet-lined case which has kept it in fine condition. The outside of the case is shagreen (fish-skin). At 2⅝in/6·6cm, it is small and was probably intended to open scent bottles, rather than bottles of wine.

3/14 & 15 Two folding corkscrews which are probably late 18th century. The left hand one is an all-steel folding bow, but of English proportions rather than Irish.
The right hand example folds for portability. These models were both made over a prolonged period, and while they have the feel of being 18th century, they could well be made in the first half of the 19th.

3/16 A folding corkscrew similar in design and form to 3/14 (above right). The folding mechanism is made of silver and is hallmarked for 1808; the maker was William Thompson. It is another rarity, as are all silver corkscrews made before the beginning of the 20th century.

Chapter 3 Corkscrews

It is clear that the plain T-shaped corkscrew had been in use in the 18th century, although exactly when it was first introduced is unclear. The type is still made today. From the number of 19th century examples to be seen in junk shops, antiques markets and in the collections of enthusiasts today, it is clear that they were made in huge numbers. Many models were made to the same designs over a prolonged period as they appear in trade catalogues from as much as 100 years apart, and seem to have changed very little over that time. The same applies to peg and worm, and sheathed corkscrews.

Henshall found collaboration for realising his design with no less a figure than Matthew Boulton the man who, more than any other, revolutionised production techniques at his Soho factory on the outskirts of Birmingham, and who was a major figure in the Industrial Revolution. Boulton, unlike some of his contemporaries in Birmingham, made items of high quality, and the button on his corkscrews to Henshall's design bear the legend OBSTANDO · PROMOVES – SOHO · PATENT.

Original Boulton-made examples are rare, because Henshall's patent expired after 14 years. However, many made to his design can be found from the period 1810–1850 or even later, and these are generally termed Henshall-type corkscrews.

It is clear from his notes that Matthew Boulton had been interested in corkscrews many years previously, and they imply that mechanical corkscrews were being made in the 1760s. It is also evident that he was importing corkscrews from France and buying in England, presumably to copy or improve in his factory.

3/17 Two all-steel corkscrews intended for the pocket. The upper one has the helix enclosed in a sheath which doubles as a handle when it is inserted in the hole at the top of the shank. The lower example is known as a peg and worm. The peg slides out from the helix (worm) and engages with the hole as above.

3/18 An unusual peg and worm corkscrew made of heavily gold plated steel. The faceted decoration is an attractive feature. It is quite small, 3¼in/8·3cm, and while it may get to the contents of a wine bottle it was probably intended for scent bottles which were much smaller.

◁3/19 A Read's Coaxer. This is a very rare corkscrew made in Ireland in the late 18th century by Thomas Read who took over his father's business at 4 Parliament Street Dublin in 1776 and who died in 1803. Conventional T-shaped corkscrews were also made by him and have similar buttons. It is quite probable that Read's corkscrews, which employed the same principle as Henshall's, were produced earlier, but as he did not patent them Henshall received all the glory.

3/20 A Henshall patent corkscrew made at the Soho factory of Matthew Boulton. The button at the top of the helix is cast with the legend OBSTANDO · PROMOVES · SOHO · PATENT. The first two words, roughly translated, mean 'advancement by resistance' which may have been Henshall's family motto. It can be safely dated between 1795 and 1809 when the patent expired.

◁*3/21 Another Henshall patent corkscrew with a cast button like 3/20 but with a different handle and with a suspension ring. The handle is said to be similar to those made by Robert Jones & Son, but that firm appear not be recorded before 1841, a fact which poses a conundrum as Henshall's patent had expired long before then. While this would appear to be a later, but more rare version of the Henshall patent and in fine condition, there are many thousands of corkscrews like this which do not have the button cast with the motto. They are called Henshall-type corkscrews. The brush is to clean away debris often seen when a lead or wax capsule is removed. A brush does a better job than a damp cloth.*

◁*3/22 A very unusual Henshall-type corkscrew made in Edinburgh in 1851, probably by James Smith. It has a shagreen (fish-skin) covered handle with ivory end caps and a silver band about the middle, and a silver shank and button. Like most Henshall-type corkscrews, the button is radially grooved on its underside, unlike the original Henshalls which are not.*

◁*3/23 Another by the same maker made a year earlier (1850). The handle is clearly a less expensive one, and shows how the ribbed barrel handle spanned several decades of popularity.*

Chapter 3   Corkscrews

3/24 A cartwheel of Henshalls. Two of the three without the Henshall-type buttons originally had them, but what makes these a group is the fine quality faceting of the shanks. It is probable that these were all made in Birmingham where much good quality steel was manufactured in the 19th century. If they were not all made by the same firm, the makers must have known of each other's work.

The second British corkscrew patent was taken out by Edward Thomason in 1802. He was a prolific inventor of hearth brushes, umbrellas, whips and medals, among other things, and at the age of 21 had started the manufacture of buttons. He was the first manufacturer from Birmingham to be knighted (in 1832) in recognition of his work. His was a mechanical corkscrew with a brass or bronze barrel made at his Church Street factory. The ingenious mechanism allowed the cork to be penetrated by turning the handle clockwise and, by continuing to turn the handle in the same direction, to pull the cork from the bottle. This was achieved by the helix being at the end of two threaded screws with opposite handedness and rotating within the barrel, so that when the helix was fully driven into the cork by the first, the helix and shank, together with the attached cork were lifted by the second. It sounds complicated, but it was very easy to use.

Many Thomason and Thomason-type corkscrews survive as they were fine and robust tools. To the barrel was usually soldered a badge of lacquered brass which was die-stamped with the royal arms and the legend *'ne plus ultra'*. Thomason's apt motto can be translated as 'nothing better'. Many Thomasons are still working after a century or more.

3/25 A mechanical corkscrew by Robert Jones and Son. The design was not patented, but registered which, for a smaller fee than patenting, gave the inventor limited security for three years. It was registered as No.425 in 1840.

△ *3/26 The first mechanical corkscrew to be patented was that by Edward Thomason on 7th May 1802. This is one of the earliest versions and has Thomason's motto, NE PLUS ULTRA, on a plate at the top of the barrel, and another at the top of the helix. Note one end of the handle is brass.*

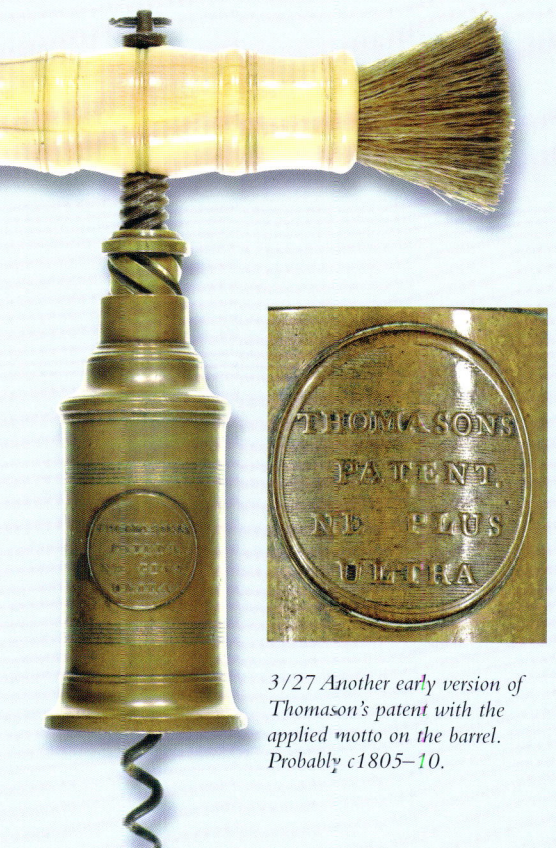

3/27 Another early version of Thomason's patent with the applied motto on the barrel. Probably c1805–10.

Chapter 3   Corkscrews

3/28 Two Thomason-type corkscrews, the left hand one with a plaque showing the royal coat of arms (but that is not significant), the right hand one made by James Heeley & Sons. They are impossible to date accurately as Thomason-type corkscrews were made continually for over a century. These appear to be about 1830–50, and in any event post 1818 when Thomason's patent expired.

3/29 Three more Thomason-type corkscrews with open barrels. The central one has PATENT beneath the coat of arms, which is not helpful as it does not say whose patent.

3/30 Two Thomason-type corkscrews with gothick window decoration cast into the bronze barrels. These are seldom seen versions and much sought.

3/31 Two more Thomason-type corkscrews with cast grape decoration on the barrels. These too, are much sought.

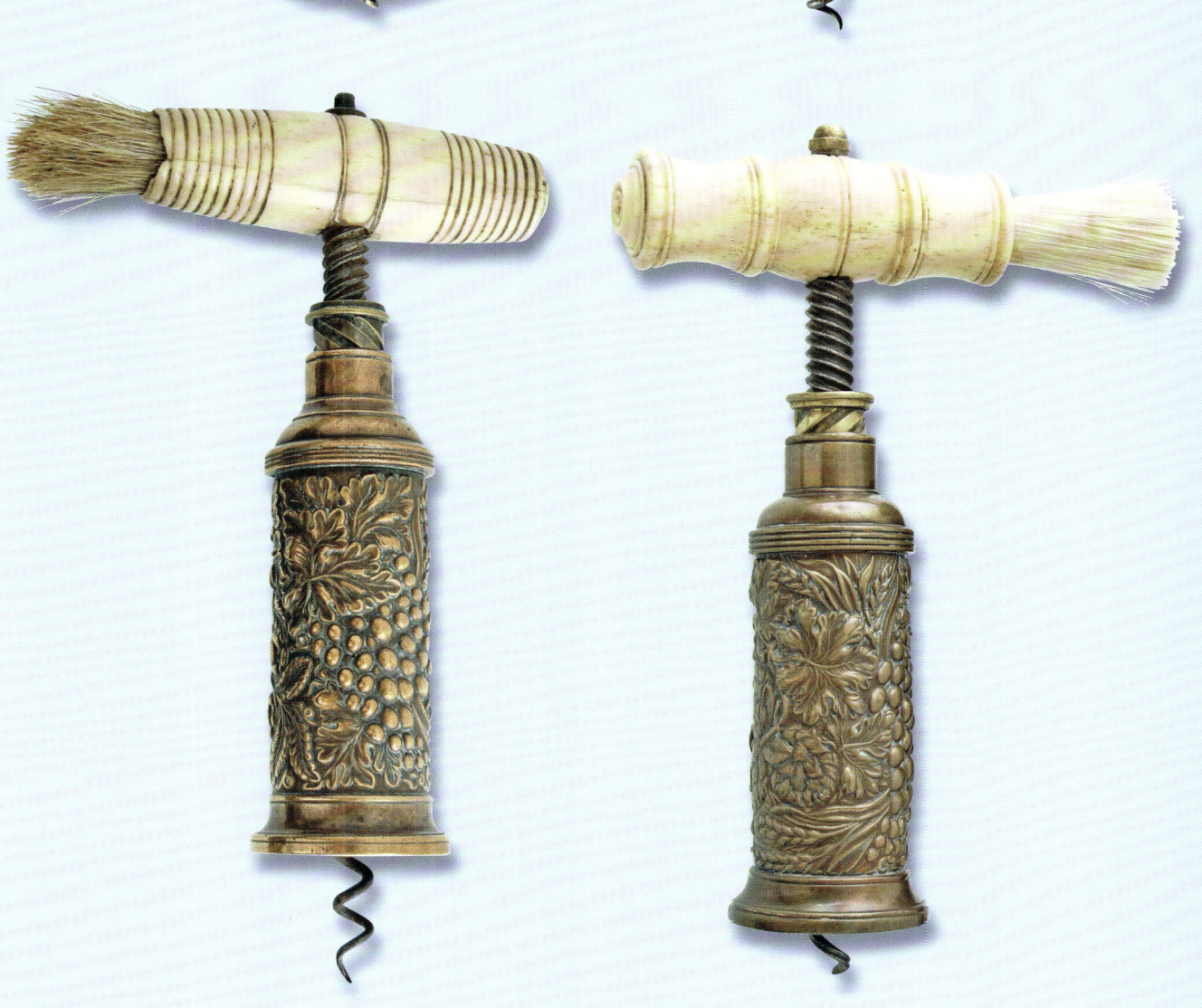

Chapter 3   Corkscrews

As Thomason's patent expired in 1816, many makers rushed to produce their versions, and these have badges vaguely similar to Thomason's but with their names – Dowler, James Heeley & Sons, Wilmot & Roberts, Barlow and several others – in Thomason's place, and with or without his motto.

Most Thomason corkscrews and their later imitators of the 19th century had bone handles, often in ignorance described as ivory, but a few have wood handles and both varieties were fitted with a brush. A few of the wooden handles are ebony, but most are of cocus wood, a rich chocolate brown timber of great density, and which takes a beautiful polish. This timber is specifically mentioned in Farrow & Jackson's catalogue of 1898. These handles are often described as mahogany or walnut, but those timbers were seldom used as corkscrew handles. Some of the most desirable of the Thomason-type corkscrews are those which have decorated barrels, either with cast gothick windows or bunches of grapes, or with japanned decoration of fruiting vines, the latter being most sought.

Very similar to Thomason's patent was the King's screw. The difference was that there was only one brass screw in the barrel; the lifting of the helix with the cork attached was achieved by rotating the side handle which engaged a rack and pinion mechanism. Just as Thomason's were made in numerous patterns, so were the King's corkscrews.

△3/32 *Two variations on the Thomason theme by Joseph Rodgers of Sheffield, the right hand one marked* THOMASON PATENT NE PLUS ULTRA *within the royal supporters. The shape of the handles begs the question of whether they were both made under the same roof.*

△3/33 *At the same time, approximately, as the Thomason corkscrew was being produced, examples of similar appearance were being made. The design was not patented or registered, but they were of fine quality and durable. They are called King's screws, and were made by all the better corkscrew makers of the time. They differ from Thomason's in having a rack and pinion mechanism on one side of the barrel to lift the cork. This one is by Dowler and has bone handles.*

3/34 A four-pillar King's screw in which the maker has demonstrated his company's ability to produce decorative turning in steel. Mid-19th century.

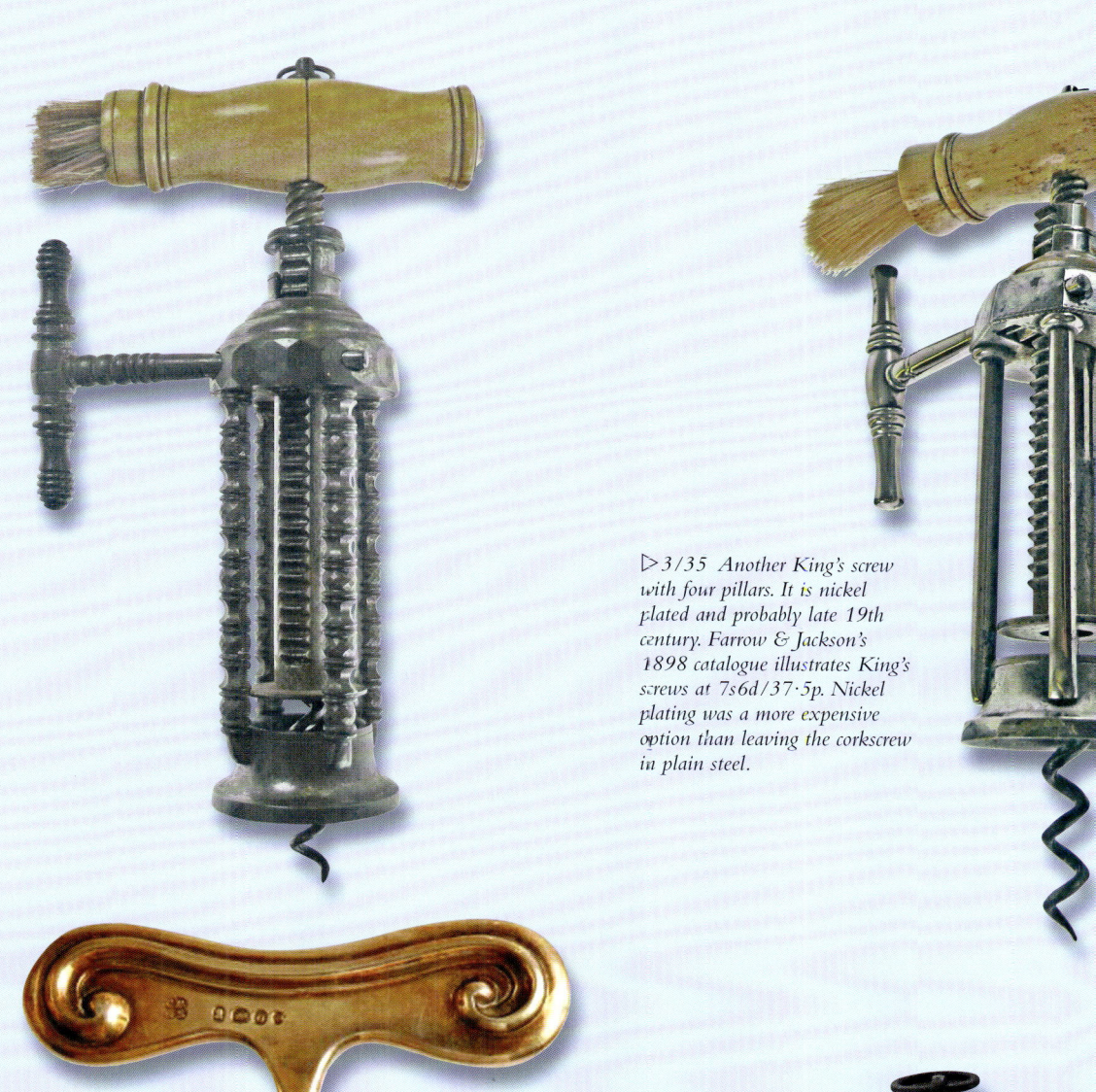

▷3/35 Another King's screw with four pillars. It is nickel plated and probably late 19th century. Farrow & Jackson's 1898 catalogue illustrates King's screws at 7s6d/37·5p. Nickel plating was a more expensive option than leaving the corkscrew in plain steel.

3/36 This is a corkscrew for the true connoisseur. The handle is silver gilt, and made by Charles Reilly & George Storer in 1829. It is a great rarity, not only for the very rare handle form and its fine condition, but because the helix is of exceptional length, which is a boon when drawing a long cork.

▷3/37 A simple T corkscrew. The shank is stamped R Jones & Son. It demonstrates that while the company was capable of producing high quality mechanical corkscrews, they also catered for the cheap end of the business. Robert Jones & Son were a very successful Birmingham firm, and although this corkscrew is very simple, it is nevertheless good quality. The handle is made of cocus wood.

Chapter 3   Corkscrews

The next corkscrew patent taken out in England was that by Thomas Lund in 1838. He was a prodigious maker, but his first patent was really an adaptation of Thomason's. It was a lighter corkscrew altogether, the barrel being replaced with a pair of pillars, and the mechanism was all steel, unlike the brass or bronze elements of Thomason's. The principal difference was that Lund's patent had three or sometimes four leaf springs which engaged with the neck of the bottle, and as the handle was turned, so the springs tightened their grip on the bottle. A simpler version by Lund, also called the London Rack, was essentially the same as his patented corkscrew without the gripping springs. While the patented spring version is quite a rarity, the unsprung versions are often seen.

Henry Shrapnel, a military gentleman, is best known for his invention of the eponymous shell which burst and scattered shot or other small metallic fragments. However in 1839 he also invented a corkscrew that has similarities with Thomason's, but with the cork fixed by spikes. Its novel feature was a pair of leather tabs which hung down over the neck of the bottle and a handle which folded to double its mechanical advantage. The finest and most famous example of Shrapnel's patent was made in silver gilt by Charles Reily & George Storer in 1840, and presented by Shrapnel to Prince Albert. The tabs are embroidered with gold braid on a red ground, and it is suitably inscribed.

It was another 16 years until Britain saw the next corkscrew invention based on an entirely novel principle. In 1855 William Lund (Thomas's son) and William Hipkins, his foreman, took out patents for two new designs. One was the lever, and the other has become known as a roundlet. Hipkins' inferior status is reflected by his name being omitted from the plaques and stampings which give Lund's name alone.

The London Lever was a very successful corkscrew because it was cheap and very functional. It consisted of two parts: the first was a helix with a small handle through which a hole was cast. The second resembled a pair of pliers, only the jaws of the pliers pivoted away from each other. One side of the jaws had a ring to fit over the neck of a bottle and the other had a hook to engage with the hole in the handle. The first part was manually driven into the cork, the lever was placed with the hook in the hole and the ring over the neck of the bottle. By squeezing the handles, the cork was withdrawn. Lund's London Lever corkscrews were being sold by Farrow & Jackson in 1898 for 2s6d/12½p, considerably less than many other models.

3/38 Two examples of Thomas Lund's patent of 1838. Both work on the same principle as the King's screw, but are fitted with springs which, when twisted, grip the bottle firmly. The right hand one is stamped LUND'S LONDON RACK at the top of the frame. London racks are often seen, but seldom with the springs so these are quite rare.

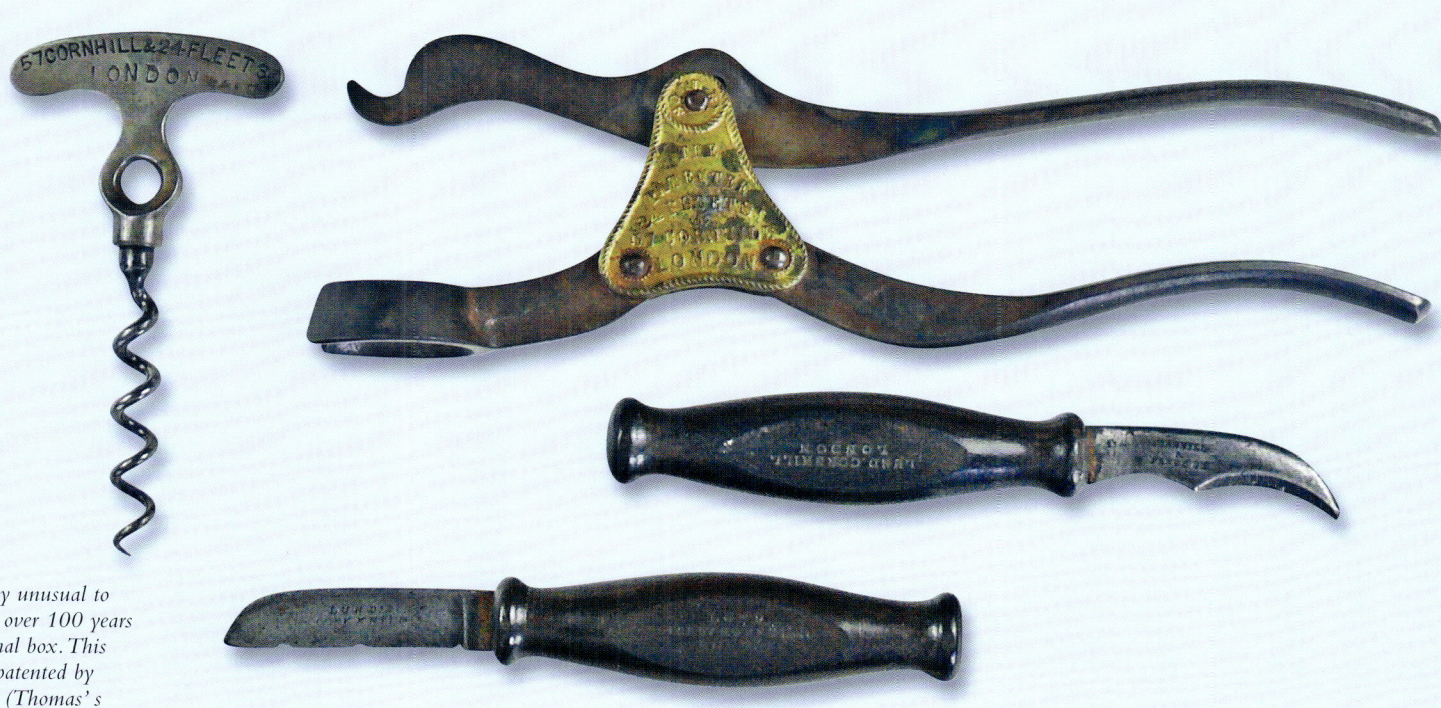

3/39 It is very unusual to see a corkscrew over 100 years old in its original box. This corkscrew was patented by William Lund (Thomas's son) in 1855. It is called the London Lever, and has two parts. This one has additional knives, one marked 'cork knife' the other 'Epernay and Hock knife'. Lund's stamps are liberally used on all parts, and it is all contained in a morocco-covered mahogany case.

Chapter 3 Corkscrews

The 'roundlet' corkscrew was similarly successful. The metal handle, in the form of a long and narrow barrel, was hollow and unscrewed in two parts at the middle. Inside was the helix which could slide out and pivot to be at right angles for use. The roundlet was the perfect corkscrew to carry in a pocket as its rounded profile had no sharp edges. Like the lever, it proved to have a long life and was made into the 20th century. Most are made of german silver, a pale metal with no silver content, but hallmarked silver examples are also seen. They were made in two sizes, the large one being quite rare.

▷3/40 One of the most durable of designs was, and probably still is, the roundlet. Originating in the late 18th century, the roundlet became very popular in the late 19th when thousands were made. Most were made in a pale base metal alloy and, at about 3–3½in/7·6–8·9cm long, are quite small. Nevertheless they were efficient and could be pocketed easily. Silver ones are relatively uncommon as are the larger versions, 4½in/11·5cm. This example is both large and silver, made in London in 1892 by Frederick & Louis Marx.

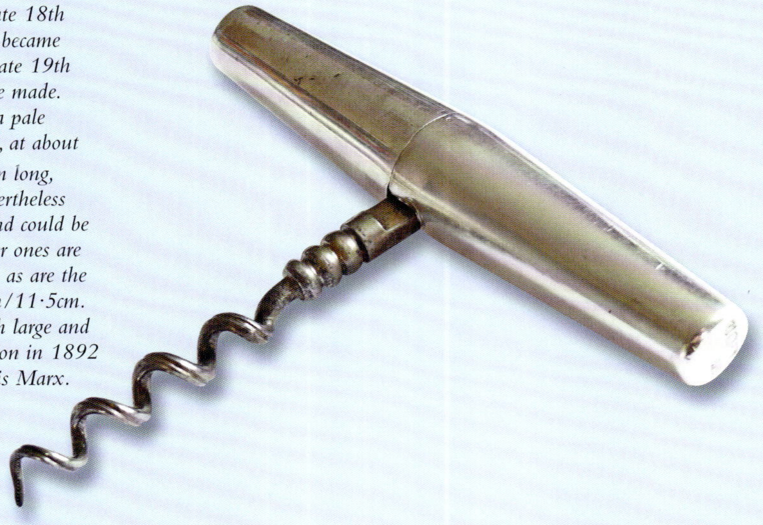

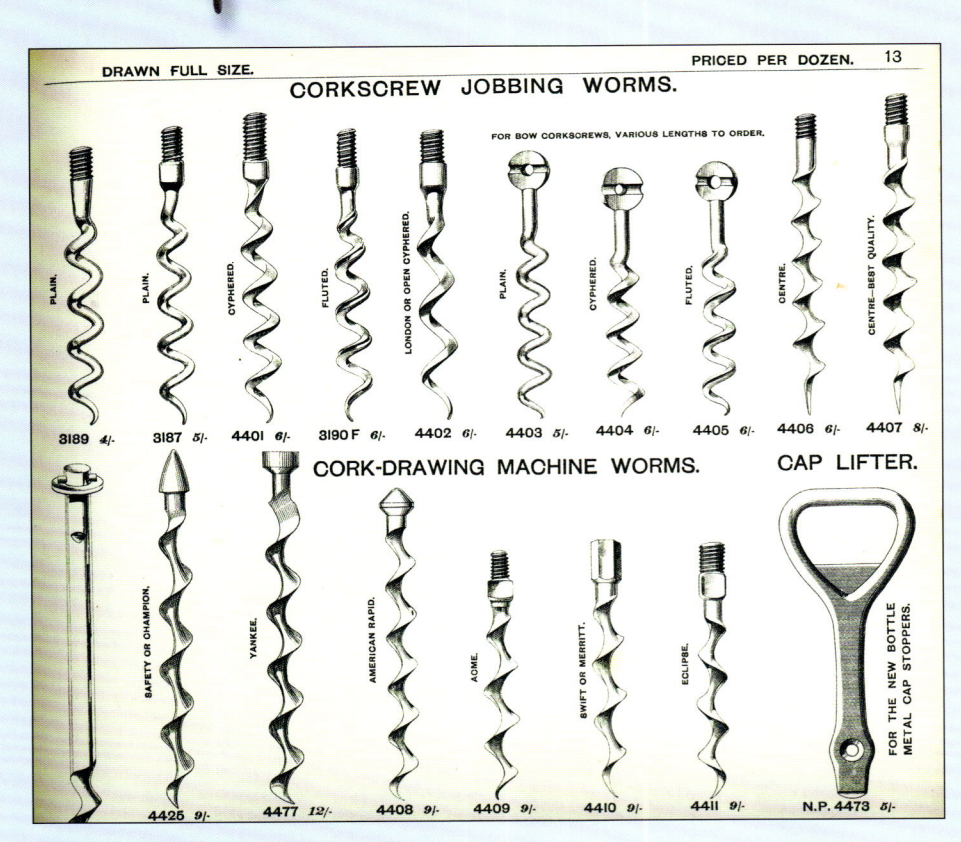

△3/41 A gold roundlet, actually made in Germany for the English market and engraved with an English heraldic crest. The mechanism of the roundlet is clearly shown as the worm is pulled from the cover and hinged to form the customary T-shape.

△3/42 Part of a page from James Heeley's catalogue showing different types of helix or worm.

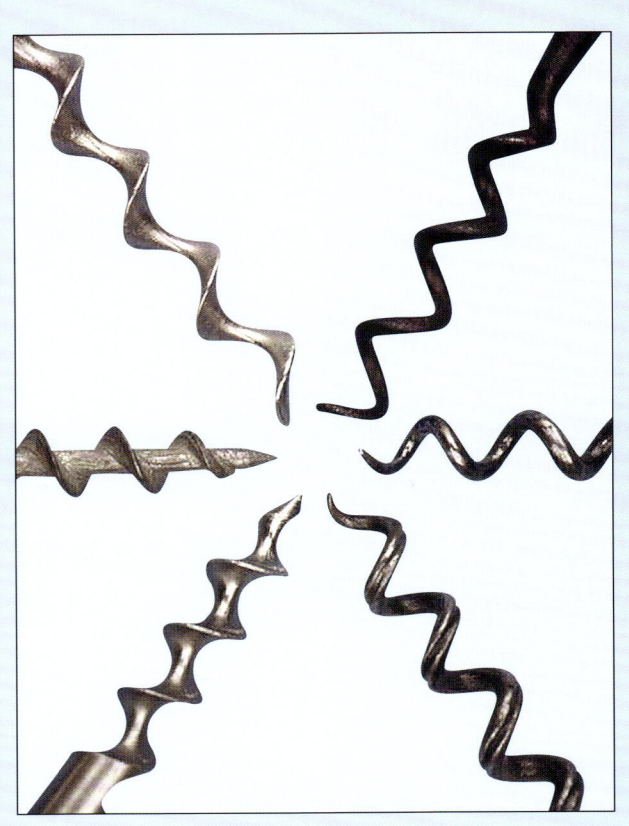

△3/43 Six examples of helix, from top right, clockwise: cyphered, plain, fluted, centred, auger and American rapid.

Within 18 months of Lund's patent, Alfred Newton patented another design, but it appears that he did not make any examples as none with his name stamped or engraved are recorded as having survived. In fact he was a patent agent handling many inventions. His design, like so many, was an ingenious one, and unlike any previous mechanism. It depended on two factors. First, the helix had a long pitch, that is it resembled a helix which had been pulled to lengthen it. Second, inside the handle was a ratchet that allowed the helix to rotate in one direction only. The ratchet could be disengaged by shifting a small button. The corkscrew worked by pushing the worm into the cork, rather than turning the handle. The long pitch and the ratchet allowed the worm to rotate. By pressing the button the worm was prevented from exiting when the corkscrew was pulled; instead the cork was withdrawn from the bottle.

Newton did not pay the stamp duty on his patent, so it lapsed after three years. It is interesting that Charles Hull made corkscrews very much on the same principle as Newton's, so much so that they look almost identical. The main difference in Hull's was that the button was nearly half-way down the shank; his alternative version had a push/pull button at one end of the handle. Hull called his corkscrew the Presto. Examples are well made and much sought. Hull's other corkscrew, the Royal Club, is among the most highly sought in collector circles. The patent for it was taken out in 1864. It has a cage to fit over the bottle neck and the worm is driven into the cork, but the extraction is achieved by a single lever.

3/44 Although this corkscrew is fitted with a gilt brass plaque at one end of the handle which states CHAS HULL'S PATENT – PRESTO CORKSCREW, the patent was never registered. Note the long pitch of the helix which is pushed into the cork rather than being twisted. The button at the end of the handle locks the mechanism for extraction. The Presto was a copy of William van Gieson's 1867 American patent.

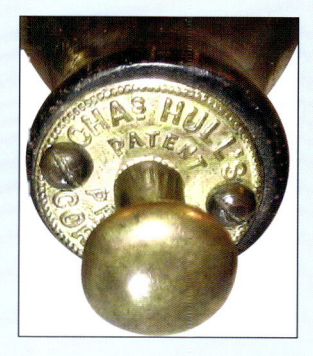

3/45 A card advertising the Presto corkscrew which reads:
  The old & tiresome process of drawing Corks by the ordinary Corkscrew is entirely obviated in the Construction and novel action of the 'Presto Corkscrew.' Its superiority will at once be seen and its use understood by the following instructions, viz: Pull the screw A out to its full extent and then insert the point of the worm into the Centre of the Cork, and by a slight pressure (without turning the hand) it will immediately penetrate the Cork, this being effected, then proceed to draw it. To remove the Cork from the worm raise the Button B and slightly pull the Cork, which will instantly be released.

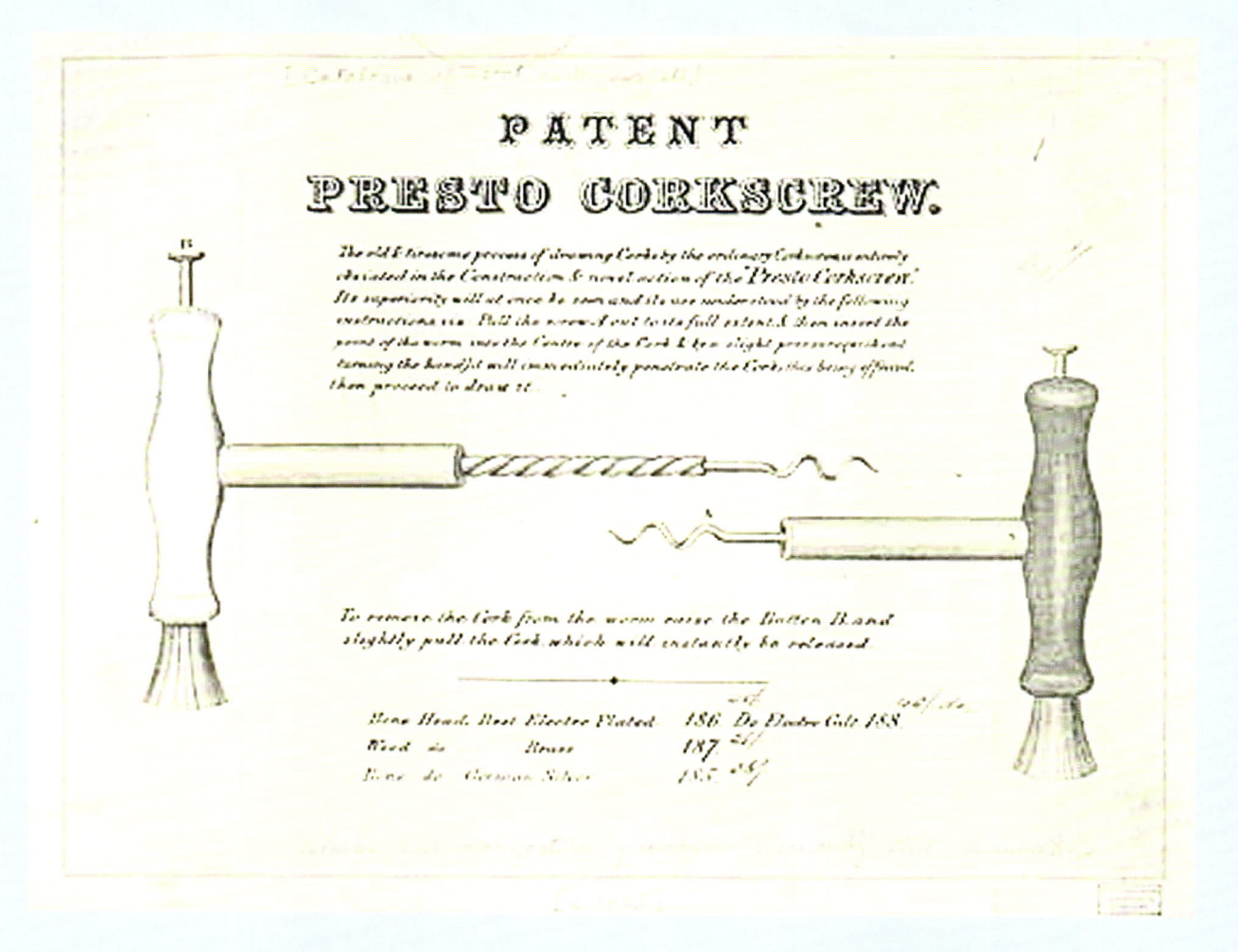

Chapter 3   Corkscrews

3/46 Charles Hull patented the Royal Club corkscrew on 26th February 1864. It works on the principle of a lever running on rollers. It is not a common corkscrew and much sought by collectors.

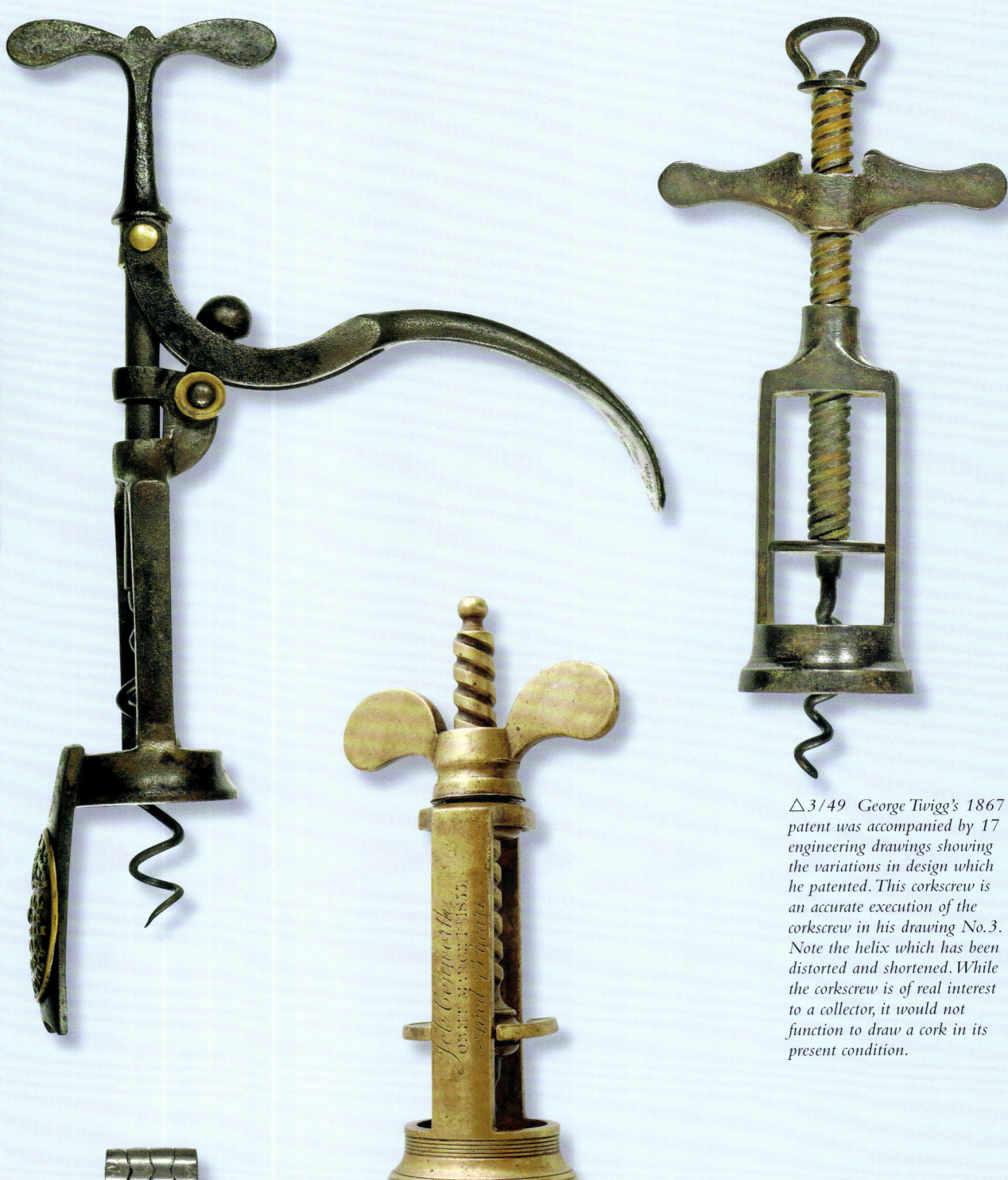

▷ *3/47 'Folding bows' are not uncommon being cheap, portable and functional. This example has two tools, the corkscrew and the button hook; some have up to nine tools.*

△ *3/48 A rare version of the Farrow & Jackson corkscrew which is engraved along one side –*

Job Conworth
OBIT MARCH 1ST 1855
aged 73 years.

Job Conworth's father had the same name, as did his son, and they came from East Retford in Nottinghamshire. Finding a corkscrew with such an inscription is very unusual. This model is often seen.

△ *3/49 George Twigg's 1867 patent was accompanied by 17 engineering drawings showing the variations in design which he patented. This corkscrew is an accurate execution of the corkscrew in his drawing No.3. Note the helix which has been distorted and shortened. While the corkscrew is of real interest to a collector, it would not function to draw a cork in its present condition.*

3/50 Two corkscrews patented by George Twigg in 1867. Note the fly nut below the handle on each. This can engage with the frame and cause the rotation of the handle to lift the cork. The nut is sometimes called a crab clutch. The idea behind this mechanism was used by other makers late in the 19th century (eg the Victor).

3/51 By the end of the 19th century, manufacturers were giving their newly designed corkscrews names, and Stephen Plant called his the Wulfrana being the Old Saxon name for Wolverhampton where Plant had his factory. The patent was registered on 27th March 1884. The copper wash version of this sold for 3s6d/17·5p, but this nickel plated version was 4s/20p.

▷ *3/52 Wilson's 1877 patent corkscrew with double helix. One helix was made shorter than the other.*

Chapter 3   Corkscrews

Two other corkscrew patents are worthy of mention here for their success, and each was made by the same company. First came the 1884 patent of Marshall Wier. Quite unlike anything previously seen, Wier's patent used the principle of 'lazy tongs': at one end, the helix was held by a lattice of short steel bars hinged together, while at the other was a loop handle. When driven into the cork, the mechanism was compressed, but as the handle was pulled the lattice expanded, so that while the helix was travelling a short distance, the handle travelled much further. The effect was to ease the amount of pull needed to extract the cork. It was so successful that it was still being offered in the 1939 catalogue of the Army & Navy Stores. It usually has a copper wash finish, but at twice the price it was available nickel plated.

Neville Heeley of James Heeley & Sons, invented and patented his very popular corkscrew in 1888. It has a pair of levers, one on either side, to lift the cork. Like the Wier patent, it was also offered with two finishes and continued to be made well into the 20th century.

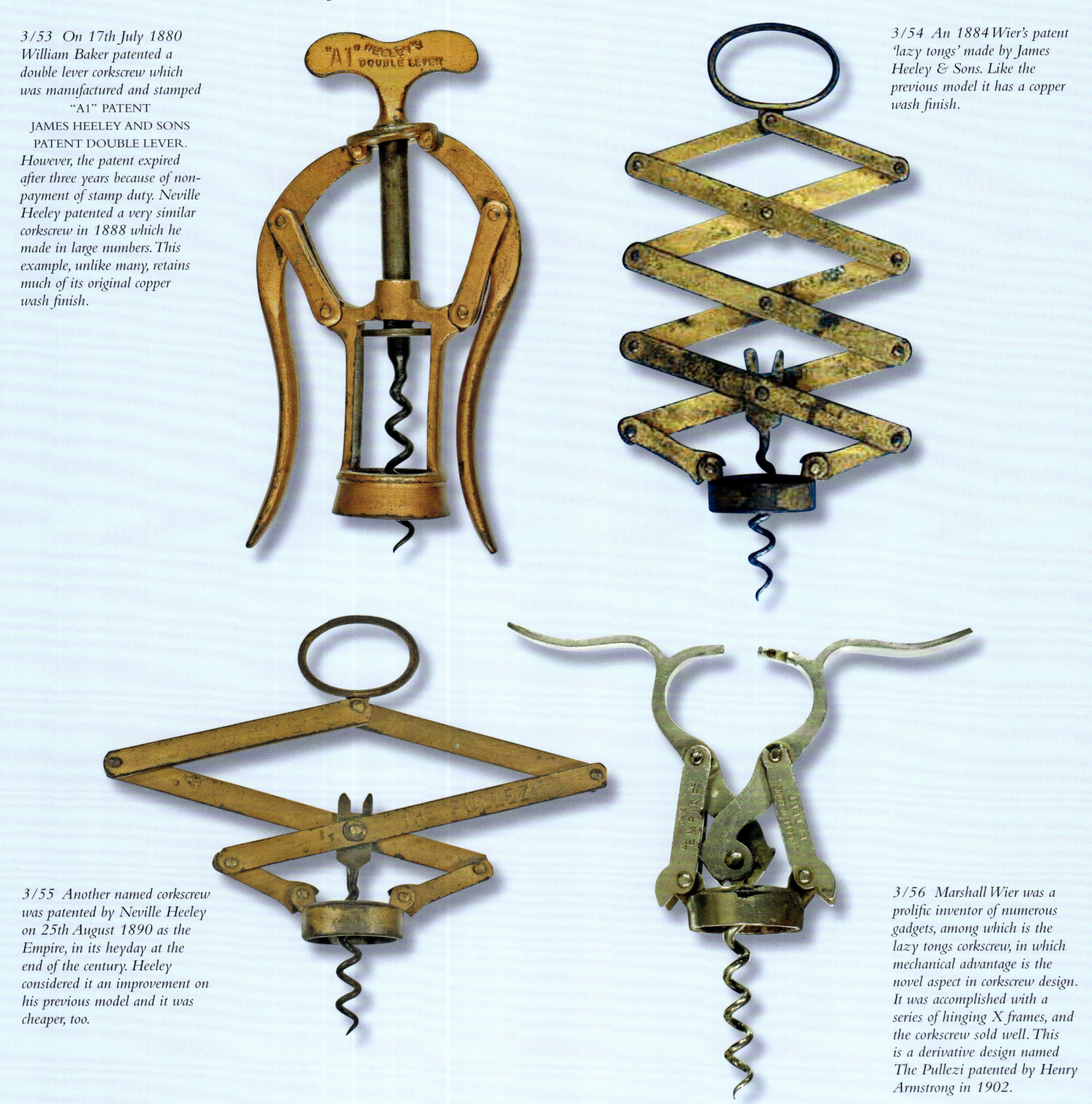

3/53 On 17th July 1880 William Baker patented a double lever corkscrew which was manufactured and stamped "A1" PATENT JAMES HEELEY AND SONS PATENT DOUBLE LEVER. However, the patent expired after three years because of non-payment of stamp duty. Neville Heeley patented a very similar corkscrew in 1888 which he made in large numbers. This example, unlike many, retains much of its original copper wash finish.

3/54 An 1884 Wier's patent 'lazy tongs' made by James Heeley & Sons. Like the previous model it has a copper wash finish.

3/55 Another named corkscrew was patented by Neville Heeley on 25th August 1890 as the Empire, in its heyday at the end of the century. Heeley considered it an improvement on his previous model and it was cheaper, too.

3/56 Marshall Wier was a prolific inventor of numerous gadgets, among which is the lazy tongs corkscrew, in which mechanical advantage is the novel aspect in corkscrew design. It was accomplished with a series of hinging X frames, and the corkscrew sold well. This is a derivative design named The Pullezi patented by Henry Armstrong in 1902.

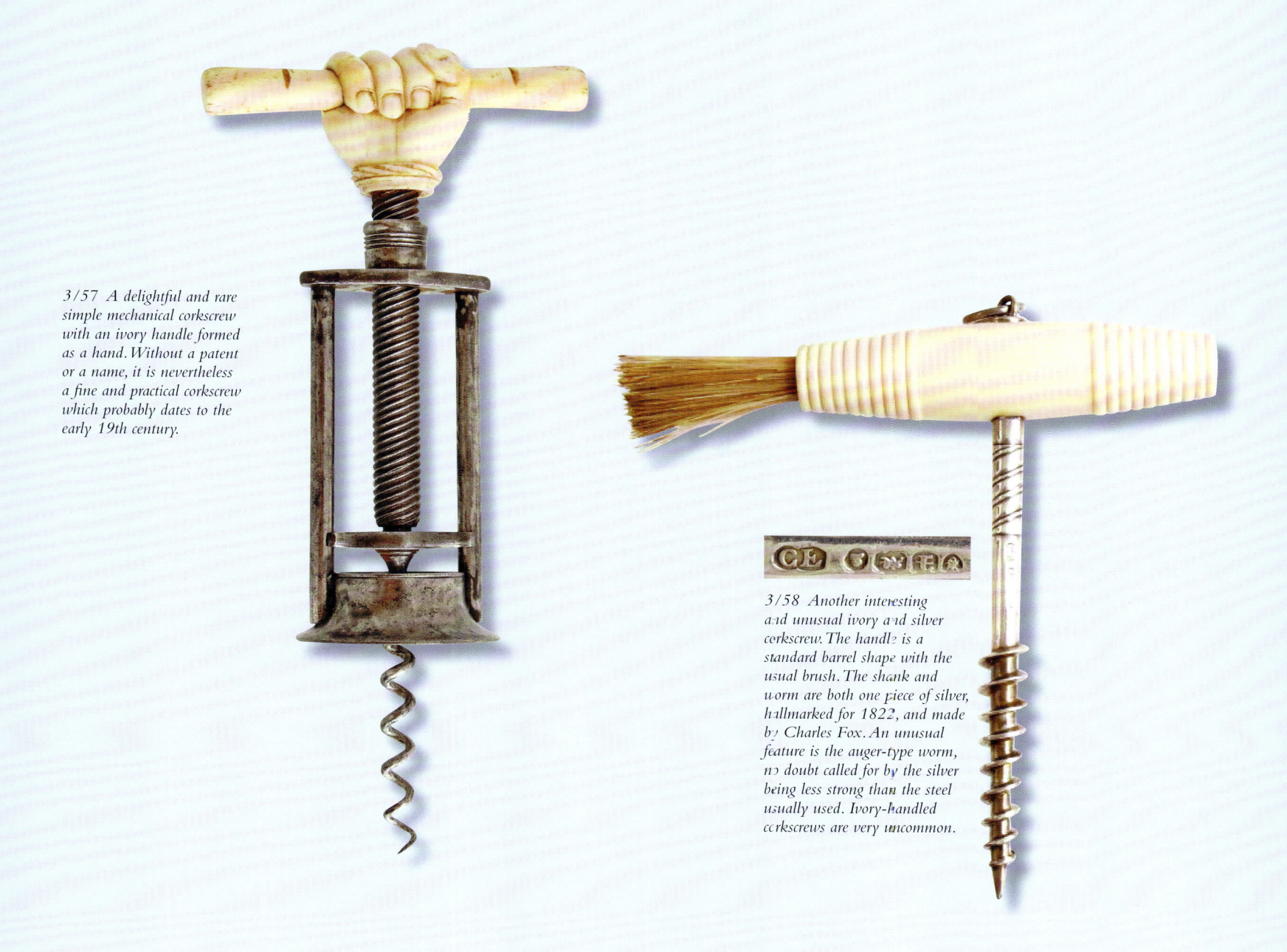

3/57 A delightful and rare simple mechanical corkscrew with an ivory handle formed as a hand. Without a patent or a name, it is nevertheless a fine and practical corkscrew which probably dates to the early 19th century.

3/58 Another interesting and unusual ivory and silver corkscrew. The handle is a standard barrel shape with the usual brush. The shank and worm are both one piece of silver, hallmarked for 1822, and made by Charles Fox. An unusual feature is the auger-type worm, no doubt called for by the silver being less strong than the steel usually used. Ivory-handled corkscrews are very uncommon.

3/59 A pair of champagne pliers. These were very popular at the end of the 19th century. The nippers were to cut the wire and the end of the handle was serrated to ease the removal of the foil. Few were made with a folding corkscrew, but not all champagne pliers had a corkscrew. This rarity has its original case and is stamped JAMES WRIGHT NOV 5 1879. Traditionally they have been dated somewhat later.

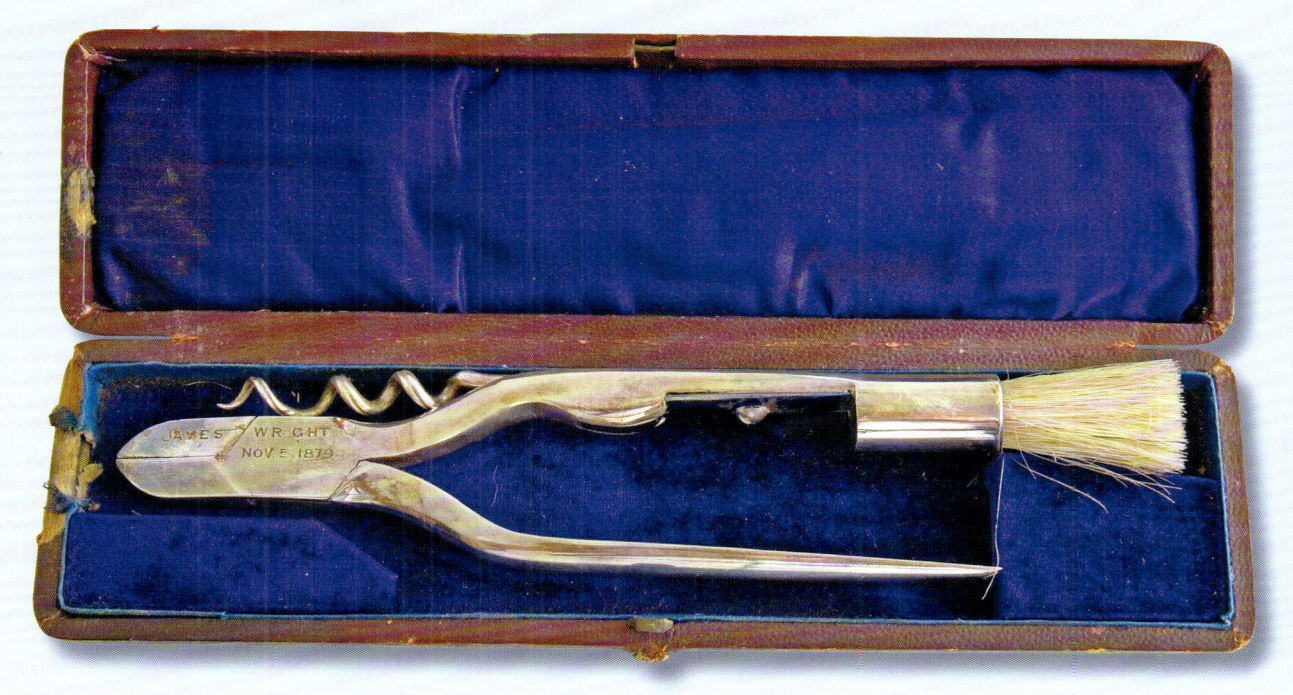

Chapter 3   Corkscrews

As already mentioned, there are numerous books on corkscrews, and it is intended that this is a general overview of them as used in Britain up to the 20th century. There are however, two types that were not patented and one which was, deserving mention here. First there exist, but only rarely, left hand corkscrews which have to be rotated anticlockwise to be driven into a cork. Also there are corkscrews hidden in walking sticks, some of which also hide a long narrow drinking glass. These are sometimes known as 'dipsomaniacs' delights'. The corkscrew differing from any others is Wilson's 1877 patent with its twin helixes which may be of unequal length (see 3/52). While these corkscrews were intended for domestic use, another more sturdy version was needed for use in bars and hotels. As bar corkscrews were intended for commercial premises they should not perhaps be considered here, but they are an integral part of the British wine scene, and so merit a mention.

Bar corkscrews are much larger, heavier and sturdier than domestic models, and first appeared in the middle of the 19th century. They were designed to be fixed to the bar or counter in licensed premises. Put simply, using a bar corkscrew, the bottle is brought to the corkscrew with one hand, and the lever is pulled with the other, uncorking the bottle and releasing the cork in one pull/push action. It is quick and, if the corkscrew is properly maintained, easy. Their makers gave them some delightful names: The Unique, The Don, The Quick & Easy and The Acme are just some, and there were others without names. Some were all polished brass, while others were decoratively-cast iron, but they were all designed to remove corks with speed and reject the cork, ready for the next bottle. Many can been seen in clubs and bars today, and while some are new, others are old, even antique.

There are many other patented designs, and some that were not patented, but the ones mentioned in this chapter are the principal British models. Late 19th century corkscrews and those made in the first half of the 20th century are often, but by no means always, of

3/60 Bar Corkscrews were invented in the mid-19th century. Fast and efficient at drawing corks, they are still often seen in bars. Frederick T Marwood patented THE ECLIPSE on 26th March 1885 and the patent was also registered in France and the USA. It can probably claim to be the most elegant of all bar corkscrews, but that is no great claim.

poor quality. This is manifested in light, locally-grown wood handles replacing cocus wood, and thinner steel used for the helix which more easily bends out of shape. Some are novelties, but the lasting impression of most is that they were cheap to make and intended to be ephemeral. More recently (since 1979) coating the helix with Teflon has made cork penetration and extraction significantly easier. The new technology has resulted in a rash of patents, mostly from America; some of these examples are very well made, and are highly effective.

Since the millennium there has been a move away from the use of cork to stopper wine bottles. This is because some wine is tainted by a mould introduced into the bottle by affected cork. The proportion of wine so affected may be small, but it is significant. Synthetic cork (made of plastic) is used by some wineries, but it can play havoc with corkscrews. Others have chosen screwcaps to seal their bottles. However, the cork producers are improving their production techniques, and it appears that traditionalists will be able to continue to use corkscrews for many years yet.

Although this book is concerned with British wine paraphernalia, it has to be said that France, Germany, Italy and America were all sources of numerous patents: many of of their products were sold in Britain and are frequently seen here. There were also occasions when patentees collaborated between different countries, just as there were those who copied foreign patents.

Corkscrew collectors take their interest right up to the present time and while some may be interested only in mechanical corkscrews, others focus on those made before 1800. There are collectors of figural corkscrews and those who collect examples made as promotional material. The subject generally is a very large one even before considering the products of each country. In this chapter, consideration has been restricted to British corkscrews made to open wine bottles, and while mention has been made of a German corkscrew, it is only because it is engraved with a British crest and therefore clearly made for use in Britain.

3/61 This model, The Acme, was advertised by Cornelius Chambers in 1929, but he was registering patents from 1891. As these were made over a long period, they are very difficult, if not impossible to date accurately. The side away from the camera is stamped THE ACME.

Tasters

British wine tasters are seldom seen outside museums or the more exclusive antique silver dealerships in London. They were probably never numerous. The reason for their scarcity is that they were not made for general use by amateurs or end-users; they were made for vintners and wine merchants for use in their trade although, no doubt, some were ordered for non-trade use. Europeans in the wine trade, particularly in France, used tasters (or tastevins*) to a much greater extent, and often wore them on ribbons around the neck, not merely because it was convenient but because they were almost regarded as a badge of office.*

By definition a taster or tastevin *only accommodates a very small amount of wine. It must be made of a material robust enough to withstand the rigours of daily use in a commercial environment and that material must not taint the wine in any way; it must either reflect light well or it must be of a pale shade in order that the colour and clarity of the wine can be truly judged.*

What are called porcelain wine tasters exist, but it is not surprising that by far the majority of surviving examples are silver. Indeed the history of silver wine tasters reaches back over six centuries and there are several recorded references to them in 14th and 15th century manuscripts. A will dated 1426 mentions 'A tastour of selver with my owne merke ymade in the bottom'. Later in the 15th century, during the Wars of the Roses, an Act of 1477–78 placed an embargo on the export of gold and silver from England to mainland Europe but wine tasters were specifically exempt from this order when used professionally: 'Any Merchant going over the Sea to buy any Wine to be brought into the realm, as far to carry with him only a little Cup called a Taster (un taster ou shewer) for wine.'

4/1 This is currently the earliest known British wine taster. It was dredged from the Thames near Vintners' Hall at Vintry Wharf and predates the next earliest known taster by some 30 years. It was made by Lawrence Gilbert (or Gilberd) in either Colchester or Ipswich. A study of the marks suggests that it was made in Ipswich either before 1567 or after 1570 and probably the latter. It follows the Bordeaux model and is very solidly made of high quality silver (92.722% pure). Any wine tasters of the 17th century, let alone the 16th, are very rare. It is 3⅝ in/92mm diameter.

Chapter 4 Tasters

During much of the 12th and 13th centuries the English kings, through marriage and military conquest, ruled Aquitaine and its most important city, Bordeaux. Although this hegemony was temporary, the trading between Bordeaux and England burgeoned, so when English wine merchants and vintners felt the need for wine tasters, they looked to Bordeaux for their model. This is a circular bowl or dish about 3½–4½in/9–10 cm) in diameter with sides raking outwards at an angle of about 45° while the entire base is occupied by a low dome. The shape allows a good sight of the wine, the sides and base giving various depths for assessing the strength of colour and clarity without the need to pour too much wine. Many tasters are engraved around their outside edge with the name of the owner, a practice probably imported from France although, unlike some of their Burgundy counterparts, the tasters are often devoid of decoration.

Although this book is concerned with English wine paraphernalia, this chapter would be incomplete without a mention of French tastevins. The Bordeaux model has been described, but it is unique in France; other towns and cities made tastevins in profusion, but they looked very different. While they were of similar size (3– 4in/7·5–10cm diameter), the sides were rounded, and with a horizontal or vertical ring handle sometimes with a thumbpiece attached (see 13/7). Many, particularly 19th century examples, have two patterns of indentations in the base, one being small circular depressions, the other a row of longer indentations, each occupying one half of the base of the bowl. These are for the wine merchant to gain the best possible reflections of light to assess wine.

The earliest English taster was thought for many decades to be one of 1631, but in 1985 a 1603 London-made taster was discovered in an outstation of Bristol City Museum & Art Gallery where it had been on loan from a church, unidentified for what it was. The sides of the bowl are punch-decorated with radiating beads beneath a ring of smaller beads, and the base embossed with a bunch of grapes within a band of scallop shells. Very solidly made, it rests on a shallow collet foot. Its claim as the earliest known English wine taster was not long lived.

In the closing years of the 20th century, an even earlier taster was dredged from the river Thames near a wharf known as Vintry, close to Vintners' Hall. This is where wine was unloaded at the Port of London. Nearby was a famous tavern, the Three Cranes at Vintry, frequented and esteemed by Ben Johnson, although Samuel Pepys took a poor view of the dinner served there on 23rd January 1662. The taster was plain, again of heavy gauge, and was made by Lawrence Gilbert (or Gilberd) who worked in both Ipswich and Colchester. From recent research, it would appear from Gilbert's movements that the taster was made either in Ipswich sometime before 1567, or after 1570, or in Colchester between these dates.

4/2 The second earliest British wine taster so far recorded, made in 1603 in London. The maker is not known. Unlike the Colchester/Ipswich taster, this is profusely decorated with a bunch of grapes within a band of scallop shells and the raked sides have radiating dimples. The taster is of heavy gauge and for many years was the property of a Wiltshire church. Its claim as the earliest known taster lasted only from 1985 for about 10 years. The stylised form of the scallop shell is the emblem of St. James and of pilgrims to Santiago de Compostela.

4/3 Strictly speaking this is not a wine taster but that does not stop many, including dealers and auctioneers, using the name for small dishes like this. They were made in very large numbers in the mid-17th century (this one dates from 1641), and from records at the Goldsmiths' Company it can be ascertained that they were called wine dishes. They were probably for drinking brandy, the Dutch equivalents being known as brandewijn (literally 'burnt wine') dishes and the Scottish equivalent for usquebaugh (modern term: whisky) known as a quaich. Brandy had become very popular once the distillation of wine was discovered. Of all 17th century British silver domestic objects, these are probably the most numerous. At the same time, wine tasters were rare. It is 4¾in/12cm over the handles, 3⅝in/92mm. diameter. The maker, whose mark is ES within a dotted circle, has not yet been identified.

4/4 This is another wine dish, made in York by Samuel Casson in 1640. Like the previous dish it has a band of punched decoration and the base is given the same finish, that is, the decoration is made by striking a blunt tool against the silver to leave a pattern of indentations, a common practice in the mid-17th century. It also has 'wire' handles of flat section which again is typical. It is 4½in/11·4cm across the handles. York had an assay office from the 12th century until 1858.

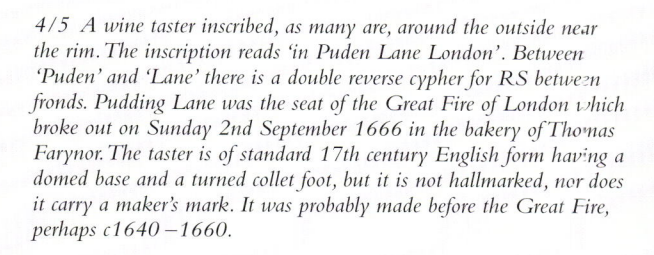

4/5 A wine taster inscribed, as many are, around the outside near the rim. The inscription reads 'in Puden Lane London'. Between 'Puden' and 'Lane' there is a double reverse cypher for RS between fronds. Pudding Lane was the seat of the Great Fire of London which broke out on Sunday 2nd September 1666 in the bakery of Thomas Farynor. The taster is of standard 17th century English form having a domed base and a turned collet foot, but it is not hallmarked, nor does it carry a maker's mark. It was probably made before the Great Fire, perhaps c1640–1660.

4/6 This small two-handled bowl is probably a late example of a wine taster in a different sense from that usually encountered and was probably originally called a cup of assay. In medieval households, wine would be tasted by a servant to demonstrate that it was not poisoned before being offered to guests and the host. This small bowl dates from around 1670 and has the maker's mark of SS beneath a crown (the maker has not been identified), while the underside is engraved DP. It is not robust enough to be a wine merchant's taster, and at only 3½in/9cm over the handles it is not large enough to be a wine dish. While this dish is English, Parisian examples were made to a similar pattern.

Chapter 4   Tasters

Most wine English wine tasters (Scottish and Irish ones are extremely rare) date from the 18th century, and remain almost unchanged in design, with very few exceptions, for over 100 years. An atypical and therefore very rare silver example of 1701 by Samuel Wastell which resembles the Burgundian model, but deeper, has a double-scroll handle in the form of a caryatid. Such handles would have been bought in from a specialist handle maker and normally used on porringers and small mugs. An equally rare taster of similar general form but made of glass is also recorded, and likewise has a gadrooned lower band. However in this case the handle has a thumbpiece (see 4/9). There are also two recorded Channel Island wine tasters of the Parisian model. One by IH of Guernsey was made in about 1740 with a scallop-shell thumbpiece and a finger ring beneath.

The few British porcelain wine tasters that do exist all appear to be either from the Derby or Worcester factories. Welsh, Scottish and Irish examples are unknown. Typically the Derby tasters are shallow bowls with a single flat handle set horizontally to the rim. The earliest have pierced handles, while later 18th century ones have moulded handles formed as shells or stylised foliage; all are decorated in underglaze blue in imitation of Chinese porcelain. The Worcester model is very different and has a handle formed as a twig while the bowl is a hemisphere of basket-weave overlaid with polychrome flowers and foliage. The inside of the bowl has a narrow band of polychrome floral decoration just below the rim.

4/7 A pewter wine taster dredged from the river Thames near Vintners' Hall. The two dredged tasters illustrated in this chapter and found at the same location, do cause one to wonder about the effects of too much tasting… It is very hard to date this one, but it seems reasonable to put it in the 17th century at the latest. It is 2¾in/7 cm diameter. The decoration in the base has been substantially degraded by its immersion, and is indecipherable. When this taster was new, it would have closely resembled silver, but pewter tarnishes much more quickly than silver.

△ *4/8 This may well be a wine taster, but if it is, it is like no others. It was made in 1707 by John East in Britannia standard silver (95.84% pure silver) and is 3⅛in/7.9cm diameter. The argument that it may be a wine taster is strengthened by the base having a pronounced dome, and it is decorated with embossed plain swags, each ending in a ball. The rim is nicely caulked, that is, it was hammered in the making to add thickness where it was most needed.*

△ *4/9 A very rare glass wine taster. The lower part is gadrooned in a way very similar to silver of the late 17th and early 18th centuries. The scroll handle has an oval thumbpiece, making its use undoubted. Stylistically it can be dated to about 1700.*

▷ 4/10 *This is a French wine taster (tastevin) from Bordeaux. It is the model that English wine tasters emulated, rather than those from the rest of France which have rounded sides and handles (see 13/7). The similarity of form between the 16th century English model and that from Bordeaux should not be surprising as Aquitaine (of which Bordeaux is the principal city) was under English rule for many years during the medieval period. This particular tastevin was made in 1730–32 by Gabriel Tillet, but the design stretches back long before that date.*

△ 4/12 *A Worcester porcelain wine taster. The bowl has basket-weave moulded sides overlaid with polychrome flowers and foliage loosely modelled. The inside of the bowl is plain except for the narrow band of stylised polychrome foliage near the rim. The handle is modelled as a twig. It was made c1765–1768. While several of this model and palette are known, blue and white examples are much more rare.*

△ 4/11 *A Derby porcelain wine taster decorated in underglaze blue in imitation of Delft pottery. The centre of the bowl is decorated with stylised foliage and a flower, while the rim has a narrow band of formal decoration. The handle is formed as an irregular A with a flat apex. It was made c1762–65.*

4/13 *A Derby wine taster with a shaped rim and flat moulded lug handle. It is painted in deep underglaze blue with a stylised flower and with a border of repeating sunbursts. It was made about 1770.*

Chapter 4   Tasters

4/14 Two Derby blue and white wine tasters and a creamware taster (below). It may also be Derby, but creamware is notoriously difficult to ascribe to one factory as it was made in many locations in the north of England. They all date from about 1775.

While the porcelain collecting fraternity have always called these shallow dishes wine tasters, there is debate about their original intended use because of the fragility of porcelain and the need for a taster to withstand rigorous use. Not only that, but there are two recorded sets, one of four and another of five. Perhaps it was because porcelain tasters were only intended for domestic use in the dining room or that gentlemen had wine tasting sessions at home. Certainly they cannot have been put to use by vintners in a commercial setting. The only other explanation for their existence is that they were not wine tasters but small handled bowls for some other use, although that notion would fly against received wisdom. What is certain is that Derby was the main factory to produce them and that their principal market was in London. The Worcester model was copied from Chinese bowls originally used on scholars' tables for washing calligraphy brushes. All English porcelain tasters (see captions 4/11 and 4/12) were made in the period between about 1760 and 1790.

Silver wine tasters from the 19th century are seen even more rarely than 18th century examples and usually mimic earlier forms. A pair made in 1800 was noted with reeded rims and vertical ribbed decoration, and we illustrate two others from the mid-century, but these are all rarities. It has to be wondered who may have wanted a pair of tasters.

△ *4/15 A small porcelain wine taster from the Caughley factory with blue and white transfer printed decoration in a pattern known as the Fisherman. It has a moulded triangular lug handle and was made about 1785–90.*

4/16 A silver wine taster made in London in 1788 by Thomas Daniell. Unusually he made it in Britannia standard silver, and quite typically it is engraved around the outside of the rim with the owner's name and the date 1790. The pattern in the bowl is a standard form. Britannia standard silver is 95.84% pure silver and was obligatory from 1697–1721, remaining an option thereafter.

4/17 A silver wine taster which, while not from exactly the same pattern as the Thomas Daniell example, is very similar. It was made in 1794 by Thomas Phipps & Edward Robinson who also made other wine paraphernalia of a uniformly high standard. It is 4⅛in/10.5cm diameter and weighs about 3oz/100g.

4/18 A wine taster of 1861 made by Edward & John Barnard who traded as Edward Barnard & Sons. The taster has 13 lobes – an unusual configuration – and is 4¾in/12cm diameter. The underside is engraved in script H. & C. S. Parker Hull. Parkers were wine merchants of that city during the second half of the 19th century.

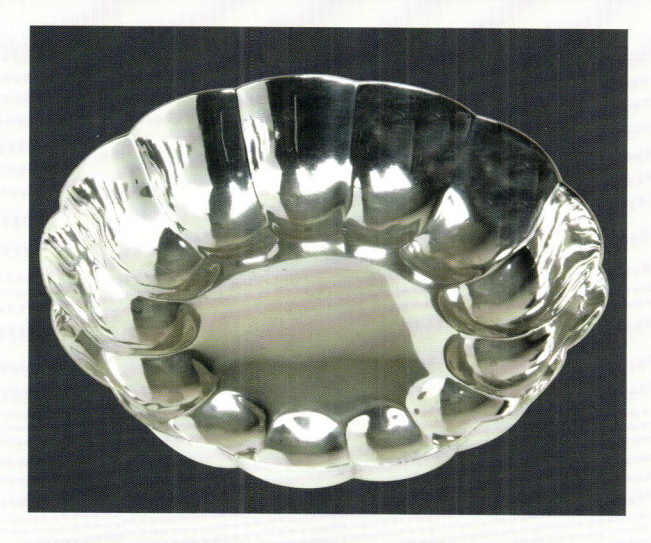

4/19 A Victorian wine taster made in 1866. It is devoid of any decoration, nor does it have the engraved name of its original owner. While the proportions have been adjusted, it is of very similar form to the one made 300 years earlier.

There is a category of small silver bowl or dish with a pair of handles, made in the mid-17th century, that has frequently been called a wine taster. Examples are numerous and visually unlike the standard, but rare, wine taster. Their purpose was unclear until it was discovered in the records of the Court of the Goldsmiths' Company. An entry for 1st January 1639 states '24 small wine dishes 1 dwt* worse than standard, are broken'. This can be transcribed into modern English as 24 small wine dishes have been found to be slightly below the legal standard for silver to be hallmarked and have been broken beyond repair. More to the point here is the evidence that someone had sent 24 wine dishes, for assay at one time. This would only have occurred if wine dishes were being made on a large scale. It therefore seems probable that the dishes referred to were similar to those that have been called wine tasters for so long.

Wine dishes do have parallels in Scottish quaichs and Dutch brandewijn dishes or bowls, and these are the clue to the popularity of wine dishes for a few decades in the middle of the 17th century. The reason is that the distillation of wine to make brandy was discovered, and brandy drinking from small dishes became very popular at this time. The Dutch brandewijn literally means burnt wine, that is, distilled.

There is another variety of small cup that should be mentioned here. It usually dates from the late 17th century, is sometimes deeper than the standard wine taster, has two small handles, and is about 1½in/3.8cm in diameter. Examples are very rare and are probably tasting cups used in grand households where a servant would taste wine publicly before the wine was poured for the host and his guests. It is probable that the ritual was a remnant of medieval practice to ensure the wine was not poisoned.

* dwt. is the usual abbreviation for pennyweight which is one twentieth of an ounce (troy). Sterling standard silver is 92.5% pure and 1 pennyweight worse than sterling standard would be 90.5%. This is not very much less than it should be, but nevertheless was considered at the time to be a serious offence. The troy ounce has remained the standard measure for bullion metals and is about 10% heavier than the avoirdupois ounce used for all other purposes.

Wine coolers, cellarets & cisterns

Wine coolers come in two forms; those that hold a single bottle or, rarely, two and are placed on a table or sideboard and those that may hold several bottles and stand on the floor. In addition there are floor-standing objects which look like wine coolers, but were designed to hold bottles at room temperature in the dining room: these are cellarets. Wine coolers have metal linings to hold iced water; cellarets do not have waterproof linings, but interior divisions to separate bottles. In the homes of the rich, even in pre-refrigerator days, ice was a commodity used all the year round. To supply ice to a household, a special ice-house was constructed in the grounds. It had thick walls with no windows, and often only the entrance and roof, which was usually turfed over, were above ground. Ice was collected in the winter from ponds and lakes and stored under straw for insulation. Some ice was imported.

5/1 Arguably the grandest British wine accoutrements ever made, with the possible exception of the Jernegan wine cistern (see 5/6), are these wine coolers wrought from 22 carat gold and weighing 365oz, 6dwt/11·36kg. The pair was made for John Churchill, 1st Earl of Marlborough about 1700 before he was created Duke (1702) and in 1744 were bequeathed to the Hon. John Spencer of Althorp. They descended through the Spencer family until they were acquired by the British Museum in 1981. They are not hallmarked, nor do they have a maker's mark, but they were part of the plate issued from the Jewel Office to Churchill for his role as ambassador to the States General (Holland) in 1701. The craftsmanship is clearly Huguenot, deriving strong influences from French models.

Chapter 5 Wine coolers, cellarets and cisterns

5/2 A massive silver wine cistern made about 1710–20 by Phillip Rollos. Although it bears his mark, it is not hallmarked. The scale of it can be judged from the chairs beyond. It is actually 45in/114·3cm long excluding the handles. The decorative detail of lambrequins, masks, floral swags and shells is cast as are the interior embellishments and the richly gadrooned rim. The handles are formed as heraldic rampant lions standing on scrolled elements, while the feet are formed as complex scrolls with dragons emerging from them. This massive cistern is among the largest known, and may have been the largest when it was made.

From the 16th century and perhaps somewhat earlier, wine was served cool. This applied to both white and red wine. In renaissance tapestries, wine coolers can be seen made of pottery (faience) or metal in the foreground. The positioning may be artistic licence, but what can be noticed is that bottles or flasks of both red and white wine were being cooled in water (presumably iced). In England, the earliest surviving vessels for cooling wine are cisterns. They were oval in outline, and usually made of silver, although a few examples in japanned or silvered base metal also survive. Pottery wine coolers as seen in tapestries appear not to have been made in England before 1700 or, if they were, none appear to have survived. It is perhaps difficult, from our perspective in the 21st century, to appreciate that in the top levels of society in the 18th century and earlier, large items of silver were bought or commissioned, and assembled for display in the dining room. These grandest of pieces were seen and judged by discerning and competitive standards. Before the 18th century, it was considered that members of the aristocracy had to appear noble in all their attributes, even when they were away from their estates. The silver and gold in their dining rooms was often described in accounts like those of Celia Fiennes, who travelled around Britain in the 17th century. The notion that showing one's wealth was vulgar was a 19th century idea that persisted for almost all of the 20th, although it may be convincingly argued that obviously expensive motor cars and ostentatious jewellery and watches have begun to reverse that trend. Wine, a commodity epitomising good living and wealth, was a natural vehicle on which to lavish money. In the early years of the 18th century and at a time of prosperity, huge silver wine cisterns and fountains were commissioned from newly-arrived Huguenot craftsmen whose skills were seldom matched by native goldsmiths. The most lavish houses of the aristocracy had suites comprising fountain, wine cooler and cistern, all matching and with applied coats of arms emblazoned so they could not be missed. Wine coolers of silver were heavy as well as grand; the Duke of Marlborough even had a pair of solid gold wine coolers (see 5/1).

By the very end of the 17th century, wine coolers were being made to hold a single bottle, a notion imported from France. These were usually made in pairs and were used or displayed on a side table or buffet; their production continued for the next two centuries. Their development followed fashionable styles, but by the late 18th century Sheffield plate was being used to make less expensive wine coolers for those who could not afford solid silver. Naturally, being cheaper, they proved popular.

Mahogany began to replace walnut as the prime cabinet-making timber in the mid-1720s, and within a decade it was being used to make floor-standing wine coolers capable of holding several bottles of wine at once. This coincided with a substantial increase in wine consumption in England, with a corresponding development of the decanter, and the introduction of wine labels. While silver wine cisterns did continue to be made, in general mahogany replaced silver as the principal medium. In the early 19th century, after silver wine cisterns ceased to be made, rosewood, oak and other woods as well as mahogany were used to make wine coolers.

5/3 A silver wine cistern which at first sight appears to have been made abut 1720. The design and style are typical of Huguenot work at that date, but this one was made by Carl Bojanowski of St. Petersburg in 1861. It is very closely modelled on another made by Philip Rollos in London in 1712 in the Wilding collection at the British Museum. It is 27in/68·6cm wide over the handles. The handles are formed as the supporters of the coat of arms of the original owner of the 1712 cistern, but perhaps Bojanowski's customer was ignorant of the allusion.

The term wine cistern traditionally refers to a large wine cooler made of silver. Similarly shaped objects were made in brass (although these were probably close-plated in silver) or in decorated base metals, but then they are termed wine coolers. The nomenclature is probably recent and is certainly confusing.

Standing on collet feet or, soon after the start of the 18th century, on four legs, silver cisterns could hold upwards of a dozen bottles. The earliest surviving example was made in 1667 and can be seen in the Victoria & Albert Museum. As cisterns became more popular, so the size of these magnificent objects grew. By the early years of the following century they became decidedly grand and sometimes excessively so. Indeed the largest item of wrought English domestic silver ever made is the wine cistern made by Charles Kandler to the design of George Vertue, modelled by Michael Rysbrack for Henry Jernegan (or Jerningham), a banker and retailer of silver and jewellery. It was conceived in about 1730 and completed by 1734. It had a convoluted and fascinating early existence and following its eventual purchase by Empress Anne of Russia, is now in the Hermitage Museum in St. Petersburg. It is 66in/167·8cm long and weighs 8,000oz (about 250kg) and was made in Britannia standard silver. When compared with a tea or coffee pot, say, which usually weighs between 12 and 30 oz, the scale of its grandeur and ostentation may be appreciated.

Wine cisterns were a passing fashion, and by 1750 their popularity was dwindling. As with almost all wrought silver, cisterns followed the prevailing styles with the baroque giving way to rococo, followed by neoclassical, although by this time very few cisterns were being made, and almost none were made after the beginning of the 19th century apart from a fine silver-gilt example made for the Duke of York, now in the Victoria & Albert Museum.

The handles of wine cisterns were often formed as the heraldic supporters of the family by whom they were commissioned; this could cause problems if the cistern changed hands. It is perhaps a wonder that they were not all melted down to be fashioned into more practical wares, or to be turned into coinage to pay for wars, as happened to so much pre-revolutionary French silver.

Chapter 5 Wine coolers, cellarets and cisterns

5/4 The grandest houses of the aristocracy had wine fountains and cisterns en suite. A few had a second larger cistern or cooler. The fountain and cistern here were used to wash wine glasses between toasts. The cistern could have been used separately for cooling wine. They are conceived in high baroque fashion having been made by Thomas Farren in 1728. The bowl of the cistern is 24in/61cm wide, and the fountain is 28in/71·1cm high.

5/5a An oval wine cistern of japanned tin. The cistern is waisted and has a strongly everted and corded rim with boldly embossed gadrooning which is repeated on a larger scale on the lower half of the body. Each lobe of the gadrooning is decorated with gilded sprays of flowers. It rests on four claw feet and has lion mask and ring handles at each end. Japanning was very fashionable from c.1685 and was promoted by Stalker and Parker's *Treatise of Japanning and Varnishing* published in 1688. By 1700 the brief fashion for chinoiserie had waned, but was revived twice more over the following 100 years. This wine cooler dates from about 1690, although the bottles are later.

5/5 A wine cistern made of copper and brass close-plated with silver. Like silver models, it is oval and has a waisted profile. It has lion-mask handles at either end and short legs with claw and ball feet. It is tempting to say, as it has been said in the past, that copper and brass objects post-date silver ones of the same pattern, but this may not be the case. Traditionally the more serious members of the antiques trade tend to date their stock conservatively, and a date of c1720–40 may have been given to this cistern. A date of c1690–1710 would probably be more accurate if it were a piece of unmarked silver. Actually it does bear a maker's punched mark, I P above a mullet in a heart-shaped shield, but although this maker is recognised from at least seven other cisterns, his identity remains unknown.

5/6 An engraving of the Jernegan wine cistern executed in 1735 by Gerard Scotin after a drawing by Hubert François Bourguignon, a Parisian who lived in London from 1732–45 and who was known as Gravelot. The original drawing cost Jernigan five guineas and he had the engraving made to promote the sale of the cistern. It has a Latin inscription. A second state of the print was run in 1740, published by Robert Clee with wording in English. The actual cistern can now be seen in the Hermitage Museum, St. Petersburg and there are electrotype copies in the Victoria and Albert Museum (London) and the Metropolitan Museum of Art (New York).

Chapter 5   Wine coolers, cellarets and cisterns

The first table wine coolers were made in the closing years of the 17th century, around 1695. A pair of 22 ct. gold examples from the collection of the Earls Spencer, (see 5/1) but made for the Earl of Marlborough in about 1701 (they are unmarked) may be seen in the British Museum. Early 18th century wine coolers were never plentiful but there are examples from the first three decades. It seems extraordinary and is as yet unexplained, that no silver wine coolers appear to have been made in the period 1740–1760.

Usually made in pairs, or occasionally in sets of four, wine coolers were substantial objects, and were intended as much for display as use. Almost all silver examples made before about 1740 were made by Huguenots and, as one would expect from these immigrant craftsmen, they were of heavily cast construction. In the 1760s until the end of the 18th century the bucket form was popular, often with engraving to simulate the staves of a wooden bucket. The 19th century saw the introduction of the vase-shaped wine cooler which developed with prevailing fashionable detail from rococo to gothick. Silver table wine coolers were seldom made in the second half of the 19th century nor in the 20th.

Although the Sheffield plating process, in which a thin layer of silver is fused to a base of copper, had been invented in 1742, it took some years before the process was perfected and its use became widespread. The advantage of Sheffield plate over solid silver is that objects could be made more cheaply, and the appearance of silver was open to a wider public; the heavier the item, the greater the saving. Wine coolers were perfect subjects for this new medium as solid silver examples have considerable weight.

After about 1780 plated wine coolers were being made in ever larger numbers and their popularity further increased from about 1805. However with the invention of electroplating in 1840, plating in silver was further reduced in price, and the Sheffield plating industry went into decline and final demise quite quickly. The electroplating industry burgeoned and has been thriving ever since. Many electroplated wine coolers have been made since the mid-19th century, usually in the style of earlier models, although there were many novel designs in the art nouveau and art deco periods.

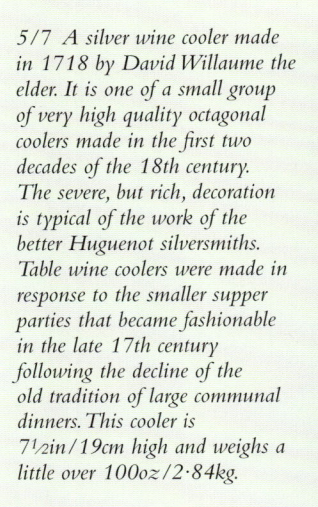

5/7 A silver wine cooler made in 1718 by David Willaume the elder. It is one of a small group of very high quality octagonal coolers made in the first two decades of the 18th century. The severe, but rich, decoration is typical of the work of the better Huguenot silversmiths. Table wine coolers were made in response to the smaller supper parties that became fashionable in the late 17th century following the decline of the old tradition of large communal dinners. This cooler is 7½in/19cm high and weighs a little over 100oz/2·84kg.

5/8 A pair of silver wine coolers of plain, slightly tapering cylindrical form, the sides simulating staved construction with horizontal hoops. They have silver collars and flat loop handles, and the liners are of Sheffield plate. They are slightly later engraved with the coat of arms of George Ackers (1788–1836), and they were made in London by William Pitts & Joseph Preedy in 1797. They are 8in/22·5cm high.

5/9 One of a pair of neoclassical ormolu (gilt brass or bronze) wine coolers. A design by J J Boileau in the Victoria & Albert Museum depicts a wine cooler of similar general outline and with an almost identical base. Other variations in silver gilt are known to have been supplied by Rundell, Bridge & Rundell, suppliers to the royal family. The ornament on these coolers derives from Egypt, a theme much used in decorative art following Nelson's routing of the French fleet off Aboukir Bay on 1st August 1798. The Egyptian taste remained popular for much of the succeeding decade.

Chapter 5 Wine coolers, cellarets and cisterns

5/10 A pair of silver-gilt wine coolers of neoclassical vase shape. Like almost all other coolers they have detachable collars and liners, these being cylindrical sleeves giving insulation between the bottle to be cooled and the visible outside surface. These coolers have a band of finely cast vine decoration with Bacchic masks at intervals beneath snake handles. They also have applied drapery cartouches enclosing the coat of arms of Lonsdale of York impaling Heywood. They were made by Digby Scott & Benjamin Smith in 1803, and stand 13in/32·8cm high.

5/11 A huge ancient Roman marble vase (10ft/3·05m high including the plinth) with Bacchic ornament was discovered in pieces at Hadrian's Villa at Tivoli about 1771 by Gavin Hamilton, a Scottish artist-antiquarian and dealer. Hamilton sold the fragments to his namesake, Sir William Hamilton, British envoy at the court of Naples, who had it restored; later it was sold to his nephew the Earl of Warwick. Since its installation at Warwick Castle, it has been known as the Warwick Vase, although it now rests in the Burrell Collection, Glasgow. First engraved by Piranesi, the vase became famous and has been much copied in reduced scale. The first copies in 1812 were a set of 12 in silver-gilt for the Prince Regent. This pair by Paul Storr of Storr & Co. for Rundell, Bridge & Rundell are 14½in/36·8cm across the handles and were made in 1814. They are fitted with liners as wine coolers.

5/12 The Portland Vase is one of the most famous works of art from the classical Roman period having been made in cameo glass around 30–50BC. It was excavated intact about 1582, was bought by Sir William Hamilton in 1778 and later by the dowager Duchess of Portland. In 1810 it was loaned to the British Museum, where on 7th February 1845 it was smashed by a drunk and later restored. The iconography of the figures in low relief has been variously interpreted. The vase was copied by Wedgwood in 1790 and this very rare pair of silver-gilt copies by Philip Rundell was made in 1820 and 1823. Each has a detachable top with a bayonet fixing which allows a bottle to be inserted, while remaining waterproof when inverted.

5/13 This pair of silver wine coolers was made in 1819 by Paul Storr, probably for Rundell, Bridge & Rundell. The inverted vase-shaped bodies are fluted and have applied cast sprays of oak-leaf decoration to the out-scrolled handles and around the shell and volute scroll feet. The rims are decorated with cast shells and scrolls. The liners and collars detach for cleaning and emptying the melted ice.

Chapter 5 Wine coolers, cellarets and cisterns

5/14 Made in 1835 by Robert Garrard for R & S Garrard, these wine coolers stand 10½in/26·7cm high. They are in the exuberant French neo-rococo fashion, the bases being decidedly asymmetrical. The handles are formed as foliate scrolls and the rims as more everted foliage. The liners and the rims can be removed.

◁*5/15 Sheffield plated wine coolers proved very popular during the first quarter of the 19th century as they were considerably less costly than solid silver ones. This is a typical example. The fruiting vine decoration was a favoured style and is given full treatment here. Note the rectangular patch in the middle of the side, an area of solid silver to accept an engraved coat of arms (in this case never engraved); engraving on the standard plated surface would penetrate to the copper beneath. The rim is removable for access to the liner inside in order to empty melted ice and for cleaning.*

5/16 A Pair of Victorian silver wine coolers formed as tall baskets of ribbon-tied reeds or bamboo, and all overflowing with vine leaves and bunches of grapes, the stems forming the handles. The rims and liners are detachable, the former being engraved with the crest and motto of Henry Bolckow who emigrated from Mecklenburg and later became the first MP for Middlesbrough. The coolers were made by Jean-Valentin Morel & Co. of London in 1851.

◁*5/17 This is one of a pair of electroplated wine coolers of about 1860. They are very heavy and are formed as baskets of osier-work with vine rims. As with their silver counterparts, the liners are detachable.*

Chapter 5 Wine coolers, cellarets and cisterns

Despite their fragility, porcelain, pottery and glass wine coolers were made from the late 18th century. In the world of porcelain, the distinction between wine coolers and ice pails is not always clear. This is a problem made worse by the propensity of those in the early 20th century antiques trade for making up names for objects. Glass wine coolers are a rarity, but pottery was an inexpensive and decorative alternative to silver and Sheffield plate. However, like Sheffield plate, pottery gave way to electroplated models from the mid-century.

Wine coolers are very occasionally seen in other materials. Among the most attractive are those in decorated tinware or tôleware (japanned tinplate). They are usually painted with flowers against a black background, but other colours are almost never seen. The art of tôleware was more practised in France than in England.

Brass wine coolers are a great rarity and any from the mid-18th century were probably originally close-plated in silver. Close-plating is a process in which silver is attached to a base metal (brass or bronze). It was not done electrolytically, nor was it the same as old Sheffield plate, but it was practised for about 50 years from about 1695.

5/18 If the gold Marlborough wine coolers are the grandest of antique wine paraphernalia, then this Davenport ceramic wine cooler for a single bottle must be among the more modest, and yet it fulfils the same purpose. With its terracotta barrel shape, dolphin handles and decoration of greek key and paling in a dark brown it is a striking object. It was made c1810–20.

5/19 A terracotta wine cooler of campana shape (bell-form, in this case inverted) with twisted handles and a lotus-leaf foot. It has applied decoration of blue vine leaves, tendrils and grapes around the body and rim, while the body sits in a calyx of acanthus leaves, echoing Greek classical decoration. Such wine coolers are fragile and usually damaged and repaired.

△ 5/20 *A pair if ice pails or wine coolers. These rare survivals were clearly intended to be used for ice as they have double walls for insulation. They are utterly simple cylinders, yet the diamond cutting gives them great presence; it also prevents any hand warming the contents. Whether they were originally intended to cool bottles or dessert fruits or ice cream is impossible to say, but it was not beyond the Georgian mind to make dual-purpose objects. They date from c1815.*

△ 5/21 *Sometimes it is difficult to say for certain if an object is English or French and this comes into that category. It has a bucket-shaped glass body mounted with ormolu (gilt brass) with a band of vine engraving interrupted by lion mask handles above a broad band of diamond cutting and another of fluting. It is mid-19th century.*

Chapter 5 Wine coolers, cellarets and cisterns

△5/22 In the 18th and 19th centuries, the dining room was considered 'male' and brass-bound dark mahogany was thought appropriate. This two-bottle wine cooler with its brass bands and coopered construction is rare, but the brass handle and borders to the hole are typical. The top hinges are to allow access for cleaning and draining water. It dates from about 1780.

△5/23 Another two-bottle wine cooler for the table. Paler mahogany was being used by the end of the 18th century and the loop handles suggest a date of about 1790–1800. Note the latch and knob to gain access for draining.

◁5/24 This pair of table wine coolers is a rare survival, but eminently practical for a small number of people dining together. While this pair was made in about 1800, there are some fakes of the same model which would deceive all but the most experienced expert.

△5/25 The similarity of this very rare four-bottle table cooler and the pair below tempt the suggestion that they were from the same workshop. They are made from the same type of mahogany and the treatment of the top edges is remarkably similar. The only major difference is the handle, but handles were bought in by cabinet makers.

△5/26 A very rare lead-lined wine cooler for a single bottle. While the lower half is conventional, the upper part is most unusual. The fan-reeded, rather than fluted top, is similar to the tops of London-made wine coolers (see 5/47). The reeding is a later form and this has a Scottish feel to it; indeed it was last seen there. Brass bands were often lacquered and over time can look like this if not restored.

◁5/27 This pair of table wine coolers is a great rarity, and their lion-mask handles and general form suggest a date of c.1810. Table coolers like these were used after the ladies had withdrawn from the dinner table and servants had been dismissed from service for the day. The baize bases of these coolers allowed the wine to be circulated around the table after the tablecloth had been removed at dessert.

Chapter 5 Wine coolers, cellarets and cisterns

Seventeenth and very early 18th century wine coolers of oak or walnut seem not to have existed. The earliest furniture wine coolers were made of mahogany and date from the 1730s, and take their form from continental European marble models. They are oval, very solidly constructed, with cabriole legs (the marble ones stand on pedestals). The legs are carved at the knee with shells or acanthus leaves, while the lower part of the body is gadrooned.

Wine coolers, as items of furniture, burgeoned in popularity during the 1740s and 50s. Of oval form with staved or coopered sides held with two or three brass bands, they were supported on separate four-legged stands. Very rarely the legs were cabriole, but the majority had square moulded or tapered legs, and all were without hinged lids. Some were lead lined and others had lift-out linings. This made them suitable as jardinières as well as wine coolers. It is probable that many were made as dual purpose furniture.

It was important that wine coolers could be emptied of water when the ice in them had melted and their job had been done. A lead-lined wine cooler full of water can be very heavy and, to lighten the load, most were made with the body separate from the stand with its legs attached. Some were fitted with taps or bungs on the underside of the body and had integral legs. Others were simply a box, albeit of furniture quality, which was supported on short bracket feet.

From the late 1760s, wine coolers developed lids and various shapes emerged. Although the oval

5/28 Positively datable and provenanced British furniture is rare, but this wine cooler is probably the earliest known floor-standing mahogany example known. The body was made from a single piece of wood by John Hodson in 1738 for the Duke of Atholl and it remains in Blair Castle, the ancient seat of the Dukes of Atholl. The oval form and the deeply gadrooned lower section are typical of earlier European marble wine coolers, but the cabriole legs with paw feet are an idiosyncratic version of the popular fashion for much of the first half of the 18th century for walnut and later mahogany furniture in Britain. They were probably fashioned from a sketch provided by someone who had seen the latest London styles.

continued to be made, new forms included square, rectangular, octagonal and hexagonal models. While square and rectangular examples could have canted corners, panelled sides, and other decoration of the period, they were not brass-bound, unlike the octagonal and hexagonal versions which often were. The more complex shapes often tapered inward toward the stand, the legs splaying out to complement the cooler above.

Wine coolers of the 1770s–1800s could be ordered in many different qualities. The top could be plain, or cross-banded, or segmentally veneered; it could be decorated with inlay, while its edge could be moulded in a diversity of forms of varying complexity and cost. The brass fittings, though normally plain, could on occasions be fancy. It was quite normal on brass-bound furniture to use a rather straight and coarse-grained mahogany, but fine flame-figured wood could be had for a premium. An inexpensive example would be fitted merely with a bung, but one of higher quality would have a tap. As far as the base was concerned, it could have a variety of mouldings to edge the join between the base and the top. The legs on a simple example would be plain, and on a better one would be moulded, while a high quality model would feature fretted brackets to support the legs. Most wine coolers, like much dining and drawing room furniture, were fitted with castors. On earlier examples the rollers would be made of laminated leather, while the rest of the castor would be brass, gilded on the best, lacquered on the less good.

5/29 An English grey-veined marble wine cooler closely modelled on those produced in 17th century Europe. Originally intended for use in the eating or dining room this one has spent some years under the skies and this has given it a patination comparable to garden statuary. The boldly gadrooned lower section of the body is very similar to the mahogany one of 1738 (5/28) and it possible that this is the precursor.

Chapter 5 Wine coolers, cellarets and cisterns

Arguably the finest brass-bound wine coolers are the oval examples made just before the introduction of lids. These had parcel-gilt cabriole legs with profusely cast and chiselled brass bands (chiselling was used to brighten up dull castings). The mask-head handles were treated in the same manner, while occasionally the body also had finely cast brass appliqués. Coolers of this form are generally ascribed to the cabinet maker Samuel Norman.

It is interesting to note that while brass-bound octagonal and hexagonal wine coolers have proved commercially popular, those without brass bands are much less so. This is an anomaly, because those without brass bands are about the most complex pieces of furniture in the cabinet maker's repetoire. This is because each side is mitre-dovetailed into its neighbour, not just at an angle that is not a right angle, but it is also tapered. These complex pieces of woodwork engineering were undertaken so that there was no visual evidence of the joint; the two pieces of joined wood appear to be held by glue only. The hidden mitred dovetail is the most complex of all cabinet joints and it allows the maximum of glued surface between one element of the joint and its neighbour.

By the 1780s and 1790s the fashion for veneering and crossbanding was being adopted by cabinet makers on a large scale and wine coolers were embellished in this way despite the dining room's association with men, a room where dark timbers without decoration were the norm, and where finely inlaid wine coolers in pale satinwood were in the minority.

The early 1800s saw pretty small wine coolers, often simply outlined with boxwood stringing lines, and the mahogany now paler than it had been 20 years earlier. A new shape from c1785 was the domed lid, particularly on rectangular models, the octagonal and hexagonal forms having fallen from favour.

5/30 Another rarity is this English oval wine cooler of c1760. With its bombé sides, carved cabriole legs and frieze, the influence is decidedly French, but the general form and some details point to an English origin. Note the finely cast brass band to the top mount, the castors beneath the hairy paw feet and the richly gilt cast brass carrying handles in the full rococo style. The brass liner is probably not original. A famous maker of wine coolers with elaborate brass mounts was Samuel Norman (fl 1759 –1767), but this would seem to be an earlier model than his recorded oeuvre.

5/30a Four designs for 'Cisterns' from the 3rd Edition of Thomas Chippendale's The Gentleman and Cabinet Maker's Director *published in 1762. These fanciful designs are in the full-blown rococo style, and although many of Chippendale's designs were executed, these are not known to have been made, or to have survived.*

◁5/31 *A simple cellaret of about 1770. The top is crossbanded with tulipwood outlined with stringing, and the moulded edge is deeply concave. The brass carrying handles and ogee feet with their brass and leather castors hidden beneath are all suggestive of its having been made in a good cabinet maker's workshop. Note that there are no dovetail joints showing: this is indicative of the use of mitred dovetails, the most complex of joints. It is not lined inside but merely divided to store 12 bottles at room temperature.*

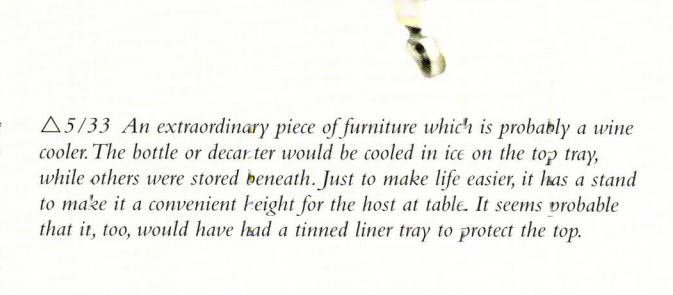

△5/32 *Furniture makers were capable of fun and making something to look like something else. This is surely an example. What appears to be an Irish peat bucket is actually a wine cooler and oyster bucket. The top tray was probably originally intended for ice to keep oysters cold, and the lower part is accessed by a door in the side. Much Irish dining room furniture has ribbed or reeded elements and dark mahogany was particularly favoured. It seems probable that it would have had a tinned liner tray to protect the top.*

△5/33 *An extraordinary piece of furniture which is probably a wine cooler. The bottle or decanter would be cooled in ice on the top tray, while others were stored beneath. Just to make life easier, it has a stand to make it a convenient height for the host at table. It seems probable that it, too, would have had a tinned liner tray to protect the top.*

Chapter 5 Wine coolers, cellarets and cisterns

5/34 This delightful small cellaret, while not unique, is an unusual form, not just for its shape, but also because the bottles rest on their sides in individual baize-lined holes. Note the scratch-bead moulding around each hole and the bespoke lock made to fit the apex of the door. The legs allow a dating in the 1780s.

5/35 The word important, often over-used by antiques dealers is actually appropriate here; clearly this cooler was made for a grand house. The sophisticated early neoclassical design embellished with ormolu mounts and handles, are an expensive touch. The top moulding is gadrooned which, with the advent of neoclassicism was a little old-fashioned, suggests that this is early in the neoclassical period, perhaps as early as 1760. The scale-inlaid legs, chevron veneered sides and block feet also hark back to earlier forms. Wine coolers of this period were without lids; hinged lids arrived a decade or so later. Open wine coolers were made as dual-purpose furniture, doubling as jardinières or, to use a modern term, planters.

5/36 This is another early neo-classical wine cooler of c1765 with many similarities to 5/35 and possibly from the same cabinet-making workshop. The white-painted surface is unusual but was used for furniture to accompany a decorative scheme. The fluted frieze edged with the bead-and-reel band and the garrya-husk handles are typical neoclassical ornament.

5/37 This is an extraordinary and probably unique wine cooler dating from about 1770. The architectonic quoins and collared legs are idiosyncratic and give much interest, but perhaps not as much as the spotted ivory inlays. The front has a pair of ivory pateræ which resemble gothic rose windows and ribbon-and-bow-tied swags of stylised foliage set against finely figured mahogany. The stepped top (see detail) is inlaid with ovals and rectangles and set within a frame of guilloche. It is tempting to speculate on the other furniture that may have originally accompanied it.

Chapter 5 Wine coolers, cellarets and cisterns

5/38 The octagonal brass-bound wine cooler illustrated here is probably everyone's idea of an antique wine cooler and many of this model were made. Sadly they are seldom in this condition. This is a fine example with its fluted frieze, moulded legs with original leather castors and C-scroll brackets. Interestingly, the most overlooked aspect of octagonal and hexagonal wine coolers is the jointing of the sides by hidden mitred dovetails cut, not at right angles but at 135°, and tapering towards the base. These are possibly the most complex joints in all British cabinet making and yet they are always made with engineering precision.

△ *5/39 Hooks are occasionally seen on the inside of octagonal and hexagonal wine coolers, between the lead lining and the top. These are to hang small bin labels (see 2/15). Sometimes the hooks have been removed or broken, leaving only marks where they once were. The appearance of old lead lining is clearly visible here, as is the style of dividing the inside of a wine cooler.*

5/38a Two designs from George Hepplewhite's The Cabinet-Maker and Upholsterer's Guide *for cellarets, also called gardes de vins. They appear in each of the three editions of 1788, 1789, and 1794. It is interesting to note that while the designs show parallel sides to the carcases, in reality almost all executed examples have tapered bodies.*

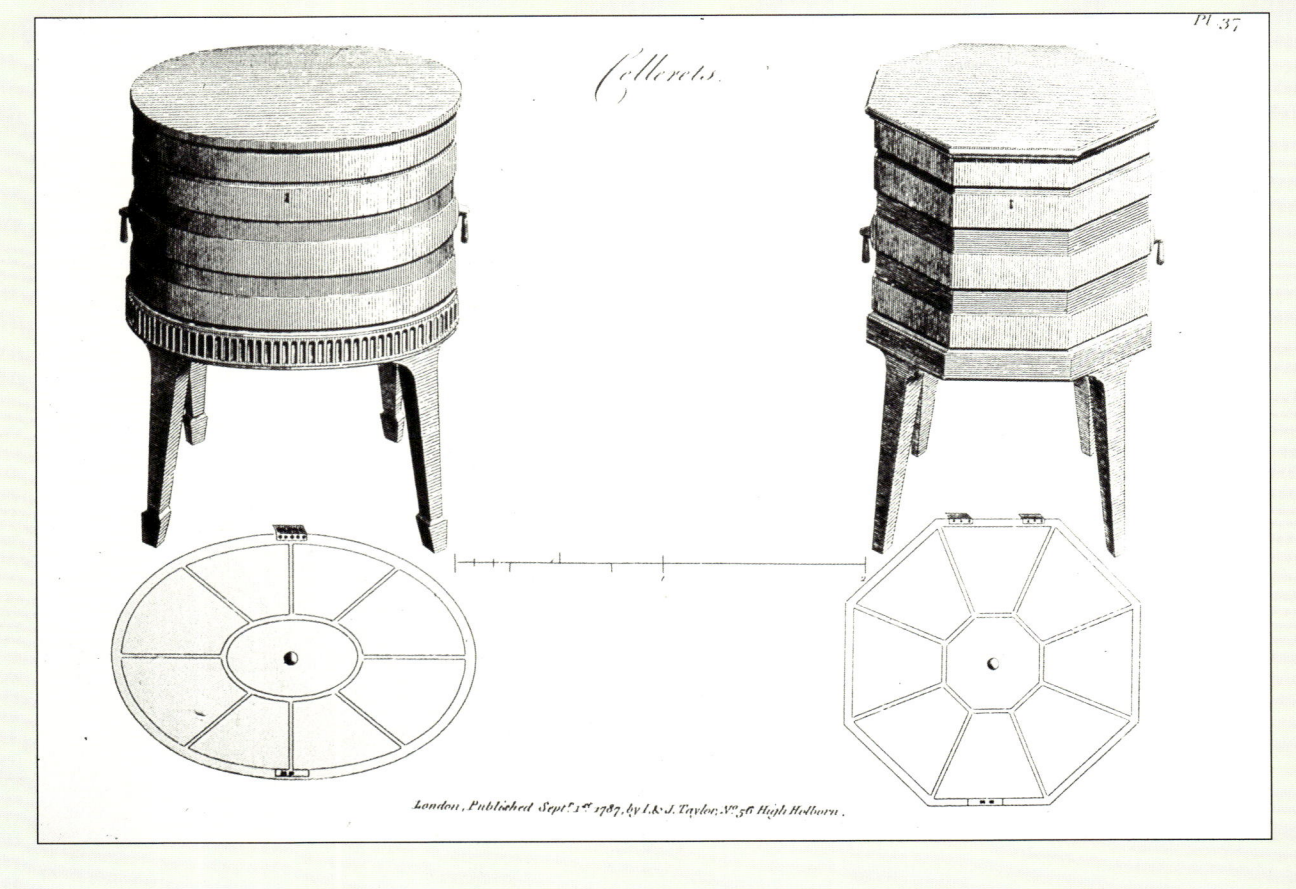

5/40 An hexagonal mahogany brass-bound wine cooler. This was a common shape in the 1770s and 1780s. The example here is better than most, with its panels of harewood (stained sycamore), inlaid paterae, fluted legs and delightful segmentally veneered top. It is interesting to see that in polishing the brass over many years, the surface of the wood has also been depleted. This is proof, if any were needed, that the piece has not been in the workshops of a restorer who would, almost certainly, have tried to make the colour of the wood the same all over. Such unrestored furniture is much prized by serious collectors, who decry the practice of preparing all antiques for mainly foreign markets where perfection of appearance has become an unfortunate obsession.

Chapter 5   Wine coolers, cellarets and cisterns

5/41 This open wine cooler, with its fluted frieze and legs headed by pateræ, is pure neoclassicism The decorative detail of the upper section has anthemia, garrya husks and more pateræ. It can be seen that the upper section is veneered in contrasting mahoganies, indicating that the husk and anthemion decoration is carved and then let into the veneer as are the corner embellishments and panel mouldings. It dates from about 1775.

△ 5/42 This detail of an open-topped octagonal wine cooler shows how decorative embellishment can add substantially to the appeal of a piece of furniture. The blind fret in the Chinese taste was promoted by Thomas Chippendale in his Gentleman and Cabinet Maker's Director first published in 1754 with subsequent editions and enlargements. Note also the cleverly designed brackets uniting the legs to the frame and the stop-chamfering to the legs which gives them a lighter profile and yet retains strength. The block feet allow leather and brass castors to be fitted almost invisibly underneath. All these details suggest that this was the production of a first-rate London cabinet maker's workshop.

◁ 5/43 Oval wine coolers first appeared in the 1730s and until the 1770s did not have lids. This example of c1780 is typical, with its brass bands and coopered or staved construction. Such coolers were made at the same time as hexagonal and octagonal forms; it was simply a matter of choice for the original customer as prices between one model and another varied little. While this one is well made with good timbers, it is devoid of embellishments such as moulded legs, carved central moulding and fancy handles. It divides into two parts to enable the melted ice to be poured away after use.

5/44 A 'Gardevine with a Trunk Lid to Hold 9 Bottles' made to a design by Gillows of Lancaster (see details). There are comparisons to be made between this drawing and the following cellaret, and the firm attribution to a well-known firm of cabinet makers makes this piece a rarity. The original drawing for the gardevine (number 4351) taken from the Gillow records is dated 1787. The records also show that this design was executed between May and June of that year. Gillows were importers of timber from the West Indies and in particular Jamaica and Barbados, and this gave them the opportunity to use the finest in their own workshops. The trunk lid became popular at the end of the 18th century and remained so for a few years in the 19th. Gillows were among the the very few English cabinet makers who stamped their work.

1 a Guardevine with Trunk Lid — 9 Bottles
2 3/4 ft of Inch Mahy and Vinear at /
9 1/4 ft of Inch do and Vinear ...
2 ft of Inch do — the Legs at 10 p/ft
2 1/4 ft of 3/4 Inch do — the Bottom at 7½ p/ft
4 ft of 1/4 Inch do — at 4 p/ft
1 Pair of Stop Hinges
1 Lock and Escutcheon
1 Pair of Lifting Handles
1 Sett of Sockett Casters — 7/8 Inch
1 Doz'n 3/4 Skrews
26 Skrews 7/8 Inch
Glew and Oil &c

Chapter 5 Wine coolers, cellarets and cisterns

Following the Battle of the Nile (Aboukir Bay) in 1797, in which Nelson gained an historic victory over the French fleet, there was a national interest in things Egyptian, which spread, particularly through the influence of Thomas Hope, to furniture. Wine coolers became sarcophagus shaped, and sprouted corner decoration of acroteria, one of the motifs associated with the eastern Mediterranean. This was also a period when dining rooms expanded in size quite substantially, with tables seating two, three or even five dozen. In response wine coolers were made to hold more bottles than previously and were sometimes supplied in pairs. With Britain ruling the waves, commerce in wine burgeoned and the effect on dining room furniture was apparent.

The Regency period had its influence on wine coolers, and the sarcophagus shape with its four outward-sloping sides was pre-eminent. Legs were abandoned in favour of lower coolers resting on plinths or bun-shaped or lion-paw feet, usually with castors hidden in recesses underneath. This was because the sideboard began to be made with pedestals and the wine cooler rested between them rather than being a separate entity to be seen somewhere else in the dining room. Mahogany remained the preferred wood, usually veneered onto an oak or pine carcase but used in the solid for the feet. Decorative elements were often, but not always, added and might consist of columns, panelling, mask handles, or gadrooned edges.

By the 1830s, a growing interest in the romantic vision of the gothic form was taking hold, and this was reflected in wine coolers, as in almost all other furniture styles. The revival is often called gothick. Oak replaced mahogany as the principal timber, and was decorated with gothic motifs - trefoils and quatrefoils in imitation of the architecture of the medieval period.

The gothic revival lasted until the middle of the 19th century, and after this wine coolers appear to have ceased being made to any significant extent, until copies of late 18th century models were reproduced in the late Victorian and Edwardian eras.

△ 5/45 *This cellaret typifies the late 18th century and dates from about 1790. It is a pretty, small size and is panel-veneered in well-figured mahogany outlined with stringing and a narrow banding of purpleheart on all sides and the top. The proportions are excellent, and while not a grand piece, this is a fine example of good Georgian taste. The similarity of the decorative treatment of this cellaret to 5/44 allows an attribution to the same makers, Gillows.*

△ 5/46 *Another example of a late 18th century rectangular wine cooler. It has a concave moulding to the lid, while the front is quarter-veneered and centered by a large oval of figured mahogany framed by boxwood stringing and a narrow band of satinwood. The short square tapered legs are panel-inlaid with boxwood stringing, including the inside surfaces, which is unusual. Unlike French furniture, much British furniture was fitted with brass castors and the flush-fitting castors seen here are standard for the last two decades of the 18th century.*

Cellarets were made to hold wine at room temperature, and therefore were not made with metal linings. They followed the pattern of wine coolers, but were seldom made before about 1780. The oval open wine coolers before that date often had removable linings, so there was no need for a separate cellaret. Like lidded wine coolers they usually had interior divisions to separate bottles, but of course they were not fitted with taps.

The duality of purpose of the cooler and cellaret, begs the question as to whether or not they were made in pairs, one a cooler and the other a cellaret. The answer is that they were; examples are very scarce and those that survive are all early 19th century in date.

Bottle canterburies are rarities that began to emerge in the 1750s. They were made to hold bottles at an angle, or upright decanters in the dining room. They usually held six or eight bottles (or decanters) and have shallow divisions with notched sides so that short cylindrical bottles of the period could be kept in an almost horizontal position. Of the few that survive, a surprising proportion appears to have the Irish cabinet-making characteristics of shallow frieze carving and shell decoration, either on the frieze or the cabriole legs. The finest London-made examples have well detailed carving on the top edges of the divisions. A few cellarets were made with lids as simple wine canterburies. The word canterbury in this context is very probably a 20th century expression coined by the antiques trade.

5/47 This is a fine oval wine cooler and cellaret (it is both) from the opening years of the 19th century. The body is carved mahogany with curved fluting or strigilation, while the top viewed from above is formed as a very large patera centered by a smaller one. It rests on four ebonised paw feet and has four lion-mask handles. It is considerably larger than many previously illustrated and was intended to be placed beneath the centre section of a sideboard. The interior demonstrates that it was both for cooling wine and keeping other bottles at room temperature. The design owes much to Robert & James Adam's Works in Architecture, *Vol III, pl. VIII, published posthumously in 1822 by Priestley & Weale. It was probably made by Thomas Chippendale the Younger.*

Chapter 5   Wine coolers, cellarets and cisterns

5/48 The 19th century saw the introduction of the sarcophagus shape for wine coolers, raked outwards, sometimes sharply from the base, and often of panelled construction. This early example of the type has no lid and was probably intended as a jardinière as much as a wine cooler. The simple form belies the high standard of making, and the finely cast satyr-mask handles emphasise the quality. It has castors hidden beneath the plinth (another 19th century innovation). It dates from about 1810 and, like most wine coolers of this date and later, is larger (31in/78·5cm wide) than most 18th century examples. This is because the fashion for bigger dining rooms and longer sets of chairs meant more wine.

5/49 This sarcophagus-shaped wine cooler is of a type often seen, but seldom in burr walnut or in this condition. The outwardly-raked carcase is balanced by the very low pyramidal lid, while the panelled body with its applied carved front decoration is counterbalanced by the thumb-moulded lid surmounted by a finial of fruiting vine and flowers, and by the paw feet. This general shape was much used in the period 1820–1840 and occasionally later, although mahogany was the usual wood used in wine cooler construction.

5/50 The revival of the motifs of ancient Greece was a popular theme among the best London designers of the early 19th century, Thomas Hope and George Smith among them. This cellaret, very much in the manner of these designers, is an interpretation in mahogany of an antique stone burial casket (sarcophagus) with applied ebonised plaster decoration of anthemia to the acroter corners and swags of laurel leaves pendant from ram's heads. It rests on fluted stump feet with castors beneath and has baize-lined interior divisions for bottles or decanters. It dates from c1805–1810.

5/51 A pair of wine coolers made of oak and carved in the rich gothick style which became popular in the 1820s and developed until mid-century. The design for this pair of coolers was published by Peter & Michael Angelo Nicholson in The Practical Cabinet Maker *in 1826.*

Chapter 5 Wine coolers, cellarets and cisterns

5/52 The 19th century saw an ever-increasing size to dining rooms and their furnishings. This cellaret holds eight double magnum rectangular decanters which were made to fit the partitions. The mahogany carcase is embellished with multiple carved scrolls, flowers and massive gadrooning, and is veneered with panels of burr elm. The decanters (see right) are engraved with a rose, thistle, shamrock and daffodil on each side: how more British can wine paraphernalia be? It dates from about 1840–50 and provides a magnificent contrast to the small elegant productions of a previous generation.

5/53 This wine cooler was made about 1860 and its cylindrical form is decorated in the grecian style with anthemia (stylised honeysuckle), pateræ, Greek key, lotus leaves and a lotus bud finial. It stands on three scrolled corbel legs with paw feet and castors. Notwithstanding the vocabulary of classical antiquity, this is far removed from the pretty and often delicate forms of the late 18th century which used many of the same motifs. It is 24in/61cm in diameter. Hardly any floor-standing wine coolers were made after about 1850 with the exception of a few reproductions.

Chapter 5 Wine coolers, cellarets and cisterns

5/54 This fine bottle stand or wine waiter (by some called a bottle canterbury but this is a recent term) clearly was made in one of the finest London workshops in the mid-18th century. The high-definition carving around the upper section and the cabriole legs with their leather and brass castors and volute scroll toes, all indicate the best London workmanship. The bottles (squat cylinders or onion-shaped at this time) could either stand upright or be laid so their necks were held at an angle. These rare objects pre-date the cellaret as somewhere to hold bottles at room temperature in the dining room. Some, with shell motifs in the middle of the long side, are Irish and these usually have faceted pad feet.

5/55 Another bottle stand. This example in rich dark mahogany with shell-carved knees, an abundance of shallow rococo scrolling foliage against a spotted background to the frieze and thin gadrooning, gives away its Irish origins. It is interesting to compare this and the previous, very English, interpretation of the same idea.

5/56 This is a simple cellaret probably of provincial origins, with charm and a delightful colour and patination. The lid with its divisions for bottles is a most unusual feature. However, comparison with 5/54 and 5/55 should leave one in no doubt about their relative merits.

Wine funnels

The apparently simple operation of pouring wine from a bottle into a decanter can give rise to problems. First, wine can easily be spilt between two narrow-necked glass vessels. Second, when one piece of glass touches another either or both can chip or crack. Third, when a corkscrew penetrates a cork, a piece of cork is sometimes dislodged into the bottle. Finally, old wine and port can throw a sediment, and this should be disturbed as little as possible.

Great care should be exercised when decanting, or wine will be cloudy from the sediment. All these problems are solved, or at least made easier, by the use of a funnel designed for the job. Funnels generally have been used for centuries, but those designed for decanting wine were developed in the mid-18th century. Many people refer to wine funnels as port strainers but whatever they are called, they can help in other ways too.

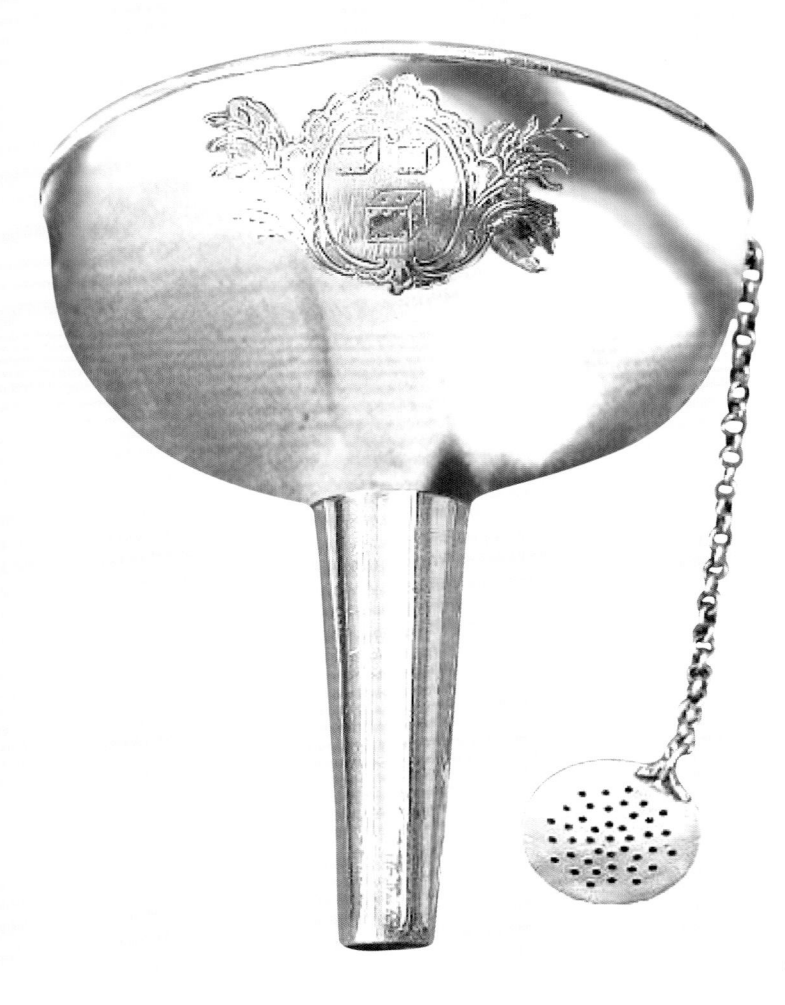

6/1 This is arguably the earliest known wine funnel. Were it not for the 'bath-plug filter', it would not be a wine funnel at all, but a funnel used for culinary purposes. However, the filter can be said to put its use beyond doubt. It is engraved with the coat of arms (three dice) of Vincent Mathias who was in the treasury of the Queen's household and who died in 1782, aged 71. It is 4in/10cm long and 3¾in/9·2cm in diameter and is marked inside the bowl. Although not clear, the date 1738 is just decipherable, but there is no maker's mark.

Chapter 6 Wine funnels

The standard English wine funnel is made of silver. It has a bowl at its upper end, and a spout which is curved or cranked at the lower end. The bowl has perforations in its base, usually holes arranged in a geometrical pattern, to catch errant pieces of cork, and the curve in the spout is to deflect the wine down the wall of the decanter, rather than allowing it to splash in the bottom. It is the cranked spout which differentiates a wine funnel from funnels generally. The bowl and spout were made separately until the end of the 18th century. However, by the opening years of the 19th century, the bowl and spout were usually made in one piece with the coarse filter inserted within the bowl. The tight fitting of one part inside the other is achieved by their being accurately sized and not needing a screw or bayonet fixing, although in rare cases a bayonet joint has been noted. There was usually a moulding around the junction which was decorative and added strength to that part of the funnel.

A third element was usually fitted but has often been lost. This was a ring, sometimes perforated, to which a piece of muslin could be sewn or otherwise held for fine filtration. The ring usually fitted within the junction of the two other parts, but occasionally formed the rim of the bowl. Being small and lightweight, it was almost always unmarked, although one inner ring with a maker's mark has been noted in a Sheffield example.

A wine funnel made in two principal parts allows the inside of it to be cleaned. This is essential if old wine stains and residue are not to taint what is being freshly decanted. The top rim of a funnel always has a decorative moulding, not merely for decoration, but primarily to add strength to a part which otherwise would be susceptible to damage. Early funnels can have gadrooned rims, but beaded and reeded mouldings were the norm from about 1770–1810. Later, during the Regency period, more elaborate mouldings became popular; shell decoration was especially so. The spouts of wine funnels were never decorated, neither were the bowls of 18th century examples, but from about 1820 some wine funnels had embossed or repoussé decoration.

Another element of all antique wine funnels is the tang. This is a small tab attached to the rim of the bowl, and logical thought suggests that it enabled the bowl of the funnel to be used as a strainer over a large vessel such as a punch bowl. A definitive explanation for the tang has yet to be made common knowledge, but what is certain is that all silver and some other wine funnels had them; some have broken away and have not been replaced.

From about 1795, many funnels had three short wires soldered to the top (bowl end) of the spout. These were usually less than 2in/5cm long and ran parallel to the spout. This feature allowed the air to escape when wine was being decanted. Occasionally cast or repoussé reeded decoration at the top of the spout performed the same function.

Some wine funnels were made with stands into which they would fit when not in use, so that drops of wine would not stain furniture. The proportion of those made with stands to those without, is unclear but, judging from extant funnels and funnel stands, it was probably considerably less than half. Few wine funnels are seen today with their original stands, but a high percentage of these appear to have been made in Edinburgh. Furthermore, Edinburgh funnels and stands were sometimes made of oval, rather than circular section, a design apparently not used elsewhere.

Wine funnels were usually made in London, but provincial assay offices also marked them. Chester and Exeter funnels are very rare indeed. So too, are those from York. A few were made in Newcastle, but surprisingly few in Birmingham. Sheffield ones are more numerous, but did not appear until the 19th century.

While silver is the usual material from which wine funnels were made, other materials were also used. Most glass funnels, and there are many of them, were not made for wine but for general culinary or scientific use. However there are rare glass funnels with curved spouts dating from the late 18th century which undoubtedly were for wine. They were made in a single piece and do not have a coarse filter (unless the few that survive have all lost their filters). Porcelain wine funnels are considerable rarities, and enamel examples equally so. Much less rare are pewter wine funnels, and these usually date from two decades either side of 1800. Old Sheffield plate funnels are uncommon, but after about 1850 electroplated examples enjoyed popularity.

The earliest extant British silver funnel dates from 1661 and those that pre-date 1700 are extreme rarities. Indeed, any examples from before 1750 are rare, and the few that do survive are usually Irish. However, most of these early funnels were not specifically made to help in decanting wine as they have straight spouts and no filters. They have often been described as wine funnels by an antiques trade keen to give their wares an appealing label, but an analytical assessment indicates they were for general, and probably culinary, use, and that if they were used in the decanting of wine it was a secondary consideration.

Wine funnels before 1760 are very scarce, but from 1765 they were made in large numbers. The earliest usually had a perforated plug attached by a chain to the bowl, as an alternative to the two-part funnel. This arrangement seems to have lost favour after about 1765. In general, early wine funnels tend to be smaller than later ones, and have ogee-sided bowls. From about 1780 until the late 1790s, the favourite bowl shape was roughly hemispherical, at which point a new model was introduced. This comprised a bowl and spout in a single long form, with the filter occupying the entire top end, and incorporating the top moulding and tang. This type remained in vogue for barely 15 years when the pre-1800 form was re-introduced, but now of larger dimensions and with a more decorated rim.

6/2 A very rare Worcester porcelain wine funnel decorated in the Chinese famille rose *palette in about 1753–4. Only 14 Worcester polychrome wine funnels are recorded and this one is 4½in/11·5cm high. Porcelain funnels do not have internal filters, so whether they were actually used for wine is debatable, but collectors of porcelain refer to them as such.*

6/3 Another very rare Worcester funnel painted with a charming vignette of a Chinese lady with a fan. The inside rim is decorated in the famille rose *palette in a trellis pattern. A Worcester funnel painted in monochrome in magenta is known.*

Chapter 6   Wine funnels

6/4 *A glass wine funnel with a curved spout. The bowl and the top of the spout are facet cut, a form which bears a close resemblance to the stems of wine glasses and the bodies of some decanters of the 1760s –70s. Facet cutting had been a form of decoration of glass since the 1720s, although this is a later pattern. Glass funnels are common, but most were not made specifically for decanting wine; those with curved spouts are for wine and are rare, facet-cut ones being the rarest.*

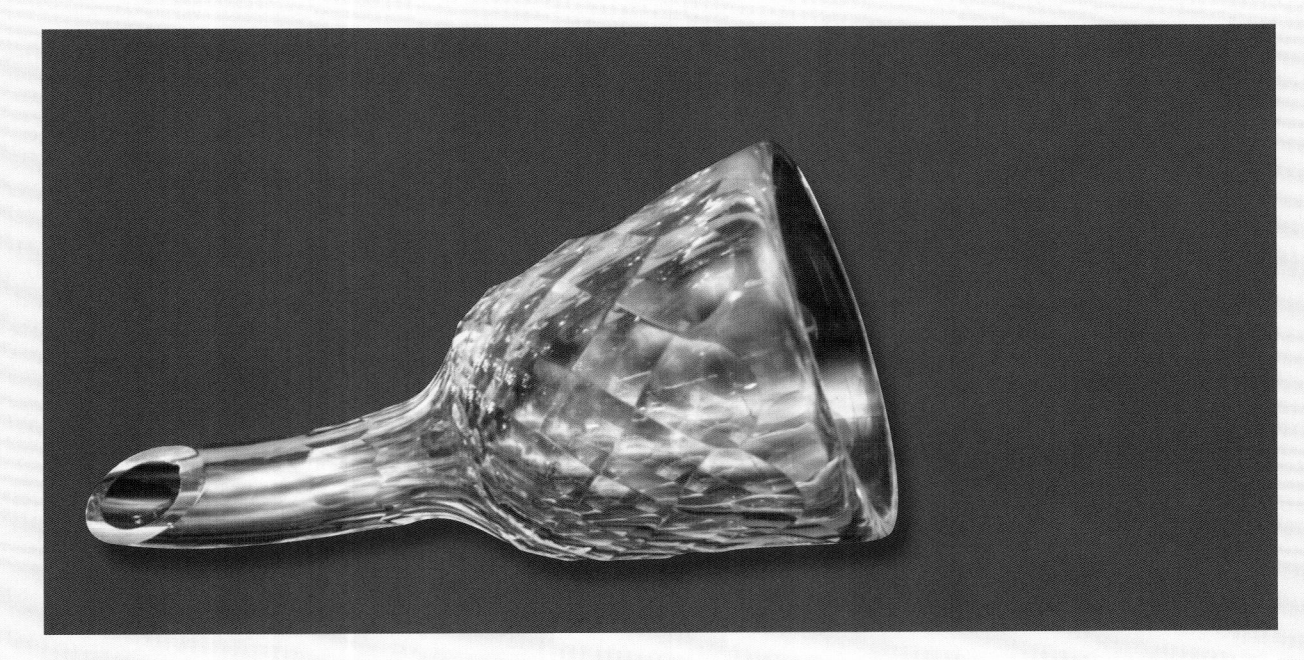

6/5 *Two glass wine funnels. These, like the facet-cut example, do not have a strainer or filter. If inverted, the bowls of these funnels look very much like the bowls of wine glasses of the period 1750–70, a dating to which these funnels also conform both in colour and glass-making technique.*

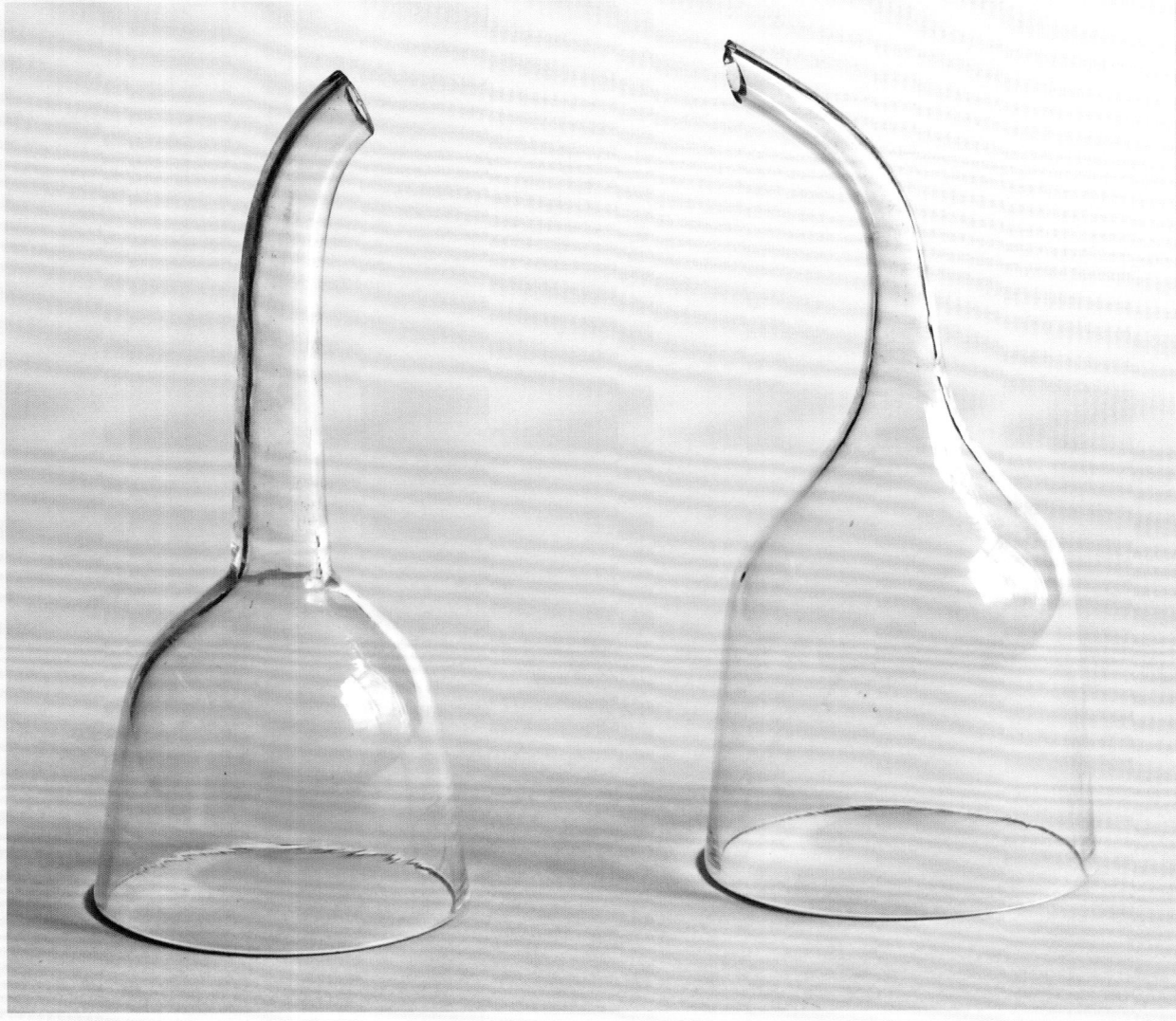

6/6 A rare enamel wine funnel. The off-white ground is decorated with a pretty blue vignette of a bird on a branch of fruiting vine, sprays of flowers and a stylised leaf motif repeated around the rim and base of the bowl. The rim is bound with an ormolu (gilt brass) moulding with a corded edge. The inside of the funnel is painted with sprays of foliage within more of the stylised leaf border. The funnel was made in copper, and the enamel is opaque white glass fused on both surfaces then decorated in blue. With such a fragile medium, it is not surprising that few have survived.

6/7 If an enamel wine funnel is rare, then a pair… Clearly these are from the same workshop as 6/6 but with decoration in pale magenta, some would say puce. It can be seen that the tangs have been removed, but they are always susceptible to damage. The bunches of grapes, both inside and outside the funnel show that they are indeed wine funnels.

Chapter 6   Wine funnels

6/8 A silver wine funnel made in Hester Bateman's workshop in 1782. Her enterprise was one of the largest in London at the time and much of its output was designed in the latest fashion, if of only moderate quality. The beaded mouldings and the shape of the tang are typical of her work, but perhaps the spout was once a little longer and with a V at its pouring end. The cup-shaped bowl was usual in the 1780s.

6/9 There are very few surviving funnels that were made and assayed in the smaller provincial cities of Exeter, York and Chester. This is one of only two known made in Chester, and it bears the hallmarks for 1784. It closely follows London-made models of the 1780s, although it is slightly smaller and lighter than most of these. Note the pronounced curvature to the end of the spout and the unusual lack of decorative moulding between the spout and bowl. The monogram was engraved at the time it was made, or very soon after.

6/10 This wine funnel is pewter and the shape of the bowl and general configuration would suggest that it was made about 1800. Like its silver counterparts, it has a cranked spout and shaped tang, although that shape is unlike recorded silver ones. The bowl shape is known as an ogee and was popular for silver funnels of the 1790s and early 1800s.

6/11 This early 19th century wine funnel was made in 1804 by William Allen who was registered at Goldsmiths' Hall as a smallworker. Note the similarity with the pewter funnel, and the top of the spout with its partial reeding to allow air to escape from the neck of the decanter. The tang is not visible in this image, but is present. The top edge of the bowl is reeded like the decoration where the spout and bowl join. Wine funnels are almost never engraved with a coat of arms, but this one, like many, is engraved with the crest of the original owner.

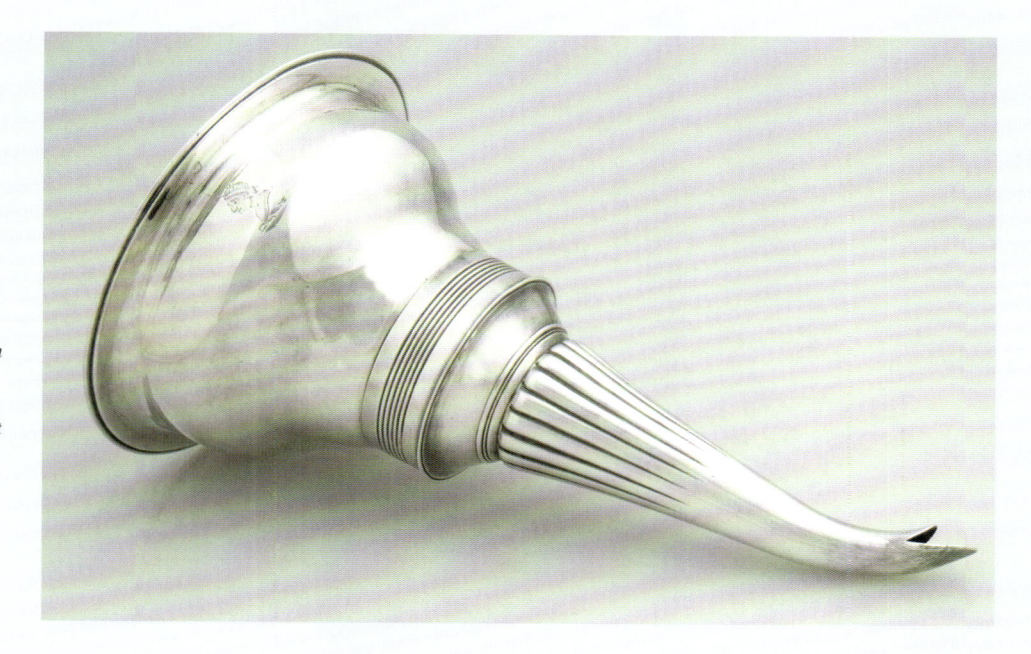

6/12 This is a very unusual silver wine funnel with its original stand. Both pieces are marked with a thistle, an unidentified maker's mark (RS) and the duty mark only. It was made in Scotland, probably Edinburgh, in about 1800 and is curious for two reasons. First it is made in one piece and has an odd arrangement of two rings for attaching gauze or muslin to strain the wine. Secondly, where the bowl meets the spout, there are three radiating, square-section spikes which allow air to escape from the decanter. The stand has a slightly domed centre and a raised astragal moulding around its edge.

6/13 It can be seen in the photograph that this wine funnel is in exceptional condition, without any dents or distortions; this is unusual as funnels generally tend not to be solidly made. This one is. The bowl is of thicker gauge than is customary and, very unusually, the spout is cast. The shape and construction is typical of the early 19th century. Note the outer shell is now in one piece with the strainer resting inside. This has its interior ring with which to attach a muslin disc for wine filtration. It was made by William Seaman in 1810.

Chapter 6   Wine funnels

6/14 This is a good Sheffield plated wine funnel of about 1810; indeed the model is very similar to 6/13. Note the seam which can be seen clearly running down the side of the bowl and less clearly down the spout. The inside of the bowl is Sheffield gilt, a much rarer sight than Sheffield silver plating. It has a gadrooned rim of solid silver to take any wear and tear without showing copper through the surface. The scribing lines setting out the pattern of piercing of the holes in the strainer are also clearly visible. The tip of the spout has been a little distorted, but overall this is a fine example of a plated funnel.

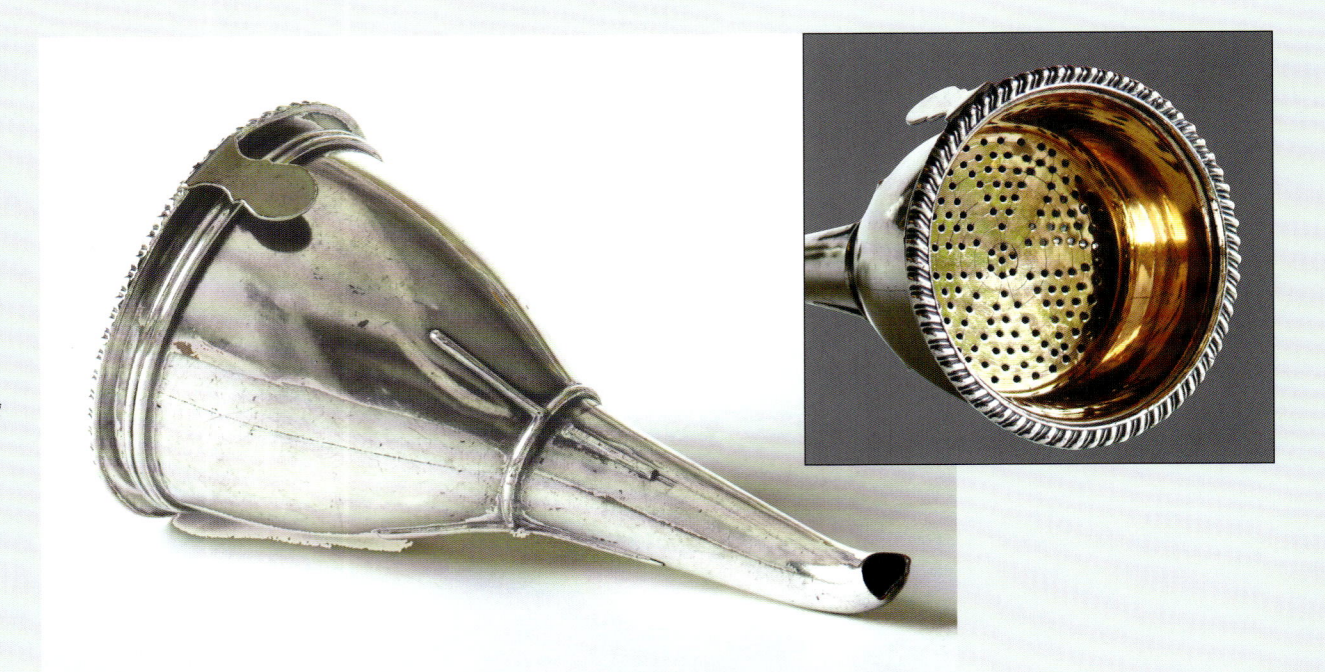

6/15 This is a good funnel made in 1820 by Robert Peppin and the lack of dents and bruises, so common in wine funnels, testifies to its heavier gauge than most. The bold gadrooning of the bowl encompasses a cartouche with an engraved crest, and the turned decoration to the spout and bowl add to its appeal. The body and spout are integral, while the filter and rim, to which the tang is attached, are a close fit within the bowl. Until this date filters were pierced in geometrical patterns; this element of the funnel was obviously re-considered by the maker.

6/16 Charles Fox, who made this funnel in 1825, was a better-than-average silversmith and a prolific one. With its deeply gadrooned bowl and cast gadrooned rim it has style, further emphasised by the shell tang. However at half the weight (3½oz/110g) of 6/13, and much lighter than 6/15 but no smaller in size, it is made of thinner silver and this has resulted in damage (and expert restoration). It has to be said that although it is a less good funnel than some, it is a good deal better than many that are both lightweight and devoid of style.

6/17 Another funnel and stand made in Edinburgh, this time fully marked on both parts of the funnel and on the stand, by J McKay in 1826–7. Each piece is plain with a border of cast acanthus foliage, and both the funnel and stand are engraved with a crest and motto. A small amount of the tip of the spout is missing, a typical result of wear and tear. Any funnels with their original stands are seldom seen, and of the few that exist, more than half were made in Edinburgh.

6/18 This is a fine and solid wine funnel made in 1828 by Robert Hennell. Like almost all early 19th century funnels the bowl and spout are made in one piece with the strainer fitting inside. The bowl is finely decorated with repoussé flowers and foliage against a matted ground, and the tang is a deeply cast shell. At 8oz/ 250g, this is considerably heavier than most, and its weight is a reflection of its quality. At 5in/12·8cm long and 3in/7·8cm diameter, it is no larger than the previous funnel.

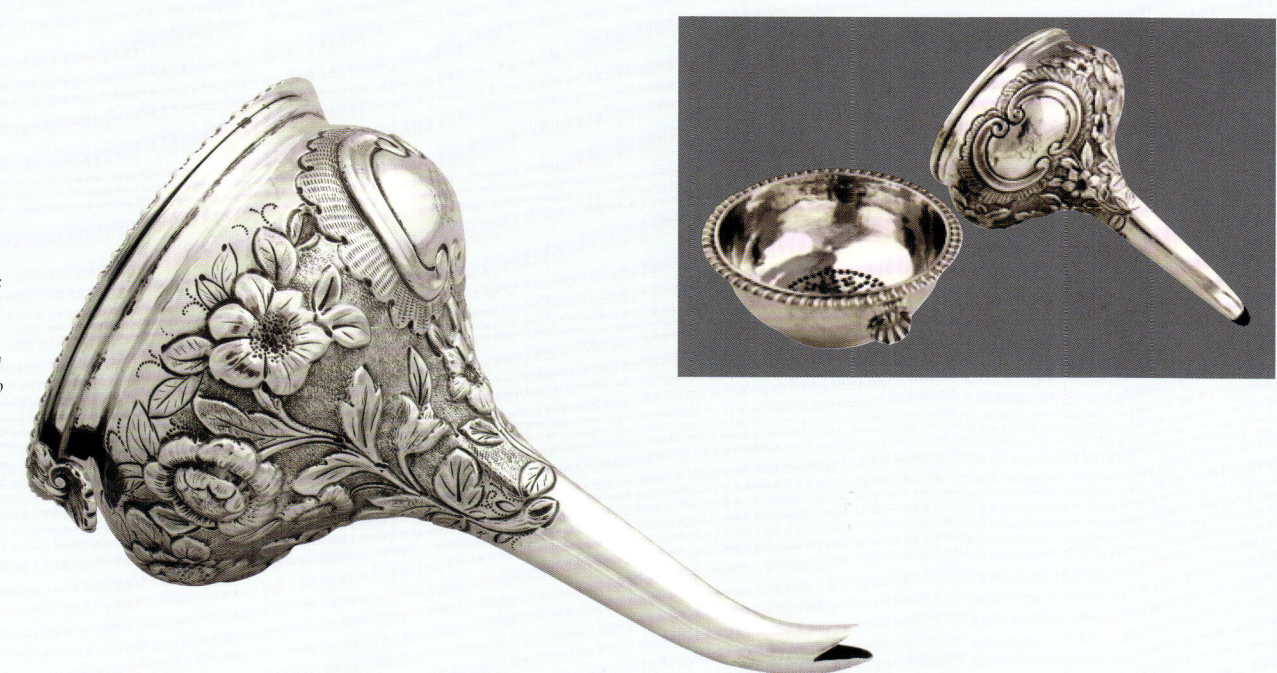

Chapter 6 Wine funnels

6/19 This extraordinary wine funnel is 12½in/31·8cm long, and must have been a special commission from someone who used large decanters. The bowl is typical of funnels made about 1820 with its ribbed side, gadrooned rim and shell tang, but the length of the spout is far from typical of any period. Note the three applied wires to allow the air to escape the decanter and the well cranked and shaped spout. An even longer funnel by Paul Storr has been noted.

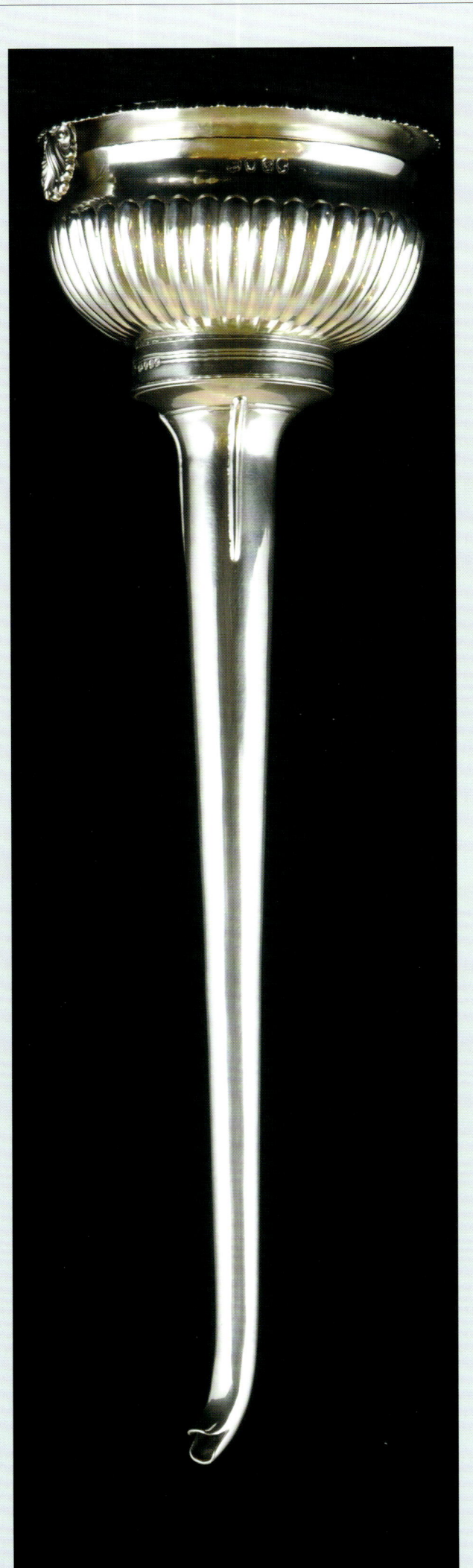

Few wine funnels were made during the second half of the 19th century, but the 20th century saw many being made in the form of earlier, usually 18th century, models.

Being made in two parts, it was obligatory to put hallmarks on both parts of a silver funnel, the larger part having a complete set and the smaller having at least the maker's mark and sterling standard mark (the lion passant). Funnels in Britannia standard silver have not been recorded. In the 18th century, the full set of marks was normally on the bowl, but this practice left the bowl seriously dented when it was returned from the assay office to the maker. To remove the dents caused by the marks, the maker had to de-bruise the marks, that is, hammer them out and polish the surface. In so doing the marks were largely defaced or degraded, so it is not surprising that few funnels of that period survive with a good set of hallmarks; often they are all but illegible. Later funnels were marked in different places which tends to result in better marks being seen today.

Because wine was (and sometimes still is) decanted in the cellar where there is poor light, a silver funnel can reflect what light there is to ensure that little or no sediment is decanted. However, decanting is normally done holding the neck of the bottle over a candle or other light source, so that the moment any sediment is seen to be leaving the bottle, the decanting process can be stopped. Fine filtration through muslin gauze is seldom practised today, and it is probably because of this that so many of the interior rings have been lost.

6/20 By the 1820s the thistle shape for the bowl of a wine funnel had become widely used. This one, by Rebecca Emes & Edward Barnard and made in 1824, has the unusual feature of the lower bowl and upper spout being slightly fluted, a more sophisticated method of letting the air escape the decanter.

6/21 A Victorian wine funnel of unusual construction with the bowl formed rather like an inside-out seashell with a cartouche left undecorated to take an inscription. This reads 'From W Kingdon to J J Tanner'. The filter, too, is unusually pierced in a floral and foliate pattern, while the top portion of the spout is deeply embossed with a band of fruiting vine above lozenge-shaped panels and further foliage. It was made in 1838 by Charles Fox the younger, whom Arthur Grimwade described as 'the last individualist plateworker before the debacle of Victorian mass production'.

Chapter 6 Wine funnels

6/22 A group of three pottery wine funnels which probably came from the same factory as they are similarly made. Rather than curved spouts, they have an aperture on one side to deflect the wine down the side of the decanter. They date from the mid-late 19th century.

6/23 A wine funnel stand of unusually heavy gauge with cast shell and gadroon border. It is engraved with the crest of the 50th Regiment, the West Kent Regiment of Foot. Wine funnel stands are often of light gauge and have been used for many other domestic purposes; this may account for few remaining with their funnels. This one was made in 1826 by William Eley.

6/24 A japanned tin-plate combination wine funnel and corkscrew. The first patent was taken out on 11th March 1618 by Aaron Rathburne, and the cheaper method of protecting an invention, the registration of it, in 1839. Combination tools had been in use since the 18th century, but the first registration to include a corkscrew and wine funnel was made by William Dainty on 22nd June 1843. In comparison to many of the wine accessories in this book, this must rank among the more rustic, but what it lacks in sophisticated materials and design, it makes up in charm and academic interest. Note the lacquered (not gilded) stamped plaque above the corkscrew.

6/25 A very unusual decanter-cum-funnel. Its shape and decoration suggest a date at the end of the 19th century. The funnel element is engraved with a band of latticework while the body of the decanter is divided into sections by ladder-like engraved divisions. The reddish hue in the handle and neck is a refraction from a piece of mahogany furniture nearby.

Decanters and carafes

Of all antique wine accessories, decanters are among the least considered by the collecting fraternity and yet they can be among the most satisfactory to study and collect. The lack of interest shown by most collectors of antiques is a boon for those who appreciate good wine. Once a huddle of enthusiasts focuses on a category of antiques, whether it is tea caddy spoons or nutmeg grater boxes, dog collars or button hooks, the prices rise sharply, usually to a degree which defies sound economic principles. Some antique wine accessories have been the subject of avid collecting, but from a wine enthusiast's viewpoint, decanters have (so far) escaped that fate. While decanters in general have been collected by very few people, there are some categories that have been keenly sought. Among these are the earliest of English decanters by George Ravenscroft and his contemporaries, enamelled decanters by the Beilbys of Newcastle-upon-Tyne, and decanters with so-called Lynn decoration. However, the reason for their being collected, and therefore highly valued, is that there are collectors of 17th century glass, of work by William and Mary Beilby, and of Lynn glass, rather than because they are decanters.

A small group of mid-late-19th century coloured decanters. The left hand example is Bohemian, the rest are English.

Chapter 7 Decanters and carafes

Before considering glass decanters, mention should be made of arguably the earliest British decanter to survive. It is made of leather and copiously mounted in silver. It has not proved possible to find an image to reproduce here, but the decanter is conical in shape. The top half of the decanter is silver and the stopper is topped by a figure of Neptune. The silver is engraved with the armorials and coronet of Lord Ogilvy of Banff. Above the arms is engraved 'Helpe youre selfe' and below is engraved 'Davide Ogilvie, Nova Scotiæ: 1644'. It was exhibited at the Wine Trade Loan Exhibition held at Vintners' Hall in June 1933.

Not only does a decanter with wine in it look appealing on a dining table, but it also enhances the drinking qualities of the wine itself. It is perhaps expedient to consider why decanters were used in the first instance. Before the 19th century, the process of making wine was less well understood than it is today and consequently it contained impurities and sediment to a degree we never now see. Decanting the contents of a bottle it allowed the clear wine to be separated from the sediment; it also allowed the wine to oxygenate, which in most instances improved it. While a few of today's fine wines throw a sediment within the time-span we allow to drink them, this mild oxygenation through decanting can usually enhance the appeal, both imagined and real, of even inexpensive wine bought in a supermarket.

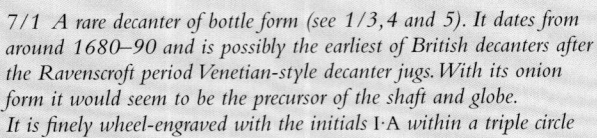

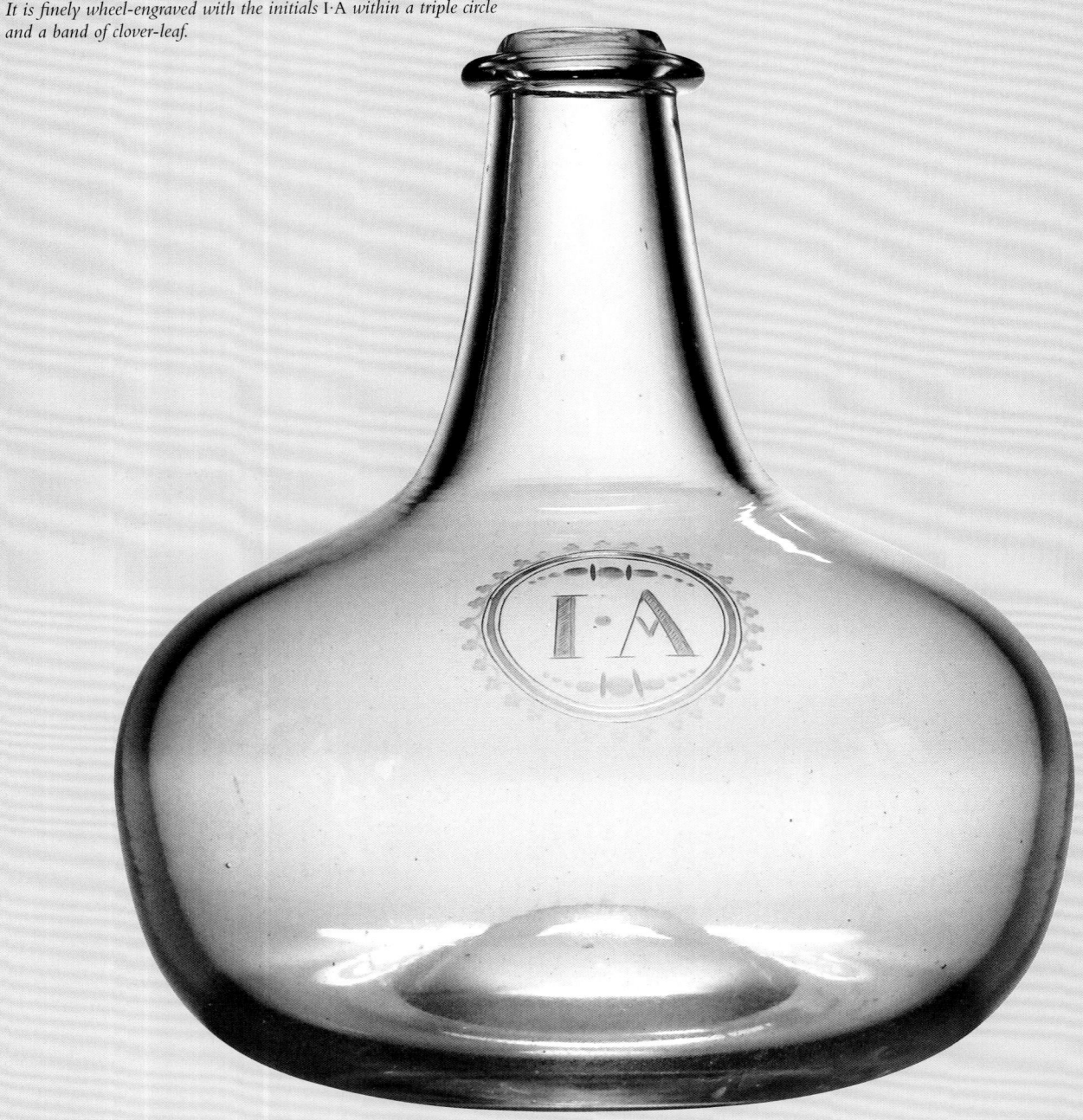

7/1 A rare decanter of bottle form (see 1/3, 4 and 5). It dates from around 1680–90 and is possibly the earliest of British decanters after the Ravenscroft period Venetian-style decanter jugs. With its onion form it would seem to be the precursor of the shaft and globe.
It is finely wheel-engraved with the initials I·A within a triple circle and a band of clover-leaf.

While corkscrews, coasters, wine labels and wine funnels all made their appearances over a brief period of time, decanters as we know them today took a long while to develop. The Romans had glass vessels from which to serve wine while later, from the 14th century, the Venetians made glass wine-serving bottles and the idea was copied over much of Europe, particularly in what today is Germany and Holland. The history and development of glass making is well chronicled elsewhere and need not appear again here.

The invention of lead glass seems to have taken place in several places at about the same time during the 1670s in the Low Countries and England. The notion that George Ravenscroft invented lead glass is now given little credence by scholars, but he was in the vanguard of its development and commercial success. He seems inextricably linked with early English glassware, but this may be due to his name which rolls off the tongue so easily like those of other celebrity makers of decorative art objects such as Hester Bateman, Thomas Tompion, and Thomas Chippendale.

Very few decanters of the 1670s, '80s and '90s are seen outside museums or famous collections, and in any event are not suitable for even occasional use. Not only are they too valuable to risk damaging, but the shapes and very constitution of the glass was improved upon in the 18th century, making earlier models best kept for study, and for collectors.

7/2 A plain shaft and globe carafe (a decanter which never had a stopper). Until recently, received wisdom was that decanters of this shape were dated to about 1730, but it appears that they can be much earlier. This example has a small degree of crizzling in the neck. Crizzling is a disease of glass in which the crystalline structure begins to break down, and was a problem when lead glass was first being developed in the 17th century. The date of this carafe is probably about 1690–1710. Carafes of this type are called serving bottles by some.

Chapter 7 Decanters and carafes

It appears that a great revolution in wine drinking occurred between about 1720 and 1740. During this time cylindrical bottles, wine labels and usable decanters were either invented or developed into forms that are easily recognised today. Earlier bottles could not be binned horizontally because they were more or less onion shaped, decanters were jug-like, and wine labels had not been thought of; this revolution saw a great increase in numbers too.

There are two forms of decanter which may have been, and probably were, made coevally and these are the oldest British decanters likely to be found outside a museum or glass collection. They are the cruciform and shaft and globe. Both forms were made between about 1690 and 1750, and either or both may have been made earlier, but it seems that the shaft and globe was the earlier shape, and the cruciform the later one.

The cruciform decanter, thus called because its plan is more or less a cross, had the body made by being blown into a mould. From those that have survived, it is clear that rods, probably of steel to withstand the heat of molten glass, were used in the shaping of these decanters as the inside corners usually have cylindrical sections. The shape does beg two questions. Why make a decanter of that form? Was it to give the surface of the decanter the greatest area so that it would cool wine more quickly, or was it to be placed between upright rods on a table for stability? Or is there another reason? It is true that much wine, both white and red, was chilled at various stages in history, but pictorial evidence of the early 18th century appears not to show the usage of these decanters. Indeed cruciform decanters hardly ever feature in drawings or

7/3 A popular early 18th century pattern of decanter was broadly cruciform when seen in plan (looked at from the top). Cruciform decanters (actually they are carafes, although nearly always called decanters) were seldom symmetrical and were blown into moulds held between vertical rods which leave clear impressions. The shape would allow wine to be cooled more effectively than conventional shapes, or it may be that such decanters are more stable when held by four spikes to prevent them toppling. Why they were made to this pattern has never convincingly been argued. These three date from c1720-40 and the neck rings allow a bung to be held securely.

paintings of the period, which makes dating them all the more difficult. Most received wisdom puts them in the second quarter of the 18th century, an assessment probably based on the colour of the constituent glass and its general feel.

What can be said for certain is that cruciform decanters were made without stoppers, and all had a string ring around the upper neck. This was a ring of glass applied in the making of the decanter a short distance (½–1½in/1·2–3·5cm) below the rim. Some string rings are 'bladed' while others are 'annulated'. In either case their purpose was to provide an anchor for a bung held fast with string.

By contrast, shaft and globe decanters are seen in contemporary illustrations and some with engraved decoration are dated, unlike cruciform decanters which seem never to have been decorated or engraved. Shaft and globe decanters seldom have string rings and later versions often had globular stoppers, most with inclusions of bubbles. Some have engraved dates that may or may not be the date of manufacture; some may have been engraved with dates commemorating earlier events, or they may have been engraved some time after they were made. As will be seen in succeeding paragraphs, shaft and globe decanters were not only made in the first and second quarters of the 18th century.

Decanter manufacture expanded and developed quite markedly from about 1755–60, and it is probably a consequence that wine funnels appeared at the same time, along with coasters to hold the decanters. This burgeoning of production continued for the following 200 years.

7/4 A pair of shouldered decanters dating from about 1740–60. These two are cut all over with shallow lozenges, each one slightly concave, which some call hollow diamonds. They have disc stoppers with scalloped edge cutting. While wine aficionados say they prefer decanters without cutting, the refractions caused by decoration such as this can enhance the ability to make informed judgements on the wine's appearance.

7/5 This shape of decanter, which was the standard from about 1750–1770 used to be known as a 'mallet' because of its resemblance to that tool. It is now classified as a 'sugar loaf' which again it resembles, but more cogently because it was called that when first made. This example is engraved, as many were, but the legend S A BERRY has defeated explanation. Whether it was the name of the owner, which would be very unusual indeed, or some long-forgotten fruit remains conjecture. The heart-shaped stopper is uncommon: some say this was a Dublin feature, but there is no proof.

Chapter 7   Decanters and carafes

Both the cruciform and shaft and globe shapes had long necks relative to their bodies. The models that followed reversed the proportion. The first decanter form to be made in large numbers used to be called the mallet shape because of its similarity to a sculptor's mallet. However, in his seminal book on the subject, Andy McConnell makes a compelling argument that they should be called sugar-loaf decanters on the grounds that that is what they were called at the time they were made. Their shape is strongly reminiscent of the standard solid block in which sugar was retailed in the 18th century.

The sugar-loaf decanter was first made about 1750, and enjoyed popularity for about 30 years. The proportions changed little from maker to maker, but as time progressed the basic shape, a tapered neck widening to a firmly-formed shoulder and a body that also tapered outwards toward the base, remained similar. By the 1780s the shoulder became less pronounced, and the 'taper' decanter evolved as the preferred shape, remaining popular for the remainder of the century. At almost the same time, if marginally later, the 'indian club' also became popular. This was similar, but the outline of the lower body curved inwards. With all these decanters, the lip of the neck was slightly everted; it had not developed into a flange.

Towards the end of the century, a clear new element of the decanter, the neck ring, appeared. These were first made by cutting into the neck of the decanter to leave two, three, four, or five slightly raised rings. These are incised neck rings. By the end of the century, neck rings were applied to the decanter body when semi-molten, and evidence can often be seen where the two ends of the applied glass meet; the joins can harbour dirt and become discoloured. The neck rings served three important functions: they allowed a good grip of the decanter; they enabled the decanter to become lighter in weight as the body no longer had to have a thick neck partially to be cut away, and they added strength to the neck of the decanter where the insertion of a stopper could exert considerable outward force. With the neck rings came a fresh decanter shape, the 'prussian', first with a target or bull's-eye stopper, and in the early 19th century with the mushroom stopper.

After about 1800, cut decoration on decanters became more widespread, so that by about 1815 many decanters were made with their entire surfaces cut. This may be a result of the then novel lighting by argand lamps using colza oil which gave a much brighter light than candles, the light being refracted in the cutting of a decanter. The shape of the prussian decanter, remained more or less the same for the first 20 years of the 19th century, albeit with slight variations of proportion. It used to be said that the increase in cutting was brought about by the invention of steam-driven cutting tools but, as mentioned previously, steam power was around 50 years earlier. Certainly light refracted through wine in a well-cut decanter is well displayed with glints and sparkle effectively showing the colour and clarity of the wine.

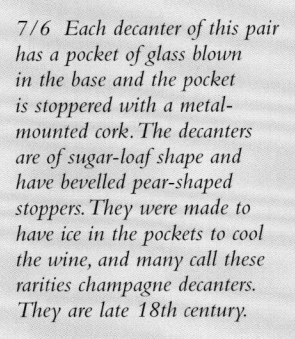

7/6 Each decanter of this pair has a pocket of glass blown in the base and the pocket is stoppered with a metal-mounted cork. The decanters are of sugar-loaf shape and have bevelled pear-shaped stoppers. They were made to have ice in the pockets to cool the wine, and many call these rarities champagne decanters. They are late 18th century.

◁ 7/7 The image of this decanter is deceptive as its scale is not immediately apparent. It holds six bottles and stands 18¼in/46cm high which, as antique decanters go, is very large indeed. Larger ones are recorded, but anything bigger than a magnum is very uncommon. While the shape is still a sugar loaf, the decorative detail of flutes and panel cutting is 10–15 years later than 7/5.

▽ 7/8 The date of these baluster-shaped or 'Indian club' decanters is very similar to 7/7, about 1775–85. The notion of putting a decanter on a pedestal foot was very seldom executed in the 18th century, but it re-made its appearance about 100 years later when it was advocated by Dr. Christopher Dresser as a way of lifting the decanter above the white table cloth for better viewing the wine. These are decorated with light wheel engraving of a guilloche band of darts enclosing stars and they have facet-cut necks.

Chapter 7 Decanters and carafes

Sometime before 1820, the prussian decanter was overtaken in popularity by the cylindrical model, and by large areas of simple panel or pillar cutting where there had previously been the more complex diamond, strawberry, blaze, and other forms. The universal mushroom stopper became hollow and of greater volume, and always had cut decoration (later French mushrooms were plain). Some decanters were being mould blown, a method of decoration that was relatively cheap to produce and gave the impression of having been more expensively cut.

The remainder of the 19th century saw numerous fresh designs and the re-appearance of some old ones. While the tall heavy decanters of the 1830s and '40s bore a resemblance to the indian club models of the 1780s and '90s, they were often heavily cut, and many had single neck rings before the neck ring eventually went out of fashion. Similarly, the shaft and globe decanters which began to appear in the 1840s bore little resemblance, apart from their general shape, to the decanters of 100 years previously. They were usually decorated and fitted with stoppers quite unlike their predecessors. On its second time round, the shaft and globe was popular for a prolonged period lasting until the early 20th century. The later examples tend to have a more squat globe than the earlier ones, with cut decoration bordering on the fussy.

There are too many decanter designs from the second half of the 19th century to describe in detail in this chapter, and they are best studied with images rather than words, but there is one dating feature of note. This is the introduction of a foot in the late 1840s, but not in general use until the 1860s. Dr Christopher Dresser advocated making decanters and jugs with feet, the better to see the contents against a white tablecloth – something always in place on a Victorian dining table.

Apart from the general evolution of decanter design, two other forms are essential to the understanding of British decanters. The first is the so-called ship's decanter and the second is the icing decanter; neither are common.

In the 1790s the form of decanter with a conical body was first seen. With its relatively broad base it was clearly more stable than the standard decanter, but whether any sensible naval officer would take one on a sail-powered ship with seldom-horizontal decks is open to question. Decanters were used on ships, and a well-known Cruikshank cartoon shows a highly inebriated and dissolute party in a ship captain's cabin with decanters and glasses hanging from the ceiling

◁7/9 Green decanters are less usual than blue, and this one is a transitional shape between a sugar loaf and a taper. It has a bevelled pear stopper and is a full bottle size. Coloured decanters are mostly thought to have held spirits, but occasionally one with a gilded label bearing the name of a wine is seen. When made in half-bottle size they were usually sold in sets of three (occasionally four) and gilt labelled for brandy, rum and hollands (gin). The fourth, if there is one, is usually shrub, a cordial made with rum and orange peel.

▷7/10 A pair of 'Bristol blue' taper decanters. The blue colourant for glass was cobalt oxide and the natural mineral was mined in Saxony. The monopoly of import was in the hands of William Cookworthy, proprietor of the Bristol porcelain factory and a merchant of that city. To make blue glass, the cobalt oxide had to be acquired in Bristol – hence the epithet. It can have a very rich, slightly purplish hue to it, quite different from other blues. Not all Bristol blue glass was made there. These date from c1785–95.

on a tray suspended by a rope. However, they are not broad-based decanters. It also has to be mentioned that some ship's decanters are engraved with anchors or inscriptions to sea captains while others are engraved with non-maritime initials.

Whatever the outcome of the debate over their original use, they have been called ship's decanters for a considerable time, and without a concise alternative it is convenient to keep a term that almost everyone recognises. Some call them Rodney decanters after the naval hero of the late 18th century, and indeed this was a term used at the time, so perhaps more correct.

Ship's decanters have long been popular, but those made before about 1820 are rare. They seem not to have been made between about 1830 and 1890. More than 90% of ship's decanters were made after 1890 with a large number made between 1900 and 1940; green or blue ones are always of late date. It is amusing to note that in the 21st century, when glass manufacturers fashion glasses and decanters to maximise the qualities of wine, broad-based decanters are enjoying a revival.

Icing decanters are even more seldom seen than ship's decanters. Sometimes called champagne decanters, they have a pocket of glass blown into the side or base into which ice can be placed without coming into contact with the wine inside. The earliest known is a shaft and globe of about 1730, and a few sugar loaves and tapers are known from the 1770s–90s. The ice is usually retained with a silver-mounted cork, although the mount is sometimes absent. After about 1800 the pocket is usually on the underside and, with cutting, is often difficult to see at first sight. After about 1830 they appear not to have been made until the closing years of the 19th century when, like ship's decanters, they enjoyed a revival.

Carafes

In large measure, carafes follow the same patterns as decanters. The simple difference is that carafes do not have, and never had, stoppers. In addition they are characterised by wider necks, although this is not always the case. When a decanter is fitted with a stopper, the neck is offered up to a lathe with an abrasive core to widen the neck to accommodate the stopper. The stopper is similarly placed in a chuck to abrade the peg until it is the correct size and taper. The operation on the decanter leaves a ridge on the inside of the neck which will be absent on a carafe, and this can easily be detected by feeling it with a finger.

◁ 7/11 *Decanters with a pocket blown in the side or beneath are known as 'icing decanters' or, for those who wish to aggrandise them, as champagne decanters. They are rarities and usually date from the late 18th century, like this one, from the 1820s or the early 20th century. The indian club shape and the restrained cutting suggest a date a little before 1800. The plug for the icing pocket is made of silver.*

▷ 7/12 *Decanters that never had stoppers are carafes, and this one is a magnum. The style of the wheel-engraved cartouche for CLARET bears more than a passing resemblance to the much earlier S A BERRY (7/5). However, the two applied neck rings and everted lip suggest a date of around 1790. The neck rings allow a good grip when the carafe is in use.*

Chapter 7 Decanters and carafes

◁ 7/13 *Towards the end of the 18th century, the bases of tapered decanters became broader and glass was sometimes blown thicker to take deeper cutting. The introduction of steam-driven cutting tools allowed this. The necks have four rings cut into the glass, and each body has a band of wheel-engraved drapery suspended from alternate foul anchors and oval paterae above a band of flutes. They are stoppered with plain target or bull's-eye stoppers. Note the lack of an everted rim, which places these firmly in the 18th century, perhaps as early as 1780.*

△ 7/14 *While this pair of decanters bears more than a passing resemblance to the previous pair, there are notable differences. The four neck rings are incised and the rim has become slightly everted suggesting a later date of 1795–1800.*

△ 7/15 *A similar pair of decanters with slightly everted lips. They have applied neck rings, a feature that follows incised ones, and they have pear-shaped stoppers. The necks are unusually narrow; that is not significant, but it does single them out as somewhat different from the norm. They were made c1800.*

The rarest of decanter models are Hodgett's or Hogget's decanters. They do not have flat bases, but are rounded or pointed so that they cannot be put down on the table; they have to be placed in a special stand or frame. They were favoured in officers' messes and in clubs, and the stand was set in front of the senior officer or chairman. The point was that when the port was circulating, it could not become stuck with someone who either forgot to help himself and pass it on (to his left), or was 'hogging it', it had to continue circulating until it reached the head of the table. Few have survived, but those that have often appear to be magnums.

Arguably the earliest known has a stand of iron covered with morocco leather, but most had rounded bases and were set in mahogany stands. A pair of these decanters is known with engraved stoppers, one for port and the other for sherry. It begs the question as to which way sherry was circulated and was any other wine given similar treatment?

▷ 7/16 *A decanter that cannot be set down on a table, but has to be held in its specially made frame is called a Hodgett's (or Hoggett) decanter; this is a very early example of c1800. Most were made about 20–40 years later. It is magnum size which further increases its rarity. The frame is made of steel covered with morocco leather (which has been replaced).*
The ovoid body means that when the port has been started on its journey it cannot be put down until it reaches the frame in front of the host. Traditionally, the wine is passed 'port to port'. The host will pour a glass for the person seated at their right and then pass the decanter to the left (the port side); this practice is then repeated around the table.

△ 7/17 *Occasionally an antique decanter is encountered which does not fall neatly into a category. Is this a ship's decanter? With its conical outline it may be, or is the proportion of its height to width too great? In any case it is a very unusual model and was made around the turn of the 18th and 19th centuries. Note the faceted neck rings and only slightly everted rim which allow such a dating.*

Chapter 7 Decanters and carafes

7/18 Very broad-based decanters are called ship's decanters, but how much this epithet is based in historical accuracy is open to question. At least everyone seems to know what a ship's decanter is. Sadly well over 90% of ship's decanters were made in the 20th century and distinguishing a modern copy from an early one is not always easy. This pair, with their incised neck rings and flute-cut bases, date from about 1800–1810. Modern copies tend have neck rings that can be felt from the inside of the decanter and they are usually a little larger than earlier models.

7/19 A pair of plain ship's decanters of the type most often copied, although these date from about 1800. They have three applied neck rings and bull's-eye or target stoppers. It is satisfying to see that modern glass factories are making broad-based decanters, not in an attempt to copy, but because oenologists say that the ship's decanter is the best shape to develop a wine once the bottle has been opened; it unlikely that late 18th and early 19th century glass makers thought of that.

7/20 Decanters that are almost the breadth of a ship's decanter, but not quite, are sometimes called semi-ship's decanters and these are examples. The incised neck rings and only slightly everted rims suggest an 18th century date, but the panels of diamond cutting around the body put them just into the 19th.

7/21 Another pair of semi-ship's decanters. The firmly everted rim puts them into the 19th century, about 1810–15. The band of finely hatched lozenges or strawberry diamonds confirm the date. Note also the star-cut mushroom stoppers which appear from about 1800 and remain the standard, although with numerous variations, for most of the next half-century.

Chapter 7   Decanters and carafes

◁ 7/22 A decanter shape which developed around 1800 is now known as the 'prussian' although it used to be given various names. The low shoulder, the (usually) three neck rings, and slightly incurving lower part of the body proved extremely successful because it functions superbly. It provides a good grip, is stable, pleases the eye and pours without gurgling. This is an early version with a pear-shaped bevelled stopper, but most have mushroom stoppers, and are not green, but clear.

▷ 7/23 This prussian decanter has blue neck rings which are a very rare feature. It is not known where they were made but various enthusiasts have suggested they were made near Sheffield as part of a whole range of glass made with blue rims, from tumblers and bird feeders to jugs and bowls. The idea of giving glass a coloured rim or band first occurred in Venice in the 16th century.

◁ 7/24 Another early prussian decanter and with a target stopper. Many who eschew decoration would say a decanter like this is perfection and it is not surprising that in recent times the model has been copied. Because of their popularity, it is not easy to find plain prussian decanters today.

▷ 7/25 Another prussian decanter with panel-cut neck, fluted base and star-cut mushroom stopper. Decanters like this were made in their thousands in the early 19th century although there are minor variations in shape and decoration. It is not difficult to find any number to form a matched set. This one was made about 1810 and has annulated neck rings, each ring comprising three smaller ones.

▷ 7/26 *An Irish decanter with two 'bladed' neck rings and panel-cut shoulders. The base is moulded with narrow flutes. Many Irish decanters have two neck rings although they were not all made in Belfast as some say. This one has a faint impression of a glasshouse moulded mark on the base, but it is not clear which one. It has a radially moulded target stopper.*

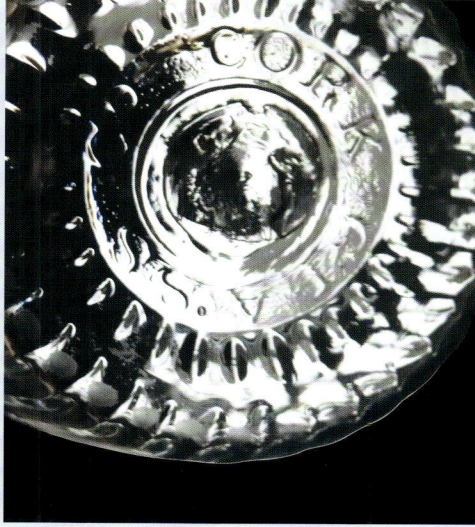

◁ 7/26a *This is the underside of a prussian decanter which was blown into a mould and so gained the impressed legend* CORK GLASS CO. *Other Irish decanters are occasionally seen impressed* WATERLOO CO CORK, B EDWARDS BELFAST, PENROSE WATERFORD *and others.*

▷ 7/27 *A rare and collectable form of prussian decanter does not have three neck rings, but a single one which spirals several times around the neck. The panel cutting at the shoulder follows the coil, becoming shorter towards the end. Spiral neck rings are often call snake neck rings. This one dates from around 1800.*

◁ 7/28 *Prussian carafes were also made and this one has a magnum capacity (two bottles). When a decanter is said to be a bottle size or magnum it will hold that amount comfortably, not to the brim. In this case two bottles would bring the wine to about mid-shoulder or about half-distance from the base to the rim. The panel cutting of the shoulders is taken over the neck rings to give an even better grip.*

Chapter 7 Decanters and carafes

Glass cutting had been used to decorate decanters since the beginning of the 18th century, but the practice became widespread from the 1750s. Although called cutting, the glass is not actually cut or sliced with a sharp instrument but is abraded away by being brought into contact with a rotating abrasive wheel, and polished by using ever finer abrasives. Obviously this can be done using one foot to power a treadle, but greater accuracy and speed can be achieved if the cutting and polishing wheels are rotated using water or steam power (today electric power is used).

It is not surprising that when steam-driven power was first invented and used in the 1760s it gave rise to cut glass. Birmingham and the West Midlands were the seat of this new invention, and Matthew Boulton and James Watt were the first to use and to sell steam-powered tools. Indeed Matthew Boulton's Soho factory was world famous and a tourist attraction when it opened its doors in 1762. It was the first factory capable of what became known as mass production, a catalyst for the industrial revolution. The Soho factory produced fine works of art in many media.

Glass cutting on decanters of the 1760s and 70s consisted of shallow slices arranged in geometrical patterns. Because of the curvature of a glass decanter, these slices appear as crescents. At the same time another form of cutting was used – faceting. Small shapes such as squares, hexagons, and octagons were popular not only on the necks of decanters but all over; sometimes an entire decanter was facet cut (see 7/4). Of course, because each facet was formed on an abrasive wheel it was slightly concave, but this gave it added brilliance which could refract and reflect light from a flickering candle.

Later in the 18th century, and in the 19th, a wide variety of cutting was used to decorate decanters, more meaningfully illustrated than written about.

7/29 *A slightly later decanter of about 1810–15 with a spiral neck ring. This one is cut like a snake and even has an engraved forked tongue (see detail). The decanter is finely cut in circular panels of diamond cutting with step-cutting above and below. It is very unusual for a star-cut base to turn the corner and be seen from the side, but when it does, it always indicates a decanter of very high quality.*

△7/30 *The crisp cutting in diagonal 'blazes' and the perfectly cut 'diamonds' set this carafe apart as of very high quality, further enhanced by its capacity. It is a double magnum (that is, it holds four bottles) and dates from about 1815. Large capacity and well cut Georgian decanters are particularly sought by collectors and serious wine enthusiasts alike.*

△7/31 A pair of decanters with all-over diamond-cut bodies beneath step-cut necks and star-cut mushroom stoppers. Diamond-cut glass proved very popular in the Regency period, particularly between about 1805 and 1820; these date from about 1815. The sparkle generated by the cutting shows wine well in candlelight.

△7/33 This illustrates the difference between a magnum (on the right) and a standard quart or bottle-size decanter. Probably from the same glasshouse, they date from about 1815–20 and have cylindrical bodies and step-cut necks. The smaller decanter will hold a quart (1·136l) but as it was intended to take a bottle (75cl) the wine would reach lower shoulder level allowing proper aeration of the wine.

◁7/32 These prussian decanters with barrel-shaped bodies have a narrow band of fine diamond cutting around the middle. This, together with the general shape, indicates that although these are probably Irish, much glass that is attributed to Ireland was probably made in mainland Britain. These are a very early example of decanters and stoppers being numbered, in this case 15 and 34. This does not infer that they are two from a long set, but that the glass makers decided that these two (from perhaps 60 made in one day) were most similar to one another to form a pair (see detail).

Chapter 7 Decanters and carafes

◁7/34 A pale green decanter the shade of which was much favoured from about 1820–1850. This is a large decanter, although not quite a magnum, and is all-over panel cut but with raised cut lancet panels. It has an early example of a hollow mushroom stopper. Green decanters are very suitable for serving white wine.

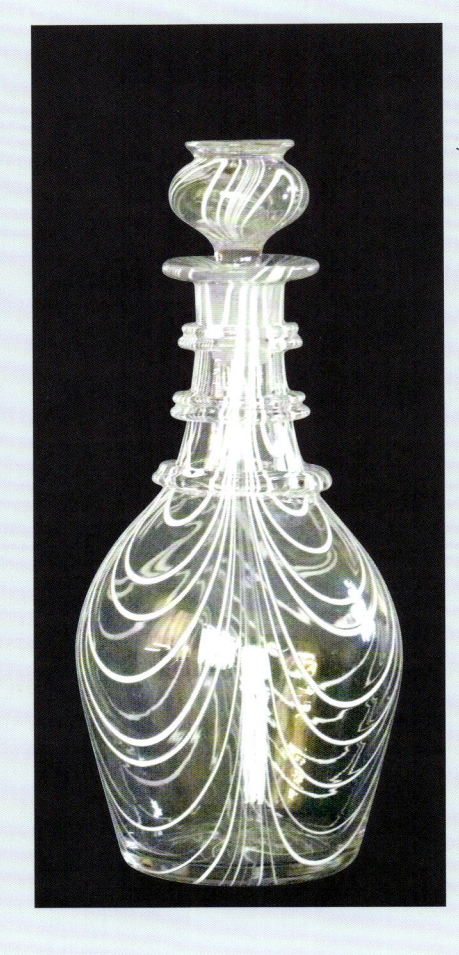

◁7/35 A prussian decanter with trailed white line decoration of a type sometimes associated with Nailsea glassworks a few miles south of Bristol, but probably made elsewhere in England. It has a hollow stopper and dates from about 1820–30.

◁7/36 A pale amethyst prussian decanter with three annulated neck rings and a moulded mushroom stopper. This type is often reputed to have a Newcastle origin although it is usually in clear glass.

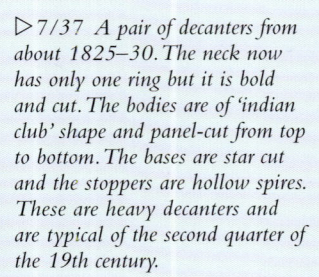

▷7/37 A pair of decanters from about 1825–30. The neck now has only one ring but it is bold and cut. The bodies are of 'indian club' shape and panel-cut from top to bottom. The bases are star cut and the stoppers are hollow spires. These are heavy decanters and are typical of the second quarter of the 19th century.

◁ 7/38 A green decanter of similar form to 7/37 although the neck ring and stopper are more rounded. The green is much more vivid than the shade of 7/34. Decanters like this are, at the time of writing, very undervalued. It is perfect for white wine, which is usually served too cool and often ruined by being chilled.

▷ 7/39 This pair of decanters typifies the decade of 1830–40. While the prussian shape persists, these two have pillar-cut bodies and panel-cut shoulders. The stoppers are unusual in being acorn-shaped and bold; the decanters are also very heavy, weighing 7kg for the pair, although they are only bottle size.

◁ 7/40 A ruby red decanter. The colour does not run through the glass but is formed by a thin layer of red glass encased by a thicker layer of clear glass. The clear layer has been cut all over with diamond facets but the cutting has not reached the red layer. The layering can be clearly seen at the base of the stopper. Usually a thin layer of coloured glass is to be found outside the thicker clear layer. This decanter was made about 1840–50.

◁ 7/41 Two tall cylindrical decanters all-over panel cut and with sharply everted rims which have been cut and scalloped to provide pouring lips. The stoppers are facet cut and hollow. They are not a pair, but decanters of this type were made in pairs or sets of three and they were often supplied in silver plated frames. They date from the 1840s.

Chapter 7 Decanters and carafes

7/42 The middle of the 19th century saw the re-introduction of the shaft and globe shape, first seen at the end of the 17th century, but now the decanters were usually decorated with cutting. This one has the spherical body deeply and sharply diamond cut while the neck is cut with slightly concave hexagonal facets. The stopper is a faceted ball, a pattern which became very popular over the following 30 years. The decanter dates from about 1855.

△ 7/43 A shaft and globe decanter of conventional form, but the wheel-engraved floral decoration is unusual on a decanter. It is more often seen on wine jugs.

△ 7/44 The proportions of this shaft and globe decanter suggest a late date of between 1880 and 1900 and the solid ball stopper confirms this. It holds a magnum and functions well, but the compressed shape of the body means that wine gurgles when it is poured.

7/45 The globe of shaft and globe decanters became steadily compressed with time. These are quite shallow and date from 1880–1910. They are lightly engraved with small stars both on the bodies and the stoppers, and each underside is cut with a complex star. Such decanters may have been originally supplied with matching glasses in numerous sizes.

Chapter 7 Decanters and carafes

Engraving. Glass can be engraved by drawing an image on it with a diamond; this is diamond-point engraving. A diamond can also be used to great effect for stippling, or creating an image with numerous tiny dots. Wheel engraving of glass is carried out in much the same way as so-called cutting: the glass is brought into contact with a fast-revolving abrasive wheel (not the other way round), and a pattern or picture is made either by being left as a matt image on the glass, or by being polished to restore transparency. Sometimes both matt and polished wheel engraving are employed to create a livelier image or pattern.

Etching. The fact that hydrofluoric acid will etch glass had been known since the 1770s, but it was not employed commercially in England until the 1850s. The glass to be etched was covered in wax, and the design was etched into the wax revealing the glass. It was then immersed in the acid, and the design appeared on the glass when the wax was removed.

Acid-etched glass should not be confused with wheel-engraved glass although the two terms are often muddled. Etching produces a shallower impression, tends to be less clearly defined, and appears semi-polished. (see 8/36).

Enamelling. The application of opaque or coloured glass onto a base, usually copper. However it is possible to enamel onto glass, and this can be a highly effective form of decoration. While enamelling on glass had been practised on the European continent for a considerable time, it was rarely used in Britain until the advent of the brother and sister team of William and Mary Beilby from Newcastle. Apart from being the most famous practitioners, their style is easily recognisable, and is of high quality. While most of their work was on wine glasses and goblets, they also decorated decanters.

Colouring, casing and staining. Glass is coloured by adding a colourant to the 'melt'. For example, cobalt oxide will make the glass blue. In the 18th century blue was fashionable, as was green and purple (usually called amethyst). Blue and green colourants were mixed to produce a dark teal or turquoise for decanters and glasses, the hue being determined by the proportion of the mix and the shade by the amount of colourants added to the mix.

It has often been observed that while blue decanters were common, blue glasses were rare, while the opposite is true for green – rare decanters and common glasses. It is probable that most blue and green solid-colour glass decanters were used for spirits rather than wine. Indeed blue (and rarely green) half-bottle decanters were often made in sets of three and occasionally four, and with gilt faux labels for brandy, rum and hollands (gin) with the occasional shrub to make up the four.

Blue glass is frequently referred to as Bristol blue, and many assume that it was all made in that city. This is not true, although blue glass was made there. There is much in a name, and 'Bristol blue' runs very easily from the tongue. How the phrase came about is interesting.

Cobalt oxide occurs as a natural mineral in what is today Germany but in the 18th century was Saxony. When mixed with glass and crushed to powder it is called smalt. When the Prussians overran Saxony in the Seven Years War, they sold the entire Saxon production to William Cookworthy, a Bristol merchant and owner of the Bristol porcelain factory. Thus anyone wanting to make blue glass had to buy the smalt (colourant) from Bristol. In fact there was an alternative supply in Cornwall, but it was much more expensive. The Bristol colour has rich overtones of purple when blown thickly, and even when thin is retains a fine brightness.

From about 1840, coloured glass decanters (and wine glasses) began to be made in a novel way. A thin-walled coloured decanter (or glass) was blown, then clear glass was blown inside it. When the decanter was cut, the clear glass was revealed beneath the colour, and a pattern or pictorial image was created. This is known as cased glass. More than one colour was sometimes used, a particular favourite being opaque white glass on the outside, with another inside, usually red or green. This technique was brought to Britain from Bohemia with migrant workers who also influenced designs. Red became a popular colour for casing because when it was used as a colourant for glass it appears black unless it is very thin.

In the early 19th century it was realised that glass could be stained, the favourite colour being yellow in shades from pale amber to yellowish brown. Later, inexpensive versions of cased decanters were made by staining in various colours; this technique is rare in British glass, while common in the Bohemian equivalent.

7/46 Various tall cylindrical coloured decanters. Each is clear glass 'cased' in a coloured glass and cut to reveal a pattern of clear glass. This form was very popular for a few years around 1845–1855 and examples are surprisingly numerous. The blue and white decanter, probably made by F & J Osler of Birmingham, and the pink and white decanter each have three layers of glass and are of a type much less frequently seen. Many tall and narrow decanters were made for fitting in frames.

Chapter 7 Decanters and carafes

△7/47 This variety of carafe is called a mell although the word in this meaning is not given in the Oxford English Dictionary. The shape proved popular and is usually stoppered with a cork, often with a silver-plated mount or one incorporating mother-of-pearl. Some put their date at about 1845, while others feel they were made in the 1870s and 80s. This example is of magnum capacity.

△7/48 A pair of turquoise mells for which the same remarks apply as for the previous carafe. They are a particularly attractive colour while most are rich dark blue or green. Some say that mells were favoured in Scotland.

△7/49 The idea of putting a decanter on small scroll feet is attributed to the Webb family of glass makers; a design of theirs with such feet was registered in 1867. This one was probably made in the 1870s and may originally been part of a set which would have included a claret jug.

△7/50 A pair of decanters with rich cutting and of heavy weight. The ovoid bodies are quite deeply cut with stylised fern motifs in panels below faceted necks. The stoppers are similarly cut. They are 'white' when compared with earlier decanters and date from the 1880s.

△ 7/51 *A fine set of eight decanters in bottle and half-bottle sizes. The baluster bodies are wheel engraved with foliate decoration and stand on collet feet. The long necks are panel cut and notched which is a feature of the 1880s and 90s. The hollow stoppers are inverted miniature versions of the bodies without the engraving.*

△ 7/52 *A set of three decanters and matching claret jug. Their attenuated form resembles the shaft and globe and seen previously, but the shaft has become a long cone. The band of fine diamonds on the shoulders of the bodies is repeated mid-neck and again on the hollow balloon stoppers. The squat bun feet and lower bodies are cut with fine flutes. They date from the 1890s.*

Chapter 7 Decanters and carafes

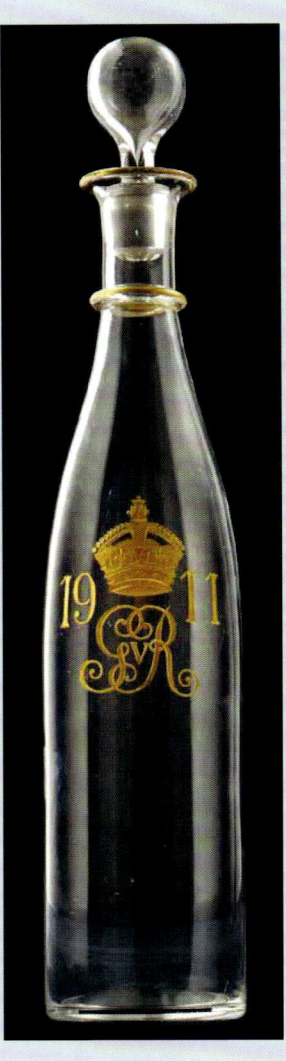

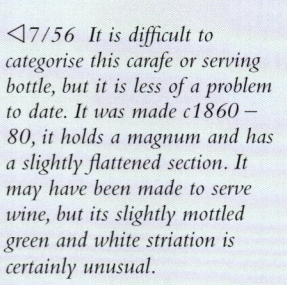

◁7/53 *In the Victorian age, both clean lines and exaggerated displays of decoration could find favour during the same period. Of similar date to the ultra-plain magnum decanter (see 7/44) is this shaft and globe, probably made by Stuart around 1900. The very thickly mould-blown decanter has been deeply cut and acid-etched to produce a rock crystal effect in a vaguely renaissance style. Other 'rock crystal' decanters and ewers could take up to 30 months of work by the engravers.*

◁7/54 *A plain tall decanter with a single neck ring to aid grip and gilded with the cipher of George V and the date 1911. It was probably made at the Whitefriars glasshouse under the ownership of Harry Powell whose ancestor, James Powell, had been a London wine merchant.*

▷7/55 *A rare turned cocus wood decanter. Like the few others known, it unscrews at the base of the neck, and probably dates from the late 18th century.*

◁7/56 *It is difficult to categorise this carafe or serving bottle, but it is less of a problem to date. It was made c1860 – 80, it holds a magnum and has a slightly flattened section. It may have been made to serve wine, but its slightly mottled green and white striation is certainly unusual.*

▷7/57 *A pretty serving bottle or carafe of a type often ascribed to Nailsea (actually the Nailsea Crown Glass and Bottle Company) a town a little south of Bristol. The swagged striations of blue are boldly conceived and can be easily felt if fingers are run over the surface.*

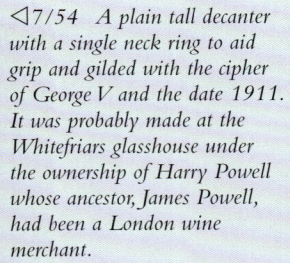

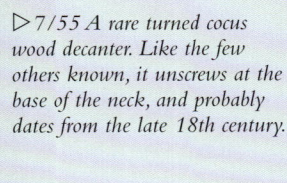

151

7/58 A group of large format decanters.

a A three-bottle (marie-jeanne) capacity decanter which dates from c1870. b A nearly magnum of c1790, which some call a port magnum because port throws more sediment. c A magnum prussian decanter which should have a mushroom stopper. d An early 20th century carafe cut with oval printies which glass cutters called 'olives'. e A three-bottle (marie-jeanne) capacity carafe, c1770.

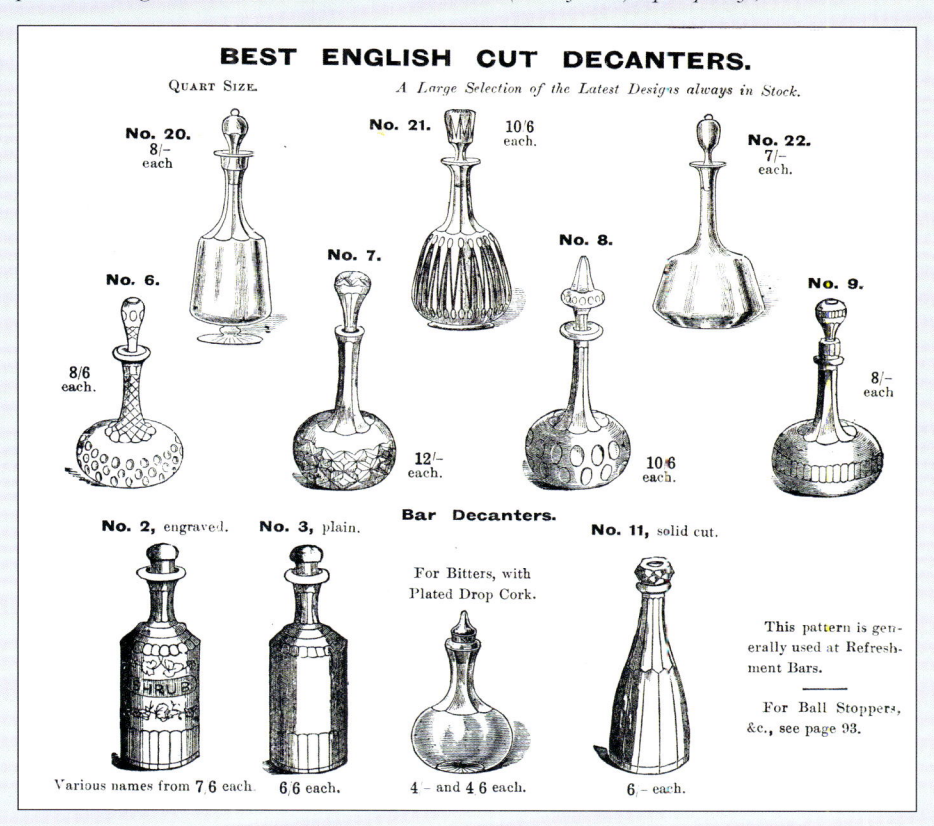

7/59 A page from Farrow & Jackson's 1898 catalogue showing decanters. Some of those shown were being made nearly 50 years earlier, and the selection is not as great as that offered by specialist glass companies. It should be remembered that the company was principally a supplier to the wine, spirit and beer trades, rather than retailers.

Wine jugs and claret jugs

Jugs have been used for many centuries, and there can be little doubt that many Greek, Roman and medieval jugs were used for serving wine. The latter were made of bronze, silver or pottery which was sometimes enhanced with dull green or brown glaze. Many were certainly large enough for a sizeable party, others were small and were in all probability made with varied uses in mind.

8/1 A magnificent set comprising a pair of wine jugs and six goblets. It was made in 1780 by Andrew Fogelberg & Stephen Gilbert, and is silver gilt, but very unusually, the gilding is in three colours. The jugs, in high neoclassical style are vase-shaped and rest on spreading feet matching those of the goblets. Each piece is set in a calyx of acanthus leaves and the feet are decorated with fluting, vitruvian scrolls, matting and beading. Each is also applied with a medallion of Greek mythological figures or putti, while the leaf-capped handle is decorated with garrya husks and the finial is a bud issuing from foliage. With the matching goblets these were definitely intended for wine: wine jugs of this date are very rare, unlike hot water jugs and coffee pots with insulated handles.

Chapter 8 Wine jugs and claret jugs

Large ovoid jugs of brown salt-glazed stoneware with short necks, sometimes impressed with an image of a bearded man below the rim, were popular in Britain as well as other parts of northern (Protestant) Europe from the 15th to the 19th century. The miserable caricature impression is that of Cardinal Roberto Bellarmino, a loathed Counter-reformation zealot. Because of this, they are known as bellarmines. They were produced in their millions.

Jugs of middle eastern and oriental pottery or porcelain of the 15th and 16th centuries and mounted in Europe, including England, with silver or silver-gilt mounts were probably used for serving wine. They may also have been used for toilet water, ale or other liquids; we have no way of knowing. One form, the tiger-ware jug, is commonly thought to have been used for wine although it, too, was probably intended for less expensive drinks. The body of a tiger-ware jug is made of mottled brown stoneware from the Rhineland and, typically, has English silver-gilt mounts to the foot, and matching rim, lid and handle decorated with strapwork and renaissance motifs. They appear to have been particularly popular in London and the south west of England, and most date from about 1550–1620. The expression 'tiger-ware' is a misnomer as the body is never striped, but mottled or spotty. More correctly, these jugs are nowadays referred to as brown salt-glazed stoneware.

8/2 Jugs of this type were made in their millions in the Rhine valley, for export all over northern Europe. Made of brown salt-glazed stoneware and usually with a bearded face below the rim and opposite the flat-section handle, they were for serving all forms of drink, both beer or wine. The face is said to be a caricature of Cardinal Roberto Bellarmino, a loathed Counter-reformationist zealot. This is an early example of c1550, and a small one at just 5in/12·7cm high. Many are up to three times the height.

8/3 A Rhenish brown salt-glazed stoneware jug with silver-gilt mounts made in London in 1562. These were almost always hallmarked for London or the west country. Commonly, but incorrectly, known as tiger-ware jugs most have exposed stoneware handles covered only near the thumbpiece. This example is unusual in that the whole handle is silver-gilt which suggests that it may have been broken. It stands 7¾in/19·7cm high.

8/4 A very rare and early English bellarmine made at Woolwich in about 1650. It is reputed to have been discovered in fishing nets off Eastbourne. It stands 8⅛in/20·7cm high.

The middle of the 17th century saw the first jugs specifically made for serving wine. They are earthenware with a whitish tin glaze (delftware) and made in London although the exact location has yet to be firmly established. They are most distinctive, with globular bodies, shortish necks and handles of flat section which were usually ribbed. They vary in size but range from about a half-bottle to magnum capacity. Their distinctive feature is the inscription on the upper part of the body in upper case letters and opposite the handle. The legends in underglaze blue read 'Claret', 'Whit' or 'Sack', with the date below. The dates are almost all between 1640 and 1665, and they have a scrolled flourish which seems invariably to start below the first figure (1) of the date. Indeed the similarity of style suggests a common factory and painter. They appear to be the only wine vessels to show the name of the contents until some decanters were engraved a little over 100 years later. Other jugs from the same factory, though exactly which one is a subject for research, have the monarch's monogram beneath a crown, or a coat of arms with initials. These jugs are much sought by collectors of early English pottery.

8/5 A London-made tin-glazed wine jug with underglaze blue lettering for SACK and the date 1650. Jugs like this were very popular for about 25 years from 1640 although few survive today. They almost always carry a date between the wine and a flourish which starts attached to the 1 of the date. This peculiarity suggests they were made in the same factory or even by the same hand. Sack was strong dry wine from Spain, principally from Jerez and Malaga; Canary sack was sweeter and much prized.

8/6 Another tin-glazed wine jug for WHIT and the date 1651. Whit is, by the standards of these rare jugs, a common name, and it is never written as 'white'. Note the flat-section handle and style of calligraphy which varies very little from jug to jug.

Chapter 8 Wine jugs and claret jugs

In the late 17th and 18th centuries silver jugs, with or without hinged lids, and of a capacity to hold a bottle or two, are not common. The antiques trade is given to calling them beer jugs but they may well have been used for wine, as decanter production was in its infancy. Most are of bold baluster form with a hollow scroll handle, and often with a waist moulding. Tall cylindrical jugs with lids are usually church flagons for holding the communion wine. By about 1770 the neoclassical taste held sway, and while earlier jugs had a distinctly masculine feel about them, the neoclassical models have a lighter, more feminine appeal; they are delicate and pretty.

When does a jug become a ewer, or vice versa? The answer is not simple, and indeed there are times when the terms are interchangeable or even downright confusing. Traditionally ewers were accompanied by a basin, and used for rosewater to refresh those having dinner. Ewer is the term also used to refer to a pouring vessel for washing before the days of plumbing and bathrooms. Pouring vessels for wine are usually called claret jugs but it would be wrong to assert that only wine from the Bordeaux area should be decanted into them. The Oxford English Dictionary has no entry for claret jug so it is quite probable that the phrase was an invention by the antiques trade in the early 20th century to give additional glamour to what was previously simply called a wine jug or a ewer. That some were clearly intended for wine can be deduced from the fact that they are embellished with fruiting vine, whether engraved or applied, as in the silver-mounted jugs of the 19th century. And there are some who call wine jugs wine ewers. For the sake of clarity, jugs for wine are referred to as wine jugs throughout this book. The term claret jug is used here because it is understood, but it should be reviewed. It is probably safe to use the

8/7 An early decanter jug which clearly shows the crizzling that occurred in the experimental years following the discovery of flint and lead glass in the late 1670s. This example is smaller than average at 8in/20.3cm, but the funnel-shaped top, while different from some, was a common feature. The decoration of the body is called 'nipt diamond waies' between pinched vertical ribs while the neck collar is described as vermicular. It probably had a loose-fitting conical stopper and the metal mount is probably an old repair, although others with similar bases are known.

8/8 Large silver baluster-shaped jugs resting on collet feet were made from the mid-17th century and for much of the 18th. While they are usually called beer jugs it is probable that they were intended for wine or other liquids, even for water for washing. This Irish example has a waist moulding which is common to many. It is 8¾in/22.3cm high, was made in 1718 and has a prettily engraved coat of arms.

term for wine jugs made after about 1830 as that appears to be how they were known at the time.

Silver jugs of the 1770s, without insulation to the handle, are considered by many to have been made for wine, but like so many antiques they were probably intended for any cold liquid. Hot water jugs and some coffee pots are similar, but they had wood handles, or the silver handles were covered in wicker (osierwork) for insulation. Later in the 19th century, ivory insulation elements were inserted in the handles for the same effect. Where the wicker has perished and been lost without replacement, such handles look thin and out of proportion to the jug, but those keen to sell are occasionally given to calling them claret jugs.

The earliest silver jugs indisputably for wine date from about 1775 and they had ovoid or vase-shaped bodies decorated with the usual vocabulary of neoclassical ornament such as bright-cut swags, paterae, guilloche, rams' heads and bell-flowers, and with borders of beading or reeding. However, the fashion for silver wine jugs appears to have been short-lived, lasting only for a decade or so.

Decanters with handles and a pouring lip, which we call claret jugs, were made in large numbers throughout the 19th century and into the 20th, but were substantially outnumbered by conventional decanters. The fashion for all-glass wine jugs did not firmly establish itself until about 1815–20; most were fitted with stoppers, but a few were clearly made without. They were often made with decanters to match as a set of three or more, but it seems that most sets have been split. By the late 1860s, the designs for wine jugs and decanters parted company and those jugs that did not follow decanter design are certainly claret jugs.

8/9 A curious handled decanter of pear-shaped form fitted with a beaded ball stopper. It does not conform to standard types and, like many such objects, is impossible to date with any certainty. Perhaps the best informed guess is that it was made sometime between 1710 and 1740.

8/10 This small jug is really little more than a wine bottle with a handle but made in clear glass. It is a rare survival and holds about a pint/half litre. One of the enduring joys of the subject is seeing some objects of great sophistication and others with abundant charm. This falls in the latter category. It is similar in general proportion to the bottle dated 1737 (see 1/11) but the octagonal bottle of 1770 (see 1/15) has even more similarities.

8/11 Another octagonal decanter jug, but this one has a stopper with air bubbles included which is probably original to it. While still exhibiting greater charm than sophistication, this is a more considered type and probably pre-dates the previous jug by 20 or more years.

8/12 A wine jug from c1805 with wheel engraving of the highest quality: perhaps that was expected by the Prince of Wales whose arms are emblazoned opposite the handle and his crest beneath it. The delicately depicted fruiting vine which encircles the jug is both realistic and artistic. The engraver, Lee, signed his work on the underside. Two engravers of that name, both J Lee (father and son) had premises in Half Moon Street, Bishopsgate in London. This version of the royal arms was in use between 1802 and 1816.

8/13 A fine wine jug of about 1815. The form is similar to decanters and may have been en suite with a pair or more. The broad 'indian club' shape is decorated with bands of cutting including fluting, panel-cutting, diamonds and, above them all, step cutting. Note that the handle is drawn from the top to the bottom in contrast to later claret jugs, the solid stopper has cutting to match the body and the everted rim forms the pouring lip. Both the base of the jug and the top of the stopper are star cut.

8/14 Another wine jug, the body of which is almost of ship's decanter form. The neck is cut with horizontal pillars while the lower body is panel-cut. The rim is notched and it is fitted with a star-cut mushroom stopper which is taller than would be fitted to a standard decanter. It dates from about 1820 and is an unusual design.

Chapter 8 Wine jugs and claret jugs

8/15 Wine jugs followed the patterns of decanters for most of the first half of the 19th century, and this one dates from the 1830s with its single neck ring and still a solid (not hollow) mushroom stopper. Parallels with decanters having all-over panel-cut bodies and necks are common, but the bright amber colour is much less often seen.

8/16 This is an unusual jug because the top half could easily be 18th century. The lower half tells a different story, with its melon-like ribbed body that is partially matted. It probably dates from the middle of the 19th century, a dating reinforced by the amount of wear on its underside: not enough for an 18th century jug.

By the 1830s a new form appeared: claret jugs made of glass with silver or silver-gilt mounts. Among the first makers were Charles Reily & George Storer who also made numerous wine labels as well as the famous corkscrew which the inventor Henry Shrapnel presented to the Prince Consort. Their claret jug designs were avant garde and incorporated the latest fashions. The glass they used was often coloured and made at the fashionable factories of the West Midlands and, unlike decanters for several decades, they had feet. Another early maker was the celebrated Paul Storr, who in 1836 made a claret jug in the form of an ancient Greek *askos*, a model which other makers followed. He made the model both with a silver body and with a glass one.

Silver-mounted glass claret jugs were slow to become fashionable, and few were made before about 1850. By the 1860s they were being made in profusion, in all probability because the new service *à la Russe* was gaining acceptance. This novel way of eating arrived in England in the mid-century, and in place of wine glasses being brought to each diner by a footman for each toast, several glasses were laid at the top right hand side of each place setting. There were numerous other differences too, but they do not concern us at this point. Decanters and claret jugs were put on the table enabling a servant to serve three or four diners instead of the previous custom which required a footman for each.

8/17 This shape of claret jug derives from the askos of ancient Greece. This one has a frosted glass body and silver-gilt mounts by Paul Storr for Storr & Mortimer, the leading retailers of their day. It is among the first claret jugs to be made of glass and silver, a combination which became increasingly fashionable during the 19th century. It was made in 1836, two years before Storr retired.

8/18 Another askos claret jug, this time with a panel-cut green glass body and with silver mounts by John Figg who was among the leading London silversmiths of his time. The handle is formed as a vine branch with grapes and foliage issuing from it. It was made in 1840 and is 8½in/21·6cm long.

Chapter 8 Wine jugs and claret jugs

8/19 One of four claret jugs with silver-gilt mounts on partly gilded clear glass. Two were made in 1834 and the others in 1838 and 1843. The mounts are cast and chased as vine sprays with fruit and tendrils, and the glass is decorated with fine trellis-work in panels and with addorsed monograms C beneath a marquess's coronet. They bear the mark of Robert Garrard and R & S Garrard and they are 10½in/26·7cm high.

△*8/20 From the 1830s claret jugs in mounted glass became very popular. One of the earliest makers of this new genre was the partnership of Charles Reily & George Storer. This example has a claret-coloured glass ovoid body encased by a silver cage of vine foliage, grapes and tendrils. The hinged lid has a cast bunch of grapes as a finial and the jug has a scrolled handle. It was made in London in 1840.*

▷*8/21 These two similar large jugs or ewers are an extraordinary expression of opulent neo-baroque grandeur. The profuse decoration is dense, in each case cast with festooned masks, husks, acanthus, flowers and other motifs against a matted ground. Each has an applied vignette of the* Rape of the Sabine Women *and the* Reconciliation of the Sabines and the Romans *about the middle of the globular body, and a female mask beneath the spout. The scrolled handles are embellished with serpents and dragons in combat. One was made in 1835 by Maurice & Michael Emanuel, the other in 1843 by John Wilmin Figg, both in London. They were probably made more for display than for pouring wine, but jugs like this, such as the Open Golf trophy, are called claret jugs. These are 29in/73·7cm high.*

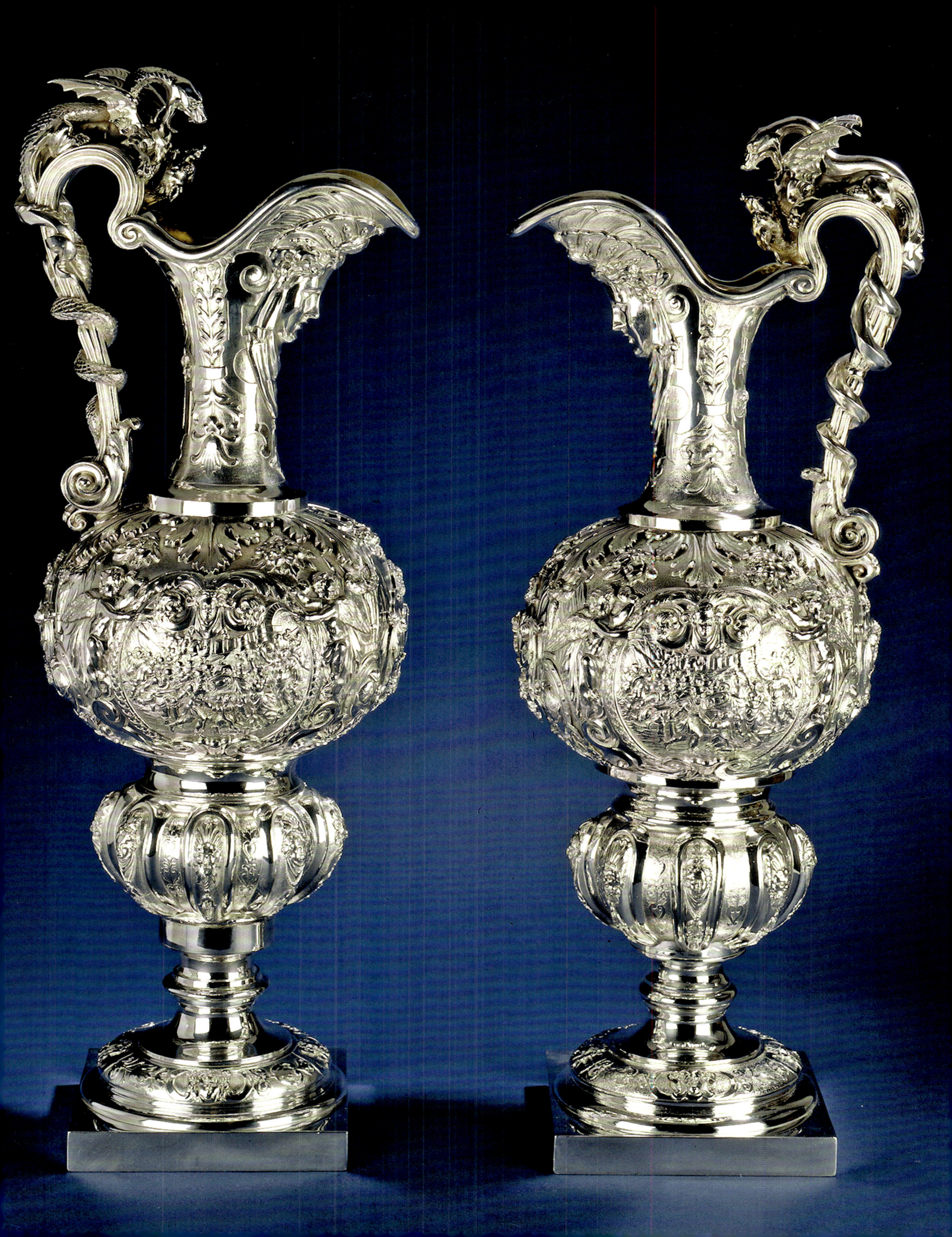

Chapter 8   Wine jugs and claret jugs

8/22 A pair of claret and burgundy jugs with baluster bodies of remarkably similar shape to those of 1780 (8/1), although these were made by Charles Reily & George Storer in 1847 and the bodies are frosted glass. The silver-gilt mounts are formed as swags of pendant vine leaves and tendrils and the handle as a loop of vine branch with a bunch of grapes as a pendant. Suspended around the necks are matching labels for CLARET and BURGUNDY while the feet are encircled by plain bands engraved GREEN & CO LONDON FECIT: these would have been the retailers. Burgundy is seldom seen on English wine labels although it is more common on Scottish ones.

◁8/23 This claret jug was also made in 1847, by James Charles Edington. It has a gourd-shaped body of red cased glass cut with lancet panels below elliptical panels with stars. The silver mount and handle is formed as a fruiting vine branch and the hinged lid is similarly treated. It stands 11⅜/28·8cm high.

▷8/24 This is another jug from Charles Reily & George Storer, this time with a teal glass body of vase shape and with silver mounts of vine foliage and tendrils. The frame upon which the vine is entwined has a slot opposite the handle where a wine label can be secured; space is left for this addition. It has a hinged lid with a grape finial and it was made in 1849.

◁8/25 This all-glass claret jug was made about 1850 and is cased in red. The body is panel-cut with broad slices and it is wheel engraved with a band of fruiting vine around the shoulder. It has a swan-neck handle drawn from the top towards the base, a technique reversed in the 1860s.

▷8/26 This heavy claret jug is deeply cut with gothic lancet panels and circular printies. Its single neck ring dates it before 1850 and the hollow stopper, after 1820. Claret jugs like this, without silver mounts, are very under-valued as they do not fall within the expectations of those who collect claret jugs, nor those who simply imagine that all claret jugs have metal mounts. Nevertheless, this and many examples roughly similar are equal in quality to the more obvious forms.

Chapter 8 Wine jugs and claret jugs

◁8/27 The shaft and globe decanter began to be re-introduced in the late 1840s and claret jugs followed as they were made in sets with decanters. With its almost spherical body, this is an early model which is cut with a lattice design and wheel engraved with flowering roses around the shoulders. The hollow stopper is a miniature inverted image of the body without the engraving. It dates from about 1855–65.

▷8/28 This shaft and globe claret jug with its more compressed body is a later form than 8/27; the more fussy cut decoration is another indicator, as is the faceted ball stopper. Like many all-glass jugs, this was probably part of a set with decanters which may have included wine glasses of various shapes and sizes. It comes from a period when decanters and jugs were put on the dining table as is shown in many contemporary paintings and drawings. Its date is about 1870.

◁8/29 This is a wine jug with an icing pocket. The simple baluster shape and the frosted surface give it a date of about 1860. Water jugs, which became popular at this time, usually have wider necks, so this is probably for wine to be served chilled. There is no sign of it ever having had a stopper.

▷8/30 An all-silver claret jug of attenuated baluster form on a spreading foot. It has a spray of fruiting vine with coiled tendrils spiralling round the body and a vine branch cast handle. It was made in 1863 by the largest firm of manufacturing silversmiths of the 19th century, Edward Barnard & Sons.

8/31 Oval flask jugs were first made in the in the mid-19th century and this set of three are in an electroplated frame which has a registration mark for 1867 on the underside. It is interesting that the ribbed handles are drawn upwards, a feature often said to have been introduced c1880. Flask jugs were probably intended for spirits but many, particularly the clear ones, are used for wine as they hold a full bottle comfortably. The shape originated in Franconia where it had been known as a bocksbeutel as long ago as the 17th century.

8/32 Askos-shaped claret jugs were made from the 1830s onwards; this one, made by Andrew Crespel & Thomas Parker, dates from 1871. All-silver models were made during the earlier period also. This one has a matted body, but the handle is similar to 8/17 although the elements beside the handle at the rim are quite different. It has a large shield of un-matted surface opposite the handle with an engraved coat of arms.

Chapter 8 Wine jugs and claret jugs

Claret jugs of the second half of the 19th century were made in several basic qualities. At the cheap end there were jugs with undecorated glass bodies with or without mounts of pewter. Next up the scale were those with silver-plated mounts; Sheffield plating had been superseded by this time, so they are all electro-plated. Silver, often mounted on decorated glass with cutting, acid etching or engraving, was the next standard. The best claret jugs had silver-gilt or very occasionally gold mounts.

Much of the finest glass in the second half of the 19th century was made in the West Midlands towns of Stourbridge and Dudley, with firms like Richardson's, Stevens & Williams and Thomas Webb & Sons employing large workforces to create fine bodies for claret jugs. Some of the most skilled craftsmen are known by name and their craft is recognisable from familiar patterns and factory records. The designs of claret jugs in the second half of the 19th century were numerous and, to an extent, difficult to categorise. Many were approximate copies of the silver-gilt-mounted tiger-ware jugs of the late 16th century (see 8/3), with glass replacing the stoneware. They boasted neo-renaissance strapwork and heraldic lions, these usually holding a shield to accommodate a crest or coat of arms. Some had plain glass bodies, or they were decorated with small engraved stars, while others had star-cut bases and wheel-engraved bodies. Some had mounts to the rim which included the handle and lid, while others had a ring at waist level to secure the handle at its lowest point, making for better security.

Many claret jugs engraved with portrait busts of ancient soldiers or gods offered an interpretation of classical Greek vases or Roman wine jugs; others had egg-shaped bodies. After about 1870 acid etching was used for less expensive jugs and they sometimes had electroplated mounts while copying the form of the more luxurious models. A rare and very attractive type of claret jug has a baluster-shaped body made of cameo glass This was cased red or green glass with a matted surface and wheel engraving to reveal translucent uncoloured glass beneath; with silver or silver-gilt mounts, these jugs are much sought.

8/33 The design of this flask jug was registered on 20th May 1874 and has a delightfully parsimonious aspect to its invention. Any wine that dribbles from the spout is caught by the slanting neck ring which, at its lowest point, has a hole drilled through the glass to let the dribble back into the jug. As the prim Victorian parlour song went:
  Waste not, want not, is a maxim I would teach.
  Let your watchword be dispatch and practice what you preach...
The registration mark, diamond-point engraved on the base of the jug, does not infer that the jug was made on that date, but at some time later and probably only a short while after the registration.

◁ 8/34 A great many flask jugs had bodies of coloured glass, either cased or with the colour running through the glass. This one has an amber body and turquoise handle and stopper. It is also finely engraved with flowers and ferns which became very fashionable in Victorian Britain both in gardens and as decoration. There are flasks with the opposite colouring, turquoise bodies with amber handles and stoppers, but the most common colours are red, green and blue, the red ones being very practical for red wine.

▷ 8/35 Most flask jugs have an oval section, flattened on either side of the handle. This one has a globular body, a panel-cut neck, star-cut base and a faceted ball stopper. The star-cut base refracts light to enable the colour and clarity of the wine to be better observed.

▷ 8/36 Two flasks, each with fern decoration over most of the body. The left hand one is wheel engraved while the right hand one is acid etched. This entails covering the glass with a wax resist and cutting the pattern away to reveal the glass beneath. It is then immersed in hydrofluoric acid which etches the glass. This technique was used extensively after about 1870 as it was less expensive than wheel engraving. The twisted handle became popular at about the same time.

Chapter 8 Wine jugs and claret jugs

8/37 A fine pair of double-handled wine jugs with silver-gilt mounts. The glass bodies are engraved with fruit and urns and the necks are mounted with pierced scrolled strapwork; like the loop handles, the mounts are engraved with foliage. The stoppers are topped with figures of trumpeters in 16th century costume. The jugs were made in London in 1877 by George Fox.

8/38 This pattern of claret jug was very popular although few are of this quality. The cheapest have electroplated mounts but all the better examples have silver ones. The finest are silver gilt, and of these the best have finely engraved glass. The glass here is engraved with swags of fruiting vine, vases of flowers and griffins. The parcel-gilt mount is repoussé decorated with more griffins and acanthus foliage. The gilt foliate scroll handle has a silver flower on either side and the lid, which sits in a coronet, has a griffin finial holding a shield. It was made in the workshops of Elkington & Co. in 1877 and stands 11in/27·9cm high.

▷ *8/39 One of the most innovative designers of the 19th century was Dr. Christopher Dresser who was among the first to advocate simplicity in the face of the vogue for complex decoration. Many of his designs would not appear out of place in the art deco period. This pair of claret jugs, 8½in/21·6cm high, may at first sight appear to be 50 years later than their 1881 origin. They were made, like many of his designs using silver, by Hukin & Heath in 1885. The handles are dark wood.*

Chapter 8 Wine jugs and claret jugs

Perhaps the most keenly sought claret jugs are those with bodies in the form of animals and birds, the silver mounts being the head, feet and sometimes the handle. It appears that the idea was that of Alexander Crichton who, with his partner John Curry, started making these delightful objects in 1881. Crichton and Curry were not successful businessmen: they became insolvent and the partnership was dissolved in 1884. Their zoomorphic claret jugs are rare, but the most often seen model is the duck.

Others include various birds such as pheasant, owl, parrot, penguin and cockatoo, as well as animals, notably walrus, monkey, squirrel and crocodile.

At about the same time as bird and animal claret jugs were being made, the designs of Dr Christopher Dresser were introduced. They were strikingly modernist, of undecorated glass made in simple shapes with angular handles; they have a distinctly art deco air about them although they pre-date that style by half a century. Many of his designs were made by Hukin & Heath.

△8/40 The fashion for wine jugs formed as birds and animals began in 1881 and the credit for it is usually given to Alexander Crichton who registered his first design (for an owl claret jug) in August 1881. This cockatoo has a registration number 374238 for 3rd December 1881. It also has the hallmarks for 1881 and was made by Crichton and retailed by Henry Lewis of 172 New Bond St. It has a glass body and well cast and chased head with naturalistic eyes, and it is gilded inside. It is 13½in/34·3cm high.

△8/41 Just a year after the clear glass claret jug, Alexander Crichton made this one. While the head is from the same casting as 8/40, the body is enamelled green glass with the plumage outlined in gilt. The feet and tail are quite different, and made in one piece. The claws now grip pebbles and the tail and lower body are of finely cast and chased silver. It is 13¼in/ 33·7cm high.

◁ 8/42 Alexander Crichton's second of many registered animal and bird claret jug designs was a walrus, registered in 1881. This example has ivory tusks in addition to the silver and glass body and is little different in shape, apart from the head, from the duck which became the most popular of models. It was made in 1881 by him.

▷ 8/44 Of all birds and animals, ducks proved to be the most popular, and copies of the general design are being reproduced in the 21st century. This is another of Crichton's productions made in 1882, but is a finer example than most with feathers precisely engraved in the glass and a well-detailed tail in silver. It is 9¾in/24.8cm long.

△ 8/43 Pheasant claret jugs are among the rarest of the genre and were made by S Mordan & Co; this design was registered by them on 27th October 1882, the year this was made. The modelling of the feathers of the glass body suggest that it was done by the same hand, or at least in the same workshop as the duck by Crichton. Interestingly, this one was supplied with a spare body in case the original was broken.

▷ 8/45 Of all the zoomorphic claret jugs, the crocodile is one of the least seen. This monster, which measures 15in/38.1cm long, was made by S Mordan & Co. in 1884. It will be noted that in order for the wine to be poured and not interrupted by the reptile's teeth, it has been given a smooth tongue.

Chapter 8 Wine jugs and claret jugs

8/46 The 1880s saw the peak of claret jug production, but not all were zoomorphic. This one, with its acorn-shaped body, is of conventional form but with the silver mount simulating an oak tree stump with leaves and acorns issuing from it. It has a glass handle cradled by oak leaves at either end.

8/47 Not all claret jug bodies were either glass or silver; this one of 1883 is Parian porcelain, a novel ultra-white unglazed porcelain invented by WT Copeland & Sons in 1844 and mainly used for reproduction marble busts. The body, with scenes of bacchic putti disporting themselves in a vineyard, drinking from saucers and surrounded by baskets of grapes, is silver mounted with a figural finial and a bold egg and dart edge. The silver is by the celebrated London silversmiths, Hunt & Roskill, successors in title to Paul Storr and Mortimer & Hunt.

8/48 There were several firms that specialised in making claret jugs, among them William & George Sissons. This jug with its ovoid body is finely engraved with foliate scrolls and flower-filled baskets on one side and a charioteer (Phaeton?) drawn by four horses on the other. The silver-gilt mount is embossed with baskets of flowers and scrolls and the beaded handle links the top to the base mount. It was made in 1883 and holds a magnum (1.5l).

8/49 Cameo-cut glass is seldom seen in claret jugs, but this is a delightful baluster-shaped example. The claret-red ground, overlaid with white and cut away to depict a bird on a hazel branch about to eat a fly, is masterful work. The silver mount, chased and pierced with scrolls and acanthus foliage, has a Bacchus-head spout. The glass was probably made in the Webb workshops and the mount bears the marks of John Goffe & Son of Birmingham (Webb's business was nearby in Stourbridge) with the date letter of 1884.

8/50 Another cameo glass baluster jug, probably from the Webb workshops, cut to reveal a gerbera flower with vigorous foliage and a butterfly. The silver mount and high domed lid are embossed with sprays of roses, the double-scroll handle is cast with stylised leaves and the spout is a Bacchus mask. The silver is marked for London, 1884 and the maker's mark is that of the manager of the Army & Navy Cooperative Society, Frederick Bradford McCrea.

8/51 The baluster body of this claret jug is frosted glass overlaid with rich ultramarine blue. The cameo cutting has revealed garden flowers and broad leaves with remarkable effect. The silver mount is relatively simple; while the neck is engraved with sinuous flowers, the flat lid and pouring spout are plain. The unadorned long handle unites the neck and the base with a narrow ring. It was made by William Hutton & Sons in 1894.

176   Chapter 8   Wine jugs and claret jugs

△8/52 Edward Barnard & Sons' day book entry for 19th November 1889 records these as follows: '4 Jug mounts with nude female figure handles supported by vine stem, Louis XVI mask lips, chased processional boy figures round bands, masks and scrolls on lower part, boy figure buttons'. The cost was £58 and the gilding cost an extra 8 guineas (£8/8s/0d). No mention was made of the glass, and they were sold to Mallett & Son of Bath and Bond Street London, who would have commissioned the glass themselves. Each claret jug (there are two magnums and two of bottle size) is finely cut and incorporates the monogram AMC within a circle of plain glass. The magnums are 12in/30·5 cm, the bottles 10in/25·4cm high.

▷8/53 A pair of claret jugs of plain cylindrical form with spreading bases, decorated all over with diamond cutting. Each has a plain silver mount, a beak-like spout and a flat lid surmounted by a finial/thumbpiece formed as a bear shackled to a tree stump. They were made by Hukin & Heath in 1890 and are 13¾in/34·9cm high.

The end of the 19th century saw claret jugs made in Britain in the French art nouveau style, with its sinuous decoration in shallow relief both with bullion and base metal mounts. Many claret jugs from the second half of the 19th century have a distinctly French rococo revival element to their design, so it is not always easy, at first glance, to say where one was made. While the French models tend to be more free in their design, the English were more robustly made.

Although slightly outside the title of this book, mention should perhaps be made of the fashion for claret jugs that occurred after 1900 as, unlike many other wine-related objects, they were made in developing art styles rather than as reproductions of earlier forms. The radicalism of art deco was less of a novelty when considering claret jugs than it was for many of the decorative arts. The plain glass bodies blown and cut to severe geometrical shapes and mounted with angular handles, bore more than a passing resemblance to the designs of Dr Christopher Dresser, but they were evolved designs, more rounded at the corners, and often with a greater volume of material in them. Many claret jugs of the early 20th century are worthy of consideration as serious interpretations of the fashions of the period. They were immensely popular from the 1870s until the outbreak of the First World War and in a huge diversity of styles. A book about claret jugs is one just waiting to be written.

△8/54 *A near pair of cranberry claret jugs made in the closing years of the 19th century. They have optically moulded bodies, reeded loop handles and tricorn rims. The stoppers are hollow and multi-knopped. Such jugs were inexpensive when made and are still to be found at modest prices.*

△55 *This very colourful claret jug and stand is silver-mounted enamelled glass, sometimes known as verre sur verre. The glass is the work of Charles Herbert Thompson while the plain silver mounts were made by Heath & Middleton. Thompson pioneered this technique in glass in 1895 and both the stand and jug are signed by him. The silver carries the hallmarks for London, 1898.*

△8/56 *The dull green glass of this claret jug was made at the Whitefriars Glasshouse in East London and the silver mounts are by the Guild of Handicrafts of which Charles Robert Ashbee, one of the leaders of the arts and crafts movement, was founder. The hallmarks are for London, 1903 and it is 8¼in/21cm high. Ashbee's sinuous curves were a move away from Victorian traditions and many would say the claret jug was in the art nouveau style, although Ashbee himself would have denied it.*

△8/57 *The final claret jug in this chapter is well past our dateline of 1900, but the simplicity of its design is a commendable juxtaposition to the dizzy complexities that have gone before. It was made in 1919 and has the mark of Hukin & Heath. The body is a thin cylinder on its side, and the silver mounts, while plain are solidly practical. The form is almost a prototype for art deco.*

Wine labels

Wine labels were first used in the early 1730s following the introduction of the horizontal binning of bottles. As seen in Chapter 2, the bin label indicated the contents of the bottles in the same cellar bin; a method for identifying the wine in a bottle once it had left the cellar and had been decanted was now devised. This took the form of a small label suspended from a chain placed around the neck of the decanter.

Wine labels are the subject of eager collection and study, and the Wine Label Circle has been very active since its formation in 1952. In 2004, after many years' preparation, its members produced a substantial book on their subject. While silver is the predominant medium for wine labels, other media were also used.

179

9/1 Part of a collection of wine labels demonstrating the variety made in Britain over a period of about 200 years. Some of the labels are for spirits and sauces, but most are for wines.

Chapter 9 Wine Labels

Until the 20th century wine labels were known as bottle tickets. The earliest, called escutcheons by wine label collectors, were usually made of silver and had a complex outline comprising a series of symmetrically composed baroque S and C scrolls about a vertical axis. Some escutcheon labels have a smooth surface with the name of the wine engraved, while others are decorated with flat-chasing. This takes the form of a fruiting vine covering the entire surface except for a central area where the name of the wine is engraved. Many of the better quality labels in the early days of their introduction were made by the specialist wine label maker Sandilands Drinkwater, who in later life (1761), rose to be the Prime Warden of the Goldsmiths' Company, but there were other makers doing similar work. His inappropriate surname may have something to do with his fame, but he was a prolific and specialist maker of wine labels, and the earliest.

Wine label shapes, while being classified by collectors according to one type or another, allowed variance within each classification. However, all labels were made to be placed around the necks of bottles or, more probably, decanters. Decanters burgeoned in popularity at the same time as labels began to be made. To fit the decanter shape, each label bowed outwards in the middle to rest easily on the shoulder of the decanter. The same attention to detail was given to almost all wine labels throughout the period when they were made. The few exceptions usually originated far from London, either in the provinces or the colonies.

Another design of early label relied on a casting technique rather than cutting from sheet metal. The molten silver was poured into a mould, and this resulted in more substantial labels than those wrought from sheet silver. The technique allowed a three-dimensional quality not seen in escutcheons. This early form of cast label took the form of a putto (cherub) reclining among scrolls and fruiting vines, holding a bottle in one hand and a goblet in the other. The name of the wine is engraved on a banner or scroll across the centre. A variant has two putti disporting themselves in a similar manner. It should be remembered that Dionysus or Bacchus (the Greek god of wine and his Roman equivalent) were traditionally depicted with putti in attendance, hence the allusion; or perhaps the putto is the young Bacchus.

Towards the end of the time when bacchic labels were being cast, some makers were producing simple rectangular forms with or without gadrooned borders, some completely plain, others with more or less shaped edges. Furthermore, old Sheffield plate was being used for cheaper labels after its invention in 1742 by Thomas Bolsover. The rectangle in varying proportions continued to be used for several decades. All early labels have the name of the wine engraved on them, but by the end of the century, names were also being pierced.

After the initial fashion for silver wine labels in the second half of the 1730s and the following decade, their popularity seems to have waned somewhat, for there is a relative dearth of surviving examples dating from about the late 1740s to the early 1760s. This period coincided with the flowering of the rococo in England and the complete absence of labels in the rococo style at this time is a mystery. While furniture, especially mirror frames, porcelain and other work of silversmiths reflected the rococo vigorously, it seems to have been ignored by wine label makers. The early cast labels with putti are asymmetrical and somewhat florid, but they are hardly rococo; they do not have the exuberance of the gilt brass fittings on furniture of the period, which are remarkably similar in size, and frequently display far more imagination.

Having almost shunned the rococo, wine label makers embraced neoclassicism. This a decorative art form had first appeared in London in the late 1750s and seems to have been adopted by wine label makers soon after. A variety of designs characterised by pretty symmetry and often with bright-cut decoration appeared. Variations on the crescent shape were very popular but other forms also found favour. They included the scroll, the wide vase (sometimes known as the goblet), the kidney, the simple narrow rectangle and the oval (both pointed and rounded). These shapes coincided with the introduction of bright cutting, a form of decoration much favoured by neoclassical silversmiths in which very small slivers of silver were removed from the surface, each slice leaving a facet reflecting bright light – hence its name. Bright cutting was sometimes enhanced by the additional technique of wrigglework, a repetitive zig-zag line used as a border or frame.

9/2 A very early wine label from a period soon after they were first made. It was made by Sandilands Drinkwater (how appropriate a name is that?) who is among the first, if not the first maker of wine labels, and he made little else. This one has his first mark entered on 20th January 1735 and the sterling standard mark that was used until 19th May 1739. It was not necessary to mark wine labels fully until 1790, so the closest it can be dated is between 1735 and 1739.

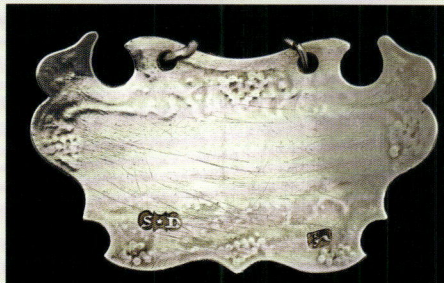

9/3 A similar label by Drinkwater with his second mark, and therefore post-1739. This and the previous label are called escutcheons in wine label collecting circles. The name of the wine, in this case claret, is engraved, and the fruiting vine border is shaped from sheet silver and flat-chased. Drinkwater was pre-eminent in the Goldsmiths' Company, becoming its Prime Warden in 1761.

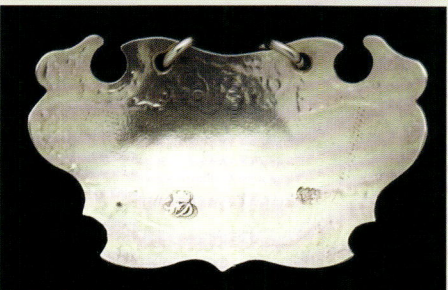

9/4 Drinkwater produced only a few designs, and escutcheons outnumber all others by a large margin. His second label is very different, being cast with two putti either side of a banner with a jug above and a satyr mask below, amid a profusion of grapes and foliage. These examples for CYPRUS and CAPE are rare and fine specimens dating from about 1750. The Cape label is the earliest known with that name.

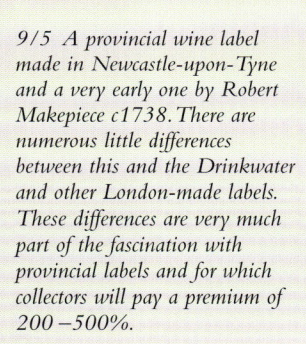

9/5 A provincial wine label made in Newcastle-upon-Tyne and a very early one by Robert Makepiece c1738. There are numerous little differences between this and the Drinkwater and other London-made labels. These differences are very much part of the fascination with provincial labels and for which collectors will pay a premium of 200–500%.

9/6 A group of four Sheffield plated wine labels, plated on one side only – an early feature. The labels are stamped from a sheet of plated copper, the silver being quite thick. The detail shows the back of the CYDER label and how the die has given a sharp edge to the pattern. Note the apples on this label. MOUNTAIN, a wine from the hinterland of Malaga, was a sweet wine that Nelson ordered in large quantities for his navy. W·PORT was the popular white port and RHENISH was hock.

Chapter 9 Wine Labels

9/7 Wine labels with mis-spelt names are always eagerly sought by collectors. This is another escutcheon from about 1750 and made by someone whose initials were JA, but whose name has not been ascertained. It is probably provincial rather than London-made. The wrigglework within the lettering is a very unusual feature.

9/8 The most sought wine labels are those made over a short period at the York House Factory in Battersea between 1753 and 1756. Probably designed by James Gwin, an Irish artist, and engraved by Simon Francis Ravenet, they are unlike any other labels. This one for LISBON is typical, with putti and a barrel. The engravings were transfer printed and hand coloured. It is 2¾in/7cm wide.

9/9 Rarely seen are black Ravenet labels. This one with its putto leaning on a barrel, is of typical outline and somewhat larger than most silver labels of the time. They were made by stamping the template out of copper and coating it with powdered opaque white glass before firing to set the glass on the copper.

9/10 Two further Ravenet labels, the transfer prints in shades of brown and magenta. The LISBON label is from the same engraving as 9/8, but while it is more clearly defined, it lacks the visual appeal of the hand-coloured one. It can be seen that the names of all Battersea labels were done by hand, only the pictorial aspect of the design being transfer printed.

9/11 This wine label is not a Battersea Ravenet example but probably from Birmingham or South Staffordshire and made in the 1760s or early 70s. The name MALAGA, while not quite rare, is certainly not often seen and refers to wines from that part of Spain; they were popular during the second half of the 18th century. This one measures 2¾in/7cm wide.

9/12 This is another enamel label probably from the South Staffordshire area. Its outline is a little different from the usual and the spelling is amusingly incorrect that it suggests that the person instructing the artist, presumably spelling phonetically, was speaking in a way not heard in the 21st century.

9/13 This is an escutcheon-shaped label made of mother of pearl. It is engraved and the engraving filled with gilding in an unusual and attractive manner. It is also among the earliest of mother of pearl wine labels, dating from about 1750. It is 2¼in/5.7cm long.

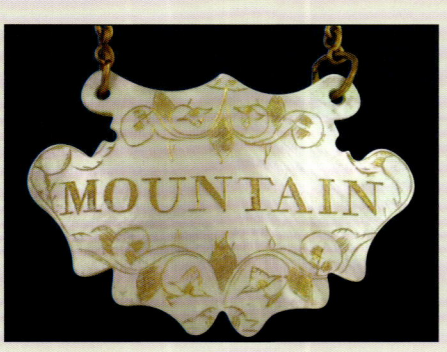

9/14 At first sight this pair of labels would appear to date from about 1740–60, but handling them produces a different opinion. The sheet silver from which they are cut is noticeably thinner than that used in Britain, so thin that the engraving has punctured the E of WHITE. They are probably colonial and the bunches of grapes are punched rather than flat-chased.

9/15 The bearded goat peering out over the banner for WHITE is unusual, as is the garland of vine leaves and grapes which forms the border. It is solidly cast by Thomas Heming and has his second mark, before he became principal goldsmith to the King in 1760 and registered his third mark surmounted by a crown. This enables a dating of between 1758 and 1760. It must be remembered that wine labels were not fully hallmarked before 1790 because they fell below the threshold weight of half an ounce.

9/16 As many engravers of wine labels were not highly literate in the 18th century, and almost certainly never drank wine or knew foreign place names, it is not surprising that some labels were mis-spelt. SETJUS should read Sitges, a town to the south west of Barcelona that produced Malvasia and Malmsey wines. The kidney shape began to be used in the late 1760s, and this one, by Jane Dorrell & Richard May, was made in the 1770s.

▷9/17 The long narrow rectangle was a popular shape for wine labels and many were utterly plain (see 9/26). Some, however, had a hump added to their top edge and were decorated with a variety of piercing and bright cutting. This group, all dating from the last quarter of the 18th century, show the range of embellishment to be seen.

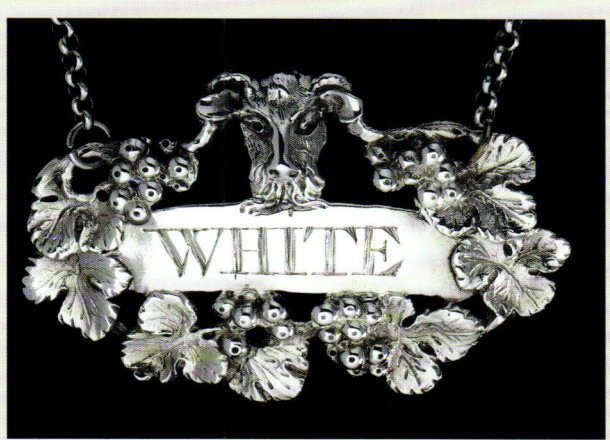

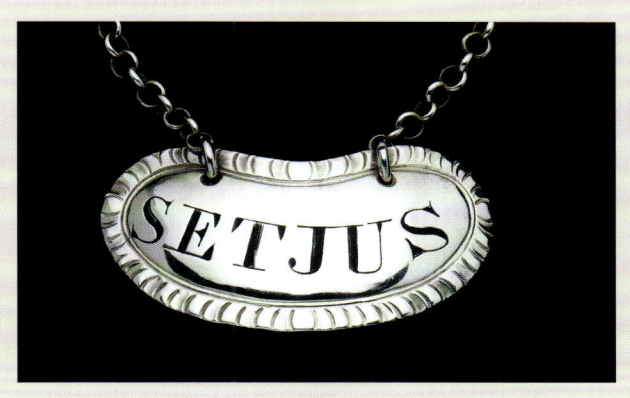

Chapter 9   Wine Labels

9/18 This label for SHERRY is a rare example of rococo decoration despite its symmetry. It was made by William Turton in about 1775. Often makers followed the trading pattern of the masters to whom they were apprenticed. It is interesting to note that Turton was apprenticed to William Dorrell, the husband of Jane who made 9/16 in partnership with Richard May; he was also apprenticed to Dorrell. It can reasonably be presumed that Jane took over the workshop on the death of her husband.

9/20 If the label for PORT is the simplest of those known in collecting circles as crescents, then this label for CLARET must be among the most complex. It was made by Benjamin Taitt, another specialist label maker, but from Dublin. It is a good example of neoclassicism with its vase, swags of bell-flowers, ribbons and bright cutting. It dates from about 1785.

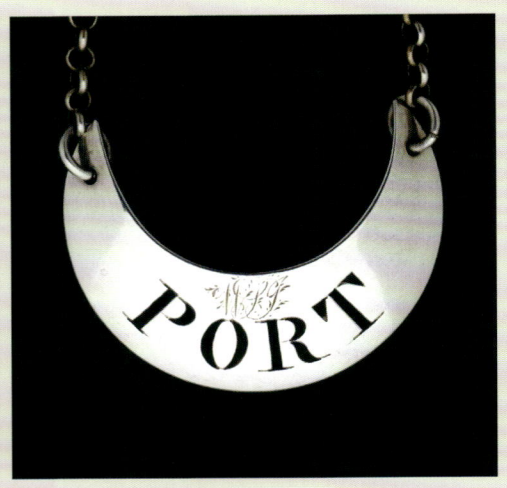

△ **9/19** One of the most fashionable shapes for wine labels in the late 18th century was the crescent. It tends to sit well on a decanter and is capable of interpretation and embellishment. This one for PORT has had the owner's initials, WSJ, engraved above the wine. Labels of this form are usually quite lightweight as they were made from thin sheet. This one was made by Thomas Hyde, a specialist wine label maker.

9/21 LISBON was a wine name often seen at the end of the 18th century and this label was made by one of the most famous British silversmiths, Hester Bateman. Her workshop produced good wine labels, and this example takes the crescent and elaborates on the idea. The form of bright cutting around the border is called feather edge and the top of the label has an oval cartouche engraved with a crest.

△ **9/22** This is a mother of pearl crescent label made in China for the British market. Shrub is a cordial made from rum or brandy with the peel of oranges and it was very much in demand for about 25 years either side of 1800. Decanters with SHRUB engraved or gilded are not uncommon and were made en suite with brandy, rum and hollands (gin). It is interesting to see how the Chinese have interpreted the crescent and engraved the legend and the coat of arms. Difficult to date, this was probably made after 1800.

9/23 Another mother of pearl label, but made in Britain. The crescent has a peculiarly notched lower edge not seen on silver counterparts, but it can be dated to the late 18th century on stylistic grounds. At 2in/5cm wide it is a normal size for British wine labels which typically measure between 1¾in and 2¾in/4·4–7cm.

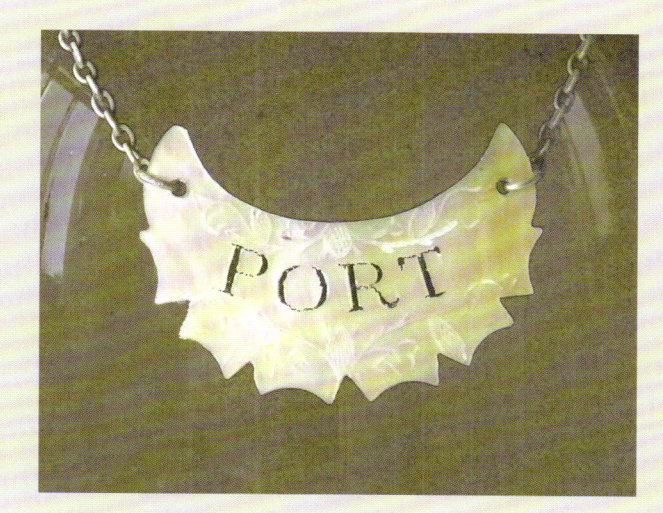

9/24 Two more mother of pearl wine labels. The left hand one for SHRUB is a simple late 18th century example whose design might easily have been executed in silver. The right hand MADEIRA may be an early one of c1750, but the escutcheon shape did have a revival in the early 19th century and may date from c1820; there is little to choose between dating this example in the 18th or 19th centuries.

9/25 Foul anchor wine labels are among the most sought by collectors. Like this one, they are very seldom stamped with either the maker's mark or hallmarks but there are sound reasons to date them from the 1790s or thereabouts. An anchor is 'foul' when a length of rope is wound around its various parts, and it is the emblem of the Admiralty as well as the crest of many families. It seems just as possible that labels of this model were commissioned by members of those families as by naval officers or by the Admiralty itself.

▷*9/26 This small label for BRANDY has the Edinburgh assay office mark but no others, which is unusual. The label is pierced to take the chain while most Scottish labels have small lugs attached to the top edge for this purpose. This label is about as modest a piece of wrought silver as there could be, and yet it has both charm and interest. It was made around 1800 or possibly a little earlier.*

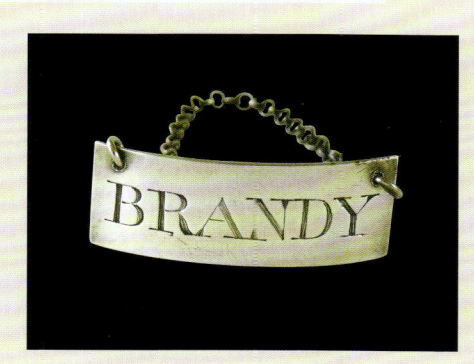

Chapter 9   Wine Labels

One of the most sought after forms today is the heraldic wine label. Examples from the 1770s were occasionally surmounted with a small oval, round or shield-shaped cartouche engraved with the crest or, more rarely, the coat of arms of the owner. Another type shows the family crest with the name of the wine on a scroll, crescent, rectangle or wreath beneath it.

A pleasing type that enjoyed a degree of popularity from about 1780 –1830 is the neck-ring. One form is simply a narrow section of a cone which rests on the neck of the decanter, with the name of the wine engraved on the outer surface. Other labels have a thick wire in place of a chain with a label of a standard pattern suspended from it.

Towards the end of the 18th century wine label design seemed to be losing some of its novelty and repetitions of earlier forms are seen, but in the opening years of the 19th century, a totally new approach was evident. In place of the thin, light-calibre tickets, pierced and shaped from sheet metal, bold cast labels of substantial size and weight, brilliantly chased and often gilded, either totally or in part, were being manufactured. Such cast labels take the form of garlands of fruiting vines, leopards' pelts with fruiting vines, shells, four-leaf clovers, or bacchanalian figures with grapes. These heavy and grand labels were made by silversmiths usually associated with substantial dinner services rather than specialist label makers, and were made for use with such services. Digby Scott, Benjamin Smith and Paul Storr are among those whose marks are found on some models.

While a few heavy cast examples were made by Edward Farrell and others after about 1815, the size and weight of labels diminished. From about 1820 a single vine leaf became a popular design, and the majority of these were die-stamped from sheet metal unlike the weighty labels mentioned in the previous paragraph. Triple vine leaves are also seen. Their production was occasioned by the manufacture of presses capable of delivering sufficient force to stamp them from sheet silver. This novel method of manufacture reduced the amount of silver used in each label and therefore the cost, and was also capable of speedy mass production.

Many wine labels from the period 1820 - 1850 were made in Birmingham by die-stamping thin sheet silver. The thinness of the sheet allowed quite sharp and three-dimensional detail, and the depth of the pattern gave strength. A popular pattern was a broad rectangle with a border of gadrooning, scallop-shells or acanthus leaves or any combination of these. Their very light weight seems to have preserved many in excellent condition. London-made labels of this period tend to be of heavier gauge, many in the rococo style that label makers had shunned 60 or so years earlier.

Around 1830 the initial label became popular, although the form had been briefly used very late in the 18th century. Early examples have initials pierced or engraved with Roman letters in a small plain rectangle (rarely a disc or oval) of about postage stamp size, often with a reeded edge. With the exception of the Scottish ones, which can be plain, later examples are cut-out letters of the alphabet, and usually reflect the florid taste of the times. They are usually cast with decorative outlines or engraved with scrolls and foliage. Most seem to have been for fortified wines and spirits: P, S and M for port, sherry and madeira (or marsala or mountain, once very popular), and W, G, R and B for whisk(e)y, gin, rum and brandy. Occasionally a C is seen, presumably for claret, and H for hollands (gin) or hock. Other letters exist but are very rare. Could it have been that strong liquor was considered a drink to be concealed with a degree of anonymity whereas wines were heralded with their full names? Today initial labels not in the safe keeping of collectors are often worn as pendants to necklaces, which does not do them much good.

By the 1840s and '50s, wine label manufacture was in decline. The process of electroplating, married with the die-stamping process, had made labels cheap and plentiful. The relatively few silver labels were mostly made in London, and were either versions of previous designs, or in the angular gothic taste. The inexpensive plated labels made in the second half of the 19th century were mainly for spirits and fortified wines which would have been kept, sometimes for prolonged periods, in or on the sideboard.

The printed paper label on bottles after 1861 dispensed with the need to identify the contents. But a few silver and plated labels were made after this date.

9/27 This is a very interesting wine label for two reasons. First, it is a very unusual form having a raised moulded edge and being an oval nearly 3in/7·6cm wide. Second, it is engraved with a spurious coat of arms. Quite why someone wanted to have a wine label engraved with a coat of arms which does not exist is anyone's guess, but it has been meticulously checked. The arms are similar to those of the Hall family, but the tinctures (colours denoted in engraving with hatched lines) are incorrect which is very unlikely to be a mistake. The label was made in 1791 by Edward Fernell.

9/28 Few wine labels were made of this form and as a result the 'button' is another type favoured by label collectors. This one for MADEIRA is well engraved above a crest, on a rock a fire beacon proper, one which is shared by 22 families; it has a reeded edge. It was made in 1794 by Robert Barker and is nearly 2in/5cm diameter.

9/29 Another variety of wine label which is high on the list of collectors' desirables is the armorial label. This example is in the form of a family crest (note the wreath upon which the peacock's neck rests), the family being Arbuthnot. It was made by Peter & Ann Bateman (a son and daughter-in-law of Hester) in 1796.

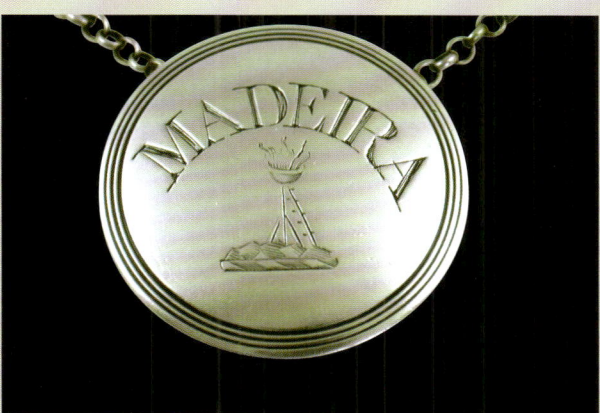

△ 9/30 Most wine labels were suspended around the neck of the decanter by a chain, but a few were attached to a ring which performed the same function. The oval form was a common one around the 1790s and 1800s and here it can be seen attached to a ring with a hinge and bifurcated link. It was made by a firm that produced many wine accessories and whose work was of a uniformly high standard without being grand. They were Thomas Phipps & Edward Robinson and they made this label in 1804.

Chapter 9 Wine Labels

9/31 This set of three labels is about as grand as wine labels go. They were made by Digby Scott & Benjamin Smith in 1806 and are silver gilt. Although this was the firm's standard best model and they made many of them, this set has an additional detail of interest. Each has an additional oval above the name of the wine and this is engraved with a cypher. This is beneath a crown and is that of Queen Charlotte, wife of George III.

▽ 9/32 Although these are the same model and size as Queen Charlotte's labels, they are white silver. Three were made by Benjamin Smith with the date letter for 1806, and three in partnership with his brother James in 1809. These labels and the ones before are large and heavily cast, being 3¼in/8·3cm wide and weighing about 2oz/60g each; this is several times the weight of most labels. As a set, they give a good indication of what wines were being consumed at that time.

9/33 Another of Benjamin Smith's label forms was the four-leaf clover. It is a solidly made cast label with the legend SHERRY engraved, and it was made in 1809. It is said that the first three leaves represent hope, faith and love, while the fourth represents luck.

▷ 9/34 The age of the grand cast wine labels was short-lived and of these, many were made by Benjamin Smith with his first partner Digby Scott or later with his brother James. This one was made in 1808 and is finely cast in the form of a scallop shell. Some objects in silver or silver-gilt were cast directly from natural objects, but the symmetry of this scallop looks too perfect to be natural. Note the heavy-duty belcher chain which is always a sign of high quality in a wine label.

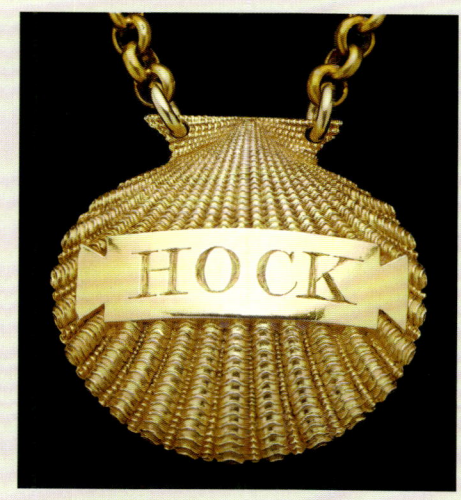

9/35 Benjamin Smith may be over-represented here but his labels, whether made on his own or with his partners (this time again with his brother James), deserve their inclusion. Here, working in 1809, he had a commission to create a label for Thomas Egerton, 1st Earl of Wilton with his crest of three downward-pointing, ribbon-tied arrows beneath an earl's coronet. OLD HOCK must have been an esteemed wine in the early 19th century although today it would be consigned to a less dignified end than being offered to a guest.

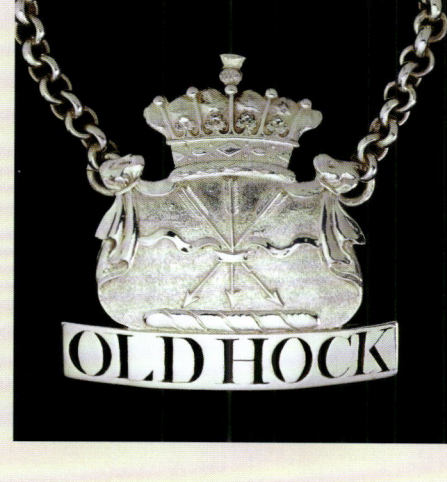

▷ 9/36 Wine label collectors can be excited by different criteria, such as unusual wines, mis-spellings, or place of production to name just three. This label is rare because it was made in Dumfries. Scottish provincial silver is keenly sought and wine labels especially so. It was made by John Pearson in about 1810.

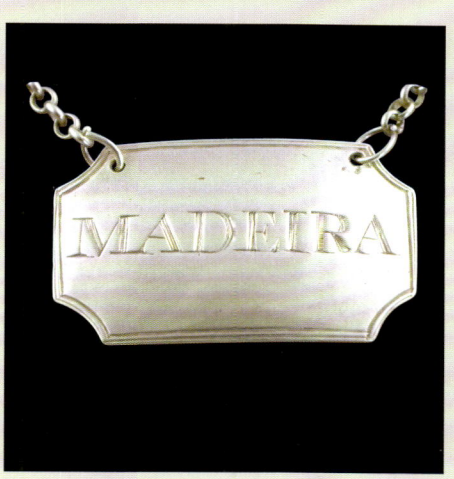

9/37 Not all wine labels produced in the early 19th century were grand. Many, like this simple long octagonal label for BUCELLAS, are lightweight and thoroughly unpretentious; indeed it is only silver plated. Bucellas was a wine from Portugal, south of Lisbon. The Methuen Treaty gave tax incentives for the British to buy Portuguese wines in preference to French ones and it resulted in a longstanding trade relationship. The Scots in recognition of the Auld Alliance continued to drink more French wine, relatively, than the English.

▷ 9/38 Another large cast label, this time made by Edward Farrell in 1815. It may be that the elephant was a family crest, but the animal is not on an heraldic wreath. Perhaps the person who commissioned it had Indian connections, possibly with the East India Company. Other versions of the elephant label by Farrell are known. This one measures 3¼in/8·3cm long.

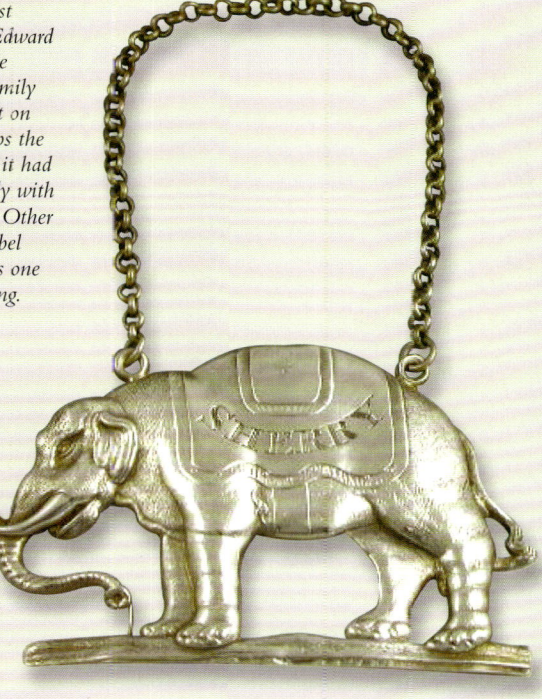

Chapter 9 Wine Labels

▷9/39 Whereas in the 18th century few of the great silversmiths made wine labels (they probably bought-in for customers when asked), considerable numbers were produced by the most eminent in the following century. This one was made by Paul Storr in 1815. It is formed as a lion's or leopard's pelt festooned with bunches of grapes and vine leaves. A wine label could hardly be more grandiose. The legend CLARET is cast and raised on a matted pelta shield.

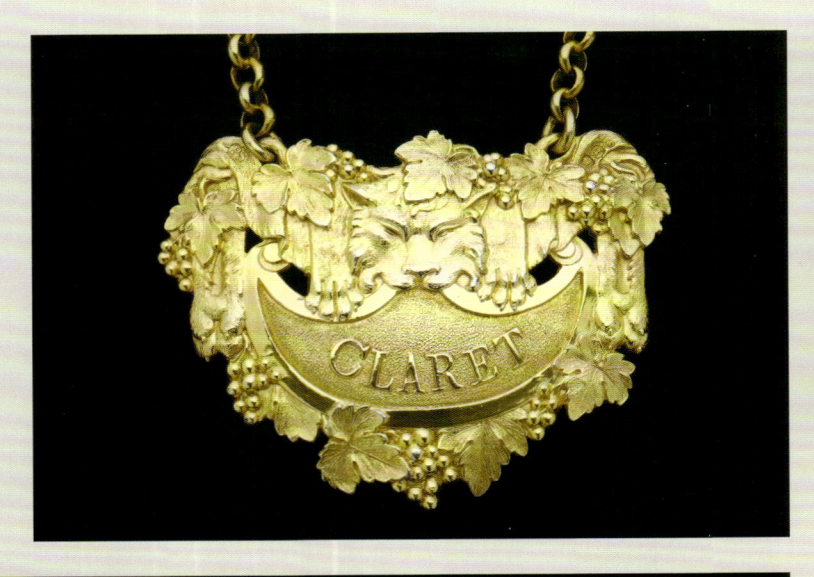

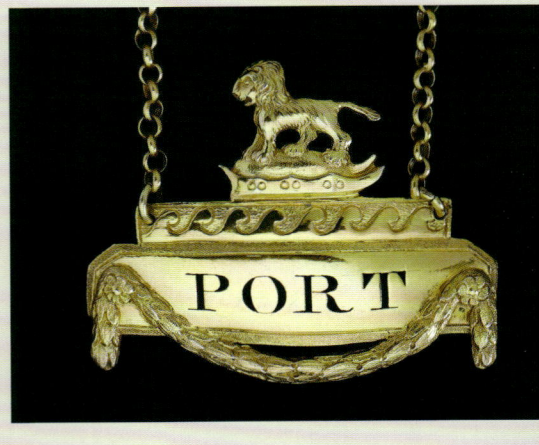

△9/40 This cast silver-gilt wine label was made by the specialist label maker John Reily. The plain rectangular label of 1817 for PORT is embellished with a swag of laurel leaves draped over paterae and surmounted by a line of vitruvian scrolls and a crest which is probably that of George Percy, 5th Duke of Northumberland. Other families had similar crests so it is impossible to be certain for whom it was made.

△9/41 These labels have larger than average chain links so it may be supposed, particularly as they were made by Paul Storr, that they were heavily cast. They are actually die-stamped and quite light. They are well proprtioned and the gadroon border and shell and acanthus cresting are both precisely defined. They were made in 1817. Note the mis-spelling of 'CHAMPAIGNE'.

△9/42 Initial letters began to be used as wine labels in the late 1790s. They started as small vertical rectangles with the letter engraved and filled with blacking and usually with two lines of reeding around the edge. During the early 19th century cut-out letters appeared. This pierced M was made in Edinburgh in 1819, but the maker forgot his own mark. It is unusually bowed.

△9/43 CAPILARE is a very rare label, strictly not a wine, but a substance used to sweeten wine, made from maidenhair fern. The label was made by Daniel Hockley in London in 1818. At about this time he became bankrupt and moved to South Africa where he again set up business as a silversmith. The form of the label, an oblong with rounded corners and reeded edge, was a very popular one.

△9/44 NEECE is presumably a phonetic spelling of Nice and the wine is presumably from that area on the Côte d'Azur. The label is a very rare one and is quite similar to early labels of the 1760s, although not as large or long. It was made in Newcastle-upon-Tyne in 1823 by Thomas Watson.

9/45 Perhaps the most obvious form for a wine label to take is that of a vine leaf. Oddly, that did not occur until the early 1820s unless the labels of Benjamin Smith (see 9/31 and 9/32) are counted. The first vine leaf labels seem to have occurred in 1818 and were in the form of a single leaf, but the idea did not become fashionable until about 1823. Multi-leaf labels are much less common than the single leaf variety, making this pair if not rare, then at least uncommon. They were made in 1824 by John Reily and are larger than most at 3in/7.6cm wide.

9/46 BUSHBY is not just rare but apparently unique and has so far defied all attempts at identification. However it may be a mis-spelling of Busby, a Scot who emigrated to Australia and is regarded by some as the father of viticulture in the antipodes. The label was made by Charles Rawlings in London in 1826, two years after Busby emigrated. Charles Rawlings was a prolific label maker who produced some innovative designs.

9/48 This splendid silver-gilt disc label was another made by Charles Rawlings & William Summers in 1835. Once again the crest is shared by several families so cannot be identified positively. It is in fine condition and a former owner of it once said that silver being antique was no excuse for it being worn out: how true.

9/49 Doubt can be a virtue when it comes to wine label collection. This label for red port looks to be from an early period, say about 1750, but the mark, WF struck twice, is not among those of makers known to have produced labels at that time. The nearest marks with these initials would seem to be those of William Ferguson, working in Elgin and Peterhead around 1830. That makes it a very rare and therefore collectable label.

▷9/47 This label for SHERRY was made in 1831 by Charles Rawlings & William Summers. It is die-stamped from thin sheet, but it has not become worn. This is because it had remained undisturbed in a drawer for many years and had not been used. With quick cleaning it looked almost new. Many labels have survived in fine condition for this reason. The gadroon and shell border was a very popular one at this time.

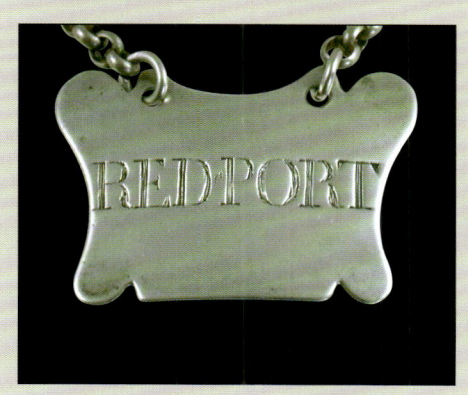

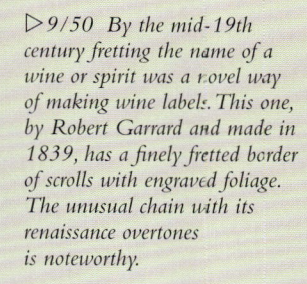

▷9/50 By the mid-19th century fretting the name of a wine or spirit was a novel way of making wine labels. This one, by Robert Garrard and made in 1839, has a finely fretted border of scrolls with engraved foliage. The unusual chain with its renaissance overtones is noteworthy.

Chapter 9 Wine Labels

9/51 One of the better designs for wine labels is the ring. With its raked sides it sits well on the shoulders of decanters of the period. The first rings were made by Sandilands Drinkwater in the 1750s but examples earlier than 1790 are very uncommon. This was made by William Eaton in 1831 and is typical. Later in the century, some ring labels were made of ivory but they tend to be flatter. (see 9/60).

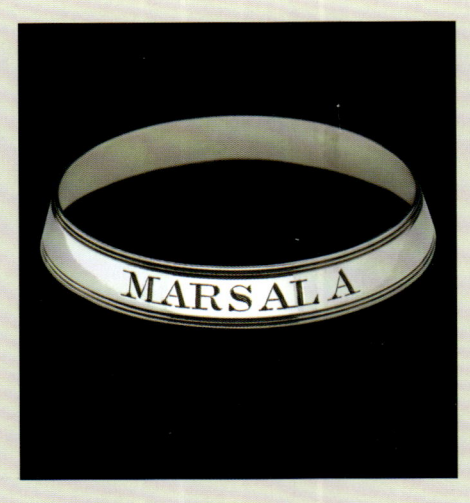

▷9/52 The postage stamp label had been fashionable in the 1790s and 1800s, but it was revived. This small wine label S (for sherry) was made by Charles Rawlings & William Summers in 1840.

9/53 An ivory ring wine label for PORT. It is probable that these were made in India for the large British population supporting the Indian army and the infrastructure of the British Raj from 1858. The steep rake of the label suggests an early date for this type, and it probably dates from around 1840–60. It would have fitted an early shaft and globe decanter of that date, or even a decanter of the 1830–40 period.

▷9/54 MANZANILLA is a very rare name to find on a wine label. It can be seen that it was cast from the thickness where the name has been pierced. Although it can be discerned that the label was made in London, the date letter and maker's mark have been rendered illegible by the piercing of the name. This is not unknown by any means.

9/55 This set of four silver-gilt labels were made by Charles Rawlings & William Summers in 1844. The leaf pattern was arguably the most common by this date, although most were very light in weight and almost all were die-stamped. These are significantly heavier than most, and it makes a pleasing change to see a set which has not been split among collectors.

9/56 The black letter font of this P is indicative of the interest in all things tudor or gothick which pervaded English taste in the early Victorian period. This label is another of Rawlings & Summers' prolific output and was made in 1846.

9/57 While handles of furniture were being made in the full-blown rococo style of the 1760s, it seems that wine label makers unanimously eschewed it. However, when the style returned, albeit with differences, they joined the theme. This utterly rococo label was heavily cast in 1849 by John S Hunt with a profusion of scrolls and acanthus leaves against a matted ground.

◁9/58 If the previous label exuded high quality with its heavy casting, this one is the antithesis. It is very lightly die-stamped and electroplated on copper and the plating is so thin that much has worn off. It was made around 1860–70.

9/59 William Summers continued business after Charles Rawlings left the partnership in 1863 and this label was made by him alone in 1872. Its design of a banner spanning five rings is unusual but evokes the spirit of the time well.

9/60 Another ivory ring wine label for HERMITAGE. By the 1870s the shaft and globe decanter shape had flattened, and this flatter ring was designed to sit at the top of the body of such a decanter. Hermitage is not a common name on a wine label, but neither is it particularly rare, – except there cannot have been a great deal of hermitage wine on the subcontinent of India.

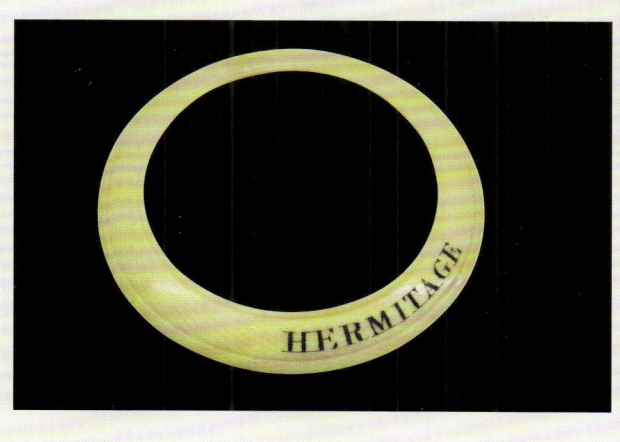

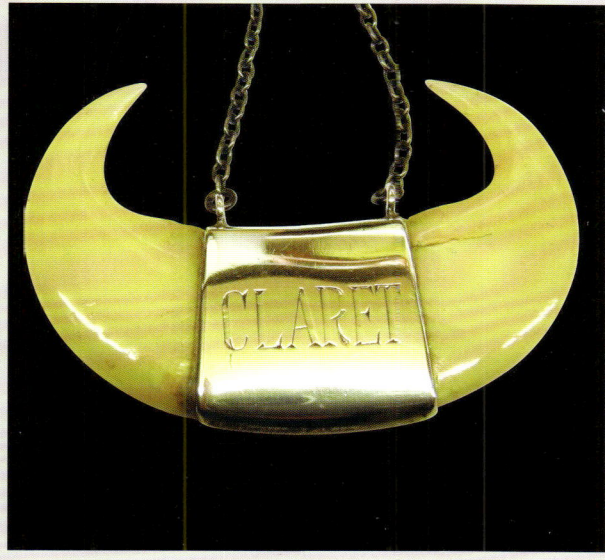

△9/61 Tiger's claw wine labels were another favourite among gentlemen of the British Raj and were perhaps only a slightly less ostentatious trophy than having the whole animal's skin on the floor. It seems probable that such items were mainly made by Indian craftsmen as most have complex filigree decoration, making this one a bit unusual. The letter form of CLARET is typical of the very late 19th century.

Coasters and decanter trolleys

A coaster is a small circular tray in which a decanter is placed on a dining table or other polished surface. The term 'coaster' is derived from its ability to 'coast' along the polished surface of the dining table and, according to the Oxford English Dictionary, was first used in an 1898 catalogue of the antique dealers Mallet & Son of Bath (more recently of London and New York), but it is quite possible that the word in that sense is older. Coasters had previously been known variously as bottle or decanter slides or stands. Many terms used in the decorative arts were invented by antique dealers in the late 19th and early 20th centuries, including phrases like 'grandfather clock', 'bachelor chest', 'brandy saucepan' and so on.

While many of the objects concerned with wine drinking evolved only gradually over a number of years, coasters, like wine funnels, seem to have mushroomed in popularity rather suddenly during the 1760s following their first introduction some years earlier. Their purpose is quite simple – to protect the decanter and what it is standing on. A dribble of wine down the side of a decanter will stain the surface upon which it is placed, and by resting the decanter in a coaster this problem is solved. Also, if two or more decanters are on a table together, coasters prevent them from touching one another and becoming chipped. This is a common occurrence, as can be seen from the numerous small blemishes around the widest diameter of old decanters. For some reason that has yet to be explained, Scottish coasters are decidedly uncommon. While they are not quite in the rare category, they certainly are not seen often, and those that appear were mostly made in Glasgow rather than Edinburgh, and tend to be early 19th century in date.

We have already seen that serving bottles preceded decanters. Of these, some had rounded bases and were kept in silver holders. While not actually coasters, they perform a similar function and therefore can be regarded as the precursors. They are also very rare.

10/1 A double coaster without wheels. It may even be described as a decanter tray. It is Sheffield gilt, that is, it was made in the same way as old Sheffield plate but using gold instead of silver, a technique very seldom seen. It is 17¼in/43·8cm long, and was made about 1820. The small rings are to hold the decanter stoppers when the decanters are being used.

Chapter 10 Coasters and decanter trolleys

Silver coasters followed the prevailing fashions of rococo, neoclassicism and the various revivalist movements in the 19th century. Almost all were designed to hold a single bottle-sized decanter, and most had wooden bases. The idea of putting a common bottle in a silver coaster would never have occurred to a Georgian gentleman. Coasters for magnum-size decanters do exist but are not common.

The wood base, usually beechwood after about 1800, but mahogany before, was almost always turned with a decorative pattern of concentric rings, and a central button of silver for an engraved crest or monogram. The underside was always fitted with a baize lining and there was usually a groove about 3/8in/9mm in from the edge into which the baize fitted to give a clean edge (see 10/36). The highest quality coasters had silver bases covering plain, unturned wood, but the undersides were still baize-lined; such coasters were often engraved with coats of arms. From extant examples, and there are many, it may be assumed that coasters were originally sold in pairs and sets of four, six, or eight, although singletons are seen on the market today.

Rococo was still popular in the early 1760s when coasters first gained widespread acceptance, so it was natural that they should reflect this. While the general shape was that of a squat cylinder, and remained so until the early 19th century, the decoration was decidedly lively and asymmetrical in feeling. Most 18th century coasters have pierced sides, and the early form typically showed scrolling foliage, sometimes inhabited by birds and set against railings. This was an attempt to bring the illusion of a rustic garden into the eating room (dining room is a modern phrase), an idea much in fashion that popularised Martial's phrase (XII.57.21) *rus in urbe* (the country in town). In the 1760s, the top moulding was often wavy and capped with gadrooning, and most coasters were about 1½–2in/3·8–5cm high. An alternative to rustic rococo decoration was chinoiserie in which the sides were pierced to form Chinese railings.

During the 1770s the rococo fashion in coasters gave way to neoclassical inspiration, resulting in the top wavy moulding becoming straight, and the gadrooned rim being replaced by beading, and later reeding. The piercing was often plain vertical paling, rounded at the top. Coasters also became less deep. More sophisticated examples were decorated with engraved rams' heads, paterae, vases, swags and other elements of the neo-classical vocabulary. In better examples the decoration was cast and applied to the basic shape while later in the 1780s and 1790s, economy often resulted in the decoration being engraved and pierced from sheet silver. It is curious that while neoclassicism was first introduced in London in the late 1750s, and silversmiths were usually among the first craftsmen to embrace new design ideas, coasters were still being made in the almost-defunct rococo style a decade later. Date letters in the hallmarking confirm this chronology.

10/2 A very rare bottle holder. It was made in 1716 by the Huguenot, Simon Pantin, and is engraved with the arms of Fenwick of Northumberland and Durham. It is of oval section and was designed to take a flask-shaped bottle with a rounded base (which has not survived). A well known example of 1723 by Augustine Courtauld is in the Ashmolean Museum in Oxford, and illustrated in several books.

10/3 A small wine bottle stand and a precursor of the coaster as an object. Silver bottle stands are very rare and this, dating from 1733, is later than the other known examples of 1716, 1717 and 1723. The last is well recorded in various books and has its original bottle. This one was made by John Gamon and has a plain elliptical body on a tall moulded collet foot; the bottle is probably a 19th century replacement.

10/4 A pair of unmarked and large magnum silver coasters of 6½in/16.5cm diameter. The sides are pierced with a trellis pattern interrupted by quatrefoils enclosing stylised foliage, all beneath an ovolo top moulding. The silver bases are engraved with the arms of Walter Calverley who took the name of Blackett on marrying the illegitimate daughter of and heir to Sir William Blackett in 1729, and who died in 1749. The decoration can be dated stylistically to the mid-1730s making these the earliest currently-known coasters.

10/5 A set of four coasters with panels of stylised rococo foliage beneath wavy gadrooned rims. Very unusually, they have wine labels for PORT, CLARET, SHERRY and MADEIRA set into the sides. They were made in London by John Langford & John Sebille in 1757. Notwithstanding the coasters in 10/4, these are among the earliest known.

10/6 A silver coaster made in 1767 by William Lestourgeon, and 4⅝in/11.8cm diameter. It is decorated with finely pierced paling entwined with foliage and flowerheads, and an asymmetrical cartouche with a double crest, all beneath a gadrooned moulding. It is typical of the rus in urbe mood of the time, to bring rustic decoration executed in fine silver into the smart home.

Chapter 10 Coasters and decanter trolleys

A particularly pleasing form, not relying on decoration for its appeal, occurred in the 1790s. It was utterly plain and of low profile; such coasters are sometimes of heavy gauge, and owe their good looks to classic proportion, understatement, and the high quality of their manufacture.

In both the early rococo and neoclassical models, it was common for a small area of the side to be left undecorated or the pattern of piercing to be halted, to leave a small circle or rectangle so that a crest or monogram could be engraved (see 10/6 & 10/7). Quite often the engraving was never applied (see 10/17) indicating that in general coasters were produced for retailers' stock as standard items to be engraved at the customer's request, rather than being made to special order.

10/7 At the same time that rococo decoration was fashionable, so too was chinoiserie. This pair of coasters were made in London in 1766 by John Langford & John Sebille, and are formed as Chinese railings. Similar patterns are seen in Thomas Chippendale's designs for garden railings and fretwork in furniture.

10/8 A fine quality pair of neoclassical coasters with silver bases engraved with a coat of arms and crest. The sides are cast with amthemia, within heart-shaped reserves, between rams-heads with pendant husks. The rims are beaded and the bases are pierced with vitruvian scrolls. They were made in London by Peter Desvignes in 1774.

10/9 A pair of silver coasters with turned mahogany bases made in 1785 by Robert Hennell. The decoration is pierced and engraved on thin sheet silver with a strengthening reeded top moulding. While pretty, these coasters do not compare in quality with 10/8.

10/10 This pair of plain coasters was made in 1802, but could have been made 20 years earlier as the pattern was popular for a long period. Their fine quality in good gauge silver demonstrates that there was always a demand for plain objects concurrently with those decorated in the prevailing fashion. Shallower coasters were fashionable during the last 25 years of the 18th century.

10/11 Soon after 1800 there was a fashion for gilding silver tablewares. Among the makers who were most given to this were Benjamin Smith & Digby Scott. These coasters from 1803 are en suite with other parts of dinner services also modelled with fruiting vine decoration. The work is die-stamped, but of heavy quality and with added cast elements. The bottom of each coaster is silver gilt over a wood base. The difference in quality of top London silversmiths' work over the lighter weight un-gilded Sheffield-made coaster should be easily apparent.

10/12 This silver coaster appears grand, but the decoration of the sides, rather than being heavily cast, chased and pierced, is die-stamped from thin sheet to form a continuous band of fruiting vine. The top and base mouldings are different sizes of cast gadrooning which give much strength to the otherwise frail construction. It was made in Sheffield in 1807 by John Roberts & Co.

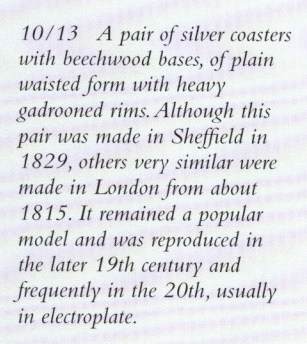

10/13 A pair of silver coasters with beechwood bases, of plain waisted form with heavy gadrooned rims. Although this pair was made in Sheffield in 1829, others very similar were made in London from about 1815. It remained a popular model and was reproduced in the later 19th century and frequently in the 20th, usually in electroplate.

10/14 One of a set of six silver-gilt coasters made by Paul Storr of Storr & Co. for Rundell, Bridge & Rundell in 1810. These large and tall coasters have sides cast and pierced with bacchic putti and leopards amid scrolling fruiting vines, and support a ribbon-tied reeded top moulding. The plinth is decorated with radiating foliage, above the plain base which is stamped:
RUNDELL BRIDGE ET RUNDELL AURIFICES REGIS ET PRINCIPIS WALLIÆ REGENTIS BRITANNIAS.
The base is engraved in the manner of Walter Jackson with the royal arms of George III, and they came from the collection of the Earl of Lonsdale. This model epitomises the luxurious grandeur which was popular during the Regency of George III.

Chapter 10 Coasters and decanter trolleys

Soon after 1800 the bulbous or waisted side became popular, usually surmounted by heavy gadrooning. This model remained popular into the 1820s and was frequently reproduced in electroplated copies much later in the century and in the following one.

The grandest, even grandiose, coasters were the silver-gilt models, made in the workshops of Digby Scott & Benjamin Smith or Paul Storr, from about 1810. These were particularly favoured in royal and aristocratic households, having been ordered from Rundell, Bridge & Rundell who had their retailer's mark stamped in Latin around the base. These coasters are high-sided with heavily cast decoration of bacchic boys under profusely fruiting vines, and with very tame-looking leopards (or perhaps lionesses). The classical decoration is underlined by the ribbon-tied reeded top moulding and the foliate base. The engraving of royal arms does not necessarily indicate royal provenance because ambassadorial plate and that used by holders of high government office was also engraved with royal arms. The issue of plate by the Treasury (that is silver and gold objects for use by high officials) was a perquisite of their office.

As a general rule, apart from the basic and grand, the fashion for silver during the latter part of the Regency period was for rococo revival, a French-inspired and heavy form of decoration. The bulbous sides became embossed with complex decoration, while the gadrooned rims had shells and floral motifs added.

Almost all 19th century coasters were made with swelling or everted sides, as opposed to the strictly vertical sides seen on those of the 18th century. This did not apply to the grandest Regency models which had tall straight sides. Concurrently, turned beechwood replaced mahogany, lignum vitae or the rarely seen rosewood bases used prior to 1800. It has been noted that these beechwood bases illustrate one of the earliest uses of varnish rather than polish to seal wood and enhance its colour. Being circular, coaster bases of all dates were easily produced on a lathe and, with the exception of a few Sheffield-plated examples, had ribbed or other concentric turned patterns.

By about 1825, coasters developed sharply everted sides reflecting the shapes of decanters. They had rims which often had cast vine-leaf, shell and tendril decoration. These models and those with gothic decoration lasted almost until the mid-century, after which silver coasters waned in popularity until the 20th century, when Georgian models were reproduced in large numbers.

△ 10/15 *A set of five old Sheffield plate coasters in different sizes. Four are the standard size for quart decanters, while the fifth is for a magnum, or possibly double magnum. Sets of coasters in varying sizes are a great rarity.*

10/16 A pair of silver-gilt coasters very similar to the magnum (10/17) and made in 1823. While silver elements are probably from the same designs and moulds, although on a smaller scale, the bases of this pair are mahogany, and the silver has its original gilding. They are for single bottle-sized decanters. It is interesting that the Dublin-made coaster (below) was 12 years later.

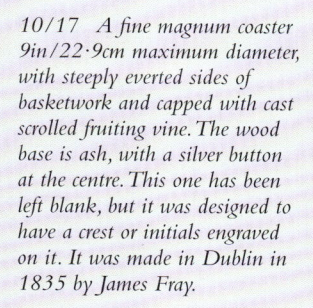

10/17 A fine magnum coaster 9in/22·9cm maximum diameter, with steeply everted sides of basketwork and capped with cast scrolled fruiting vine. The wood base is ash, with a silver button at the centre. This one has been left blank, but it was designed to have a crest or initials engraved on it. It was made in Dublin in 1835 by James Fray.

10/18 A magnificent pair of silver-gilt coasters made in London by Paul Storr for Storr & Mortimer, and assayed in 1836. The cylindrical sides with everted rims are delicately cast, pierced and chased with fruiting vines and olive sprays, and with acanthus scrolls. The coasters have wood bases.

10/19 A fine pair of silver coasters made in London in 1836/7 by Mary & Richard Sibley. The sides form a fretwork of scrolls and are topped by further scrolls and shells in the neo-rococo style. The bases are finely engraved with the arms, crest and motto of Captain Charles Waldo-Sibthorp within a baroque cartouche and a border of vigorous scrolls, shells, fish-scales and masks, very much in the manner prevailing in the 1720s –40s.

Chapter 10 Coasters and decanter trolleys

The Hallmarking of Coasters

The positioning of hallmarks on silver objects, including coasters, followed standard practices. The earliest were hallmarked somewhere on their vertical sides, and an unpierced section was often left specifically to hold the marks. Coasters with silver bases were usually marked somewhere on that surface. By 1780, the hallmarks had been moved from the side to the moulded rim of the base. These marks were stamped before the piece had been finished and in particular before the wooden base was added. As a result, and in order to fit the base and complete the process of finishing the silver itself, it was necessary to rework the base moulding. In doing so, the silversmith quite frequently defaced or otherwise damaged the hallmarks. This process, together with subsequent zealous or frequent cleaning, has meant that most late 18th century coasters now have very poor hallmarks. Good, clear hallmarks on coasters must be regarded as a bonus if they are ever seen.

Silver-plated Coasters

Silver-plated coasters followed a similar pattern to their more expensive silver counterparts. Very few survive from before about 1780, but neoclassical models with repetitive decorative detail are seen. These are all of old Sheffield plate. However, a clear distinction must be drawn between these and later electroplated models (see glossary). A lot less common was the plain Sheffield plated coaster from the 1790s. The bulbous sided or waisted model already seen in silver was very popular for much of the 19th and 20th centuries, but only those made before about 1840 are old Sheffield plate; all later examples are electroplated.

Rarely seen in solid silver, although not unheard of, are wirework coasters. These enjoyed brief popularity in the closing years of the 18th century. They are more frequently encountered in old Sheffield plate and electroplate.

10/20 The marks from 10/6. It can be seen how the pattern of piercing and engraving has been modified to allow the maker's mark and hallmarks (for 1767) to be read clearly.

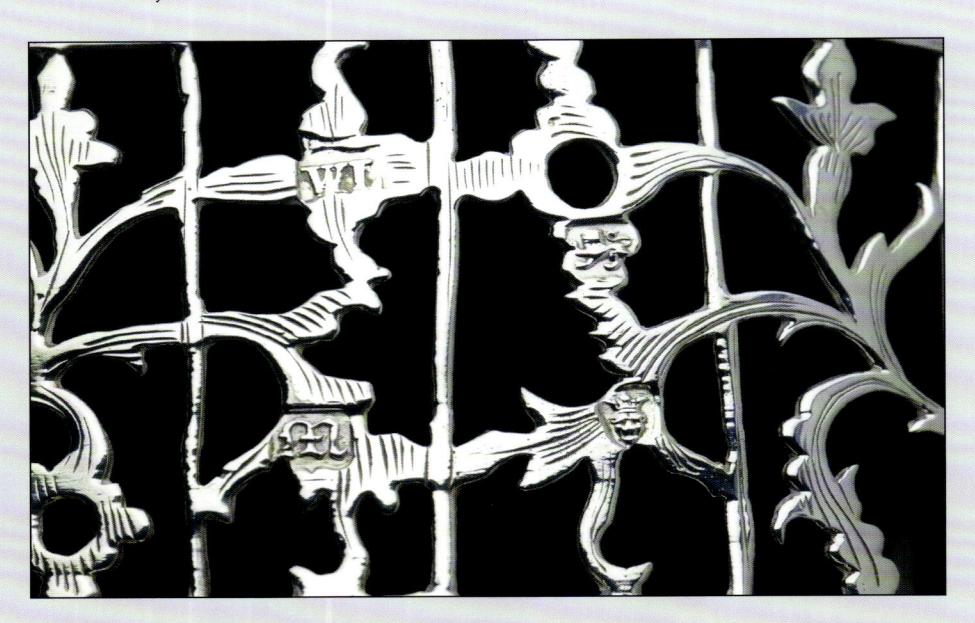

10/21 A detail of 10/13 showing the usual positioning of hallmarks on coasters made after about 1775. In this instance the marks are very clear, but the insertion of the wood base of the coaster and bending it under to ensure it stays there with the subsequent re-working by the silversmith, usually results in the marks being distorted and degraded; frequently they are all but illegible.

10/22 This is an electroplated coaster made by Elkington & Co. in about 1860. It has a much thicker plating than most, which is to be expected of the leading manufacturers of their day. The base is solid satinwood, an expensive imported wood seldom used except in fine furniture.

10/23 This pair of silver coasters was made in 1794 by John Edwards. Wirework coasters were usually plated and silver ones are uncommon. They well demonstrate that simple designs and economy with materials can still result in highly satisfactory works of art. They would be equally attractive if made in old Sheffield plate.

10/24 A pair of silver and oak coasters by Omar Ramsden. While they are outside the dateline suggested by the title of this book, their original design and superlative quality should be noted. They are hallmarked for 1936, three years before Ramsden died. He had a large workshop in Fulham where he employed 20 workmen and ensured stringent quality control. Like all his work these are signed in small engraved upper case:
OMAR RAMSDEN ME FECIT.
They are also inscribed:
MARTIN DODD ME DONAVIT.
They are 5¾in/14·6cm diameter, and the underside is also applied with a Tudor rose.

Chapter 10 Coasters and decanter trolleys

Papier mâché and lacquered coasters were very popular from the end of the 18th century and for the following few decades. The first were straight-sided and made of papier mâché: layers of lightweight, re-constituted paper and cardboard, were compressed with glue. They were decorated with lacquer, plain on the inside surface and usually decorated outside. While black is the most commonly seen colour, various shades of red, green and occasionally cream are found; blue very rarely so. Arguably the earliest papier mâché coasters are those with horizontally ribbed sides. With their scarlet (or sometimes black) lacquer and Sheffield-plated rims, they are very attractive and some have small hooks and rings so that they can be attached to one another.

Around 1800–1825, a very large number of coasters were made with decoration in polychrome or gilding and often with both. The typical decoration was floral, but chinoiserie, and repetitive geometric motifs were also popular. Occasionally the decoration resembled lustre ware with a subtle sheen. Within 20 years bulbous sided coasters were favoured, but these were usually turned wood and lacquered, and heavier than their papier mâché counterparts although they are often mistakenly called papier mâché.

One of the earliest manufacturers of papier mâché in Britain was Henry Clay of Birmingham who had perfected and patented the process of pasting layers of paper under pressure in 1772, although the first recorded reference to papier mâché coasters is dated 1792. Clay frequently stamped his work and although he died in 1812 the firm remained in business for a further 50 years. Another firm that signed much of their papier mâché was Jennens & Bettridge who took over Clay's workshop in Birmingham after the latter had moved to London.

While papier mâché coasters have long been collected and are very decorative, it should be remembered that when made, they were very much the inexpensive alternative to silver or Sheffield plated ones. At the time of writing, a good pair may cost almost as much as the equivalent in silver, and more than a plated pair, which begs the question of whether or not our priorities are where they should be. While black lacquer is most often seen, it is the least wanted, while cream, green, and red are more eagerly sought.

▷10/25 A pair of sealing-wax red papier mâché coasters with horizontally ribbed sides. Sometimes this model has narrow Sheffield-plated rim mounts with hooks and latches to connect two coasters together. Dating papier mâché coasters is an inexact science, but these may be the among the earliest made in Britain from c1790–1800.

▷10/26 A pair of black papier mâché coasters decorated with sprays of flowers in two-colour gilding. The rims are bronzed, a common feature of papier mâché coasters. Unlike most, these are in excellent condition with the inside (plain black) still quite shiny. They date from around 1800.

▷10/27 A black-lacquered coaster decorated with panels of stylised flowers and foliage with alternating panels of black trellis decoration against a gilt ground. Its pristine state both outside and in, is most unusual.

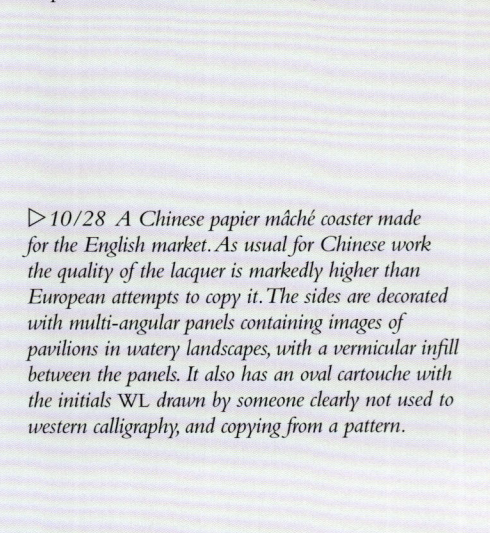

▷10/28 A Chinese papier mâché coaster made for the English market. As usual for Chinese work the quality of the lacquer is markedly higher than European attempts to copy it. The sides are decorated with multi-angular panels containing images of pavilions in watery landscapes, with a vermicular infill between the panels. It also has an oval cartouche with the initials WL drawn by someone clearly not used to western calligraphy, and copying from a pattern.

▷ 10/29 *A pair of red papier mâché coasters with slightly bulbous sides. The lacquer has a lustrous, almost metallic finish and the gilding is dull, probably an intentional contrast. They date from about 1820.*

▷ 10/30 *An extraordinary set of 18 papier mâché coasters. It is thought that they were ordered by a civic authority for use in municipal functions. The decoration is very clearly in the chinoiserie style which was fashionable in the opening years of the 19th century.*

▷ 10/31 *A pair of coasters lacquered in dark green. Although they are almost universally called papier mâché, they are in fact turned wood and only the rims are papier mâché. The detail (below) shows the subtle effects of the bronzed lily pads contrasting with the vivid polychrome of the foreground leaf background decoration.*

▷ 10/32 *A red papier mâché coaster with gilt decoration in at least three shades. The condition of the inside of the base is typical: it has been wetted with drops of wine, and this has degraded the lacquer. It was made around 1815.*

▷ 10/33 *A papier mâché coaster with steeply everted sides and a shaped rim. Unusually the decoration is on the inner sides, and includes foliage and flowers that would have been seen in a Victorian garden – roses and morning glory among others. It also has delicate gilded scrolls in the neo-rococo taste. The decoration and feel of it suggest a date of c1830–40, but the everted sides suggest it was made for a decanter of comparable form, such as shaft and globe of c1850 or later. It is a not-so-common example which is difficult to date.*

Chapter 10 Coasters and decanter trolleys

Treen coasters, or those made of wood (treen is literally tree-en, like wood-en), are an attractive alternative to silver or papier mâché. They were usually made in the period up to about 1830, although they are becoming increasingly difficult to find. Typically the early ones, made of mahogany, were not as tall as silver models and had short, ogee-turned sides, while the rims were astragal moulded. The best were inlaid with chequer stringing around the top moulding while others, equally good, had brass stringing lines. These are very rarely seen as pairs. Another very rare and attractive type has plywood sides (ply was an invention of the mid-18th century) with fretwork in the rococo style.

A particularly attractive variety of treen coaster was made in Ireland in the period 1810–1830. Quite substantial and sometimes of rosewood, although usually of mahogany, it was about 1½in/3·8cm) tall – slightly higher than usual – and closely resembled the shape and size of lacquered wood models.

10/34 An early mahogany coaster of simple form. The height, about ¾in/2cm is typical for this type. This one is large enough to hold a magnum, being 6in/15·3cm diameter. It is inlaid on its top edge with a brass stringing line, while the sides are turned with an ogee moulding. These are very rarely seen as pairs. Some brass-inlaid coasters have a wavy edge (see 10/38), and are considered to be from c1760, while this one is probably c1770.

10/35 The underside of a wood-based coaster was always fitted with a baize lining, and there was usually a groove about ⅜in/1cm in the edge into which the baize fitted to give a clean edge; the baize in this example has frayed.

10/36 An early mahogany coaster with a brass-inlaid and shaped rim. While the model is well known to furniture specialists, it is not yet known who made this type; several candidates have been put forward.

10/37 A mahogany coaster with ribbed sides. The top and bottom ribs are stained and polished black in imitation of ebony. The centre of the base has concentric ring turning, and it is large enough to hold a magnum. The ribbed decoration strongly suggests an Irish origin, and would have matched the edges of other dining room furniture when it was made.

10/38 A pair of mahogany coasters. The sides are deeply ogee in outline, effectively a squat baluster shape, while the inside edge curves outwards. They are probably English, although they may have been made in Ireland, where bolder versions of the same form are known. They were made about 1820.

10/39 A mahogany coaster made by James Mein of Kelso, whose identity is known from the paper labels on the undersides of his coasters. Typically they are large (9in–10in/23–25·4cm. diameter), and most have heavily gadrooned edges. While they may have been intended for large decanters, it does seem more likely that they were intended for some other, probably culinary, use. Invariably they are fitted with three brass and leather castors underneath.

10/40 A mahogany magnum coaster with bobbin-turned supports for the rounded rim, and with a concentrically turned base. It is an unusual type, and its steeply raked turnings clearly indicate its use with a shaft and globe decanter. At 7·5in/19cm. diameter it might even be large enough for a double magnum decanter. It dates from about 1830–60.

Chapter 10 Coasters and decanter trolleys

Yet another rare form of treen coaster has a tall plywood extension to one half. The purpose of this was to shield the decanter from the heat of a fire. The shield coaster was used after dinner when the ladies had withdrawn and gentlemen would gather round the hearth to drink. Shielded coasters were sometimes part of a horseshoe-shaped drinking table. Exceptionally, they appear to have been made in other materials. A 'claret bottle frame, called a wine shade' has recently come to light. Made of silver, and of semi-cylindrical form with a domed top, it has a flat, circular base resting on four claw feet. It was made by John Emes in London in 1806 and was given to Magdelene College, Oxford by Farrer Grove Farrer Spurgeon that year.
(See *Silver Society Journal,* No 14, 2002, pp126/127)

10/41 This is a rare mahogany shield coaster. Shield coasters protected the decanters that would have been placed in them from the heat of the fire around which those who used them would have been sitting. Shield coasters have usually been found in the north of England which suggests that they may have originated there. It probably dates from about 1800, although it looks earlier.

10/42 A pair of mahogany shield coasters with wide brass bands, and carrying handles. The quality of the mahogany and the colour of the brass indicate a very late 19th century date.

10/43 A fine pair of mahogany shield coasters. The pointed shields suggest an early date, even 18th century, but the turning of the bases put them early in the 19th century. The backs of the shields are crisply carved with stylised classical foliage which is a rare feature. They are 11ins/ 28cm high and as all antiques must be dated from their latest feature, they can be dated to about 1810.

10/44 A very rare pair of large shield coasters with knurled or beaded mouldings. The backs have pierced hand grips and boxwood reserves inlaid CLARET and PORT respectively. Each coaster features a pocket which would not only further insulate the decanter from the heat, but would also accommodate a cloth or corkscrew. They date from about 1820–1840.

Chapter 10 Coasters and decanter trolleys

Coasters of brass, pewter, and other materials are not often seen. An extremely high proportion of brass examples were made in the early 20th century in imitation of Georgian styles. Many of these closely mirror the illustrations in the catalogues of Pearson Page, brass founders and copyists of old base metalware, and can probably be attributed to that firm (see 13/12). However, a few genuine and very rare examples exist.

Pewter coasters are occasionally seen and are almost always late 18th century in date. They tend to be relatively high-sided and are engraved with wrigglework in the neoclassical style. When new, they must have looked similar to silver and would almost certainly have been polished to retain that appearance. In his monograph *Old Pewter*, H. H. Cotterell illustrates a pair of pewter coasters which apparently have painted decoration of fleur-de-lis. They have tall straight sides, are unmarked and date from the late 1790s. Much more rare are paktong coasters; very few of these are known to exist. They were made from an alloy first invented by the Chinese for imperial use, and look similar to silver. They almost always date from about 1765–85, and approximately follow silver models. Very recent research has shown that paktong coasters are probably Chinese made for the British market; their construction differs slightly from the English silver models that they imitate.

While researching this chapter, an advertisement was noticed for an antique coaster made of rhinoceros horn. Its simplicity would seem to date it to about 1800. It is a great rarity and was possibly made in India to an English design for a member of the East India Company. If it were made in India, its date may be a few years later, as fashions were inevitably slow to travel 5000 miles.

Coasters in other media are also seen occasionally. Among the most delightful, are those made of rolled paperwork or paper filigree (called quillwork in the USA). This form of decoration was done by ladies of leisure, and they could buy prepared coasters from artists' suppliers requiring only the application of the rolled paper to complete the effect. Most examples were varnished to protect the surface when finished and this process is likely to have been carried out by professional craftsmen. Originally brightly, almost garishly coloured, no rolled paperwork coasters appear to have survived in pristine condition.

10/45 This curious brass object may be a coaster for a bottle. It was made late in the 19th or very early in the 20th century and is finely hand-crafted, not, as it might appear, adapted from a WWI shell case. Most tall coasters were not for wine bottles or decanters, but for soda syphons, and were usually electroplated but a few were made in silver. Perhaps this is a wine cooler?

10/46 This is a paktong coaster. It is neatly designed in the neoclassical taste of the 1770s–80s with a vacant cartouche to take a crest. While this looks utterly British, it was actually made in China for the English market. This can be deduced from the constructional techniques which vary slightly from English ones. Note the pinholes to keep the wood base in place because paktong cannot be worked like silver, from which this was clearly copied.

10/47 Two pewter coasters. The left hand one has pewter sides and a papier mâché base. The pewter is lacquered black, but the detail (right) shows the bright-cut decoration. The right hand coaster is papier mâché, and is inlaid with pewter in the prevailing neoclassical fashion with swags of bell-flowers. They each date from the closing years of the 18th century.

10/48 A coaster made of rhinoceros horn. Its simple design, with straight sides, would indicate a date of about 1800, but as it was possibly made in India, it is probably up to 20 years later. It is a great rarity.

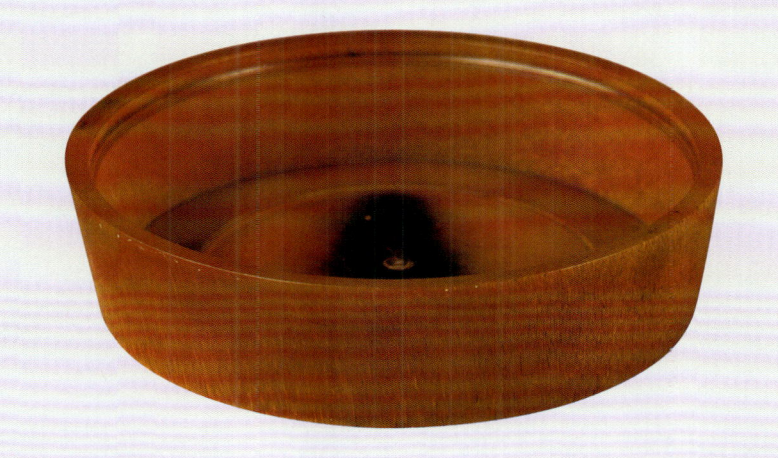

10/49 A rolled paperwork coaster. In fact the body of the coaster is turned wood inlaid on its top surface with checker stringing. The recessed sides are applied with gold-edged rolled paper of different colours which are now sadly faded (as all the few known examples are). It is late 18th century.

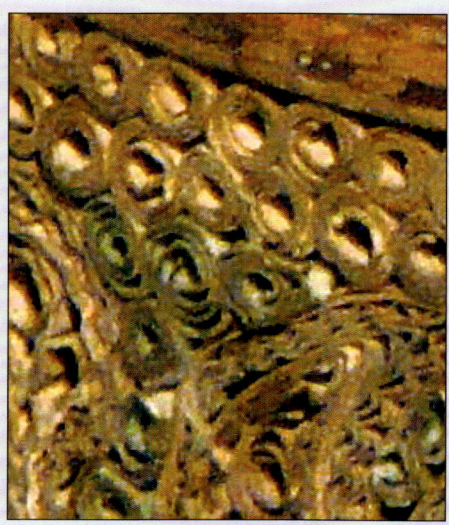

Chapter 10 Coasters and decanter trolleys

Leather coasters are very rare, but we do illustrate two very different forms. Similarly, pottery coasters are uncommon but examples by Wedgwood are occasionally seen. Most creamware coasters are French or Italian, but English ones are usually marked with a stamped impression on the underside.

Whether straight-sided glass dishes were ever coasters for decanters is debatable; it does seem unlikely but nevertheless possible, and the illustrated example is as good a contender as any. With wine-related items becoming increasingly popular, labelling such glass dishes as coasters is inevitable; they may have been stands for other objects, or simply shallow dishes.

10/50 A leather coaster, one of a set of three, of rare type. The leather has been pressed into shape so that there are no seams. It has then been dressed with a thick black lacquer. The rim has been finished with a narrow silver mount which is unmarked. It is impossible to date accurately but it seems probable that it was made within 20 years of 1770.

10/51 A pair of papier mâché and leather coasters with painted decoration of writhen stylised leaves in cream and green alternating with cream panels, some of which are painted with flower sprays. The bases are papier mâché, but the sides are leather – a combination that may be unique.

10/52 A pottery coaster with the sides formed as simple paling or simulated fluting beneath a moulded rim. While this coaster closely follows an English model, it is probably Italian or French in origin, and made for the English market.

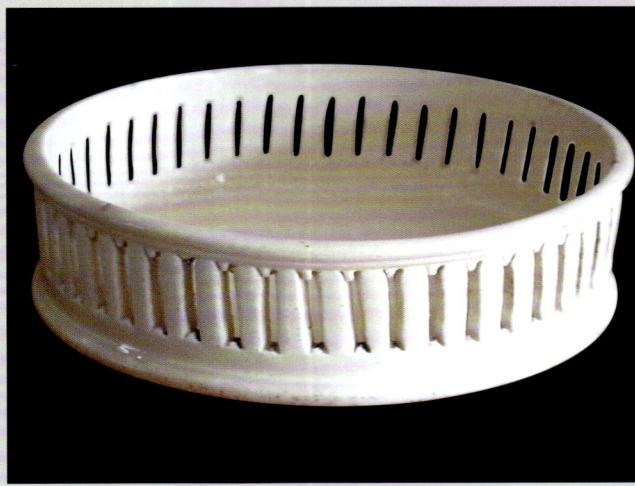

▷ 10/53 *A Bristol blue glass coaster of the late 18th century. It is quite plain with relatively tall and slightly splayed sides. This may be a stand for some other object but its size is about right for a Bristol blue decanter (see 7/10), and it is about the same date. The colour is called because the colourant, cobalt oxide, could only be bought from William Cookworthy of Bristol.*

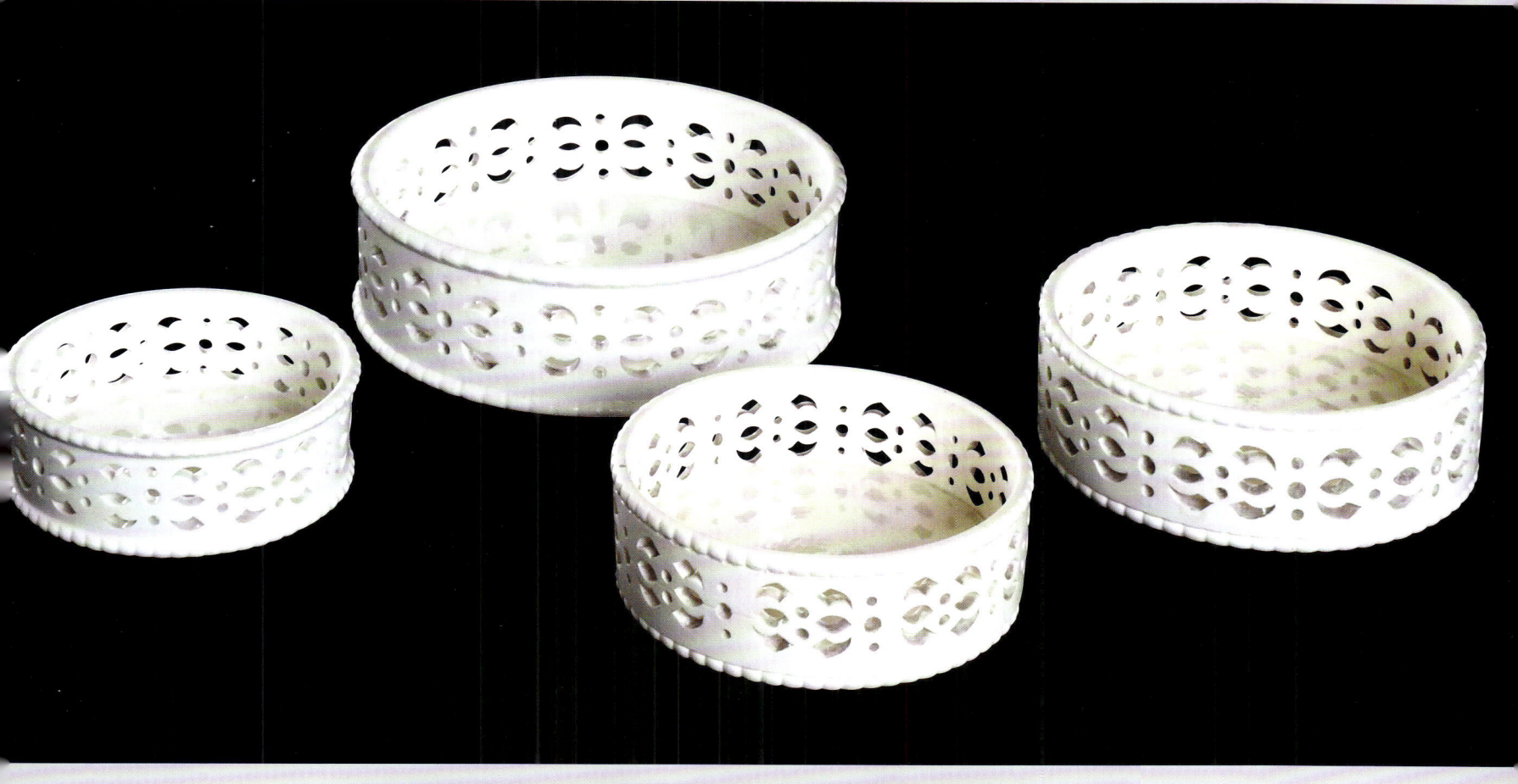

10/54 *An extraordinary set of four pottery coasters, each impressed WEDGWOOD. They are pierced with a geometric pattern between beaded mouldings. Coasters are very rarely seen in sets of different sizes, and then usually one is for a bottle-sized decanter with the other for a magnum. The largest in this set is the standard bottle size, but matching decanters in sizes to fit the other coasters have yet to be seen by the author. They date from the closing years of the 18th century.*

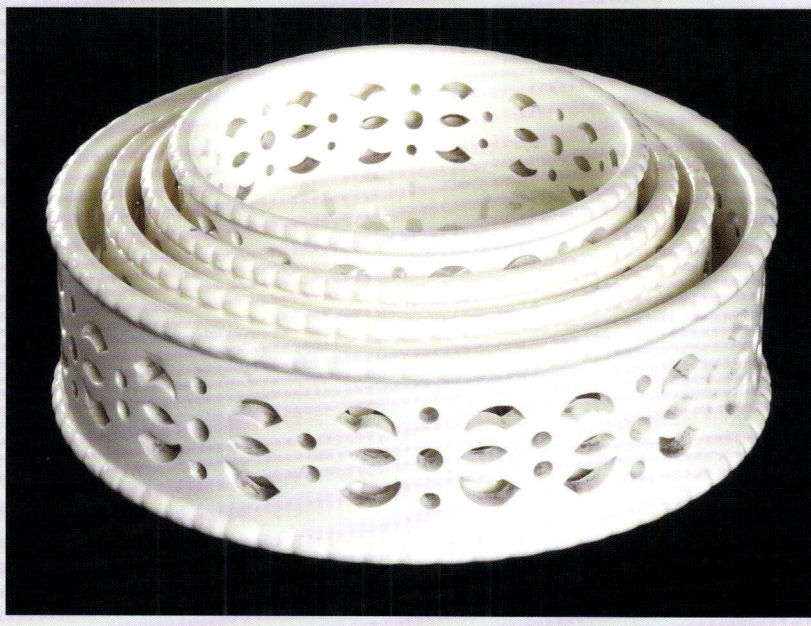

Chapter 10 Coasters and decanter trolleys

Towards the closing years of the 18th century, the consumption of wine in England was increasing at an alarming rate. Until the 1780s the practice in most grand households was to have dinner at several small tables in the eating room. From this date, tables became fewer and larger and soon a single table was the norm. This change of fashion engendered more conviviality and competitive spirit among gentlemen, resulting in the increase in wine consumption. Certainly wine drinking was traditionally competitive among gentlemen until the 20th century.

Dining tables progressively increased in length until the Regency period when it was common in grand houses to seat two or three dozen people, or even more, at one table.

The production of decanters burgeoned in response, and the need for coasters followed. It was at this time that a fashion developed for coasters to be joined together and put on wheels to form wagons or trolleys. Most wagons had two coasters, but a few had three.

Arguably the earliest form was the jolly boat, a model of a small rowing boat fitted with two circular recesses to hold the decanters and smaller holes to accept the decanter stoppers. The earliest had wood bases, usually baize-lined, but soon small castors or rollers were fitted underneath. Silver was the usual medium, but papier mâché also took this form, and the boat shape was stylised to have a bow at each end. Mahogany examples are very rare.

10/55 A rare papier mâché double coaster boat. It has a raised prow at each end and encloses a pair of low plain coasters. The sides are lacquered with finely detailed bunches of grapes with tendrils and leaves. The proportions and design suggest an 18th century date, perhaps as early as 1785, but probably nearer to 1800. The author had this in the early 1970s, selling to a well-known London dealership. It re-surfaced on the market some 35 years later in Vancouver, and has since returned to England – a well-travelled boat.

10/56 A three-bottle coaster boat probably from the same workshop as 10/55. It has the unusual feature of the individual coasters being removable.

10/57 A mahogany jolly boat. This great rarity is fashioned from a solid piece of mahogany, and inlaid with pale and dark stringing lines (probably boxwood and ebony). It can hold two bottle-sized decanters and there are holes for the stoppers when the decanters are in use.

10/58 A boat-shaped silver double coaster with gadrooned borders and leaf-scrolled ends with rings. The coasters are also gadrooned and the underside is hardwood. At either end of the boat is a small ring to hold the decanter stoppers. It was made in London in 1800 by Richard Cooke. The base-plate is engraved with the crest of the 9th Duke of Hamilton.

Chapter 10 Coasters and decanter trolleys

By about 1810 the wheels that had previously been small and hidden beneath the boat, if it had wheels at all, became larger and highly visible. The boat had become a trolley or wagon. An early popular model was made of black papier mâché and had gilded or lacquered brass embellishments on wheels, handles and mounts to protect the lacquer. The wheels were fitted with leather tyres, although these have seldom survived. Decanter wagons proved popular, and were often made of Sheffield plate, with usually a handle of ivory either left white or stained green.

The best wagons were made of silver, and a few were further embellished with gilding, particularly in the period 1815–1845 when revivalist splendour was at its zenith. By about 1815 it was usual for the wagon to be articulated. During the 60 or so years that the decanter wagon enjoyed its period of fashion, the coaster element always followed the pattern of the single examples. Most wagons were made to hold two decanters, but a few, especially after about 1840, held three; of course a pair doubled the number of decanters. Some wagons had detachable coasters, but this was not usual.

10/59 This papier mâché double coaster wagon was a popular model. It has lacquered brass wheels with leather tyres, although the latter are usually missing. The two levels of papier mâché are separated by brass spindles, and it has brass handles at either end.

△ *10/60 A smaller version of 10/59 designed to hold two half-bottle or pint decanters. Additionally the papier mâché is decorated with exotic flowers and birds. The smaller version is a rarity.*

10/61 A pair of jolly boats on wheels formed as clinker-built rowing boats, each with a pair of integral coasters. Note also the small holes amidships to take the stoppers.

10/62 A double coaster trolley with a pair of claret jugs en suite. The trolley is of a type associated with a slightly earlier style being of low profile, with simple wheels and articulated. However, the richly cast, pierced and chased handle, rim and cartouches are typical of their date. The baluster-shaped claret jugs are engraved with complex strapwork and entrelacs, and have scroll handles in the form of vines to match the stoppers. The ensemble was made in 1851 by Edward Barnard & Sons.

10/63 A decanter trolley of very unusual configuration: it has one decanter in front of two in trefoil pattern. Three wood-based coasters with silver horizontally-reeded sides and with richly cast vine rims are pushed and drawn by four cherubs; the trolley has four wheels with turned spokes.
The decanters have deeply diamond-cut ovoid bodies and panel-cut necks, with silver stoppers formed as cherubs disporting themselves on vine leaves and fruit. It was made by Benjamin Preston in London in 1860. The arms are those of the Keighly-Peach family. It is interesting to observe the decanter pattern at this period: it is often thought to date from the 1890s, and sometimes does.

Chapter 10 Coasters and decanter trolleys

10/64 A pair of magnificent silver-gilt double coaster wagons made by Benjamin Smith in 1828. Each is massively cast, pierced and richly chased with fruiting vines above a reeded base and with everted vine leaf rims. The coasters are joined by scrolled tendrils which form the stopper holders, and run on wheels with turned spokes and engine-turned tyres. They can be joined to one another with a hook and eye, and have green-stained ivory handles. They were retailed by Kensington Lewis in St. James's Street, and the plates are richly engraved with the arms of Sir John Astley who succeeded to the Barony of Hastings.

10/65 Another pair of almost equally grand double coaster trolleys. The waisted oblong bodies have bold gadrooned borders and florid scrolls resting on feet which conceal wheels. The detachable coasters are cast and pierced with putti amid fruiting vines with tendrils, and are separated by cast plaques with the coats of arms of John Sawbridge who, on marrying the heiress Jane Erle-Drax-Grosvenor, assumed the surname and arms of Erle-Drax. They were made in 1829 in the workshops of Edward Barnard & Sons, and retailed by David Ellis.

10/66 *A massive (26in/66cm long) decanter wagon with three detachable coasters. The whole piece is conceived in the rococo style with scrolling foliage, and the coasters are cast, pierced and chased, with asymmetric rims. The wagon is supported on wheels, two articulated, with turned spokes, while the frame has foliate scrolled ends and a rococo cartouche on either side, engraved with the arms of Rolt. It was made in London by Edward Barnard & Sons in 1842, and the coasters are large enough to hold magnum decanters.*

Chapter 10 Coasters and decanter trolleys

10/67 *A very curious pair of coaster trolleys of triple bulbous form, the central coaster being of magnum size flanked by bottle-sized ones. They are finely engraved with gothic trellis. The central coaster has the arms of Sir Henry Durrant Bt. while the flanking coasters have masonic symbols within quatrefoils. They have wood bases and gothic pierced trefoil wheels. They were made in London in 1851 by Samuel Hayne & Dudley Cater.*

10/68 Strictly speaking this is not a coaster, but a silver-gilt decanter stand. Of shaped square outline, the tray is engraved and has a raised border of cabochons and strapwork; it rests on demi-bun feet that are similarly decorated. The frame has a central finial in the same style and panels of engraving, and it holds four large and four small rings. The four decanters have ovoid bodies on feet and are wheel engraved with Régence-style scrolls and masks. They are further embellished with silver-gilt rococo cagework and rims and are fitted with baroque finial stoppers. The ensemble was made in London by John Figg in 1850.

Wine glasses, goblets and cups

Wine whets the wit; improves its nature's force
And adds a pleasant flavour to discourse

Anon – couplet engraved on a wine glass c.1810

British or English wine glasses are the perfect subject for collection. However, before considering the history of them, it is worth repeating two short paragraphs from the introduction.

Why are 18th century wine glasses so small compared with modern ones? It is not because they drank less. During much of the 18th century, wine glasses were not put on the table; they were kept by servants on the sideboard or on a side table. During a dinner, drinking wine was restricted to occasions when a toast was given. At that point a footman would bring a glass fully charged to each diner, to be taken in a single draught. The glass would then be re-charged for the next toast and so on. If a different wine was used, the footman would rinse the glass in the dining room before it was refilled. Because a single draught is not large, wine glasses were not large either.

At the end of the dinner and after the ladies had withdrawn (to the withdrawing room), the servants were dismissed from the dining room, and the gentlemen would gather to drink and indulge in the sort of conversation deemed unsuitable for mixed company such as politics and bawdy talk. It was at this point that the serious drinking started and larger glasses, what today we call goblets, were used.

11/1 Part of a collection of 18th century English wine glasses illustrating different bowl and stem forms.

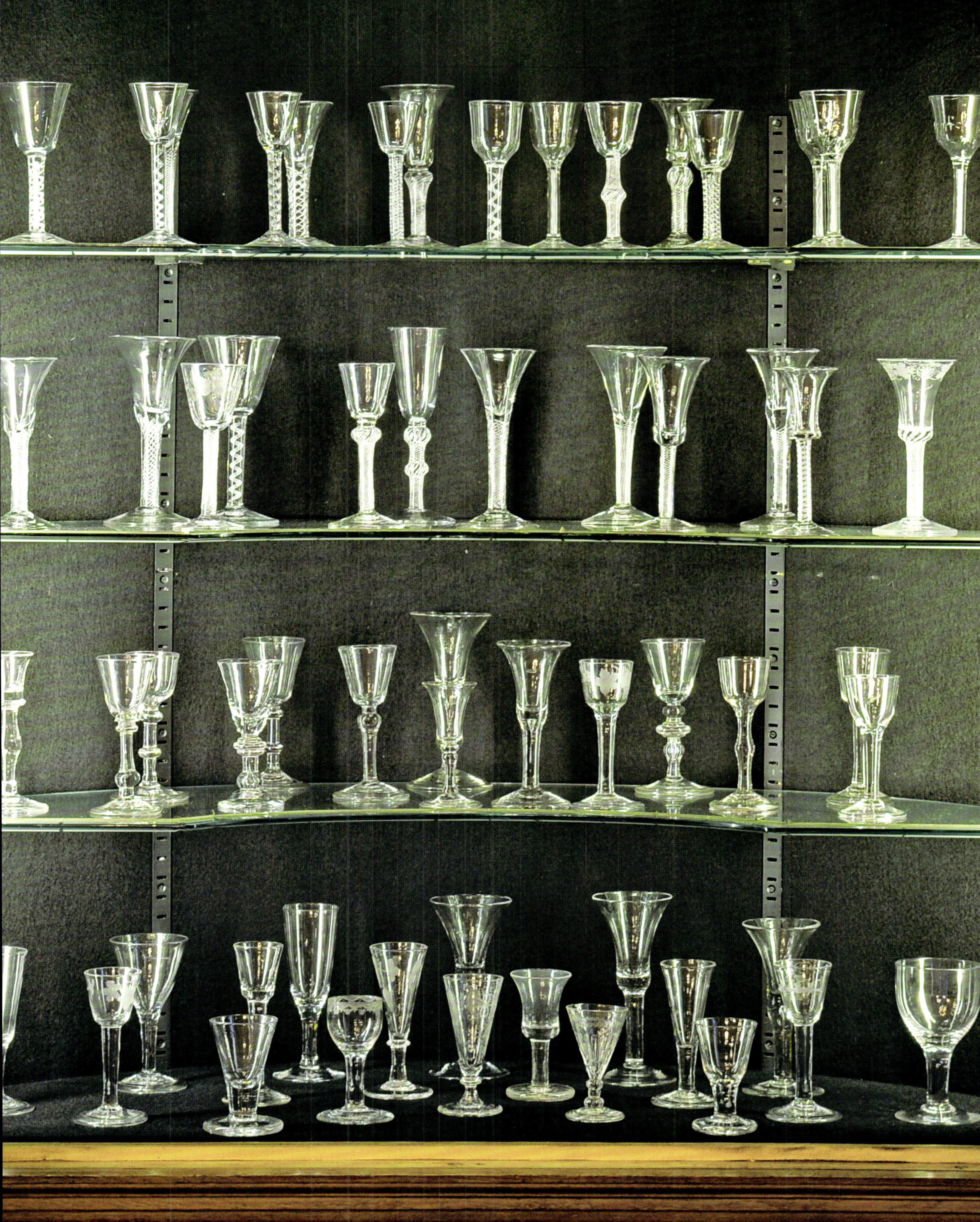

Chapter 11 Wine glasses, goblets and cups

11/2 A coconut cup mounted with silver-gilt in 1518 in the prevailing style. Coconuts and ostrich eggs were considerable rarities at the time, having been brought back on perilous voyages in small ships across oceans. They were believed to be antidotes to poison, with medicinal properties to relieve the symptoms of fever and kidney stones, and even to have aphrodisiac qualities. As late as the 18th and 19th centuries coconuts were used as drinking goblets.

11/3 This is one of a very small number of surviving glasses made in the glasshouse of Giacomo Verzelini. He was among the first to make drinking glasses in England having arrived in 1571 and taken over the glasshouse at Crutched Friars Hall in London. Although Venetian, he came via Antwerp. Decorated in diamond point by Anthony de Lysle, it is dated 1578.

The Romans were responsible for inventing the technique of blowing glass which in turn led to their making glass bottles and vessels for drinking. Following the fall of the Roman Empire, glass making continued but on a smaller scale until it was revived by the Venetians in the early years of the second millennium. From the 14th century, Venetian glass makers became pre-eminent, but they guarded the secrets of their production methods jealously. Venetians perfected the making of clear glass, or *cristallo,* and developed opaque and coloured glass which was of commercial importance in the production of beads. Once a man was apprenticed in a Venetian glasshouse there was little escape because the penalties were barbarous. However, a few men did leave to practise their craft in northern Europe and later in England.

There had been glasshouses in England since the early 16th century principally supplying window glass. At the time, this was very expensive and its use was restricted to small panes and generally small windows. The extensive fenestration of Hardwick Hall and Longleat, both built in the second half of the 16th century, must have seemed wild and ostentatious extravagances when new. Those making window glass also turned their hands to drinking vessels, although probably with limited success.

Among the pioneers of domestic glass making was Jean Carré from Antwerp, who set up his glass furnace at Crutched Friars in London around 1570. A little later he was joined by Giacomo Verzelini, a Venetian glass maker whose output of drinking vessels is the earliest certainly identifiable in England. He was granted a 21-year monopoly by the Crown on 15th December 1574. However, others were keen to get in on the act and before the patent expired he had competition. Sir Jerome Bowes, Sir Edward Zouch, and Sir Robert Mansell were all keen to follow where Verzelini had led the way to successful drinking glass production. Mansell paid huge sums to establish himself, and was producing both glass vessels and window glass, but no known drinking glasses firmly attributed to his glasshouses have survived. By contrast, several Verzelini glasses are known, most of which are now in national museums.

11/4 From medieval times many wine cups and goblets had covers, although this became less usual from the late 16th century. This covered cup dates from 1610 and has a rounded funnel bowl resting on a baluster turned stem. These terms are not used by silver specialists but the form is not dissimilar to glass goblets a century later. It is finely engraved with bunches of grapes and (out of sight here) the arms of Sir Henry Hobart of Blickling Hall, Norfolk who was Chief Justice of the Common Court of Pleas at Westminster. With its cover it is 9⅞in/25cm high.

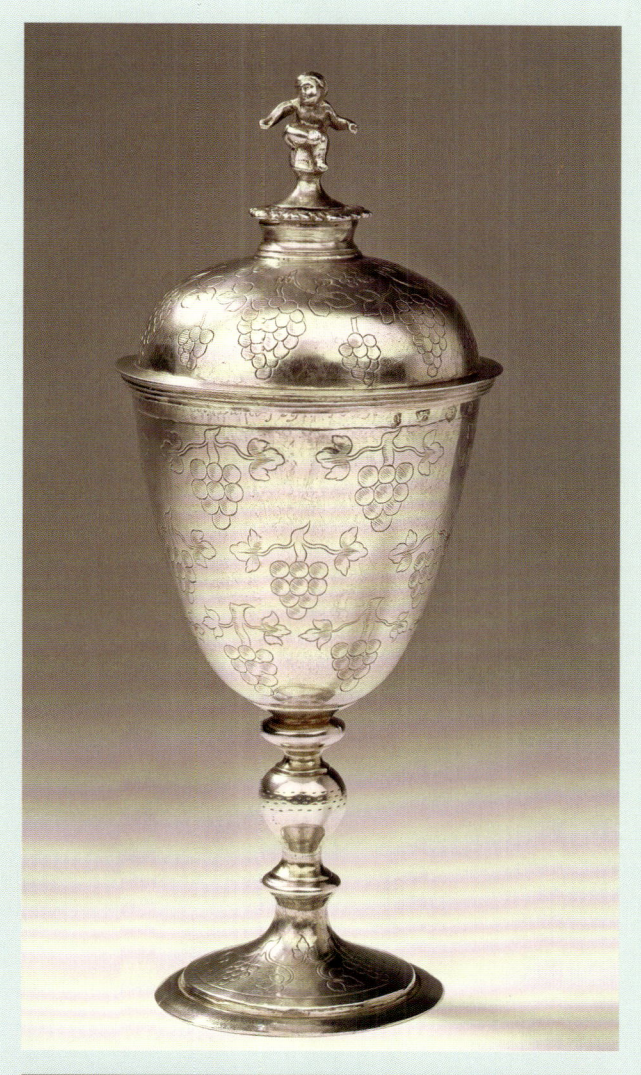

▷ *11/5 A wine cup or goblet of 1613, with a similar shape to the previous cup. The rim is slightly everted and caulked, that is it was hammered to thicken the rim and give strength. The slender baluster stem is similar in form to the legs of tables at this date and it rests on a conical foot. This type of goblet has been reproduced in recent times. It is 8in/20·4cm high.*

Chapter 11 Wine glasses, goblets and cups

◁ 11/6 Another goblet but of 1636. The bowl has become wider and the stem more bold and complex. At this date wine glasses were available from Venice, but were both expensive and fragile, so silver was a viable alternative. At 7in/17·8 cm high it is a good size for taking wine and, contrary to the beliefs of many, silver does not taint wine. Although often copied as presentation and commemorative goblets, the modern ones never have the fine proportion and balance of the originals.

▷ 11/7 A pair of wine cups in different sizes, each engraved around the rim THE GIFT OF MR. ANTHONY PALLE MERCHANT TO HIS MAJESTY'S WINE PORTTERS 1638. The cups are hallmarked for London 1638 and the maker's mark is IG over a cup, possibly signifying that he was a specialist cup maker. The larger cup is 5⅝in/14·3cm, and the smaller one 4½in/11·5cm high.

◁ 11/8 Small stemless silver cups were made between about 1640 and 1665, and this is the earliest known of the type, being made in 1640. The mark, GM above a bird, is probably for George Martin, the bird being a rebus on his name, although this has not been substantiated. It is 3¼in/8·1cm diameter and typically the bowl is lobed and punch-decorated.

◁ 11/9 Another stemless cup with a plain bowl. This one was made in 1664 by SR (it is rare to be able to identify the maker of London silver before 1697) and is quite plain except for the pricked initials WS within a cartouche of scrolls and hearts. These are often termed 'dram cups', and it is possible they were made for strong liquor.

△ 11/10 17th century English silver wager cups are very rare indeed although they were more common in Germany and Holland. The smaller cup swivels and the wager is for drinking both cups dry without spilling any wine (or stronger liquor). This one was made about 1665 by Richard Blackwell. The upper cup or bowl is typical of tumbler cups of the period with a large calyx of acanthus foliage in repoussé while the lower cup is modelled as a girl in a wide skirt. The two sets of initials probably commemorate two marriages, one a little later than the other.

△11/11 From about 1775 and for much of the 19th century, many goblets were made of silver, almost invariably with gilded interiors and often in pairs. Here are four pairs from 1794–1820; two of them were made in Edinburgh. The left hand pair were presentations and have a touching inscription to Major Holland Watson in 1803. The goblets illustrated here vary in height from 6⅜in/16·2cm to 7¼in/18.4cm. Until about 1820, silver goblets were elegantly shaped, but the proportions of later ones appear not to have been an improvement.

△11/12 This silver goblet was made in Birmingham in 1827 and stands 6¾in/17·2cm high. The fine neoclassical design and proportions of the previous decades have given way to a more decorated form of thistle shape. The decoration to the lower bowl and foot is embossed. A goblet of this type and size can accommodate almost half a bottle.

Chapter 11 Wine glasses, goblets and cups

Glasses were produced in England throughout the 17th century, but few survive, and although they developed British characteristics they remained essentially Venetian in style. The big change occurred in the early 1670s. George Ravenscroft, a member of a family of merchants and lawyers, had an interest in the Venetian trade from the 1650s, having been sent to school at the English College in Douai in 1643.

In the late 17th century, there were many people trying to improve glass manufacture. All glass before this time was soda glass which is naturally light and brittle. It lends itself to pretty trailed decoration and 'wings' on the stems of glasses; structures attached to either side of the slender baluster stem. Furthermore, the bowls and feet of glasses were thin; the glasses feel lightweight. Soda glass was not the kind of material which could be heavily cut, although it did take diamond-point engraving well.

Experiments were being undertaken in England, particularly at Ravenscroft's glasshouse at Henley-on-Thames, as well as elsewhere in the Low Countries and France. Ravenscroft's first attempts with flint glass in 1673 or '74 produced results which crizzled, that is, the structure of the glass broke down internally and the surface fragmented, causing the glass to become opaque.

By 1676, this problem was advertised as having been overcome, and Ravenscroft marked his improved formula with a seal showing a raven's head on his wares. The improved melt had litharge (lead protoxide) added, and English lead glass had begun its route to becoming prized around the world, supplanting Venetian as the most sought glass for the table. It may not have been an immediate occurrence, but within a few decades it had established its supremacy.

11/13 By the 1670s silver goblets and cups were being replaced by glasses, at first of Venetian manufacture, and later by English. This is a Venetian wine glass of a type imported to England in large numbers by John Greene between 1667 and 1672. The supplier was Allessio Morelli of Murano and Greene was very specific about the size, shape and clarity of glass, giving his supplier precise instructions. The largest glasses were for beer, the next size for claret and the smallest for sack. This, at 5½in/14cm, lies on the cusp between what Greene called a claret glass (for French wines) and sack (for Spanish wines). Few of these survive today outside museums. It has a conical bowl above a merese with a latticino trumpet foot and hollow knopped baluster stem.

11/14 This is a type of wine glass known as a heavy baluster, having a stem of solid proportions and presenting a firm statement of style. It has a rounded funnel bowl of great simplicity and it rests on a bold stem with two knops. The upper one is a teared angular knop, the lower one a ball knop. The foot is folded, that is, the glass was folded back on itself which adds much strength by inhibiting the foot from becoming chipped. This was a common feature of glasses made between 1680 and 1750 in England.

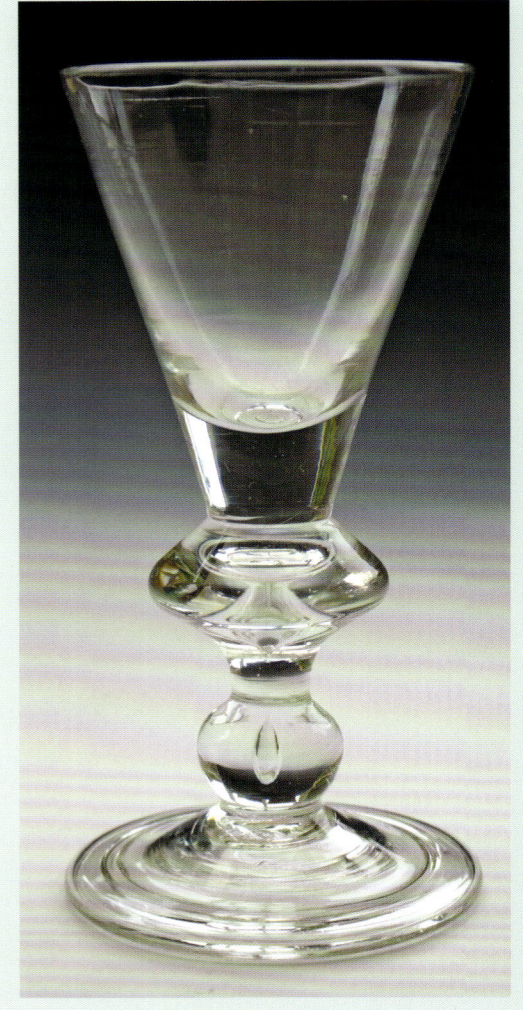

11/15 Another heavy baluster wine glass with a conical bowl on a stem very similar to the last. It also rests on a folded foot and was made around 1700 –1710. It is 6¾"/17·2cm high and is a type much sought by collectors for its form and early date. The English baluster glasses made of lead glass were a stark contrast to the lightweight soda glass of Venice and elsewhere, and lent themselves to bold forms.

Late 17th century British drinking glasses are comparatively rare and are eagerly sought. They soon developed into styles and forms well known to glass collectors. Early lead glass enabled its makers to create bold forms with a strong masculine appeal, quite unlike the pretty Venetian drinking glasses. In place of tall stems with thin bowls, the English glass houses were producing heavyweight glasses with thick knopped stems and purposeful feet, folded at the edge for strength and durability. These are known to collectors as heavy balusters. They were made in large numbers and many survive, but they are becoming beyond the pocket of novice collectors.

Most wine glasses from the period 1680–1780 were made in three parts – the bowl, the stem and the foot – and were joined while still in a semi-molten state. Some glasses were made in two parts, the stem and bowl being made in one operation. The exact method of making is well described elsewhere, but the results are important in the history of wine appreciation in Britain; it was the century when British wine glass making was supreme in the world.

Heavy balusters enjoyed the limelight for about 35 years, from about 1690. But there is a constant demand for fresh thinking, and by about 1725 the proportion of the stems was becoming lighter; the use of less glass may well have had something to do with keeping prices down too. These lighter glasses are simply known as balusters. The trend continued, and by about 1740 the stems became as light as they could be without jeopardising the strength. Glasses of this type are known as balustroids. Where a heavy baluster becomes a baluster, and a baluster a balustroid is not clear-cut, and indeed it can even be a matter of a glass being bought (or sold), balusters being more valuable than balustroids.

11/16 A small group of early 18th century heavy baluster glasses showing the great variety of bowl, stem and foot shapes and sizes. The largest glass is a goblet, while the smallest is a 'deceptive' glass; when full of wine, it holds much less than it appears. Each of the stems has knops which have names; mushroom, ball, cylinder, drop and baluster, which gives the group its generic name.

Chapter 11 Wine glasses, goblets and cups

Among the attractive features of the baluster family of wine glasses are the swellings comprising the stem. They are known as knops. Collectors categorise them by shape and where they occur on the stem, so a glass may have an acorn knop above a basal ball knop, for example. Knop names include cushion, egg, cylinder, mushroom, baluster, annular and bobbin, but these are just some given by enthusiasts. Additionally wine glass stems of this period often have bubbles of air, which may be elongated to a greater or lesser extent. Some were probably an accident in the making, but others were clearly intentional; these are arranged in a circle or at an advantageous position in the stem to enhance the appearance.

Like the swellings comprising the stems of early wine glasses, the bowl shapes also have names, including trumpet, bucket, round funnel, ogee, ovoid, bell and so on; they are all self explanatory. While some knops and bowl shapes are rarer than others, combinations of one and the other can produce an even greater degree of complexity and rarity, and it is this aspect of wine glass collection which has galvanised the attention of glass collectors for well in excess of 100 years. But their interest does not stop with balusters, whether they are heavy, light, or 'oid'.

Most baluster glasses have folded feet, that is, the glass forming the foot when semi-molten was folded back on itself. This gave the glass an extra thickness where it was most likely to be damaged and there was no edge to chip. This practice died away toward the middle of the century.

A common form of wine glass in the 1730–1750 period was very plain, without any knops to the stem, and usually with a simple trumpet bowl (see 11/21). Some have folded feet but many do not. They proved very popular as the shape was elegant and purposeful. They were made in many sizes and in two parts, the bowl usually being described as a drawn trumpet following its method of making. It is a model that has been revived since World War II, and although the modern factories do not refer to their glasses as reproductions, they could not be mistaken for antiques.

A less common form was what has become known as the Silesian stem. This is yet another modern term which has no basis in historical accuracy. Glasses of this type have moulded pedestal stems or, more accurately, inverted pedestal stems, but these are long-winded descriptions. The earliest appear to have been made to commemorate the accession of George I (of Hanover), and are moulded with the legend GOD SAVE KING GEORGE, presumably soon after his arrival in 1714. The square pedestal was soon to become hexagonal and octagonal, with or without diamond-shaped projections on the shoulder of the pedestal. The pattern was seldom made after about 1735.

11/17 This is another group of baluster glasses dating from about 1720–1730. The heavy baluster stems are becoming lighter as time progresses. There are heavy balusters, light balusters and balustroids, but they are inexact divisions which nevertheless collectors understand. (a) is a cordial, the smallest capacity made even smaller by being a deceptive; (b) has a rare waisted bucket bowl; (c) has a thistle bowl prettily engraved, and a domed foot; (d) is the earliest of the group and it has a rare knop combination; (e) is a light baluster, with four knops of which the most obvious is the annulated one.

11/18 Baluster glasses of about 1725 each with annulated knops, an unusual feature.
(a) has a cup bowl which is seldom seen, and an inverted baluster stem with a high conical folded foot; (b) is an early example of a bell bowl and a baluster stem (less common than an inverted baluster), and (c) has a rounded bucket bowl and an inverted baluster above a base knop.
All have folded feet and are excellent examples which would appeal to any serious collector of glasses; (a) would also be a delightful glass from which to enjoy a fine wine. It is 8½in/21·6cm high. Both (a) and (c) are large capacity glasses known as goblets.

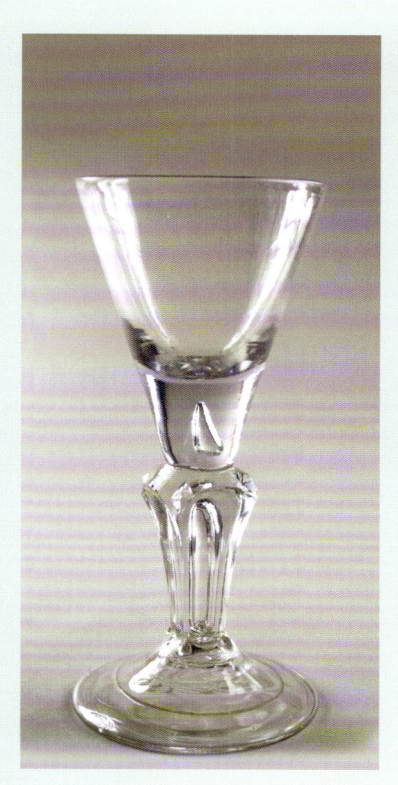

11/19 A favoured wine glass form in the 1720–1740 period had a stem of inverted baluster outline but a section that was more or less square. These used to be known as Silesian stems, but the preferred terminology is now pedestal baluster stem. This one has a conical bowl with a pear-shaped air bubble or 'tear'. The stem was made in a mould and has shoulders with projecting 'stars'. It is an early example of the type and is 6½in/16·5cm high.

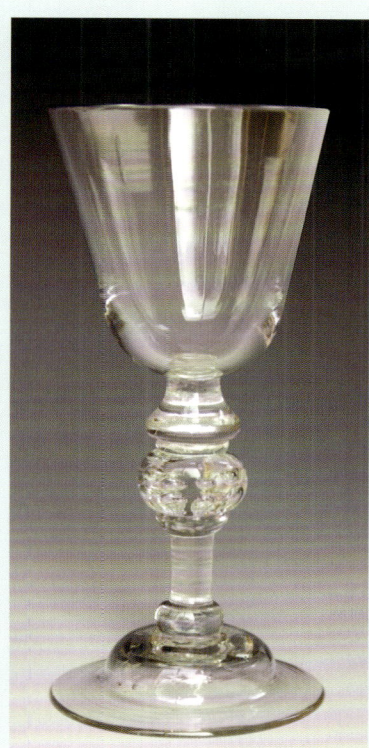

11/19a This is a baluster goblet (a large wine glass) with a stem comprising a drop knop above a ball knop with bead inclusions either side of which is a thin flat disc known as a merese. The stem ends with a basal knop and rests on a domed foot. It dates from about 1730 and is 6⅞in/17·5cm high.

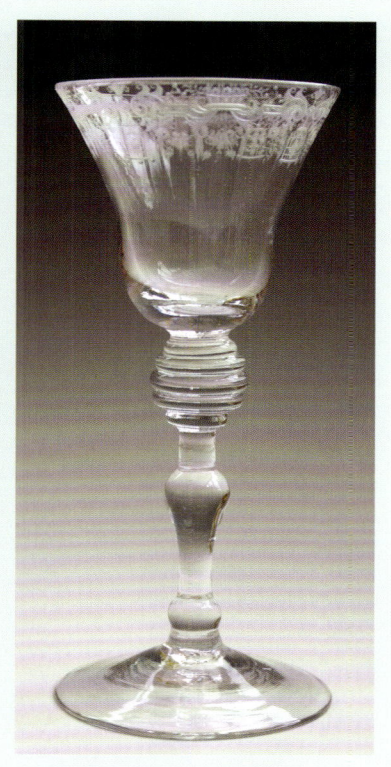

11/20 A light baluster goblet of a type often referred to as Newcastle. The more slender stem with five annulations and an inverted baluster supports a bell bowl engraved with swags, garlands and strapwork suspending bird cages. This form of decoration in a band around the top of the bowl was fashionable in the 1740s and 50s. It is 7⅜in/18·7cm high.

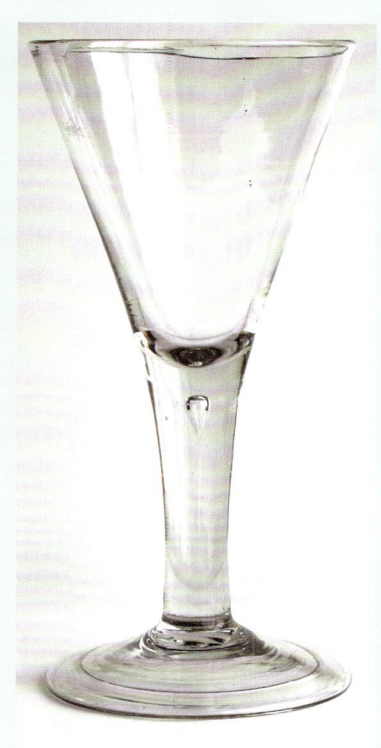

11/21 A plain drawn trumpet goblet with a small tear in the stem. These large glasses (this one is 7¾in/19·7cm high) were made in great numbers around 1740. It may be that the quantity corresponds with bottles being binned and the introduction of wine labels which signalled a general burgeoning of the wine trade in Britain. It is interesting to see that the pattern has been copied in recent times, although never with the fine proportions of the originals, nor do modern examples have folded feet which diminish the chance of chipping.

11/22 High on the list of desirable glasses for a collector is one having definite associations with the Jacobites. The Jacobites were supporters of the Stuart dynasty after the flight of James II to France in 1688 and the accession of William III and his wife Mary (the protestant daughter of James II) to the English throne. The Jacobites made several attempts at returning James II, and later his son James (the Old Pretender) and grandson Charles Edward (the Young Pretender), to the English throne and there were numerous societies or clubs to support them. Such groups were outlawed but they were encouraged by many rich gentlemen and aristocrats. Two risings or rebellions, depending on your viewpoint, took place in 1715 and 1745 in addition to several lesser outbursts in the Jacobite cause.

The Jacobite clubs and societies had many wine glasses with engraved designs with a meaning for them. Most well known emblems were the rose and two buds representing the Old Pretender and his two sons, Prince Charles and Prince Henry, although this interpretation is not universally accepted. Many Jacobite glasses have Latin mottoes which do not translate easily. It was normal in Jacobite clubs to drink the health of the king 'over the water' by passing the wine over a bowl of water on the table. For this reason finger bowls were banned in England until after the loyal toast had been given, even up to the late 19th century.

The pinnacle of achievement for a Jacobite wine glass collector is an Amen glass. While most Jacobite glasses have symbols of Jacobitism, and if discovered could be explained away, Amen glasses are quite specific in their allegiance: they are engraved with the alternative national anthem which ends 'Amen'.

This glass is a large trumpet-shaped goblet, diamond-point engraved with the double reverse cypher of James III (VIII of Scotland) and the first four lines of the anthem. The cogent adaptation of the usual national anthem is the penultimate line which, instead of 'long to reign over us', is engraved 'soon to reign over us'. It is 11½in/29·2cm high and was made about 1745–50. It has an impeccable pedigree.

11/23 More fine Jacobite glass. The decanter (a) is a late version of the early form of shaft and globe and is engraved with Jacobite emblems. The small glass (b) has a very thick foot and is known as a firing glass. Such glasses were banged on the table to signify agreement, often fervent, of a toast that has been given. The sound of many glasses sounded like gunfire, hence the name. It, too, is engraved with Jacobite emblems and the motto, FIAT. (c) is the most usual form of Jacobite glass, while (d) is a very unusual goblet with an air twist stem and waisted ogee bowl. All were made within 10 years of 1750.

Somewhere near the middle of the 18th century, whether by design or by a chance experiment, someone took a glass gather with air bubbles, and stretched and twisted it. The result was a rod with a spiral of air inclusions which looked attractive, and was suitable as the stem of a wine glass. The exact date of the earliest 'air twist' wine glasses is unknown, but most glass collectors date them to 1740–1760, so it is tempting to suggest c1760. A few air twist wine glasses have a degree of brightness much greater than most, and this is caused by the internal shape of the spiral. These glasses are rather misleadingly termed mercury twists despite no mercury being used. Of course, it was possible to put knops into these new forms, so the combination of bowl shape and stem form became ever more complex.

Not long after the making of air twist glasses, British glass makers began to use another technique that had been known to Venetians a century or more previously, the *latticino* technique. This involved the setting of thin opaque white glass rods in place of the air bubbles, and twisting to form the stem. Opaque twist stems used to be called cotton twists, but although the opaque white threads resemble cotton, it is a confusing misnomer. Conventionally, opaque twists are dated to the 1760s, but while opaque twists followed air twists, there can be no doubt that they were produced for some years simultaneously.

Chapter 11 Wine glasses, goblets and cups

11/24 This is a very fine Jacobite wine glass wheel engraved with a portrait of Prince Charles Edward (Bonnie Prince Charlie) wearing tartan and a bonnet. It is within the buckled cartouche containing the motto AUDENTIOR IBO which roughly translated means 'I shall go with greater daring', a slight mis-quotation from the sixth book of the Aeneid. The foot of the glass is engraved with a thistle. It is 7½in/19·1cm high and dates from about 1745.

11/25 Another Jacobite glass, and the most common form; not that any Jacobite glass is often seen: they are all very collectable. It has a multi-spiral air twist stem and trumpet bowl engraved with a rose and two buds and also the motto, FIAT. 'Fiat' may have been the motto of the Cycle Club, one of the most famous Jacobite clubs, but the motto seems to have been used in a wider context. It means 'so be it' which is much the same as 'Amen'.

11/26 This is an air twist stem wine glass of a type that became popular about 1750. Most air twists are 'single series', that is, they have a single spiral of twist (see 11/23 and 11/25). This one has two twists, one inside the other; there is an inner corkscrew within a multi-ply tape. The glass has a rounded funnel bowl, moulded with flutes in its lower half which, with the less often seen double series air twist, makes it a quite rare wine glass. Its capacity is sufficient for one good draught, but no more.

11/27 The upper section of this glass is said to be a drawn trumpet. This means that the bowl and stem were made in a single piece. It has a multi-spiral single series twist, but unusually it has a second stem element – an inverted baluster with air bubbles. Bubbles, intentionally put within glass, were drawn out and twisted to form the air twist stem type. When two forms of stem are found in a single glass, they are termed composite stems. It was made about 1755 and is 6½in/16.5 cm high.

11/28 This glass is wheel engraved with a ship portrait, and it is diamond-point engraved around the rim Success to the LYON Privateer. It has a single series opaque twist stem formed from a pair of corkscrew gauzes. Privateers were privately owned and armed ships, licensed by the government to attack enemy ships and plunder the cargoes in return for a share of the spoils. Many emanated from Bristol, and glasses of this type, of which there are several, may have been made in that city. It is 6in/15.2cm high and dates from about 1756.

11/29 This composite stem wine glass has a rounded funnel bowl above an annulated knop. The lower section of the stem is a double series opaque twist with an inverted baluster above a base knop. The opaque twist stems are generally considered to have followed air twists, but there can be little doubt that they were made at the same time because of the similarity of form. This particular glass is very well made with almost no flaws or striations in the bowl, indicating a high level of skill by the maker. It was made about 1760. Opaque twist stems have white glass spiralling through the stem and used to be incorrectly called cotton twists.

Chapter 11 Wine glasses, goblets and cups

◁11/30 *Firing glasses with very thick, flat feet were used in clubs and societies where toasts were given and assent was signalled by everyone present banging their glasses on the table to produce a loud noise resembling gunfire. It is surprising that so many have survived. This one, dating from about 1760, has a double series opaque twist stem and stands 3in/7·6cm high.*

The form of the twists, like other aspects of British wine glasses, are categorised. The twists can be 'corkscrews' or single or multi-ply tapes, while others can be gauzes. Further to complicate matters, many air and opaque twist glasses have one twist inside another; these are known as 'double series', while the simple version is a 'single series'. Oddly, most air twists are single series and most opaque twists are double series (abbreviated to SSAT, DSAT, SSOT and DSOT). These terms are a modern invention for the convenience of collectors and dealers to cram much information onto collection records or small stock tickets. A rare form is the glass with an air twist inside an opaque twist, or vice versa. Even rarer are triple series glasses.

Another form of wine glass is that with a cut stem. Facet cutting had been used on cruet bottles since about 1715, but its use on the stems of wine glasses is conventionally considered to be in the second half of the 18th century. Many dealers and collectors glibly date them at c1770, just as they date air and opaque twists as c1750 and c1765 respectively. This appears to be an over-simplification. It is probable that they were all made concurrently but the general principle that some air twists are the earlier form and the cut stems are the later seems reasonable.

△11/31 *This goblet stands 6½in/16.5cm high and is typical of thousands of opaque twist stem goblets and glasses which still survive intact. Its construction in three parts can be clearly seen, and the twist is, like some, not accurately made being longer pitch at the top and becoming shorter near the base. It comprises a pair of corkscrews within a nine-ply tape. The shape of the bowl is said to be ogee and is often seen.*

△11/32 *This shows the difference in size between a goblet and glass made about the same time, in the 1760s. The goblet holds about four times as much wine as the glass and was used by gentlemen when drinking on their own. The goblet is the one seen left; the wine glass is 5⅜in/13·7cm high.*

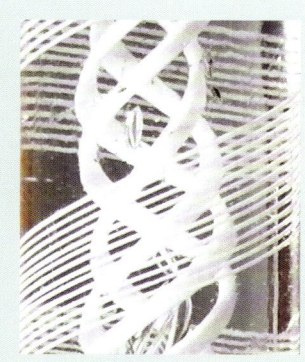

11/33 A detail of a double series opaque twist (often abbreviated to DSOT) stem. There are 14 plys to the outer layer of tapes and the inner series is three corkscrews. Interestingly, air bubbles can be discerned at the centre of the stem, tempting someone to call it a triple series glass; this would be a rarity. However the air bubble, although twisted, does not appear to have been put there intentionally and it is very doubtful that the maker intended to make a triple series composite twist wine glass.

The facets take several forms, some being approximately square, while others are hexagonal or octagonal; some have sides of equal length and some are elongated. Nor is it unknown for facet stem glasses to have knops (see 1/40).

From about 1780, wine glass stems became shorter and were often undecorated, bowl shapes were simplified usually to the ovoid and bucket forms, and the golden age of British wine glasses drew to a close. The production of wine glasses in the 18th century must have been colossal for so many to have survived, but the glasses of the last two decades seem oddly few in number and do not show the style and quality of workmanship displayed in previous decades. Certainly there were a few well-crafted glasses, but they lack the interest that is inherent in the proportion and originality of designs seen earlier.

The decoration of wine glasses adds yet another dimension to their fascination for collectors. The bowls of glasses could be wheel engraved, and some of the most desirable were stipple engraved with a diamond point. This is a very delicate art form which requires a high degree of skill and patience, as it is a slow craft. Wheel engraved glasses were accorded a number of different patterns. The simplest were repetitive circular depressions and intermediate crossed short lines, known as OXO engraving.

Among the more collectable glasses are those commemorating events and political associations. These are engraved with the symbols of the Jacobite cause, or the Williamite one, as well as those recording privateer ships (or legalised piracy). Among the most sought are those that are diamond-point engraved with the Jacobite national anthem and which because of the last word are known as 'Amen' glasses (see 11/22).

11/34 Four engraved glasses and all rarities. (a) is a wide ogee bowl goblet on an opaque twist stem engraved with a cockfighting scene and the legend THE SET TO. Originally this would have been one of a set of four glasses, the other three being THROAT, THE FIGHT and THE DEATH; (b) is another goblet with a bucket bowl on an opaque twist stem and engraved with a running fox in a small landscape; (c) is a short cordial glass engraved with a stag hunting scene in a landscape, and (d) is another fox among trees on a multi-spiral air twist stem. They all date from about 1765–1770.

Chapter 11 Wine glasses, goblets and cups

11/35 Among the rarest and most sought wine glasses are those with colour in place of white in their stems. This group of five displays various bowl shapes that were produced concurrently, as well as different colours, most having more than one colour. The least often seen colour is canary yellow which is most prized by collectors.

11/36 This pair of wine glasses on double series opaque twist stems are good, but unremarkable except for the decoration of the bowls. The gilding was done in the workshop of James Giles (1718–1780), an independent decorator of porcelain (usually Worcester) and glass. Giles became bankrupt, and his stock of glass was sold at Christie's in March 1774. From the descriptions, much gilded glass is attributable to his workshop including these glasses.

Another very collectable type of wine glass is one in which one or two of the white opaque elements of opaque twists are substituted with coloured ones, yellow being particularly favoured. Occasionally more than one colour is used. Colour twists are very seldom seen, but there have been many modern copies (see 13/18).

During the 18th century there were two important businesses engaged in decorating glass without using engraving technique but which are most attractive. First was the brother-and-sister partnership of William and Mary Beilby in Newcastle-upon-Tyne who carried out enamelling on glasses (and decanters). Most of their work is white enamel on clear ground, but the subject matter varies from idyllic landscapes to rococo scrolls, and hunting scenes to portraits. They worked mainly in the rococo style, but some of their later pieces show neoclassical influence. Arguably, their most important work was a series of large goblets enamelled with the royal arms (see Foreword).

The second decorator whose work is as distinctive as the Beilbys' was James Giles. His workshop was responsible for decorating porcelain from Worcester and Longton Hall, but his glass decoration is of concern here. Typically he gilded wine glasses, goblets and flutes with flowers and bunches of grapes, and his ale glasses with barley and hops. His workshop also engraved, and his later work is known for neoclassical decoration with the full vocabulary of that style, including paterae, garrya husks, bucrania and vitruvian scrolls.

Chapter 11   Wine glasses, goblets and cups

△ 11/37 More glasses from the Giles workshop showing the very distinctive style. Note the second glass with its 'pan top' bowl. These, and all glasses from the 17th and 18th centuries in these pages, have rough pontil marks. That is, the underside of each glass has a central sharp or jagged area where the pontil rod, used in the making of the glass, was broken off. They were not subsequently ground and polished to a smooth surface.

▷ 11/38 Green glasses of this date and pattern are not common although green glasses outnumber blue ones very considerably. This has a cup bowl and the stem is plain. The rarity of this glass lies in the bowl which is mould blown in an unusual form, fluted and reticulated near its base. It is tempting, because of the size of the bowl, to call this a wine glass, but as a great many green (and blue) decanters have gilded labels for brandy, rum and hollands (gin), it is probably safer to consider this to be a glass for spiritous liquor. It was made around 1750–60 and is 5¼in/13·3cm high.

▷ 11/39 Some glasses are difficult to date to within 20 years with any degree of certainty, while others can be pinned down to a mere 5–10 year period. This deep 'Bristol' blue wine glass with its rounded funnel bowl and plain stem was made about 1770 plus or minus 10 years. Blue wine glasses are much less often seen than green ones, and this is a very early type. Coloured glasses are thought to have been for spiritous liquor, although in the late 19th century, blue glass was reserved for poison.

△ 11/40 These three glasses demonstrate the skill and successful artistic achievement of the best English engravers. The delicate rural scenes follow the rustic style which was part of the rococo movement, reaching its most popular moment in the late 1760s. The glasses rest on facet-cut stems, one with hexagonal facets, and the pair with diamond facets. Each glass is about 5¾in/14·6cm high.

▷ 11/41 The variety of English wine glasses in the first 75 years of the 18th century is extraordinary. It ranges from the plain trumpet glasses of the 1740s with their simple bold form, to these delicate examples of the cutter's art. They were made about 1770 and unusually are facet cut all over the bowls, the stems, and even the foot of the right hand example.

Chapter 11 Wine glasses, goblets and cups

The 19th century saw a substantial change of direction. Small wine glasses, so popular in the previous century, disappear from the glass maker's output to be replaced with larger, short-stemmed goblets and 'rummers'. Ale flutes were also popular, but were they used for champagne? Probably not, but many people use them that way today.

Rummers are popularly thought to have been for drinking rum, their large size suggesting that the spirit was diluted. The Oxford English Dictionary gives the derivation of the word as probably Roman glass. Others say that rummer derives from *roemer*. In what is now Germany and the Low Countries, *roemers* or *römers* were made in large numbers in *waldglas*, an olive green soda glass, often quite pale in colour. They had hollow stems with 'raspberry prunts', and feet with trailed decoration. While the word is similar, the British rummer is quite different.

Some early rummers of the first two decades of the 19th century are finely crafted. Some have lemon-squeezer bases, square and plinth-like and their undersides moulded in a concave form with radiating ribs, rather like a mould of a lemon squeezer. The bowls are usually ovoid or bucket-shaped, and many are finely engraved, either with repetitive motifs or with pictorial engraving often of a commemorative nature. The Sunderland Bridge is one of the better subjects.

Many rummers were made throughout the 19th century with thick bowls and robust small feet. These were made for tavern use as they were cheap to produce and strong enough to withstand the wear that was expected of them. Many survive and are used today for everyday wine consumption where and when fine and elegant wine glasses would be inappropriate.

11/42 This glass marks the end of the supremacy of British wine glass making. From this point the design, the elegance and the quality of workmanship declined. This huge goblet was made about 1790 and will hold a full bottle of wine being 7½in/19cm high; most of the height is given to the bowl and very little to stem. It is actually a well made glass of good clarity and suitable for someone who wishes to indulge themselves in gluttonous fashion, or for drinking beer.

11/43 This is a small glass, just 4¼in/10·8cm high. The bowl is said to be ovoid and it is a good rich green colour. These and numerous similar examples were made in sets, and it seems likely that they were for drinking spirits rather than wine. That has not stopped many from calling them wine glasses.

11/44 This set of four goblets was made about 1810 and the fluting at the base of the bowls closely resembles the fluting seen on many decanters made at the same time (see 7/25). Their size approximates to that of a modern glass seen in restaurants – say about 250ml – and this makes them very usable. Their bucket-shaped bowls rest on short spool stems with a central blade, and the feet are flat. The pontil mark has been ground and polished away – the first time this has been noted in this chapter.

11/45 This pair of goblets are 7in/17·8cm high and date from about 1840–60. Like the glasses above, they are a good size for drinking wine in the way that it is today. The facet cutting of the stems allows a firm grip and the cutting of the bowls refracts light to show wine to advantage.

Chapter 11 Wine glasses, goblets and cups

11/46 This pair of red wine glasses is from a set of 12, but probably from a larger set originally comprising glasses for red and white wine as well as champagne, sherry, port and hock. These are very finely worked with panels of strawberry cutting below fine flutes and on notched stems and star-cut feet. They date from about 1880–90.

With the introduction of service *á la Russe* in the mid-19th century a need for more wine glasses was universally felt. They needed to be of varying shapes and sizes, although the full implication of different glasses for different wines and spirits did not manifest itself until the closing years of the 19th century. At the time that the new dining order was being introduced, the standard shape of decanter was the shaft and globe. With its dimpled 'printies' it was easy to copy for matching wine glasses. Claret and other red wines were usually served in red cased glasses (see 11/47). This produced an effect unexpected by those who had not witnessed it previously. Red wine in a red cased decanter or glass looks red; it is only when the wine level drops that the clear printies begin to show for what they are. White wine was served in either clear or green glass, as was champagne. Late in the 19th century wine glasses became very thinly made and were acid etched, often with repetitive circular and other motifs around the rim. The wide saucer-shaped champagne glasses so popular before about 1970 are said to have been modelled on Marie Antoinette's breasts, but however fanciful a notion that may be, she met her untimely end a long while before the champagne 'coupe' was invented. Some coupes are hollow stemmed while others are on solid stems, but they were all late 19th or 20th century.

All the glasses mentioned in the last two paragraphs were produced on a large scale. The designs were published in catalogues, and some models were made over a period of several decades well into the 20th century, which makes dating them accurately very difficult. It is interesting to see in Farrow & Jackson's catalogue of 1898 that 87 different patterns of glass are illustrated and that some of them bear a strong resemblance to the 'ideal' glasses made today.

11/47 This set of six red wine glasses typifies much table glass made in the second half of the 19th century. They were probably originally supplied with a shaft and globe decanter similarly cased and cut. When full of red wine, the clear glass cannot be discerned; it is only when some of the wine has been consumed that the pattern becomes obvious. Dating from about 1860–70, these are 5in/12·7cm high.

11/48 This set of six pale green champagne coupes are cut with oval printies or 'olives' and the stems are facet cut. Unlike the red glasses, these are a pale shade of green throughout the glass. Although finely made, the glasses are heavy. The champagne coupe allegedly, but improbably modelled on Marie Antoinette's breasts, was the standard champagne glass for about 100 years until the 1960s. These date from c1860.

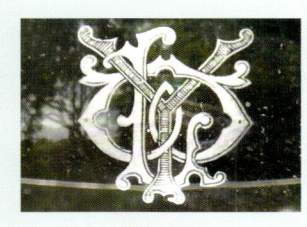

11/49 A set of six champagne coupes from about 1900. The glass is very thin and they feel (and are) fragile. Champagne became extremely popular during the period when these were made and it was common for glasses to be ordered in large sets with initials or crests engraved or acid etched. These appear to be engraved with the initials LOY.

11/50 Pages from Farrow & Jackson's 1898 catalogue showing a variety of glasses available to the wine trade. These were intended for both trade use and for selling to the general public, although the catalogues of other firms were aimed more at the retail market. Note that prices are marked per dozen, and a 1/- equates to 5p.

71   *Address for Telegrams:* "FARROW—JACKSON, LONDON."

TASTING GLASSES.

BEST CUT ENGLISH FLINT GLASS, WITH BLOWN FEET.—Per Dozen.

"Bodega" Patterns.

Large Cut.	Small Cut.	Large Plain.				
No. 24. 15/-	No. 24s. 13/-	No. 25. 11/-	No. 26. 16/-	No. 27. 15/-	No. 28. 12/-	No. 29. 12/-

					Hollow Stem.
No. 30. 11/-	No. 33. 15/-	No. 35. 16/-	No. 36. 14/-	No. 37. 18/-	No. 38. 24/-

Hollow Stem.				Hol'ow Stem.	
No. 41. 20/-	No. 41s. 18/-	No. 42. 15/-	No. 43. 13/-	No. 44. 18/-	No. 45. 12/-

| No. 46. 18/- | No. 47. 36/- | No. 48. 36/- | No. 49. 9/- | No. 51. 12/- | No. 52. 14/- |

16, Great Tower Street, E.C.; 8, Haymarket, S.W.; Factory: 91, Mansell Street,

Address for Telegrams: "FARROW—JACKSON, LONDON."

TASTING GLASSES.

BEST CUT ENGLISH FLINT GLASS, WITH BLOWN FEET.—PER DOZEN.

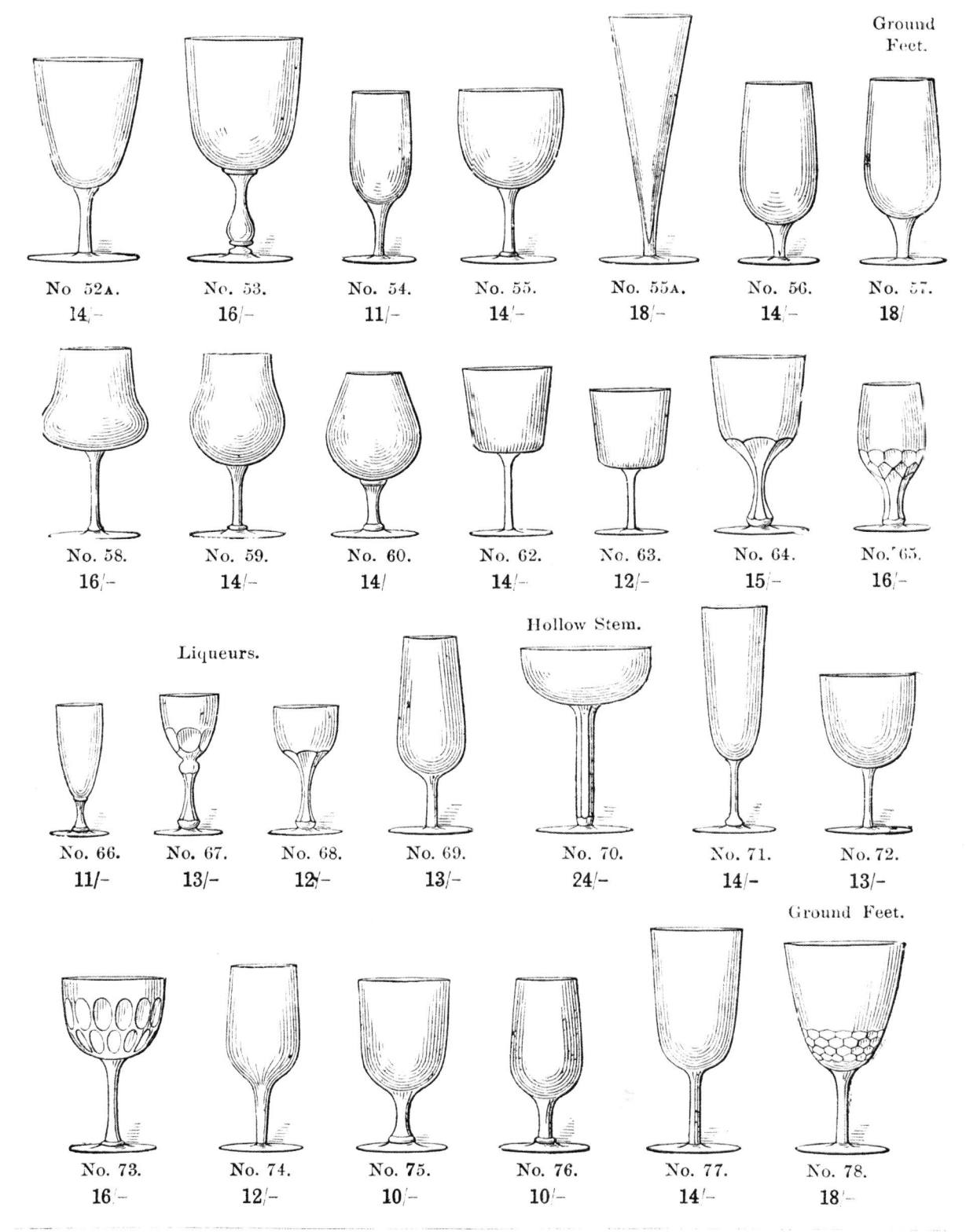

No. 52A.	No. 53.	No. 54.	No. 55.	No. 55A.	No. 56.	No. 57. (Ground Feet.)
14/-	16/-	11/-	14/-	18/-	14/-	18/-

No. 58.	No. 59.	No. 60.	No. 62.	No. 63.	No. 64.	No. 65.
16/-	14/-	14/-	14/-	12/-	15/-	16/-

Liqueurs.

No. 66.	No. 67.	No. 68.	No. 69.	No. 70. (Hollow Stem.)	No. 71.	No. 72.
11/-	13/-	12/-	13/-	24/-	14/-	13/-

No. 73.	No. 74.	No. 75.	No. 76.	No. 77.	No. 78. (Ground Feet.)
16/-	12/-	10/-	10/-	14/-	18/-

16, Great Tower Street, E.C.; 8, Haymarket, S.W.; Factory: 91, Mansell Street, E.

Chapter 12

Miscellaneous

There is a wide variety of objects, some small, others large, which had a direct connection with the storage, serving and consumption of wine in the 18th and 19th centuries. In previous chapters we have seen all the objects that are easily categorised; in this chapter the remainder are considered.

12/1 *A wonderfully eclectic selection of wine accessories formed by an enthusiast. While most pieces have a strong connection with wine, there are objects of a culinary nature and a few for use with other alcoholic drinks. Many appear within the pages of this book.*

MADEIRA
BRONTE
GOOSEBERRY
CLARET
ALE
GIN
PORTER
MALMSEY
13
SHERRY
SHERRY
RUM
MALMSEY
MADEIRA
MADEIRA
SHERRY
CALCAVELLA
CLARET
ERMITAGE
ROUGE.
SAUTERNE.
CLARET
LAFFITTE.
SHERRY
FROM EARLE & Co
59 MARK LANE & CHELMSFORD
PORT
FROM EARLE & Co
59 MARK LANE & CHELMSFORD
CHAMPAGNE
FROM EARLE & Co
59 MARK LANE & CHELMSFORD
LIQUEURS
PALE SHERRY
HOCK
MOSELLE
BUCELLAS
SHRUB
SHERRY

Chapter 12 Miscellaneous

The most obvious piece of furniture with wine connections is the wine cooler, and that is dealt with in its own chapter. However, wine coolers were not the only dedicated objects for cooling wine; many sideboards had cellaret or wine cooler drawers.

Sideboards first appeared in the 1770s when the side table and the pair of pedestals flanking it joined to become a single piece of furniture. Typically the sideboard has a central shallow drawer between by two deeper ones, or a deep drawer on one side and a hinged cupboard which looked like a drawer on the other. Often the deep drawer or cupboard was veneered and outlined with cock beads to appear to be two shallow drawers, and occasionally this was the case. Many deep drawers were compartmented inside to hold bottles. When they were waterproofed by being lined with a lead lining, they were wine coolers, while those not lead-lined were cellarets for bringing the wine up to room temperature.

Early in the 19th century, the deep drawers of sideboards were extended to the floor for additional space to house the needs of diners for more glasses, corkscrews, napery and aids for the servants to tend the whims of their masters. Sideboards also became longer and deeper for these purposes, so that by the 1850s they were massive; in many cases the elegance of plain or inlaid mahogany gave way to densely carved oak, but they still fulfilled the function of housing all the requisites of sumptuous dining and drinking.

12/2 A mahogany sideboard of typical form. Some are straight fronted, some serpentine, but this is bow fronted. It has finely figured timber veneered in panels outlined with ebony stringing lines, and it rests on six turned reeded tapered legs. It has a central drawer flanked by two deeper ones and a drawer beneath whose function is not immediately clear. Unusually the right-hand 'drawer' swivels open, and the scribing lines where bottles were intended to be can be seen clearly (see detail). It has the maker's label of George Simson whose business was at St Paul's Churchyard from 1787–1839. It dates from about 1800 and is 72¼in/183.5 cm wide.

This detail shows the pencilled marking-out of bottle divisions (never constructed) and the leaden bung (far right) to allow drainage.

A piece of furniture that was expressly made for drinking wine was the semicircular or horseshoe-shaped drinking table. It is sometimes called a 'hunt table' but this epithet has no basis. It had a particular function; at the end of a dinner, particularly in winter, and when the ladies had retired and the servants had been dismissed for the night, the men sat around to drink wine and talk of subjects not thought to be suitable in mixed company – religion, politics and sex. In some houses this would have been done at the dining table, but others had a table specially designed for the purpose. It was placed around the fire so that the last heat would warm the drinkers. On its inside edge there was usually a rail to allow a pair of decanters to pass between the diners (see 12/4). The first illustration of these tables appears in *The Cabinet Makers' London Book of Prices* in 1793 (see drawing below) but this was a relatively small table, and it was not designed to straddle a hearth.

The drinking table had a relatively short life as none appear to have been made after about 1840. While these tables were never plentiful, those that survive mostly date from the period 1800–1825. They average about 6ft/183cm wide, and while the earliest are on square tapered legs, the majority have turned ones, the earlier, the slimmer. Those with the decanter rail attachment often had a shield behind the decanter to protect it from the heat of the fire. Some have a flat leaf which folds out from the rear of the table to extend its length, while others fold for compactness.

12/3 *A 'Gentleman's Social Table' made to a design of George Hepplewhite in* The Cabinet Makers' London Book of Prices *(1793) and dating from about that time. This is the only known extant example that follows the Hepplewhite design exactly. It is made of mahogany with boxwood stringing lines which not only delineate it but also, being a tough wood, protects the mahogany. The centre part is of recent make.*

△ 12/4 Horseshoe-shaped drinking tables were probably never common. This example with its curtain rail and decanter slide is unusually complete. Such tables were placed around a fire to take heat from the remaining embers after dinner, when the ladies had withdrawn and the gentlemen gathered to drink, usually to excess. The port, sherry or madeira would circulate between them in decanters hidden from the heat of the fire by the shield back of the double coaster. A curtain would protect the gentlemen from the heat of the fire but could be drawn if it became cold.

▷ 12/5 A club existed in Yorkshire in the vicinity of Wakefield, probably about 1820–40, which was evidently given to serious excess of wine drinking. Each member had a pair of specially constructed crutches to support him under each arm when seated at the dining table. The purpose of the crutches was to prevent him sliding beneath the table or lurching forward onto it. Each crutch had a hemispherical base that was heavily lead-weighted so that it returned to upright position if let go. The style of the crutches gives a good indication of the date; at least three pairs are known. These must surely epitomise the absurd lengths to which English gentlemen were prepared to go in suffering for their love of wine. Despite many enquiries it has not proved possible to determine the name of the club.

12/6 Drinking tables, first made in the 1790s, enjoyed a life span of about 50 years or less: very few were made after about 1840. Most had flaps to extend the top at each end. This unusual model works on the gateleg principle with two large flaps hinging inwards to meet at the middle. The plain turned tapered legs are another unusual feature. Tables like this can be over 6ft/183cm wide. This one never had a curtain rail or decanter slide within the semicircle. Some examples had nets in the space inside the quadrant to catch any falling debris; these seldom survive although evidence of their having existed can be seen sometimes.

Chapter 12   Miscellaneous

12/7 Many people refer to small tripod tables as wine tables which they are not. This, however, is a wine table. In simple terms, it is a mid-18th century tripod table that has a rotating mechanism (called a birdcage by the antiques trade), but the very rare feature is the fixed galleried coaster, large enough for a magnum decanter, and eight circular depressions to take wine glasses or smaller decanters.

12/8 18th century dumb waiters were usually made with three, but sometimes two, tiers. The trays revolve, allowing the host to bring bottles and other refreshments to the table after the servants had been dismissed, and without having to leave his seat. This is a fine early example, dating from around 1750, with writhen-carved vase columns and a carved tripod base. Later models had folding tiers, while in the 19th century, they had usually two tiers divided by three brass columns near the edge of each tray.

An important item of dining room furniture, often purloined for use elsewhere in the house in more recent times, was the dumb waiter. With either two or three rotating tiers, they were first made in the 1730s or 40s, and were placed by a servant next to the host before the ladies and servants left the room. Usually the tiers, graduated in size with the smallest at the top, were separated by a central turned column, but some made in the early 19th century have the tiers spaced with three brass columns at the edge of each tray. The tiers were set with decanters, glasses and sweetmeats, and the rotating action allowed the host to reach any decanter with ease. Some Irish dumb waiters have turned coasters incorporated, leaving us in no doubt about their use. By about 1830 the dumb waiter assumed a very different form, becoming rectangular and of much greater size. This stood at the side of the dining room for the serving of food and is of no relevance here.

12/9 This unique dumb waiter was probably made in Ireland (where it was photographed) and is unusual in having four built-in coasters for decanters and a pair of galleried frames in which plates could be stacked. Its use for serving wine is undoubted.

12/10 It is surprising how often experienced and knowledgeable antique dealers, or those whose professional life is in the decorative arts, come across something they have never seen before. This (and several other items illustrated within this book) are examples. It has a revolving upper section with a cupboard occupying about two thirds, the remainder being open and with a brass rail to prevent bottles falling out. It is supported on a turned column and tripod base with, like most English dining room furniture, brass castors.

256   Chapter 12   Miscellaneous

Trays with high sides and with divisions to hold bottles, notched to take the neck of a bottle, were used for bringing bottles from the cellar to the dining room. They are called bottle trays and are designed to hold two, four, six or eight bottles, but the four and six bottle sizes are most seen. The sides of the divisions sometimes have triangular corner blocks to hold the bottles firmly. They should not be confused with cutlery trays which look similar but do not have notches for the necks of bottles. Bottle trays appear in a 1793 and an 1813 book of prices for cabinet makers (see12/16).

Another small item of furniture seldom seen is the bottle holder or bottle slope. These mahogany pieces were made to keep a bottle at an angle of about 30° so that the sediment would settle in a small area of the base, and the bottle would be presented for the easier use of the corkscrew. Indeed, the 1898 Farrow & Jackson catalogue lists one as a 'Cork Drawing Stand'. The earliest seem to date from the 1770s, but they continued to be made into the 20th century. Some have an apron at one end to catch drips (or a cork).

Butler's trays were an invention of the late 18th century. Early models were simple rectangular mahogany trays with high galleries and pierced carrying handles and with one long side lower than the others. The tray rested on a folding stand. The early stand was an X-frame made of mahogany of rectangular section and prevented from opening too wide by two or three straps of webbing. By the beginning of the 19th century the legs had become turned. The better trays had folding sides with special hinges allowing the side to be firm in either the upright or flat position. By the end of the 18th century, the oval tray had become popular, with the centre made in a panelled construction. This model was reproduced in large numbers in the 20th century and set on a low stand, as were some originals; these were termed coffee tables and became very popular after 1950.

12/11 This beautifully proportioned table appears to have two short drawers and two long ones, but that is an illusion. Only the bottom drawer actually opens as a drawer; the upper ones are dummies, and the top lifts to reveal a butler's tray and compartments. Such a piece could hold corkscrews, napkins and other accessories in a dining room. It dates from about 1760 and is 35in/89cm wide. Later furniture which performed the same function tended to take the form of a cupboard with a pair of doors and sometimes a drawer above. The cupboard doors might enclose a wine cooler.

12/12 and 12/13 I had never seen a two-bottle mahogany carrier until this (12/12 above) was shown to me recently. It has a brass handle and baize-lined interior. Within three weeks another came to the market (12/13 right), and has now joined its pair.

△ 12/14 Now very seldom seen are boxes designed to hold bottles of wine. This example has a lock and key and was made in the late 18th century when servants were clearly used to sneaking a share for themselves. It has two lids which slide to one side and a handle fretted from the projecting central division. It measures 12in/30·5 cm in each dimension and was made about 1790.

△ 12/15 Another box with four separate lids, the compartments lined with baize. It is brass banded and has a folding brass handle. Note the higher quality mahogany used in this box and the general sophistication of design and fitments. It is much the same date and size as the previous box.

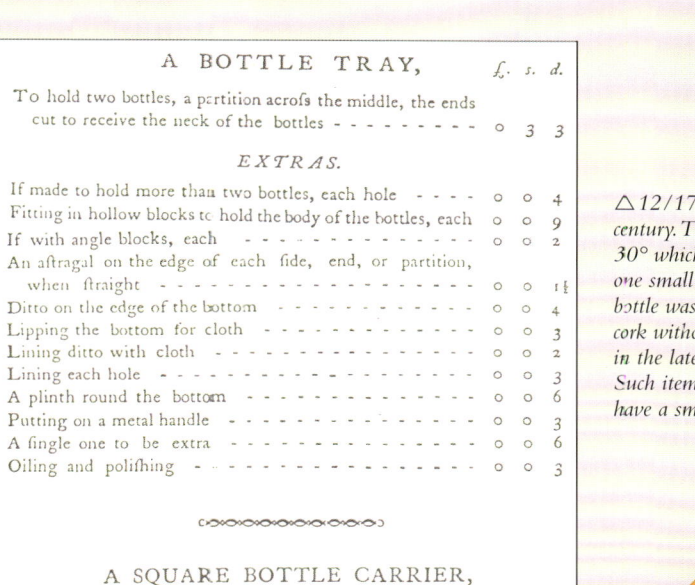

△ 12/17 Small bottle holders were being made in the late 18th century. They were designed to hold a single bottle at an angle of about 30° which allowed two functions. First, the sediment could settle in one small area at the base of the bottle and to one side. Second, the bottle was presented in a way that allowed the easy drawing of the cork without disturbing the sediment. The mahogany is of a type used in the late 18th century, giving a date for the holder of about 1790. Such items were made until about 1900, but later examples tend to have a small semicircular apron to catch any drips.

	£	s.	d.
A BOTTLE TRAY,			
To hold two bottles, a partition across the middle, the ends cut to receive the neck of the bottles	0	3	3
EXTRAS.			
If made to hold more than two bottles, each hole	0	0	4
Fitting in hollow blocks to hold the body of the bottles, each	0	0	9
If with angle blocks, each	0	0	2
An astragal on the edge of each side, end, or partition, when straight	0	0	1½
Ditto on the edge of the bottom	0	0	4
Lipping the bottom for cloth	0	0	3
Lining ditto with cloth	0	0	2
Lining each hole	0	0	3
A plinth round the bottom	0	0	6
Putting on a metal handle	0	0	3
A single one to be extra	0	0	6
Oiling and polishing	0	0	3
A SQUARE BOTTLE CARRIER,			
To hold four bottles upright, the edge of the bottom and rim rounded	0	3	3
EXTRAS.			
Each extra bottle hole	0	0	7
Fixing a metal handle	0	0	3
Lipping the bottom for cloth	0	0	3
Lining ditto with cloth	0	0	2
A single one to be extra	0	0	6
Oiling and polishing	0	0	3

△ 12/16 A page from the 1793 Cabinet Makers' London Book of Prices. Such books were produced from time to time to let both those in the trade and their customers know what any standard piece of furniture should cost. It can be seen that the basic object is cheap, but that adding the number of bottles it will hold, the fitting of angle blocks, lining each hole with baize, fitting a metal handle and polishing all add to the final cost. The bottle tray in (12/18) would have cost six shillings, a not inconsiderable sum in 1793.

△ 12/18 Mahogany bottle trays are very seldom encountered but are a standard type and typically hold four or six bottles, although two-bottle and eight-bottle trays are known. They were designed to take a bottle from the cellar to the dining room in a near-horizontal position so as not to disturb the sediment. Some are baize-lined and each division has triangular corner blocks to prevent bottles from rolling. The notched end of each division holds the neck of the bottle. They were made from about 1770 onwards but most are early 19th century. Some have been converted from cutlery trays, which did not originally have notched ends.

Chapter 12 Miscellaneous

△12/19 This little bottle rack is made of metal decorated with coloured varnish in the manner known as japanning. These and numerous other bottle carriers were made in large numbers in the late 19th century and they appear in Farrow & Jackson's catalogue of 1898. This model would have cost 7s6d/37·5p, as shown in 12/23.

◁12/20 A strange country-made oak tripod table of small dimensions. The shield fixed to the circular top was probably made to protect a decanter from the heat of a fire. While the general shape and form of the tripod is 18th century, it could have been made well into the 19th and may have been produced by an estate carpenter.

△12/21 A bottle 'boot' or, as Farrow and Jackson's catalogue would have it, a 'leather hand and bottle guard'. It fits over a bottle and allows the cork to be drawn by standing on the protruding steel lugs. Such devices have been rendered almost redundant by the introduction of teflon-coated corkscrews with easy-to-use mechanics.

△12/22 This fine and rare Chinese porcelain monteith, enamelled in famille rose colours with flowers and birds was made about 1730. It was made for the European, and possibly the British, market and was designed to keep wine glasses chilled. In use it would have been filled with iced water, and wine glasses put in each notch so that the bowl was in the cold water. Monteiths were made from the late 17th century and named after a Scottish gentleman who wore his cloak with a notched hem. Silver examples usually had a detachable rim so that the body would double for use as a punch bowl.

▷12/23 Farrow & Jackson's 1898 catalogue showing bottle carriers, decanting machines and wine coolers.

Address for Telegrams: "FARROW—JACKSON, LONDON."

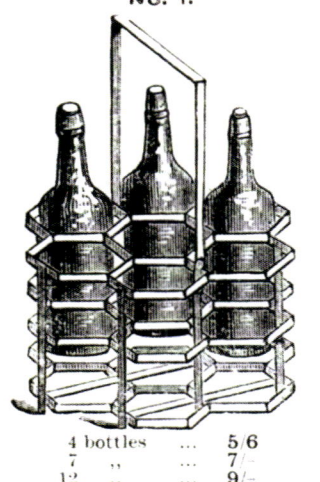

DECANTING APPLIANCES.

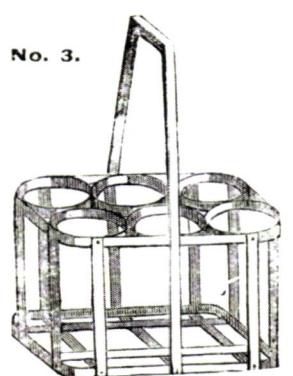

GALVANIZED IRON BASKETS.

No. 1.

4 bottles ... 5/6
7 " ... 7/-
12 " ... 9/-

No. 3.

4 bottles, 3/6   6 bottles, 4/3
To Fold for Syphons, 6 bottles, each.

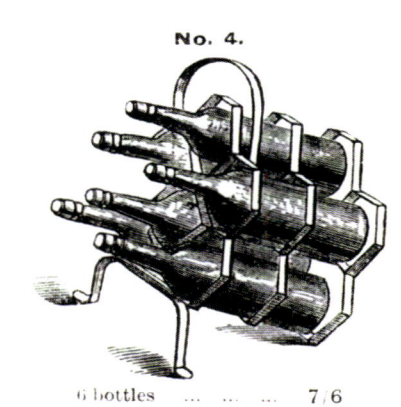

No. 4.

6 bottles ... 7/6

Japanned Carrier, with cover.

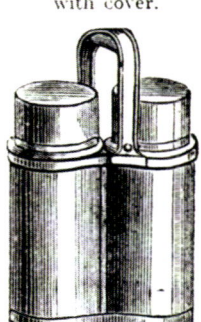

Very strong.

1 bottle ... 4/6
2 bottles ... 8/6
3 " ... 13/6

Japanned Bottle Carriers.

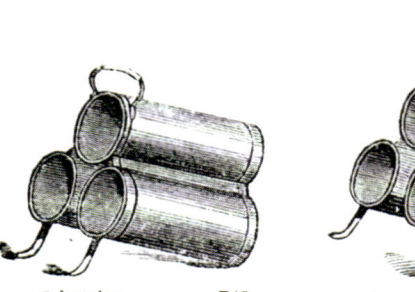

3 bottles ... 7/6
6 bottles ... 10/6
Lined with Baize.

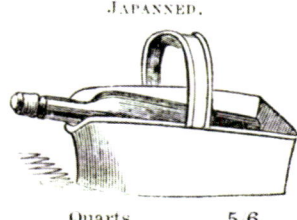

Burgundy Decanting Baskets.

JAPANNED.

Quarts ... 5 6
Pints ... 5 3

WICKER.

With handle on top or back.
Quarts ... 3/-   Pints ... 2/6

Decanter Baskets.

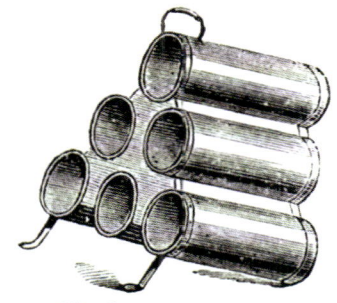

For 4 bottles, 8/-   For 6 bottles, 10/-

Wine Coolers.

Double sides and packed.

2 bottles.
Japanned ... 9/-

With Copper bottom.
Japanned Green, with Gold Lines, 12/6

Icing Frame.

Japanned, 3 bottles, 4/6

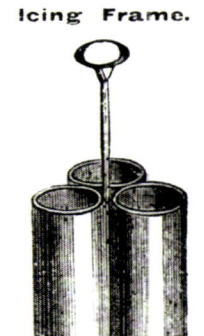

DECANTING MACHINES.

No. 1 (Recommended). With adjustment for Pints, Quarts, and Burgundy. Price 27/6.

No. 2. All Polished Brass. Price 25/-

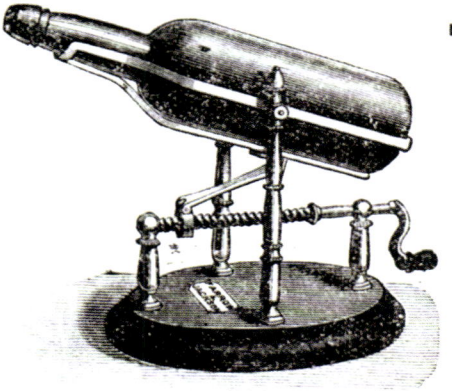

Lund's Decanterer. Price 17/6

16, Great Tower Street, E.C.; 8, Haymarket, S.W.; Factory: 91, Mansell Street, E.

Chapter 12   Miscellaneous

12/24 A rare mahogany butler's cabinet. It has two long drawers for napkins, corkscrews and other accessories that may be needed by a butler or footman, below which is a lead-lined deep drawer for cooling wine flanked by a cupboard door in which wine may be kept at room temperature. It stands on short turned legs and dates from the opening years of the 19th century. The drawers are outlined with ebony stringing lines and the lower elements have ebony inlays, which some say was done in deference to the death of Lord Nelson in 1805.

12/25a A butler's tray of simple rectangular form with rigid sides and standing on an X-frame base. Such trays are not fixed to the base, so can be lifted with whatever is on them. They vary in size, and it will be seen that the fretted handles are on the longer sides and that the edge furthest from the butler is lowered for ease of taking glasses from the tray. It dates from the late 18th or early 19th century.

12/25b An early 19th century oval butler's tray. This popular model has a panelled surface and folding sides and, like the rectangular form, rests on a folding stand. Many like this have been reproduced since about 1950 and used as stands for drinks in drawing rooms and, when fitted with low stands, as coffee tables

◁ 12/26 *A tray to hold six bottles or decanters vertically. The construction is simple, the central long division projecting and fretted to form the handle. These trays were made in the 1770–1820 period; they are now very scarce, and are eagerly collected. It is doubtful if the decanters (of about 1800) are original to the tray, but they fit the tray well and are contemporary.*

△ 12/27 *A wine tray shaped for ease of use and incorporating a pair of coasters. It is inlaid with mother-of-pearl and panel-decorated with gilt rococo scrolls. The reverse is stamped JENNENS & BETTRIDGE, MAKERS TO THE QUEEN beneath a crown. Also the back is stencilled R. REDGRAVE and REG^D DEC 19th 1847. Jennens & Bettridge were the principal papier mâché makers of the 19th century having taken over the business of Henry Clay. The artist Richard Redgrave designed this form of tray for Felix Summerly's Art Manufactures. It was produced in rich maroon as well as black. It is 28in/71.1cm wide.*

12/28 *A bottle/decanter stand or four-bottle cellaret. It is made of fine-grained mahogany and its deceptively simple form hides very high quality cabinet making. It rests on plain cabriole legs and has a pair of carrying handles. It dates from the 1740s.*

Chapter 12   Miscellaneous

Wine syphons are rarities, and come in two forms. Both draw wine directly from a bottle without the need to tilt it and disturb the sediment, obviating the need for a funnel. The least common is the type which has a pump to draw the wine from the bottle; the more usual form has a tube which can be sucked by mouth to do the same job. Both have a long U-shaped tube one end of which goes into the bottle while the other has a tap (usually) to control the flow. Most have a strengthening bar at the top. The earliest known wine syphon was made by John Harvey in about 1750, but the majority were by Phipps & Robinson around 1800.

Punch bowls fall outside the scope of this book, but some had a dual function for cooling wine glasses, in which case they were known as monteiths. Many punch bowls were made of tin-glazed earthenware (delftware), but monteiths are almost always of silver. The earliest date from after the restoration of the monarchy in 1660, but most are early 18th century. It is said that they are called monteiths after a Scotsman of that name who wore his cloak with a scalloped hem.

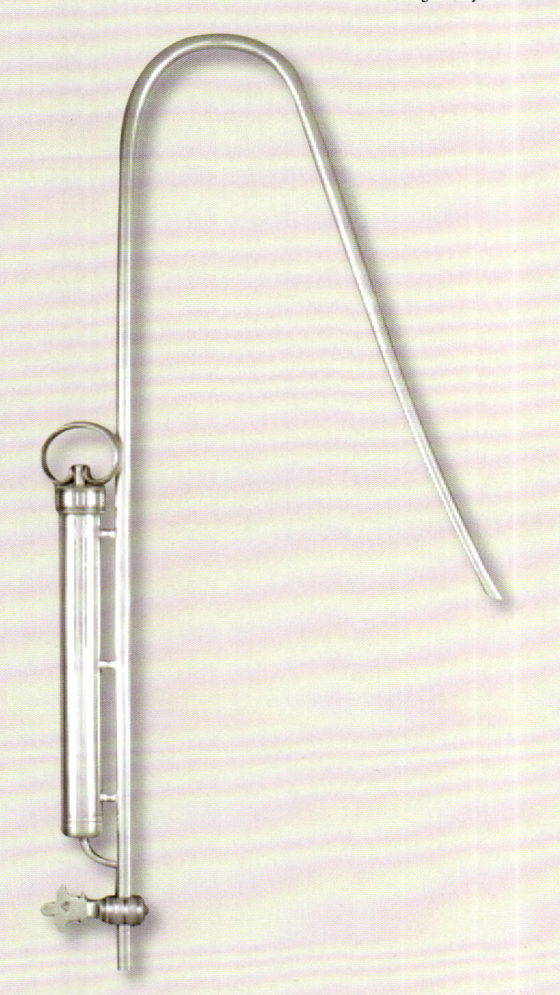

12/27 A wine syphon was an alternative way of taking wine from a bottle to a decanter without using a funnel. They are invariably made of silver and the earliest date from the mid-18th century. This one by John Harvey, who also specialised in making wine labels, is a very early example of about 1740–50 and the syphon is primed with the pump.

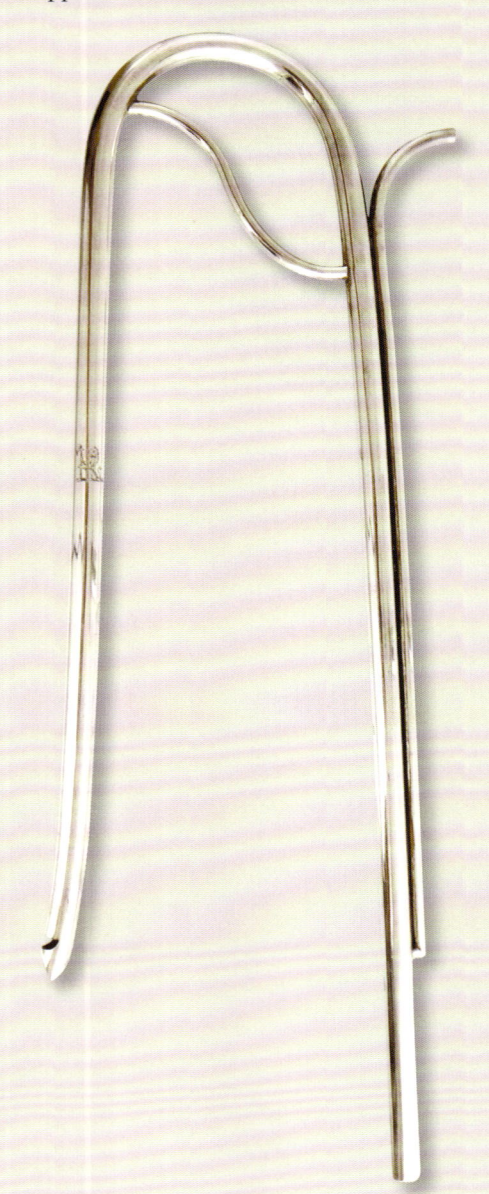

12/28 This is a second wine syphon by John Harvey but without a pump to set it working. To prime the syphon, the secondary tube has to be sucked by mouth to raise the level of the wine. It also dates to the mid-18th century. It is unusual in that it does not have a tap to stop the flow. It appears that Harvey was the only man making syphons at this date, but he did not make them with a full set of hallmarks, which was contrary to the law if they were to be sold as silver.

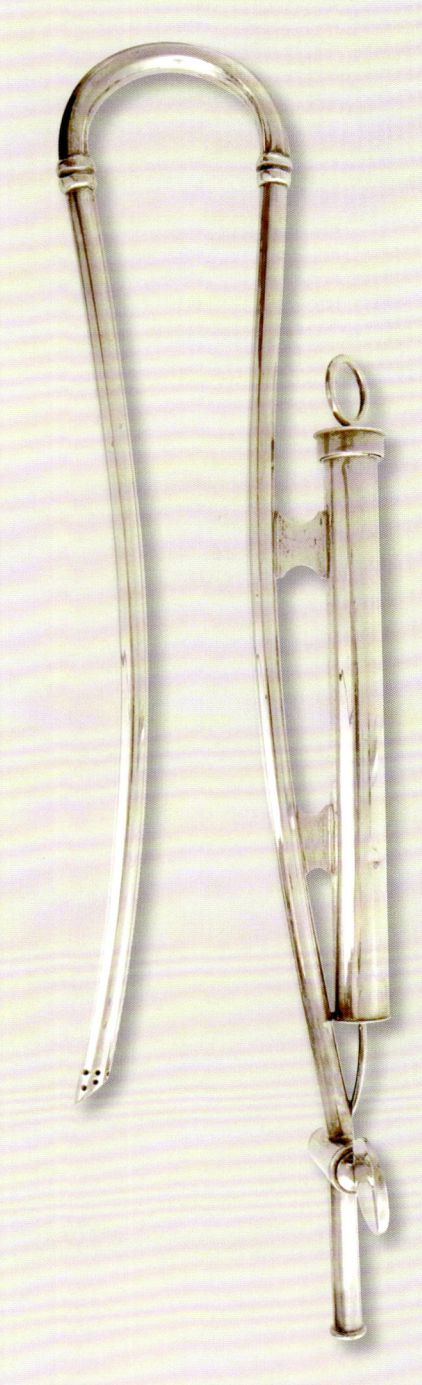

12/29 A wine syphon of unmarked silver, probably made around 1790. Silver wine syphons are considerable rarities, but they were made in America in the early 19th century, usually by Frederick Marquand of New York. Others were made in Holland but differed slightly from English models.

At the opposite end of the scale of affluence are cork mounts. Decanters or carafes were not always used, although it is probable that between 1700 and 1900 they usually were. Silver mounted corks were used to stopper bottles and carafes (though probably not decanters) after about 1780. The simplest comprised a silver disc at either end of a cork joined by a threaded rod passing through the middle of it. Some were just that and no more, but many had a silver ring to aid extraction, while the most elaborate had finials in the form of heraldic crests. The more commonly seen stoppers are electroplated and have either a flat ring with a wine name engraved on it, or a mother-of-pearl disc, also engraved.

12/32 This is a pair of silver-mounted corks, large enough to stopper a magnum. They are engraved at one end with the cypher and coronet of Princess Sophia Augusta (1768–1840), second daughter of George III. At the other end, they are engraved EA over Fs. When Queen Victoria came to the throne in 1837, her uncle, Ernst Augustus, Duke of Cumberland, became King of Hanover. He wanted the Hanover silver and jewels brought to England by George I returned to him in Hanover. However, Victoria's advisers demurred. When eventually the silver was sent, he had everything engraved EA over Fs, Fs being an abbreviation of fideicommis, the legal term for inheritance.

12/33 Not all silver-mounted corks were made for royalty or those with crests. This one is of simple unmarked silver and comprises two reeded mounts, one at either end of the cork, and a plain ring at right angles. The reeding suggests a date of about 1800.

12/34 This silver-mounted cork has a wheat sheaf finial. The wheat sheaf is the crest as it rests on a wreath., but as the crest is that of nearly 150 families, ascribing it to any one is impossible. The hallmarks are interrupted by the decoration so cannot be read. It was made about 1840.

12/35 The domed mount of this cork is surmounted with a label for BRANDY and it carries full hallmarks for Birmingham; it was made in 1892. Many mounted corks of this date have mother-of-pearl labels and the mounts are plated.

Chapter 12 Miscellaneous

Decanting cradles come in several forms. The most usually seen model has an oval mahogany base and brass pillars supporting a cradle which tilts. The mechanism is based on the fact that a screw that is turned will move a nut if it cannot rotate.

12/36 A rare decanting machine with a small plate marked 'Ellis Patent No. 94 Elutriator'. The mechanism is damped by a piston preventing the bottle from being tilted too suddenly. The frame is cast iron, the cradle wrought, and the piston is of brass, while the handles are of cocus wood. It dates from about 1860.

▷12/37 A brass decanting machine of the standard type. Rotating the mahogany handle (lower right) causes the bottle cradle to tilt gradually by being linked to the brass collar on the steel screw. The bottle would be lightly held by the spring clip to grip the neck. This model usually has a mahogany base, but after 100 plus years' use the mechanism has often become worn between the brass collar and the steel screw.

12/38 This all-steel decanting machine may well be French or Portuguese, but by about 1900 the type was made to similar patterns across Europe. The mechanism is the standard form with a long-pitch screw turned with a cranked handle and linked to the bottle cradle. This is as simple as they come; many have spring clips to hold the bottle more securely, decoratively turned uprights of brass, or metal elements electroplated in silver.

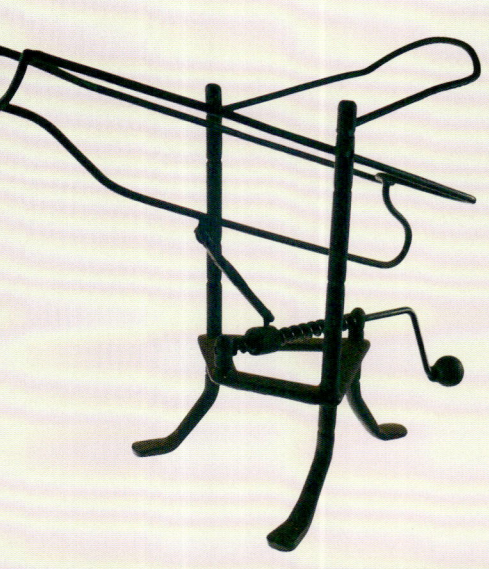

▷12/39 Decanting machines began to be made in the 19th century. The first were usually in the form of a cannon or artillery mortar and made largely of mahogany; they are very rare. The upright members and moulding of the base make this one look to have been made c1860, but it may well be a little later. It has an unusual mechanism to tilt the bottle, and the base is circular when most are oval.

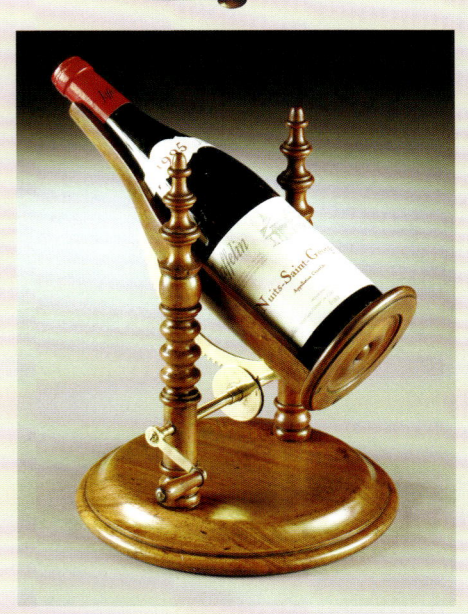

12/40 This beautifully crafted pair of decanting machines or bottle carriages was probably made for an officers' mess or for a retired army officer. They are electroplated and were made around 1890–1910. Great detail has been lavished on the design of these.

265

◁ 12/41 Barrels of glass mounted on their sides and with a spigot (tap) are usually called wine fountains and are very rare. This, known as the Shaftesbury and owned by the Vintners' Company, may be the earliest known and is certainly the most famous. The glass body is cut with daisies and shallow circular printies. It has a finial in the form of Bacchus sitting on a barrel, and rests on a scrolled base with hoof feet. The barrel has silver hoops, but the silver is not hallmarked. Stylistically it can be dated to about 1750 and it is 13½in/ 34.3cm long.

△ 12/42 In the late 19th century there were more domestic servants in British homes than at any time previously. To prevent unauthorised opening of bottles, bottle locks were invented and Burns's patent of 1881, made by Thomas Turner & Co., was the most successful of them. It is not surprising perhaps, that they were known as 'butlers' enemies'.

▷ 12/43 This pair of ½-pint mugs are finely decorated with diamond cutting and have silver-gilt mounts cast with flowing fruiting vines. They were made in 1862 by George Richards & Edward C Brown. It would be strange to cast the handles with grapes if they were for beer, but perhaps a clue lies in the date. When Albert, the Prince Consort, died in 1861, the country was plunged into deep mourning and black pervaded. The steward at Brooks's Club even put champagne into mourning by mixing it with Guinness. 'black velvet' became a popular drink. Are these black velvet mugs? Well, possibly.

△ 12/44 Another bottle lock in silver. It was made in Sheffield in 1898 by Joseph Ridge for John Round & Sons. It is stamped with the patent number, 16782.

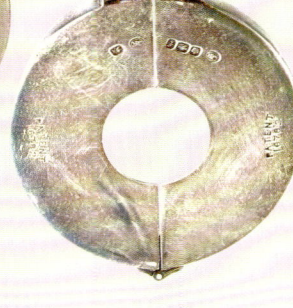

▷ 12/45 Three designs for bottle holders. It is interesting to see that they fit long necked bottles well, such as those from Champagne, Burgundy or Germany, but that Bordeaux bottles do not sit well in them. The first holder is actually labelled for HOCK.

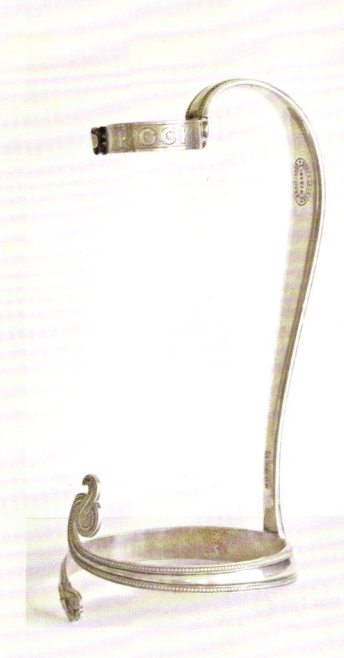

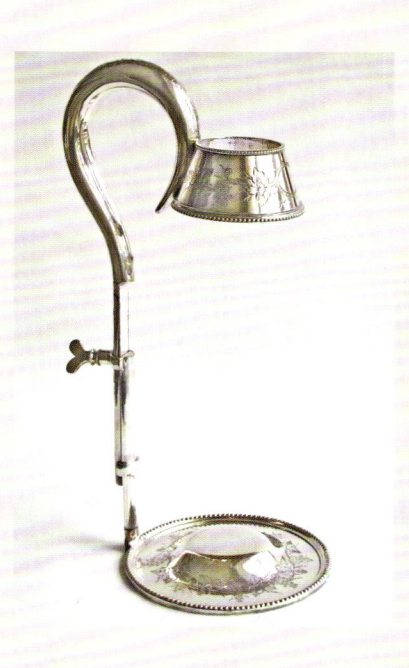

Chapter 12 Miscellaneous

'I drink it when I'm happy – and when I'm sad.
Sometimes I drink it when I'm alone.
When I have company, I consider it obligatory.
I trifle with it when I'm not hungry – and drink it when I am.
Otherwise I never touch it – unless I'm thirsty.'

Madame Lily Bollinger –1961

Champagne became the wine we know (and love) today in the 1850s when an English wine merchant tasted the unsweetened Perrier-Joüet of 1848 and realised its potential in the English market. Before then, champagne was bubbly, but sweet. It gained popularity in the succeeding decades but it must have become the drink of the moment quite suddenly in the 1890s if the accessories made for it are any indication of its appeal. Bottle holders were an effective means of handling a bottle of champagne without the hands touching and warming it. They consist of a tapered ring which fits the neck of a champagne bottle (but not a bordeaux bottle) and a shallow dish to fit the base; the two are joined by a long loop handle, and there is inevitably an adjustment feature to allow the bottle to be held securely. They are almost always electroplated, and many designs are known, all dating from c1880–1910.

Very much rarer is a bottle holder which completely encloses the bottle. An example is 12/46 and it is the size and shape of a champagne bottle. It probably had a chamois leather lining originally and this would have held the bottle firmly, although there is no evidence to suggest it. In use, it not only makes pouring very easy, but also the very reflective surface keeps the champagne cool.

Champagne decanters were a phenomenon of the 1890s, and vary in size between a quarter bottle and a jeroboam. They look like champagne bottles, but the glass is clear, and the 'foil' is silver. Typically the head of the cork hinges, either to have a cork incorporated into the lid, or a glass stopper inside the lid; this always closes in such a way that it does not pop open accidentally.

With the build-up of gas inside the bottle, a champagne cork has to be held securely. Initially the cork was secured by string and this was cut with a hook-shaped knife, serrated along much of its length. By the 1880s, wire was replacing string to secure the champagne corks. To cut the wire, pliers were needed. Some were just that, others had serrations to help remove the foil capsule, a brush to clean the bottle before opening, and even a corkscrew for opening still wines; such pliers were made specifically for opening champagne bottles.

Champagne taps and syphons became popular at around the turn of the century. *The Gentleman's Cellar and Butler's Guide* of 1899 wrote: 'A screw tap has been invented which every butler should know. In case of sickness, where only a little champagne is required at a time, this little screw tap can be screwed through the cork and you can draw off whatever is required without the rest that remains in the bottle losing its freshness'. These same taps were also used for soda water which was being used for medicinal purposes too. Larger versions were used in bars where champagne was sold by the glass. Thousands were made and can still be found in markets and shops today.

Champagne taps are often seen, but few people are aware of their purpose. The tap is screwed into the champagne cork in the turned off position. Some models have a detachable pin which drops into the bottle once it has done its penetrating job (see 12/49), while others have a perforated end to the tap. In either case, the champagne is taken from the bottle by turning the tap; the pressure of the gas inside ensures a rapid flow. A third model is shown in 12/49a. This is sufficiently long so that the bottle does not need to be tilted for the champagne to flow. A few champagne taps are silver plated, but the majority are either nickel-plated or made of a whitish alloy similar to paktong known as German silver. Like the bottle holders, they are all in the 1880–1910 date bracket.

12/46 A silver bottle holder for champagne decorated all over with bark effect and with a Georgian-style scroll handle. It hinges vertically with the handle coming in half. It was made by Rupert Favell & Henry Elliott in 1890 and has the London hallmarks. It was exported to France where it was given an import mark, and the base is stamped TIFFANY & CO PARIS: they must have been the retailers and would have commissioned it from Rupert Favell & Co. It is also stamped with a pattern number, 3746, and the design registration number 125245. It would have been lined with chamois leather originally.

△ 12/47 This is a half-bottle with a cork stopper made in 1895 by Heath & Middleton; it is engraved with a complex monogram.

△ 12/48 For a very few years in the 1890s, when champagne was at the height of its popularity, there was a fashion for champagne decanters in the form of the bottles from which it had been decanted. This magnum with a silver 'foil' was made by John Grinsell & Sons, who specialised in silver-mounted glass. It has a glass stopper inside the hinged lid and a star-cut base.

△ 12/49 Champagne taps were made in their thousands, and this is typical, if in much better condition than most. It is contained in a morocco leather case with instructions within the lid. It has two 'points' which facilitated the penetration of the cork. Once in the bottle, the point would drop into it and a glass of champagne could be taken out allowing the remainder to be kept for another day. These were made from the 1880s until about 1915.

△ 12/50 A set of four quarter-bottle champagne decanters with electroplated mounts, nesting in a realistically woven basket. Such a set might accompany a group of smart ladies going to the opera, the races or a regatta.

△ 12/49a A nickel-plated champagne syphon. It is hard to imagine how the syphon could be screwed into a tightly compressed champagne cork without first drilling a hole in it. It seems likely therefore, that the champagne cork was removed, and a pre-drilled cork put in its place with the syphon already penetrating it.

268 Chapter 12 Miscellaneous

12/51 A page from Farrow & Jackson's 1898 catalogue showing various types of bottle stoppers.

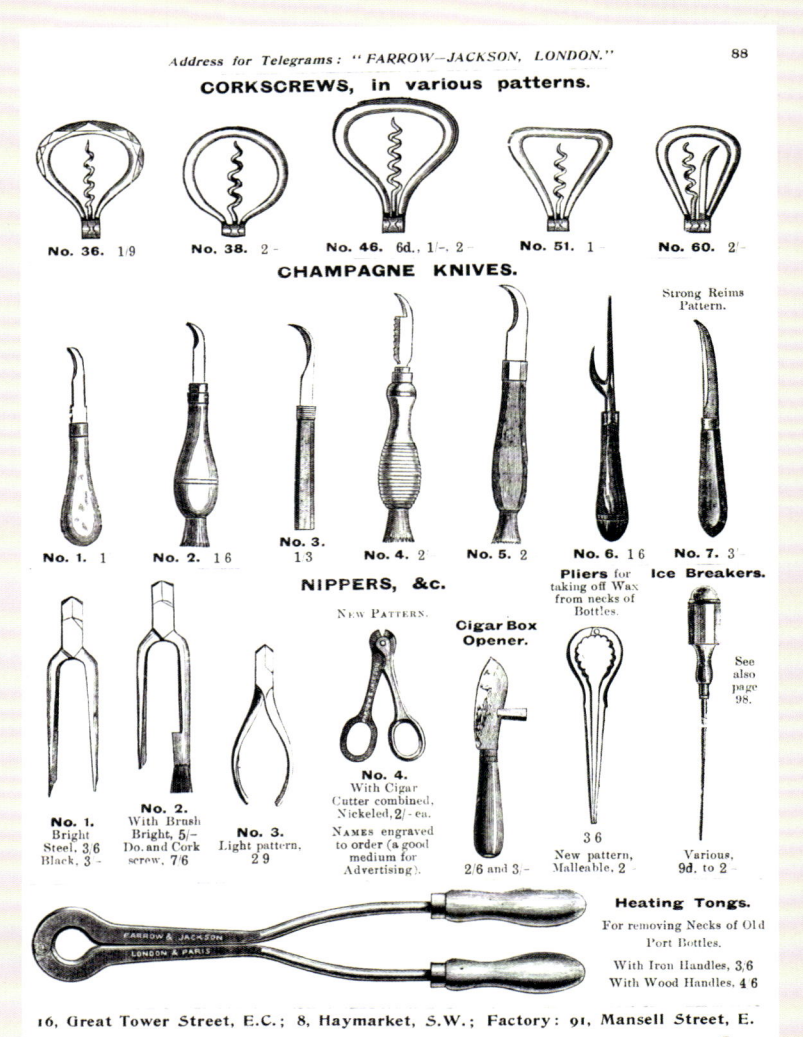

12/51a This page of the catalogue shows folding bow corkscrews, a variety of champagne knives, nippers and a pair of port tongs. It has not been possible to find a pair of old port tongs to illustrate, but the drawing in the catalogue gives a good idea of their appearance. It appears there is a need for port tongs which are being made again.

12/52 A champagne bottle sealer. It corresponds exactly to the top left illustration in Farrow & Jackson's 1898 catalogue and is similarly impressed on its top.

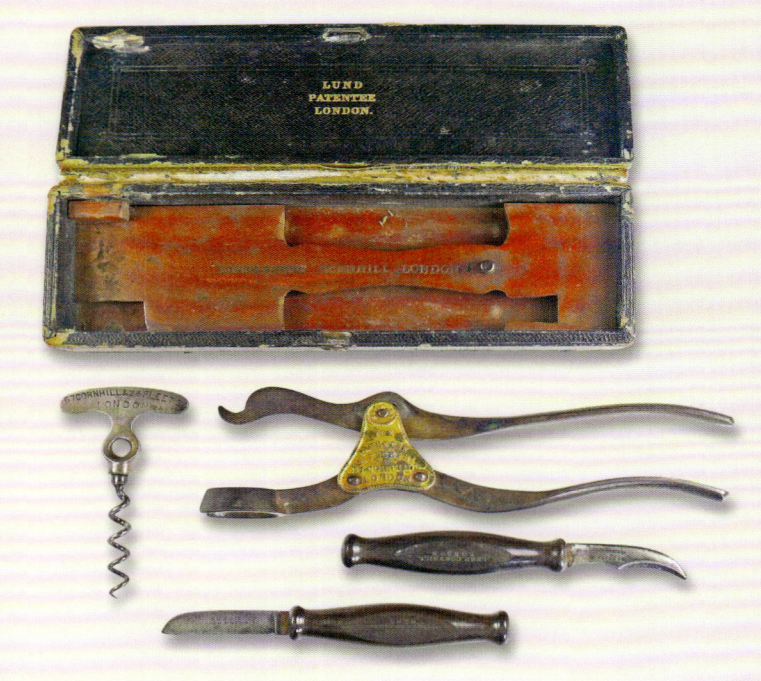

12/53 Lund's patent lever corkscrew of 1855 in its original box. Note the cork knife and the second knife stamped EPERNAY & HOCK KNIFE. These were used to cut the string before champagne bottle corks were wired in position.

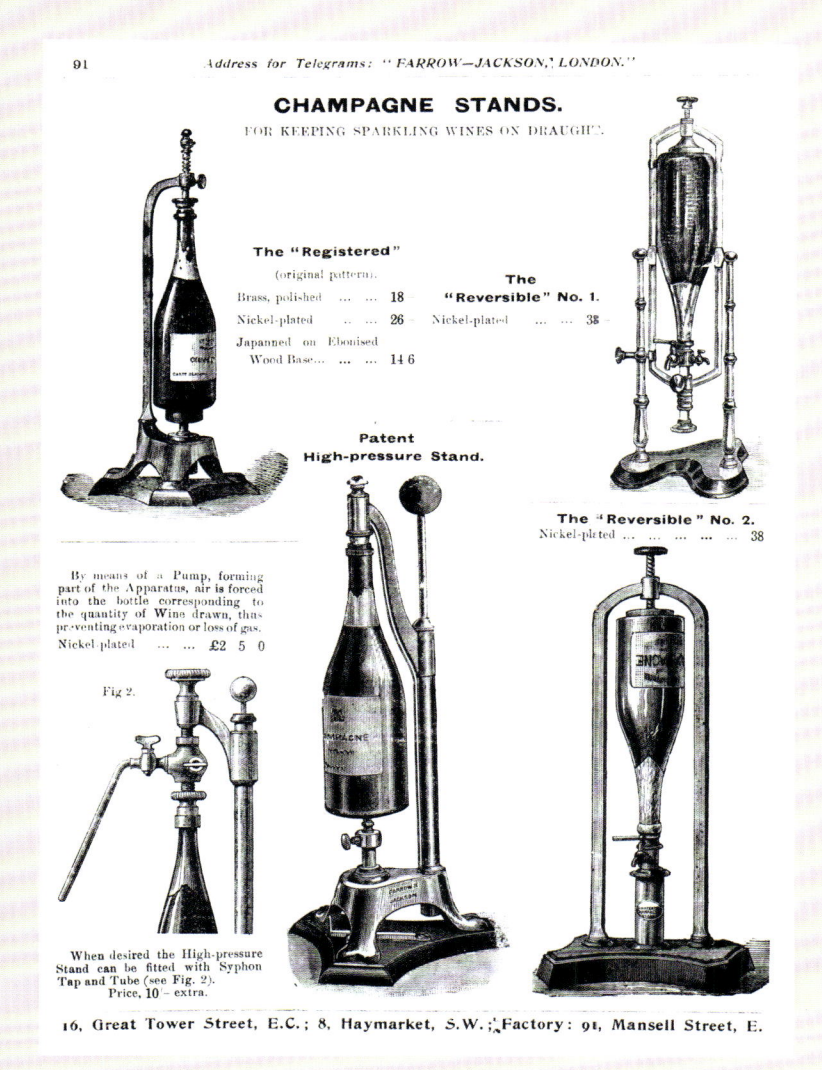

12/54 Champagne stands 'for keeping bottles on draught' are seriously scarce. This illustration gives a good picture of what they are and how they function.

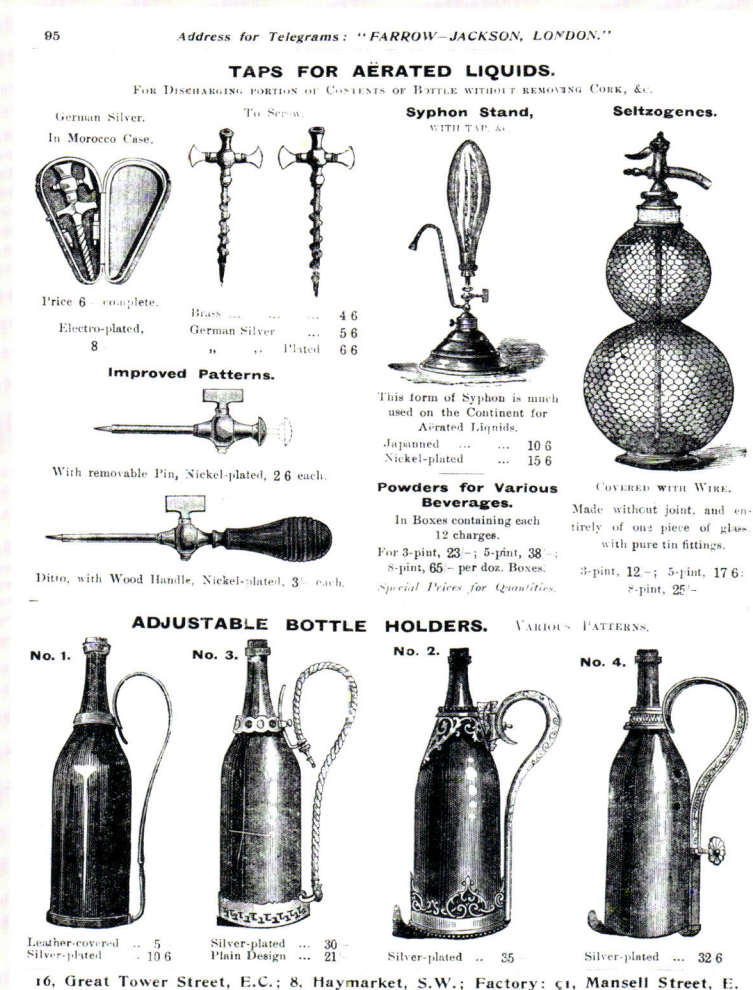

12/55 Another page from Farrow & Jackson's catalogue showing champagne taps and bottle holders.

Champagne glasses, with and without hollow stems, were considered in the previous chapter. These became fashionable at much the same time as many other champagne accessories. In addition there were champagne stoppers which would keep the fizz in an opened bottle, and champagne stands for, as the page in Farrow & Jackson's 1898 catalogue states, 'keeping sparkling wines on draught'. These are real rarities now.

It is difficult to overestimate the fervour which champagne generated in the late 19th century until the outbreak of hostilities in 1914. In part, this was because, for the British market, the Champenois began making dry wine that was not only to the British taste, but also had better keeping qualities. It represented the ultimate in luxury – we still refer to a 'champagne lifestyle' – but at an affordable cost. However the rise in popularity of champagne had started a little earlier in the 1860s, when duties on champagne were drastically reduced so that a bottle cost five shillings (25p) in 1861 and the famous music-hall song *Champagne Charlie* was composed in 1869.

12/57 A pair of champagne pliers with corkscrew and brush, stamped JAMES WRIGHT NOV 5 1879. Similar pliers and nippers appear in Farrow & Jackson's catalogue, but without any mention of a presentation box.

Fakes, forgeries and other problems

Fakes and other problems are an ever-present headache for dealers in antiques. This is not so much because dealers make mistakes of judgement: of course they do, but with experience these happen very seldom. It is the perception by the buying public that they may unwittingly be duped which is the problem. Whenever an antique can be sold for more than it costs to make an accurate copy, there is the possibility that such a copy will be made with the intention of deceiving the purchaser. There will always be those who will try to take advantage of the ignorance of the buyer. Wine-related antiques have probably suffered less than some other disciplines in this way, but fakes are not unknown. It may be helpful to take an overview of the problem. Anything that looks like an antique can be put into one of four categories.

First there is the object which was made at the date that its design suggests it was made and is the genuine article. To be genuine, an article must not have had its original specification altered or enhanced in any way.

Second, there is the object made in the manner of an older style, and this is called a reproduction. A chair designed in 1754 by Thomas Chippendale but made in 1900 is an example, and there are many like that. Chippendale furniture was very popular at the beginning of the 20th century and his designs were much reproduced to fill the requirements of the market. Reproductions continue to be made and no attempt is made to pass them off as antique.

Third, if a reproduction of an old design is 'distressed' or aged artificially with the intention to deceive, it becomes a fake or forgery. Fakes are those objects that are meant to deceive, but fakers vary in their competence. Some fakes are obvious to anyone with experience of their subject, while others are much more difficult to detect and may not be discovered for a long time after they are made, if ever.

The last category occurs when an object is incomplete or consists of one or more parts of something else: a decanter without a stopper being offered as a carafe is an example. If the top half of a wine funnel is 'married' to the spout of another, it would also constitute a problem.

It has to be said that encountering a fake used to be a rare occurence and it still is, but as the prices of all antiques continue to rise – which they rarely fail to do – the proportion of fakes and other problems appears to increase. It makes more and more sense therefore to buy from a specialist in the particular subject that interests you, whether it is an inexpensive simple corkscrew or a valuable wine cooler.

It is as well to remember that, traditionally, auctions are where dealers dispose of unwanted stock and others sell surplus possessions. A close examination of the conditions of sale, which all auctioneers are bound to display, should be mandatory for anyone who thinks of buying at auction. Bargains can be bought and many are, but there are numerous tales of people paying far more than they should for substandard antiques. Certain aspects of the Sale of Goods Act and the Trade Descriptions Act may not apply to auctions, so once the hammer falls, unless very specific conditions apply, there is no unravelling of the deal. An item bought at auction one day cannot be taken back the next day because it is the wrong colour, or it does not quite fit the decor of your room. While bidding at auction may be fun, it is also a gamble unless you have specialist knowledge.

Some of the problems specific to wine-related antiques are given below.

Wine Bottles

The only really valuable wine bottles are those with seals indicating the owner and often the date, preferably before 1750. Until now, these appear not to have been faked, but with fast escalating prices it would seem logical that it is only a question of time before a fake sealed bottle comes to the market. Of course it is possible that sealed bottles, are already being faked but at this point none has been detected.

There have been allegations that old bottles of wine are being incorrectly described and this at a very serious level. It applies particularly to those bottles purporting to have originally been in the cellars of the third American president, Thomas Jefferson, who travelled in Europe and collected fine wine. However, these bottles full of wine are of more relevance to wine afficionados and do not fall within the scope of this book.

The only real problem with bottles is their condition: the dark glass used for making bottles can easily hide cracks, so careful examination is essential.

Corkscrews

Corkscrews appear not to be objects of fakery, but numerous corkscrews are adapted or cannibalised. It is far from unknown for a collector or dealer to buy two corkscrews in poor condition, and to take the handle from one and marry it to the helix of another to make one apparently good corkscrew. Such marriages can be very difficult to detect as all the component parts are of similar date and might well have been used in an original version. Whether or not they are acceptable to corkscrew collectors is an individual decision.

Many corkscrews have bone handles (ivory is very seldom used). Bone discolours and, relative to ivory, is soft. Recently a corkscrew handle, originally thought to be bone, was found to be plastic, and stained to look like bone. It is probable that many others like it are about.

13/2 This corkscrew has both a shortened tip and it has been bent out of true. If used to draw a cork, it would probably mangle the cork or push it into the bottle. A similar problem occurs when a helix remains straight, but has become mis-shapen.

13/1 The tip of this corkscrew has been shortened. Note the abrupt coming to a point. Old corkscrews gradually taper to their tip, often over nearly 1in/2·5cm.

Bin Labels and Numbers

Bin labels are hardly worth faking, but hotel room and house numbers have been known to be offered as bin numbers.

13/3 This is not a bin label, although it was sold as one. It is a hotel room number. Ceramic house numbers have also been passed off as bin numbers.

Chapter 13 Fakes, forgeries and other problems

Wine Funnels

Wine funnels tend not to be faked, but it is not unknown for the bowl of one to be married to the spout of another. As both halves should be hallmarked even if partially, and bear the maker's mark, marriages should be easily found, but in practice this is not always the case. Wine funnel spouts are often dented, torn or shortened. They are seldom robust and were usually used by servants until the second half of the 20th century. The weakest part, the spout, is damaged more often than not. The tip of the spout should be curved to deflect wine down the wall of a decanter, and almost all have a notch at either side giving the spout a V shape when looked at from the side. If a funnel appears to be undamaged, a close inspection of the spout may reveal repair.

The other part of a wine funnel which is often damaged or repaired is the tang. As this sits apart from the bowl, it is easily snagged causing it either to be ripped away from the bowl, or the bowl to be damaged. Original tangs are usually shaped or made as a shell, so a plain rectangular tang or one simply with rounded corners should be regarded with suspicion.

Funnels made at the end of the 17th century and the first half of the 18th do not have cranked or curved spouts and are not strictly wine funnels; they were made for use in the kitchen. While they may have been used for wine, that was not their original purpose.

13/4. This wine funnel was made in 1813, but at a later date it was extended, probably in an attempt to make it more valuable. The transverse seams, where an extra length was added to the spout, can be clearly seen. The tang appears also very angular which probably indicates that this, too, has been altered. Without being re-hallmarked, it would be unlawful to sell this funnel.

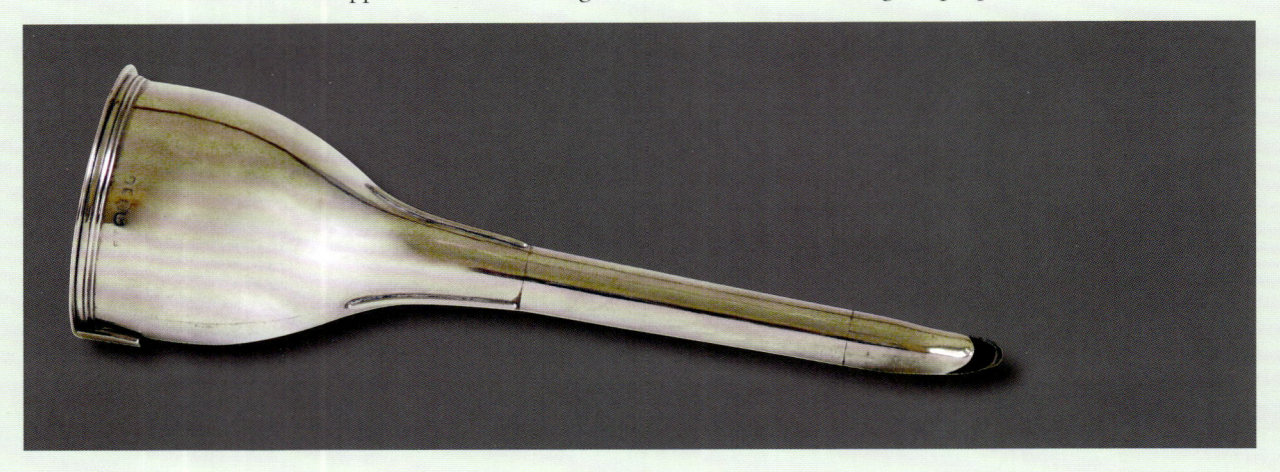

Wine Coolers and Cellarets

Floor-standing mahogany wine coolers seem not to have been faked, but many have survived in less than good condition. Being close to the floor, they have often been kicked accidentally, bruised by vacuum cleaners, or damaged by cats using them as scratching posts. Restoration made necessary by fair wear and tear is acceptable, but replacement feet or legs and badly abraded legs less so. The stands of wine coolers with legs have often been truncated, lost or replaced and these shortcomings are not acceptable. Some mahogany table wine coolers for one or two bottles have been copied and passed off as antiques and can be difficult to assess.

Silver wine coolers very seldom present a problem, but old Sheffield plated ones should have their original plating and not be re-plated. An old Sheffield plate wine cooler will show a seam down its length, and usually a rectangle of silver let into it so that a coat of arms can be engraved without going through to the copper beneath. When they are re-plated, they emerge with a very bright and seamless surface. The difference will soon be apparent to anyone with a little experience.

13/5 This brass 'wine cooler' looks to have been made around 1720, and the patination would seem to bear this out. However, it was actually made by Pearson Page and appears in their 1922 catalogue as a jardinière (far right). The dimensions are exactly as given in the catalogue. It is constructed as a genuine one would have been, and after about 80 years, the surface patination is very convincing, but the feet are poor imitations of old models.

Wine Tasters

British wine tasters are so rare and collected, that any which come to the market are subject to close scrutiny. Such detailed attention is usually sufficient to scare a faker away, but recently an English wine taster surfaced in Australia having been commissioned by a 'collector'. He even had the gall to retain the punches which gave the taster its fake hallmarks (for 1697) and the maker's mark of George Garthorne, a well-known goldsmith of that period. Both the faker and the collector have since died, but it is worrying that while the wine taster has come to light some 30 years after its manufacture, and is illustrated here, the punches have not. Fortunately the punches are not very good copies of those used in 1697, but it does show that fakers have recently been active. The faker also made the mistake of not knowing his subject: he made the taster about three times as heavy as a genuine one – enough to rouse the suspicions of any expert.

13/6 The shortcomings shown up to this point have been accidents or mistaken identities. This wine taster is a forgery – something made to deceive. It has fake hallmarks for London 1697 and maker's mark of George Garthorne, a well-known maker at this period. While the general idea might just have escaped the notice of many people, the faker made his piece three times as heavy as an original would have been. Close examination of the hallmarks confirms that these are not struck by the punches of the Goldsmiths' Company. It would be unlawful to sell this piece in Britain and the penalties for doing so, if discovered, would be very harsh.

13/7 This purports to be an 18th century French tastevin (wine taster), and so strictly speaking falls outside the scope of this book. However fake 18th century French wine tasters are probably as common as genuine ones in Britain, so this is included here. It is heavy gauge and the marks look convincing, but the wear has been 'applied in a hurry'.

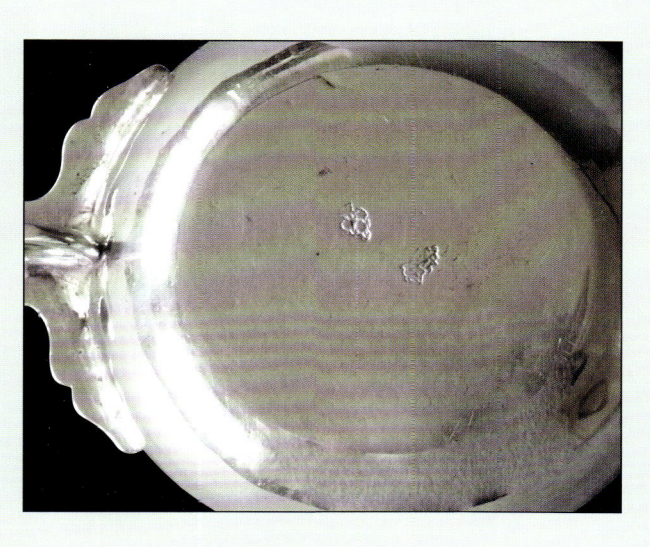

13/8 This small object (it is just 2in/5 cm long) has a bunch of grapes on its handle. It is in fine condition and made by George Unite, a good Birmingham silversmith. While it just may have been intended for tasting wine, most silver experts would say it was a tea caddy spoon. Unlike most most wine tasters, it is quite lightweight.

13/9 Small (this one is 4in/10.2cm.) two-handled shallow bowls made in the Channel Islands might be mistaken for wine tasters, but they are lightweight in comparison to true wine tasters which in any case do not have two handles. These small dishes were usually given as christening presents, but some were marriage gifts and are engraved with two sets of initials rather than one. This example dates from about 1750 and was made in Jersey by Thomas Mauger. It is not a fake and would only be a problem if someone tried to call it a wine taster.

Chapter 13   Fakes, forgeries and other problems

Decanters and Carafes

Decanters present a few problems, and damage cannot always be repaired. If the rim of a decanter is slightly chipped, it can be ground down and polished, but the result can take away the good proportions of the original shape. Georgian decanters and their stoppers are not numbered except on very rare occasions (see 7/32), so it is impossible in most cases to say for certain that a stopper is original to a given decanter. Indeed provided that the design, colour, age and fit of a stopper looks correct, it is not regarded as a problem at all.

Many decanters made in the opening years of the 20th century copied designs of 100 years or so previously, and telling the difference is not easy for an amateur. Commonly the model has three or four neck rings, and original examples had the rings added after the decanter was blown. When a finger is inserted through the neck the rings should not be felt on the inside. If they are, it means that the rings were blown with the decanter, and this is a 20th century technique.

When a decanter and its stopper part company, it may be a temptation to call it a carafe (a decanter which never had a stopper). Stoppers have to be ground into the neck to make a good fit, and the ridge caused in the grinding process, even if it is subsequently polished, can always be detected by feeling with a sensitive finger.

Carelessly used decanters tend to become scratched and bruised. Light scratches can be polished away, but deeper ones are a problem. Even a light clash of two decanters can produce a crack. Cracks can be difficult to detect, particularly small star cracks, so a good light is necessary to make an assessment. Star cracks may not compromise the use of a decanter, but they do reduce the value considerably.

Many decanters become cloudy inside. This is caused by water etching the inside surface of the decanter and the damage cannot be removed by you or me. It has to be done by a professional who can buff the inside of the decanter. The process takes a few days to accomplish. Any dealer in antique glass will know about a range of domestic solutions to this problem, but the fact is that they do not work. The old remedy of putting lead shot in the decanter and rolling it around will cause more scratches and make the professional's job impossible. The simple rule is never try to get rid of cloudiness in a decanter: leave it to a professional.

After use, a decanter should be washed in warm water and turned upside down to drain, but to dry the decanter properly, make a wick of newspaper and put it in a low oven (60–80°C) for a few minutes before feeding it into the decanter and leaving it for a half hour and repeating if necessary. The wick will absorb all the remaining moisture from the decanter. Never leave a decanter wet.

Occasionally port, red wine, or sherry is left in a decanter for several days or more (what a shame), and this can leave a dark stain in the base. This can easily be removed by adding warm water to cover the stained area and adding three or four denture cleaning tablets. Leave for an hour or so and rinse. This can be repeated if necessary, but as with all decanter washing, it is essential to dry it out thoroughly afterwards.

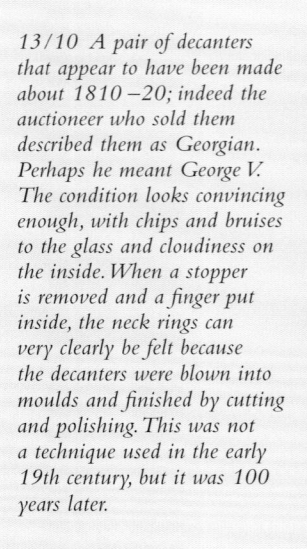

13/10 A pair of decanters that appear to have been made about 1810–20; indeed the auctioneer who sold them described them as Georgian. Perhaps he meant George V. The condition looks convincing enough, with chips and bruises to the glass and cloudiness on the inside. When a stopper is removed and a finger put inside, the neck rings can very clearly be felt because the decanters were blown into moulds and finished by cutting and polishing. This was not a technique used in the early 19th century, but it was 100 years later.

Coasters

Coasters of the late 18th century bear a strong resemblance to the frames of some models of cruet stands, and the conversion of one to the other is simple to accomplish. By removing the cruet bottles, feet and handle, a coaster-like object remains, and many examples have appeared on the market. As cruet stands with their bottles lost popularity, so the price difference between them and coasters widened, and the temptation arose for the unscrupulous to make the adaptation. The difference between the two is that cruet stands have flat wood bases while coasters have decoratively turned ones. Of course it is not difficult to lathe-turn a new base, but it will never have the colour and patination of an old one. Also if the old base is left, marks will show where the feet were attached. Some of these coaster conversions are magnum size, making the alteration all the more profitable.

Lacquered papier mâché coasters have also proved very popular for use on the dining table. The same applies to tôleware examples. Many, if not most, are in less than fine condition. Lightweight and delicate papier mâché coasters seldom survive 200 years in pristine order. The inside surfaces are usually more or less degraded and the outside surfaces worn. A careful examination is therefore recommended if one is found, and checks should be made to see if restoration has been carried out, or if it is as old as its appearance would suggest.

13/11 A cruet made in 1782 and showing its constituent parts. One bottle is missing, as are the stoppers of the oil and vinegar bottles. However, when they are all removed from the frame, the handle unscrewed and the feet removed, what is left looks very much like a coaster. Many 'coasters' started out as cruet frames, but these do not have turned mahogany or beechwood bases, and replacement ones should be regarded with much suspicion.

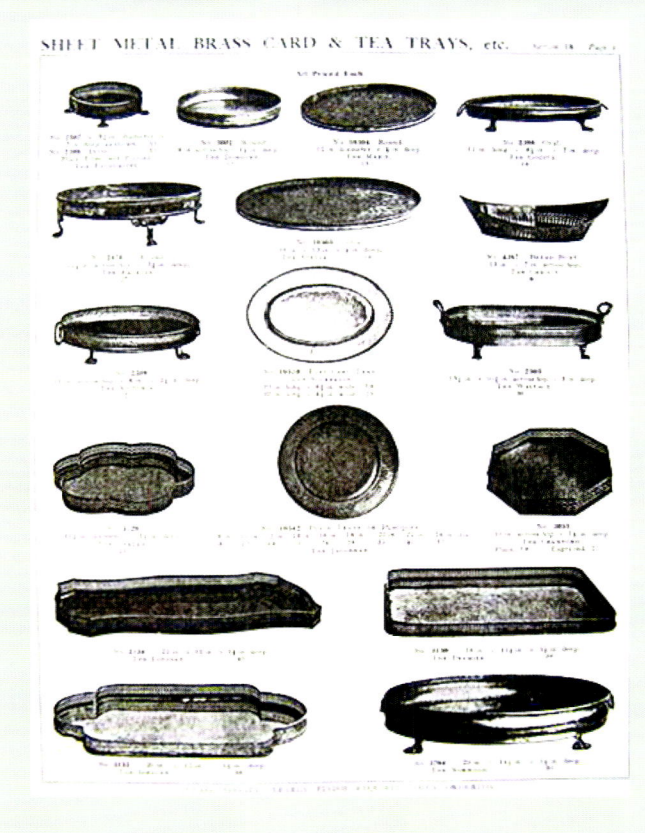

13/12 A page from the Pearson Page catalogue showing reproduction brass trays, salvers and what could be coasters. Many of the top left FAVOURITES (detail, far right) have been offered as antique coasters, but the Antique Metalware Society has done much to inform dealers and the public about these.

Claret Jugs

Claret jugs, like decanters, need to be checked for cracks and bruises. All-glass examples, that is those without metallic mounts, are usually weak at the base of the handle, so a careful check at that point is advisable. Also, like decanters, they can become stained or cloudy and the same remedies apply as for decanters.

Sometimes the glass bodies of claret jugs have been replaced. This can be very difficult to see, so an assessment of the colour of the glass should be made. It may sound strange, but even clear glass has a hue varying from grey to green or mauve to blue. Assessing the hue is a matter of experience, although having other glass for comparison can help considerably. In general, modern glass replacement bodies tend to be whiter than old ones and devoid of any shade of colour.

13/14 A silver jug with the embossed mask of Bacchus and a handle formed as a vine branch. The base of the jug has the hallmarks for London in 1759 and the maker's mark of Thomas Cooke & Richard Gurney. The mask and the fruiting vine in Bacchus' hair suggest it was intended as a wine jug, but it did not start life like this. The foot, handle and the wide top rim have all been added at a later date and the embossing done at the same time, probably in the middle of the 19th century. As the additions have not been hallmarked it may not be lawfully sold. More than one version of this jug exists.

13/15 A so-called late 19th century French claret jug which turned out to be an important Fatimid Egyptian ewer of the 11th century mounted in gold by the Parisian jewellers Morel of Sèvres. It was a problem for the provincial auctioneer who failed to recognise it for what it was (see page 279).

Wine Labels

Silver wine labels can be of very high value compared with their bullion value, so fakes should be expected. In reality it would seem that there are few. The most common name on wine labels is Madeira; it is therefore the least wanted by collectors. One way that a Madeira label may be 'improved' is to fill the engraved name with silver solder and re-engrave it with a more collectable name. This may be detected by breathing heavily on a cold label: the solder will appear lighter than its surroundings. However, if the label is electroplated after being filled, detection will be much harder. Electroplating gives silver a very white, almost bluish colour when compared with sterling standard silver, and freshly plated items will be very shiny and look almost new. A wine label with this appearance should be the cause for concern.

The very best silver and silver-gilt labels of the early 19th century are of cast construction and are often hallmarked on their front decorated surfaces. Fakers have been known to make a casting of an existing label, together with its hallmarks, so producing an almost identical label. Of course when the casting cools, it shrinks, so the new label will be nearly 10% smaller than the original. Also the marks, closely examined with a strong magnifying glass, will be seen to be cast rather than being struck with punches. To sell such a label is illegal but the rewards have tempted some.

13/16 Wine labels are small and relatively valuable so more fakes than appear to be around should be expected. This wine label was originally engraved MADEIRA, but the engraving has been 'filled' with silver solder and re-engraved WHISKEY. It is very difficult to see when polished, but the label was allowed to tarnish over a period of months and 'Madeira' can now be seen behind the 'Whiskey'.

Glasses, Goblets and Cups

Wine glasses have been collected for well over 100 years so it is hardly surprising that attempts at deception have been made. Very few glasses are so valuable that they are worth faking, but one category falls well within this group; they are Jacobite glasses celebrating the hoped-for Stuart succession to the English throne in the mid-18th century. The most valuable of all are those diamond-point engraved with the Jacobite national anthem, which, because it ends with 'Amen', are known as amen glasses. The story of the fakery and its discovery is well outlined elsewhere (see bibliography), but away from amen glasses, there are many which are later engraved with varying degrees of conviction; some are obvious fakes, others less so.

There are numerous examples of glasses made at the end of the 19th and beginning of the 20th centuries in an earlier style. A few may have been made with an intent to deceive, but many were simply reproductions. The problem with the latter is that now, 100 years later, they have acquired wear and tear, particularly where a glass meets the surface on which it stands, and the wear can look older than it is.

During the 20th century many glasses were made with stems imitating of the colour twists of the 1760s. Colour twist glasses are valuable rarities. Differentiating between them and later copies should not be difficult to anyone with even a little experience, but for the novice collector they can be deceptive. Most copies are not English and are made of soda glass so their weight is unexpectedly light, and the bowls do not ring like a lead glass example when lightly tapped.

Many glasses have been chipped, either at the rim or on the foot. Even a tiny chip can reduce the value of a glass considerably. Small chips can be ground and polished out, but it should be possible to detect such restorations. The rim of an antique wine glass was finished hot; it was not ground to an edge when cold. The rim will therefore bulge very slightly in thickness and, looked at in the light, any reduction should be seen easily. A ground rim will not bulge, but will be of even thickness right to the top.

The feet of glasses should be observed differently. To detect a removed chip to a foot the glass will need to be held in one hand by the bowl and rotated. Any slight lack of circularity or indentation to the edge of the foot should be felt with the other hand if a chip has been ground away. The foot of an old glass should always show wear where it meets the surface it rests upon. This wear should be clearly visible with the aid of a magnifying glass.

Silver goblets present few problems except, perhaps, if they have been re-engraved.

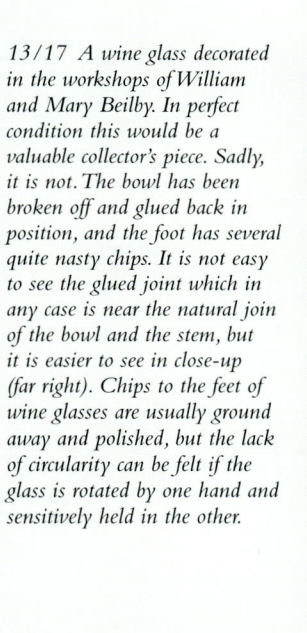

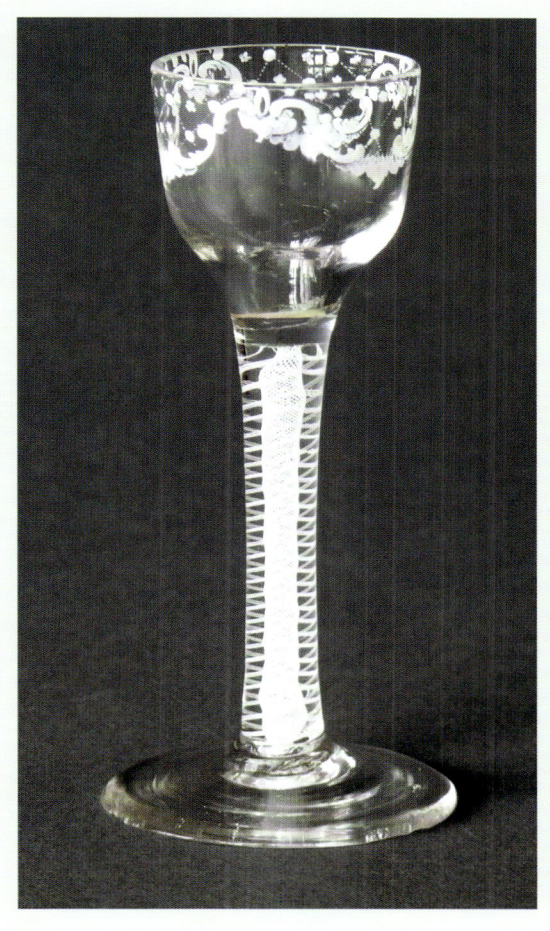

13/17 A wine glass decorated in the workshops of William and Mary Beilby. In perfect condition this would be a valuable collector's piece. Sadly, it is not. The bowl has been broken off and glued back in position, and the foot has several quite nasty chips. It is not easy to see the glued joint which in any case is near the natural join of the bowl and the stem, but it is easier to see in close-up (far right). Chips to the feet of wine glasses are usually ground away and polished, but the lack of circularity can be felt if the glass is rotated by one hand and sensitively held in the other.

Chapter 13 Fakes, forgeries and other problems

13/18 A colour twist wine glass made, probably in Holland, in the early 20th century. It is of a type of which many examples exist – more than the 18th century glasses it vaguely resembles. It is doubtful if these were made as fakes, but in view of the prices of genuine ones, some are 'distressed' to make them seem older than they are. The metal is soda glass rather than lead glass and therefore does not ring as long when tapped. Also there is a lump at the base of the bowl inside which is not to be found on genuine examples.

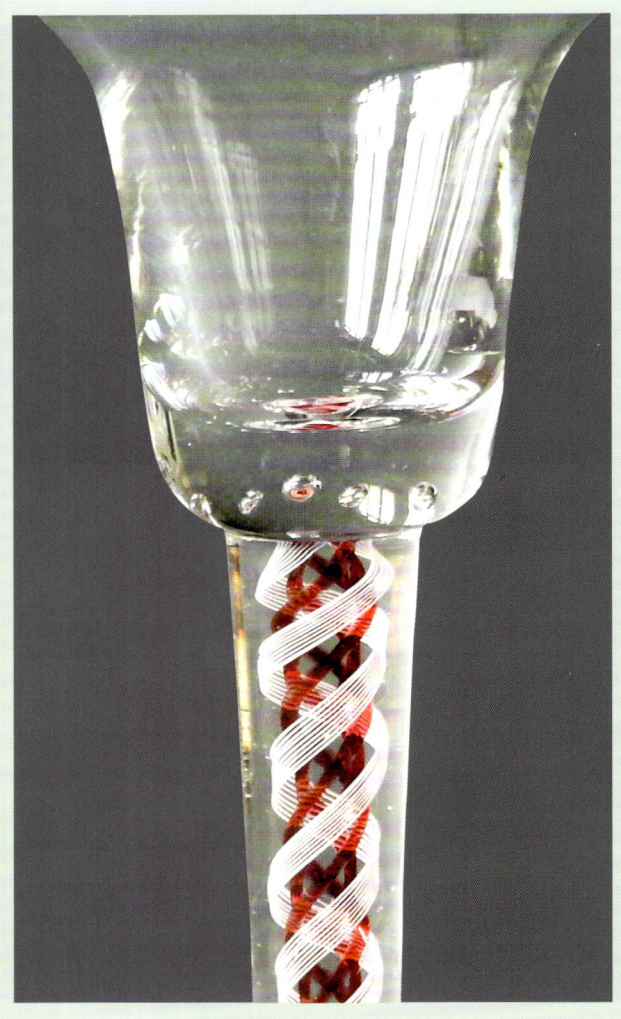

13/19 A set of four wine glasses with faceted stems. They look as if they were made around 1780–90 but are modern copies, and the undersides have been abraded to simulate the wear of over 200 years. While the bowls and stems are quite convincing, the flatness of the feet and the lack of a pontil mark give them away for what they are. In addition the colour of the glass is not quite what it should be.

Miscellaneous

Most wine-related antique furniture is unlikely to be faked. Few people feel the need for a drinking table, so the supply is sufficient to cater for the demand. Similar arguments apply to sideboards and dumb waiters. However small items like bottle trays and cork drawing stands are rare and highly sought, with the obvious inferences.

Bottle trays are similar in date, size and general appearance to cutlery trays, which find scant favour in the modern home. While bottle trays are eagerly sought and command high prices, cutlery trays are just the opposite. The temptation to make one from the other has been too great for some restorers or those who give them instruction, and a few conversions have been noted. They can usually be seen for what they are because it is very difficult to make a new surface match an old one and, to make the conversion, notches to take the bottle necks must be carved from the old wood.

Cork drawing stands or bottle holders are not complex things to a competent cabinet maker, and a few have tried to make them. However it is not easy to simulate an old patination, and this will usually lay bare the deception to an expert assessor.

It might appear that there are no end of traps into which the unwary may fall. This is really not the case especially if one is aware of the pitfalls. There have been deceivers, forgers and fakers for many hundreds of years. Some fakes are even collected in their own right for what they are. However, the faker is only equal to the level of ignorance of those he is trying to deceive. Just as murders committed many years ago are being solved by new forensic science, so too, faked antiques are being revealed by constantly increased knowledge of the decorative arts.

Societies like the Furniture History Society, the Glass Circle, the Silver Society and many others disseminate knowledge among their members. Today anyone with an academic interest in the decorative arts can have a much deeper knowledge than was available to previous generations. At the time of writing, a faker of silver has been recently discovered and sent to prison. The techniques he used and the punches he made to mark the silver have been made common knowledge in the press, among dealers and Silver Society members.

The officers of the Goldsmiths' Company have been at the forefront of the increase in learning about bullion metals and the company holds regular seminars on the subject of fakes. They were also responsible for the evidence used to convict the faker mentioned above. The company's assay office has highly sophisticated scientific equipment used not only to assay (test) silver, gold and platinum brought in for hallmarking, but also to test and date objects brought before it that may have spurious marks or doubtful origins. The service it provides is an extremely valuable one.

The surface of a faked piece of furniture may look convincing when it leaves the workshop, but it is doubtful that it will stand the test of time. This is because the surface of wood evolves through the effects of oxidation on the timber and ultraviolet light on its fibres. It is also affected by the conditions of its use and storage. A visual simulation of these effects may be successful for a short time, but any pigments used will deteriorate quite differently from naturally aged wood.

In January 2008, the following description appeared in a country auctioneer's catalogue, together with an estimate: *A French claret jug, the rock crystal body carved with animals, the silver gilt mounts with enamelled decoration, 19th century, 30cm (cracked and damaged). In fitted box of Morel à Sèvres. £100–200.*

When the auction took place the vendor was in the room to see his piece being sold. As the bids were escalating far beyond the auctioneer's estimate and the price rose not in hundreds, but thousands, to well over £200,000, the vendor realised that something was wrong and he rose and shouted aloud that he wished to withdraw the lot. The auctioneer dropped his gavel and 'sold' it to the highest bidder. Mayhem ensued.

The auctioneer, vendor and the 'purchaser' arrived at a settlement and the sale was rescinded, which is very unusual. Soon after this the 'claret jug' was re-entered in a properly catalogued auction where nine months later it sold for nearly £3,000,000. In reality it was not cracked or damaged – rock crystal has natural 'flaws'– and the mounts were gold. Most importantly, the ewer was about 1,000 years old, from Egypt and one of only a very few known. It was and remains a highly important item of Islamic art.

The so-called claret jug may not have been British and it certainly was not a claret jug, but it was traded in Britain and called a claret jug, demonstrating that problems in the world of antiques are not all about fakes and forgeries.

Glossary

A
Acroter *(pl. acroteria) an upstanding ornament or plinth to be found on a pediment; also acroterion.*
Amphora *a large Græco-Roman or Egyptian pottery wine storage vessel usually with two handles and a pointed base.*
Annulated *made in the form of rings.*
Anthemion *(pl. anthemia) a neoclassical ornament in the form of stylised honeysuckle.*
Archimedean screw *a bladed spiral screw with a central core (see chapter on corkscrews).*
Art nouveau *a late 19th/early 20th century stylistic movement characterised by sinuous curves, stylised flowers and leaves and a tendency towards asymmetry.*
Arts and crafts *a late 19th century decorative movement emphasising handicrafts and good design inspired by the works of John Ruskin and William Morris.*
Astragal *a moulding with its cross-section composed of a rectangle surmounted by a semi-circle.*
Augur *a bladed spiral screw (see chapter on corkscrews).*

B
Bacchic *relating to Bacchus, god of wine and fertility.*
Baroque *a late 17th/early 18th century art form originating in Italy and characterised by exuberant classical decoration and symmetrical curvilinear lines, particularly the C-scroll.*
Bead *a repetitive moulding comprising a sequence of conjoined hemispheres of small size.*
Bead and reel *a classical repetitive moulding comprising lengths of beading separated by oblong reels.*
Bellarmine *a Rhenish stoneware flask with a moulded mask of a bearded man opposite the handle. Made from about the 15th century onwards and later named after the counter-reformationist, Cardinal Roberto Bellarmino.*
Binning *the method of stacking bottles on their sides in pigeon holes in a cellar.*
Black glass *dark green to brown glass used in making old wine bottles.*
Blind fret *fretwork decoration that is not pierced through but set against a backing.*
Bombé *literally 'blown out'; an exaggerated swollen form popular in the rococo style.*
Brandewijn *(Dutch) literally 'burnt wine' ie distilled wine or brandy.*
Bright cut *a form of engraving, particularly on silver, whereby minute slivers of metal are removed with a graver, leaving a glistening surface.*
Britannia Standard *high quality silver alloy containing 95.84% pure silver.*
Bucranium *(pl. bucrania) an ox skull often draped with garlands; a classical and neoclassical motif.*
Button *(in corkscrew terminology) a disc at the top of the helix which can engage with the cork to aid extraction (see Henshall's patent).*

C
Cabriole leg *a leg curving outwards at the knee and tapering in an elongated S towards the foot; originating in China and popular in England from the early 18th century onwards.*
Capsule *covering over the top of a bottle, made of lead, plastic or hard wax.*
Carafe *an open decanter which was never made to have a stopper.*
Carboy *Any very large bottle, but usually with a near-spherical body.*
Cartouche *a tablet, normally in the form of a curling scroll or shield to accommodate an inscription or armorial device.*
Casting *a method of construction using a mould.*
Caulked *silver which has had its edge hammered to thicken it, is said to be caulked.*
Cellaret *a piece of furniture for storing wine at room temperature.*
Chamfer *(or bevel) an angle cut at the corner of two surfaces.*
Chasing *the tooling of a metal object from its outer surface to produce a raised pattern.*
Chinoiserie *the western imitation of oriental design, 17th century onwards.*
Cock bead *a small applied raised moulding often used to edge a drawer.*
Collet foot *a ring-like shallow foot, sometimes turned or moulded. A term used in silver and glass.*
Creamware *a variety of 18th century lead-glazed pottery with a cream-coloured body containing flint.*
Crizzling *a defect of glass in which the internal structure breaks into a crystalline form.*
Cross-banding *veneered decoration on the edge of furniture and panelling where the wood grain is at a right angle to the edge.*
Cruciform *cross-like, with a plan in the form of a cross.*

D
Delftware *English tin-glazed earthenware made from the 16th century onwards emulating products from the Dutch town of Delft.*
Die-stamping *a method of decorating and piercing metal by compressing and puncturing it in a heavy press.*

E
Earthenware *(pottery) all types of wares made from clay.*
Egg and dart *(egg and tongue) a repetitive classical pattern consisting of alternating ovals and arrow heads. It signifies life and death.*
Embossing *generic term for relief decoration on metal.*
Enamelling *a form of decoration in which a layer of glass is fused to a metal or glass base.*
Engraving *(on metal and glass) a method of decorating a surface by inscribing the required pattern with a rotating abrasive wheel or a sharp tool (diamond point or steel graver).*
E.P.N.S. *(electro-plated nickel silver) electro-plated wares (usually nickel though sometimes silver) were coated with silver by electrolysis, patented in 1840.*
Escutcheon *originally a shield bearing a coat of arms, but also a decorative plaque; also a shaped metal plate protecting a keyhole on furniture.*
Etching *the process of decorating glass or metal by the application of acids.*

F
Faience *French name for tin-glazed pottery.*
Feather-edge *a form of bright cut, fluted decoration used as a border on silver, especially spoons and forks.*
Flat chasing *a method of decorating silver by using a tool which does not remove the silver, but leaves a shallow impression (see 9/2).*
Fluting *ornamentation of close-set, concave semi-circular, vertical grooves.*

G
Gadroon *a decorative moulding of convex curves, usually used as an edging.*
Garrya husks *classical decoration of stylised bell-flowers.*
Gilding *decorating with a very thin layer of gold leaf.*
Gothic *an art form characterised by pointed arches, trefoils, quatrefoils and other medieval motifs. Originating in France in the 12th century it was revived (in a modified form) in Britain in the 18th century, when it was sometimes known as Gothick.*
Guilloche *a classical ornament formed by continuous interlocking S-scrolls.*

H
Helix *a spiral (of metal) as in the business end of a corkscrew.*
Hobnail *a variety of glass cutting whereby a grid of Vs cut in the surface leaves an upstanding pattern of squares.*

J
Japanning *the western imitation of oriental lacquer work.*

K
Knop *a decorative swelling on the stem of a glass object.*
Knurled moulding *a moulding composed of a long series of ball-like elements.*

L
Lambrequin *a fringe-like ornament usually with pendants.*
Latticino *clear glass with embedded white glass threads.*
Lead glass *glass containing a percentage of lead oxide; often called lead crystal, thereby confusing it with rock crystal which occurs naturally.*
Lignum vitae *a very hard and dense wood from the West Indies, Central and northern South America; often used for turned treen and said to have life-giving properties, hence its name.*
Lunar slices *a variety of mid-late 18th century glass cutting, particularly favoured in Ireland, consisting of the removal of shallow, crescent-shaped slices.*
Lustreware *pottery fired with an iridescent metallic glaze.*

M
Malolactic fermentation *Secondary fermentation when sharp (appley) malic acid is converted into softer lactic (milky) acid.*
Mannerism *a development of the renaissance style, characterised by elongated and contorted forms.*
Marvering *the finishing of glass by rolling the still-hot melt on a 'marvering' table.*
Mell *a form of carafe with a flattened body and narrow tall neck.*
Merese *a small flat 'cushion' delineating the swellings on the stem of a drinking glass.*
Metal *in the context of glass, its substance or composition.*
Must *the residue left after juice has been pressed from the grapes.*

N
Neoclassicism *a style which emerged in the 1750s characterised by symmetry, simple geometric forms and the use of classical Greek and Roman architectural ornament.*
Nipt diamond waies *a form of glass decoration dating from about 1660-90 in which trails of applied glass are pincered while still molten to form a trellis pattern; particularly associated with George Ravenscroft. Often abbreviated to NDW.*

O
Oenologist *a technician versed in the science of wine.*
Ormolu *gilded brass or bronze.*
Ogee *(double ogee) an elongated S shape.*

P
Paktong *an alloy of copper, zinc and nickel invented for imperial Chinese use. Used in the 18th century in England as an economic alternative to silver.*
Papier mâché *a moulded composition of compressed pulped paper and glue; commonly japanned.*
Patera *(pl. paterae) an oval or circular medallion frequently incorporating a stylised flower head.*
Patina *the effect of age, oxidation and usage on the surface of wood and other materials.*
Pennyweight *one twentieth of a troy ounce.*
Pontil rod *a solid iron rod used in a glasshouse for handling glass during making.*
Pontil mark *the sharp mark left when the pontil rod is broken from the glass or decanter.*
Pricking *a form of decoration found on 16th and 17th century silver consisting of numerous tiny dots executed by needlepoint.*
Printie *a polished circular or oval shallow depression cut in glass.*
Prunt *a small blob of glass applied to the main body of a piece for the purpose of decoration.*
Punt *the hollow in the base of a wine bottle; also known as a kick.*

Q
Quaich *a Scottish shallow dish from which strong liquor was taken; originally of staved and hooped construction and with flat lug handles.*
Quatrefoil *a four-cusped device or cartouche associated with gothic(k) ornament.*

R
Raising *a silversmithing operation whereby a flat sheet of metal is hammered over a block to produce a hollow shape.*
Reeding *a form of simple convex moulding comprising two or more closely spaced parallel grooves.*

Select Bibliography

Repoussé *the projecting decoration on metal achieved by hammering from the underside.*
Renaissance *a sophisticated cultural and artistic movement based on ancient Roman ideals which began in Italy in the 14th century and spread throughout Europe. Decorative motifs were based on classical orders of architecture and ornament found on Roman sarcophagi.*
Rigaree *trailed decoration on glass, with notches.*
Romanesque *a pre-medieval art form characterised largely by rounded arches and chevron decoration.*
Roundlet *a variety of travelling corkscrew in which the helix folds into the two-part handle.*
Rummer *a large drinking glass of a type often associated with tavern use, thus heavily constructed.*

S

Salt glaze *a glaze applied to stoneware and formed by the addition of salt during firing which produces a distinctive speckled and pitted surface.*
Scrimshaw *a rustic art form practised by sailors by scratching designs on whales' teeth or bone.*
Shank *(in corkscrew terminology) the part between the handle and the helix.*
Silesian *a square or polygonal tapered stem found on glassware; now usually called a square pedestal stem.*
Soda glass *glass in which sodium carbonate replaces potash as the flux.*
Sterling silver *the standard form of British silver alloy containing 92.5% pure silver.*
Soldering *the joining of two pieces of metal by melting lead (soft soldering) or silver (hard soldering) with a flux.*
Strapwork *a form of decoration characterised by symmetrical arrangements of simulated leather straps or carved fretwork.*
Strawberry cutting *a variety of glass cutting consisting of hobnails with additional hatching.*
Strigilation *curved or S-shaped fluting.*

T

Tang *a tab or pendant element, a projection (see wine funnels).*
Tazza *originally a shallow saucer on a stem and foot. Often incorrectly used to describe salvers on feet.*
Tiger ware *a type of late 16th and early 17th century stoneware with a heavily mottled brown salt glaze producing an appearance not unlike that of the skin of a leopard. It is a misnomer.*
Tin glaze *an opaque white glaze applied to earthenware and made from oxides of lead, tin and silicate of potash.*
Tôleware *japanned metalwares, derived from the French name for the same, 'tôle peint'.*
Trefoil *a three-cusped device or cartouche associated with got'nic(k) ornament.*
Treen *literally 'wooden', but generally used to describe domestic utensils made of wood and most particularly for items formed on a lathe.*

U

Ullage *seepage or loss of wine from a bottle or cask in its stored state through an apparently firm stopper.*

V

Vitruvian scroll *(or wave scroll) classical ornament resembling repetitive breaking waves.*
Volute *a spiralled scroll.*

W

Wirework *decoration formed of silver mouldings (often rims). Wire is the general term for metal (particularly silver) moulding of almost any cross-section.*
Worm *in this context, the business end of a corkscrew, a helix.*
Wrigglework *a form of engraving upon silver whereby the graver is wriggled from side to side producing a wavy or zig-zag line.*

What follows does not pretend to be exhaustive, but major and some less well-known works are included. Many books written before about 1980 contain information which today is considered out of date so, with few exceptions, old books have been omitted. There appear to be no books specifically on bin labels, wine tasters, wine coolers and cellarets, wine funnels, claret jugs or coasters. The catalogues of all the major auctioneers can be a very useful source of information, as can the printed and online catalogues of specialist auctioneers such as BBR Auctions (wine bottles) or Woolley & Wallis (silver). The journals of the Silver Society, the Wine Label Circle, the Glass Circle and other decorative art societies are also strongly recommended. It has been decided for convenience, to list books specifically for each chapter.

Bottles
Dumbrell, Roger, *Understanding Antique Wine Bottles*, Antique Collectors' Club, 1983.

Morgan, Roy, *Sealed Bottles, their History and Evolution 1630–1930*, Midlands Antique Bottle Publishing (nd).

Ruggles-Brise, Sheelah, *Sealed Bottles*, Country Life, 1949.

Van den Bossche, Willy, *Antique Glass Bottles, their History and Evolution 1500–1850*, Antique Collectors' Club, 2001.

Corkscrews
Bull, Don, *The Ultimate Corkscrew Book*, Schiffer, 1998.

Giulian, Bertrand B., *Corkscrews of the Eighteenth Century*, White Space, 1995.

Perry, Evan, *Corkscrews and Bottle Openers*, Shire, 1980.

Peters, Ferd, *Mechanical Corkscrews, their Evolution, Actions and Patents*, Pintex, 1999.

Wallis, Fletcher, *British Corkscrew Patents from 1795*, Vernier Press, 1997.

Watney, Bernard, and Babbidge, Homer, *Corkscrews for Collectors*, Sotheby Parke Bernet, 1981.

Decanters, Wine Jugs and Carafes
Hajdamach, Charles, *British Glass 1800–1914*, Antique Collectors' Club, 1991.

Hollingworth, Jane, *Collecting Decanters*, Studio Vista, London, 1980.

McConnell, Andy, *The Decanter, an Illustrated History of Glass from 1650*, Antique Collectors' Club, 2004.

Wine and Bin Labels
Penzer, N.M., *The Book of the Wine Label*, Home & Van Thal 1947.

Salter, John (ed.), *Wine labels 1730–2003*, Antique Collectors' Club, 2004.

Wine Glasses
Bickerton, L.M., *An Illustrated Guide to Eighteenth Century English Drinking Glasses*, Barrie & Jenkins, 1971.

Lloyd, Ward, *A Wire Lover's Glasses: The AC Hubbard Collection*, Richard Dennis, 2000.

Seddon, Geoffrey B., *The Jacobites and their Drinking Glasses*, Antique Collectors' Club, 1995.

General books which contain substantial amounts of material on the subject of British wine accessories

DECORATIVE ART BOOKS
R Butler & G Walkling, *The Book of Wine Antiques*. Antique Collectors' Club, Woodbridge, 1986.

Robin Butler, *The Albert Collection*, Broadway, London, 2004.

M. Clayton, *The Dictionary of Gold and Silver of Great Britain and North America*, Country Life, London 1971.

Farrow & Jackson – the Centenary Catalogue 1898, Reprint. Richard Dennis, 1997.

Fleming, John and Honour, Hugh, *The Penguin Dictionary of Decorative Arts*, Penguin, London 1977.

Philippa Glanville & Sophie Lee (eds.) *The Art of Drinking*. V & A Publications London, 2007.

Hartop, Christopher, *The Huguenot Legacy: English Silver 1680–1760*, Thomas Heneage, 1996.

Timothy Schroder, *The Gilbert Collection of Gold and Silver*, Los Angeles County Museum of Art, 1988.

WINE HISTORY
Hugh Johnson, *The Story of Wine*. Mitchell Beazley, London, 1989.

Johnson Hugh and Robinson, Jancis, *The World Atlas of Wine*, Mitchell Beazley 6th edn. London, 2007.

Andrew Robinson, *Vintage Years*, Phillimore London, 2008.

Robinson, Jancis (ed.), *The Oxford Companion to Wine* (2nd Edn.), Oxford 1999.

Simon, André L., *Bottlescrew Days*, Duckworth, London, 1926.

EXHIBITION CATALOGUES
Loan Exhibition of Drinking Vessels, Books, etc. Vintners' Hall, London, June 1933.

The Compleat Imbiber W & A Gilbey Centenary Exhibition, London, May–June, 1957.

The Philoenic Antiquary. G. Noël Butler, Honiton, 1978

The Goldsmith & the Grape. The Goldsmiths' Company, London, July 1983.

The Baluster Family of English Drinking Glasses, Delomosne & Son Ltd. London, May 1985.

Celebration and Ceremony, Cooper Hewitt Museum, New York, Summer 1985

Champagne Antiques, Brian Beet and Jeanette Hayhurst, London November 1985.

100 British Glasses, Asprey & Co. London, 1985.

Drinking Treasures, The Duke of Buccleuch and Queensberry, Drumlanrig & Bowhill, 1989 and 1990.

A Celebration of Wine, Dreweatt Neate, Newbury, November 1998.

English Wineglasses with Faceted Stems, Delomosne & Son, North Wraxall, 2005.

The Seton Veitch Collection of Early English Drinking Glasses, Delomosne and Son, North Wraxall, September 2006.

The Art of Drinking, Victoria & Albert Museum, London 2007.

Vintiques, Butler & Silverman, London, May 2008.

Picture credits

vi/vii BHM

Bottles
1/1 RB
1/2 VC
1/3 JH
1/4 RB
1/5 BBR
1/6 CS
1/7 BBR
1/8 RB
1/9 BBR
1/10 BBR
1/11 BBR
1/12 BBR
1/13 VC
1/14 BBR
1/15 VC
1/16 BBR
1/17 BBR
1/18 BBR
1/19 BBR
1/20 RPB
1/21 BBR
1/22 BBR
1/23 BBR
1/24 RB
1/25 BBR
1/26 KD
1/27 anon

Bin Labels
2/1 anon
2/2 RB
2/3 RB
2/4 anon
2/5 RB
2/6 anon
2/7 anon
2/8 anon
2/9 CS
2/10 anon
2/11 anon
2/12 CS
2/13 anon
2/14 RB
2/15 RB
2/16 RB
2/17 RB
2/18 RB
2/19 RB
2/20 RB
2/21 RB
2/22 RB
2/23 RB
2/24 RB
2/25 RB
2/26 RB
2/27 RB
2/28 RB
2/29 RB
2/30 RB

Corkscrews
3/1 DB
3/2a RB
3/2b DB
3/3 DB
3/4 DB
3/5 DB
3/6 DB
3/7 DB
3/8 DB
3/9 DB
3/10 DB
3/11 DB
3/11 DB
3/12 DB
3/13 DB
3/14 anon
3/15 anon
3/16 DB
3/17 JE
3/18 RB
3/19 DB
3/20 anon
3/21 JE
3/22 DB
3/23 DB
3/24 anon
3/25 DB
3/26 DB
3/27 JE
3/28 DB
3/29 DB
3/30 DB
3/31 DB
3/32 DB
3/33 JE
3/34 CS
3/35 CS
3/36 DB
3/37 RB
3/38 DB
3/39 RB
3/40 RB
3/41 RB
3/42 JE
3/43 JE
3/44 RB
3/45 RB
3/46 JE
3/47 JE
3/48 DB
3/49 DB
3/50 DB
3/51 DB
3/52 JE
3/53 JE
3/54 JE
3/55 JE
3/56 JE
3/57 DB
3/58 D
3/59 DB
3/60 DB
3/61 DB

Tasters
4/1 CH
4/2 CH
4/3 RB
4/4 RB
4/5 CH
4/6 NS
4/7 VC
4/8 RB
4/9 D
4/10 RB
4/11 B
4/12 B
4/13 B
4/14 B
4/15 B
4/16 JB-S
4/17 RP
4/18 RP
4/19 RB

Coolers
5/1 BM
5/2 BHC
5/3 MA
5/4 BHC
5/5a RB
5/5 EH
5/6 RB
5/7 CH
5/8 MA
5/9 J
5/10 MA
5/11 MA
5/12 KRA
5/13 MA
5/14 MA
5/15 RPB
5/16 MA
5/17 GH
5/18 RB
5/19 PCS
5/20 M
5/21 RB
5/22 RPL
5/23 AF
5/24 PL
5/25 RPL
5/26 anon
5/27 RPL
5/28 BCP
5/29 anon
5/30 RPL
5/31 A
5/32 RPL
5/33 RPL
5/34 RPL
5/35 RPL
5/36 RPL
5/37 RPL
5/38 PL
5/38a RB
5/39 RB
5/40 NA
5/41 RPL
5/42 PS
5/43 RB
5/44 J
5/45 RPL
5/46 A
5/47 MH
5/48 RG
5/49 RG
5/50 LC
5/51 BA
5/52 JW
5/53 BA
5/54 RPL
5/55 RPL
5/56 RB

Funnels
6/1 DBA
6/2 SS
6/3 SS
6/4 JPS
6/5 anon
6/6 AE
6/7 LG
6/88 RB
6/9 NS
6/10 RB
6/11 BS
6/12 RB
6/13 HW
6/14 PCS
16/5 BS
6/16 RB
6/17 CS
6/18 BS
6/19 VC
6/20 SL
6/21 DB
6/22 anon
6/23 RB
6/24 anon
6/25 RB

Decanters
7/01 RB
7/1 RB
7/2 RB
7/3 RM
7/4 VC
7/5 RB
7/6 D
7 VC
7/8 RB
7/9 RB
7/10 RB
7/11 D
7/12 RPL
7/13 RB
7/14 RPL
7/15 RB
7/16 RB
7/17 RPL
7/18 RPL
7/19 D
7/20 RB
7/21 RPL
7/22 RB
7/23 MW
7/24 RB
7/25 RB
7/26 VC
7/26a RM
7/27 RB
7/28 RB
7/29 RPL
7.30 M
7/31 RB
7/32 RB
7/33 RB
7/34 RB
7/35 RB
7/36 MW
7/37 RB
7/38 RB
7/39 RPB
7/40 RB
7/41 RB
7/42 RB
7/43 MW
7/44 RB
7/45 RB
7/46 RB
7/46 RB
7/47 RB
7/48 RB
7/49 MW
7/50 RB
7/51 MW
7/52 MW
7/53 AMc
7/54 RPL
7/55 RB
7/56 RB
7/57 anon
7/58 RB
7/59 RB

Wine Jugs
8/1 KRA
8/2 BBR
8/3 VC
8/4 JH
8/5 JH
8/6 JH
8/7 BHM
8/8 RB
8/9 D
8/10 anon
8/11 D
8/12 RPB
8/13 RPL
8/14 RPL
8/15 RB
8/16 RB
8/17 KC
8/18 KC
8/19 MA
8/20 KC
8/21 MA
8/22 KRA
8/23 MA
8/24 KRA
8/25 RB
8/26 D
8/27 RB
8/28 RB
8/29 RB
8/30 IF
8/31 RB
8/32 KC
8/33 RB
8/34 RB
8/35 RB
8/36 RB
8/37 KRA
8/38 KC
8/39 KC
8/40 MA
8/41 KC
8/42 NS
8/43 NS
8/44 KC
8/45 KC
8/46 EL
8/47 KC
8/48 KC
8/49 KC
8/50 KC
8/51 KC
8/52 MA
8/53 MA
8/54 RB
8/55 KC
8/56 KC
8/57 RB

Wine labels
9/1 VC
9/2 RB
9/3 RB
9/4 SHF
9/5 SHF
9/6 TG
9/7 SHF
9/8 SHF
9/9 AE
9/10 VC
9.11 RB
9/12 VC
9/13 SHF
9/14 RB
9/15 RB
9/16 anon
9/17 anon
9/18 RB
9/19 anon
9/20 RB
9/21 anon
9/22 anon
9/23 RB
2/24 anon
9/25 RB
9/27 anon
9/28 anon
9/29 anon
9/30 anon
9/31 anon
9/32 RB
9/33 RB
9/34 anon
9/35 RB
9/36 SHF
9/37 RB
9/38 SHF
9/39 RB
9/40 RB
9/41 anon
9/42 RB
9/43 SHF
9/44 SHF
9/45 SHF
9/46 SHF
9/47 RB
9/48 RB
9/49 SHF
9/50 anon
9/51 RB
9/52 RB
9/53 TG
9/54 SHF
9/55 RB
9/56 RB
9/57 SHF
9/58 RB
9/59 RB
9/60 TG
9/61 TG

Coasters
10/1 KRA
10/2 RB
10/3 CH
10/4 PCL
10/5 RPL
10/6 RB
10/7 HW
10/8 RPL
10/9 RB
10/10 RB
10/11 KRA
10/12 RB
10/13 RB
10/14 MA
10/15 DFB
10/16 JS
10/17 RPL
10/18 MA
10/19 KRA
10/20 RB
10/21 RB
10/22 RB
10/23 MA
10/24 VC
10/25 M
10/26 RB
10/2 7 RB
10/28 RB
10/29 RB
10/30 JS
10/31 RB
10/32 RB
10/33 RB
10/34 RB
10/35 RB
10/36 RB
10/37 RB
10/38 RB
10/39 RB
10/40 anon
10/41 JH
10/42 RPL
10/43 AF
10/44 anon
10/45 RPB
10/46 KP
10/47 RB
10/48 F
10/49 AJ
10/50 RB
10/51 LC
10/52 RB
10/53 D
10/54 RB
10/55 RB
10/56 AF
10/57 anon
10/59 J
10/60 AF

Glasses
11/1 VC
11/2 VC
11/3 D
11/4 MA
11/5 RB
11/6 RB
11/7 VC
11/8 RB
11/9 NS
11/10 CH
11/11 MA
11/12 IF
11/13 MW
11/14 RB
11/15 GS
11/16 D
11/17 D
11/18 D
11/19 RM
11/19a GS
11/20 GS
11/21 RB
11/22 D
11/23 D
11/24 D
11/25 RB
11/26 RB
11/27 GS
11/28 D
11/29 RB
11/30 RB
11/31 RB
11/32 RB
11.33 RB
11/34 D
11/35 D
11/36 D
11/37 D
11/38 RM
11/39 GS
11/40 D
11/41 D
11/42 RB
11/43 RB
11/44 RB
11/45 RB
11/46 D
11/47 RB
11/48 RB
11/49 RB

Miscellaneous
12/1 anon
12/2 RPB
12/3 RB
12/4 JB
12/5 anon
12/6 WL
12/7 RPL
12/8 RPL
12/9 anon
12/10 PL
12/11 AFL
12/12 anon
12/13 anon
12/14 RB
12/15 RPL
12/16 RB
12/17 RB
12/18 S
12/19 RB
12/20 SW
12/21 anon
12/22 C&C
12/23 RB
12/24 anon
12/25 anon
12/26 RB
12/27 RB
12/28 RB
12/29 DB
12/30 DB
12/31 DB
12/32 RB
12/33 RB
12/34 RB
12/35 RB
12/36 RB
12/37 RB
12/38 CS
12/39 RPL
12/40 RPL
12/41 VC
12/42 DB
12/43 RB
12/44 DB
12/45 RB
12/46 RB
12/47 RB
12/48 RB
12/49 CS
12/50 RB
12/52 RPB
12/53 RB
12/57 RB

Fakes forgeries and other problems.
For reasons that are probably obvious, the owners of all the fakes, forgeries and other problems, have chosen to remain anonymous.

Key

A	Anthemion	Cartmel, Cumbria
AE	The Antique Enamel Company	London
AF	Apter Fredericks	London
AFL	Anthony Fell	Holt, Norfolk
AJ	Anthony James Antiques	London
A McC	Andy McConnell	Rye, Sussex
B	Bonhams	London
BA	Butchoff Antiques	London
BBR	BBR Auctions	Elsecar, Barnsley, S. Yorkshire
BCP	Blair Castle,	Perthshire
BH	Anonymous collection	
BHC	Burghley House Collection	Stamford, Lincolnshire
BHM	Broadfield House Glass Museum	Kingswinford, W. Midlands
BM	British Museum	London
BS	B Silverman	London
C	Cohen & Cohen	Reigate, Surrey
CH	Christopher Hartop	Pudding Norton, Norfolk
CS	Christopher Sykes	Woburn, Bedfordshire
D	Delomosne & Son	North Wraxall, Chippenham, Wiltshire
DB	Don Bull	USA www.bullworks.net/virtual.htm
DBA	Daniel Bexfield Antiques	London
DFB	David Foord-Brown Antiques	Cuckfield, W. Sussex
EH	Edward Hurst	Coombe Bisset, Salisbury, Wiltshire
EL	Elliott Lee	London
F	Finch & Co.	London
GH	Grey-Harris	Clifton, Bristol
GS	Ged Selby Antique Glass	Embsay, Skipton, N. Yorkshire
HW	Henry Willis, Sherborne	Dorset
IF	I Franks	London www.ifranks.com
J	Jeremy	London
JB	James Brett Antiques	Norwich
JB-S	J H Bourdon-Smith	London
JE	John Ericson Esq.	
JH	Sampson & Horne Antiques	Mayfair, London
JPS	John P Smith Esq.	
JS	Jason Sandeberg	London
JW	John Walker Antiques	Rait, Scotland
KC	Kent Collection	www.claretjugs.com
KD	Balmain Antiques	Cumbria
KRA	Koopman Rare Art	London
KP	W A Pinn & Sons	Sible Hedingham, Essex
LC	Lennox Cato	Edenbridge, Kent
LG	Lawrence Gould	London
M	Mallett & Son (Antiques)	London
MA	Marks Antiques	London
MH	Haughey Antiques	Kirby Stephen, Cumbria
MW	Mark West	Redhill, Surrey
NA	Norman Adams	London
NS	Nicholas Shaw Antiques	Petworth, W. Sussex
PCL	Peter Cameron	London
PL	Peter Lipitch	London
PS	Patrick Sandberg Antiques	London
RG	Richard Gardner Antiques	Petworth, W. Sussex
RB	Butler's Antiques	Shalford, Essex. www.butlersantiques.com
RM	Marris Antiques	Sudbury, Suffolk
RP	Richard Phillips	Australia
RPB	Roderick Butler	Honiton, Devon
RPL	Ronald Phillips	Mayfair, London
S	Sothebys	London
SW	Sworders	Stansted Mountfitchet, Essex
SHF	Steppes Hill Farm Antiques	Stockbury, Sittingbourne, Kent
SS	Simon Spero	London
TG	Terry Gill Esq.	
VC	The Worshipful Company of Vintners	London
WL	Wakelin & Linfield	Billingshurst, W Sussex

Special thanks

From Martin Mortimer and Tim and Vicky Osborne of Delomosne & Son, I have, over a period of many years, learned much about glass generally and they have provided many images of wine glasses and decanters; their generosity of spirit is an example to which all in the antiques trade should aspire. Simon Phillips of Ronald Phillips is another very generous dealer in making his furniture and glass images available, and he has done so with great kindness. Phil Chaney very kindly allowed me to pore over his extraordinarily eclectic collection of wine accessories and to photograph them, having never even met me before. Mark West sent me many good pictures of his glass, and Don Bull provided me with a large number of great images of a wonderful collection of corkscrews. Without them this book would have been much the poorer.

John Culme very kindly provided me with some splendid images from Marks Antiques and helped with useful snippets of information to enrich the text, while Nick Shaw and I have had many happy hours in conversation about the world of antiques and he has allowed me to have images I would not have found elsewhere. Timo Koopman and his staff have also been extremely helpful and provided some wonderful images of fine silver and silver-gilt for which I am very grateful. Christopher Sykes and his assistant, the late Sally Lloyd, have been known for antique wine accessories for many years and have always been the epitome of generosity and help. Others who have been particularly helpful are Christopher Hartop, Jon Culverhouse at Burghley House, Kari Moodie at Broadfield House Glass Museum, David Buck, Jason Sandeberg, and Peter Cameron. In short, every dealer or individual I have approached for information and images has been utterly generous in their responses and those not named here will be found in the picture credits. Such co-operation is to be expected within a trade where trust and straightforward dealings are far more usual than most people imagine.

The majority of pictures in this book have come directly from dealers as digital images sent over the internet; some have arrived as CDs. I have taken many myself, but two professional photographers have shown me how it really should have been done; they are Henry Wilson and Douglas Atfield. They each went on assignment to London and took superb images without which the book would have been deprived of some fine glass, silver and furniture.

Finally, I would like to express my considerable thanks to the Worshipful Company of Vintners who not only allowed me to photograph fine pieces from their collections, and made their staff available to help in doing so, but also for their very generous contribution towards the cost of the images. In particular, I would like to thank Past Master, John Avery MW for kindly introducing me to the company, Brigadier Michael Smythe, the Clerk, and Major Stephen Marcham, the General Manager. They all gave most generously of their time when they were very busy.

Index

A
acid etching (see etching)
Acme 65
acorn shape 174
Adam, Robert and James 103
agate 44, 45
Albert, Prince Consort 56, 161, 265
ale (see beer)
Allen, William 117
Alloa glassworks 22, 23
amber 45
America 7, 9, 11, 25, 26, 59, 64, 65, 262
Andrews, John 19
antique/antiques 8
Antique Metalware Society 275
Antwerp 224
Aquitaine 68, 71
Armstrong, Henry 62
Army & Navy Cooperative Society 175
Army & Navy Stores 62
art deco 80, 171, 172, 177
art nouveau 80, 177
arts & crafts 177
askos 161, 167
ash 201
Ashbee, Charles Robert 177
Ashmolean Museum Oxford 196
Asprey & Co 9
Atholl, Duke of 90
auctions/auctioneers 9, 32, 69, 271
Australia 191, 273

B
Bacchus/bacchic 83, 174, 175, 180, 199, 200, 265, 276
baize 89, 94, 105, 196, 206, 256, 257
Baker, William 62
baluster shape 131, 149, 156, 164, 166, 168, 175, 206, 217, 225 (see also wine glasses)
Barcelona 183
Barker, Robert 187
Barlow 54
Barnard, Edward 73, 166, 176, 217-219
Barnard, Edward & John 73
baroque style 77, 78, 162, 201, 221
barrel 14, 26
basket 267
Bateman, Hester 116, 127, 184
Bateman, Peter & Ann 187
Battersea 182
beech 196, 199, 200
beer 25, 28, 29, 154, 156, 228, 242, 265
Beilby, William & Mary 6, 124, 277
Belfast 139
Beaune 182
bellarmine 154
binning 10, 17, 26-39, 178, 231
bin labels (see labels)
bin numbers 34, 36-38
Birmingham 48, 50, 51, 55, 112, 140, 147, 182, 186, 204, 227, 263, 273
biscuit 28, 32, 38
black velvet 265
Blackwell, Richard 226
Blair Castle 90
bocksbeutel 167

Bohemian glass 125, 147
Boileau, J. J. 81
Bojanowski, Carl 77
Bollinger, Madame Lily 266
Bolsover, Thomas 180
bone 50, 51, 53, 152
'boot and flogger' 8
Bordeaux 7, 2, 25, 32, 67, 71, 157, 265, 266
bottle
    boot 258
    box 256, 257
    canterbury 103, 108
    carrier 256-259, 264
    holder 265, 266, 269
    lock 365
    stand 108, 196
    tray 256, 257, 261, 279
    tickets (see wine labels)
bottles 8, 12-25, 77, 79, 83, 86-89, 93, 94, 100, 102, 103, 105, 108, 110, 128, 131, 157, 271
    bladder shape 14, 16
    cylindrical 17, 20-22
    globular 23
    mallet shape 17, 19
    onion shape 14-16, 18
    serving 127, 194
    shaft and globe 14, 15, 23,
    with handles 15, 17, 157
Boulton, Matthew 48, 49, 140
Bourguignon (see Gravelot)
Bowes, Sir Jerome 224
boxes 47, 57, 63, 267-269
boxwood 92, 102, 208, 215, 251
brandewijn 69, 73
brandy 10, 33, 69, 132, 147, 183-186, 190, 240, 263
brass 42, 51, 77, 79, 86, 88, 89-91, 96-99, 102, 108, 206-208, 210, 216, 264
bright cutting 180, 183, 184, 211
Bristol 8, 22, 24, 25, 132, 142, 147, 150, 235
Bristol blue 132, 147, 213, 240
Bristol City Museum 68
Britannia standard 70, 73, 77, 120
British Museum 75, 76, 80, 83
Bronte 29, 30
bronze 42, 51, 53, 152
Brooks's Club 265
brushes 42, 49, 54, 61, 63, 266
Buccleuch and Queensberry, Duke of 7, 9
Bucellas 189, 191, 192
Burgundy/burgundy 7, 9, 25, 68, 190, 265
burr elm 106
Burrell Collection, Glasgow 82
Bushby 191
butler's cabinet 260
butler's tray 256, 260

C
Cabinet Makers' London Book of Prices 251, 257
Calcavela 30
canteen 42
canterbury 103, 108
Cape 181
capilare 190
capsule 17, 42, 49, 266
carafes 124-151, 374
carboy 18, 25

carnelian 44
Carré, Jean 224
cases (see boxes)
Casson, Samuel 69
cast decoration 53, 83, 119, 122, 162, 166, 181, 183, 186, 196, 199, 200, 217-219
castors 91-93, 96, 99, 102, 104, 107, 108, 207, 214, 255
Caughley 72
cellaret 29, 32, 40, 74, 93-109, 250, 272
chalcedony 44
Chambers, Cornelius 65
Champagne/champagne 7, 9, 10, 17, 28, 30-33, 182, 190, 242, 244, 245, 265-269
    bottle sealer 268
    coupes 244, 245, 269
    pliers 63, 266
    siphon 266, 267
    stand 269
    tap 266, 267, 269
Channel Islands 70, 273
Charlotte, Queen 188
chateaux 31, 35
Chester 112, 116
China/Chinese 204, 210, 258
Chinese style/chinoiserie 72, 79, 99, 113, 196, 204
Chippendale, Thomas 92, 99, 103, 127, 198, 270
cider/cyder 14, 25, 29, 181
claret 7, 9, 26, 29, 31, 32, 35, 133, 155, 181, 183, 184, 186, 188, 190, 192, 193, 197, 208, 228, 244
claret jugs (see jugs)
Clay, Henry 204, 261
close-plating 77, 79, 86
clubs and societies 10, 19, 25, 40, 178, 279 (see also under individual names)
coasters 9, 10, 126, 129, 194-221, 254, 255, 261, 275
    bases of 196, 200-203, 206, 209, 212, 214, 215, 217
    boat-shaped 214-216
    brass 210
    Chinese 204, 210
    chinoiserie 196, 198, 204
    die-stamped 199
    double/triple 195, 214-216, 218, 219, 252
    electroplated 199, 200, 202, 203, 210
    glass 212, 213
    hallmarking of 202
    Irish 206
    leather 212
    pairs of 197-199, 201, 203-206, 209, 212, 214, 216, 218
    paktong 210
    papier mâché 204, 205, 211, 212, 214, 216
    pewter 210, 211
    pottery 212, 213
    rhinoceros horn 210
    rolled paperwork 210, 211
    sets of 196, 197, 200, 205, 213
    Sheffield plate 200, 202-204, 216
    shield 208, 209, 252
    silver 196-203, 210, 214, 215, 217, 220
    silver gilt 199, 201, 202, 216, 218, 219, 221
    treen 206-209, 215
    turned 204-207
    wheeled 216-220
    wirework 202, 203

Coalport 28
cobalt oxide 132, 147
cocus wood 54, 55, 65, 150, 264
coffee pots 153, 157
Colchester 67, 68
Collard, John 16
construction (see furniture construction)
Cooke, Richard 215
Cookworthy, William 132, 147, 213
Cooper Hewitt Museum, New York, 9
Copeland 32, 174
copper 79, 80, 115
copper wash 61, 62
Cork Glass Co 139
'cork drawing stand' 256
cork mounts 263
corks 8, 13, 17, 42, 44, 51, 65, 110, 112, 133, 148, 266, 267
corkscrews 7-9, 28, 40-65, 110, 123, 126, 250, 256, 260, 266, 268, 271
    Empire 62
    folding bow 43, 60
    King's screw 54, 55, 56
    lazy tongs 62
    London Lever 56, 57
    London Rack 56
    peg and worm 44, 48
    Presto 59
    Pullezi 62
    roundlet 47, 58
    Royal Club 59, 60
    Wilson's patent 61
    Wulfrana 61
Cornwall 147
Cotterell, H.H, *Old Pewter* 210
Courtauld, Augustine 196
creamware 72, 212, 213
Crespel, Andrew & Parker, Thomas 167
Crichton, Alexander, 172, 173
crizzling 127, 156, 228
cruet 275
Cruikshank, George 132
crutches 252
Cumberland, Ernst Augustus, Duke of 263
cups 222, 224-226 (see also goblets)
    dram 226
    coconut wager 226
Curry, John 172
cutlery tray 257
Cyprus 181

D
Dainty, William 123
Daniell, Thomas 73
Davenport, 86
decanter
    carrier 256, 261
    slide 252
    stand 221
    trolley/wagon 9, 10, 194-221
decanters 7, 9, 10, 40, 93, 103, 105, 106, 110, 114, 117, 120-151, 155-157, 180, 184, 194-221, 243, 251, 252, 254, 274
    champagne 130, 133
    coloured 132, 133, 138, 142, 143, 146, 150, 213
    cruciform 128-130
    cylindrical 132, 143, 146, 147
    handled 123, 157, 160
    Hodgett's/Hoggett 135
    icing 132, 133
    indian club 130-133
    with Lynn decoration 124
    mallet 129, 130
    onion-shaped 108, 126, 128
    pear-shaped 157
    pocketed 130, 133
    prussian 130, 132, 138, 139-143
    Rodney 133
    shaft and globe 126-130, 132, 144, 145, 149-151, 166, 192, 193, 205, 207, 233, 244
    ship's 132, 133, 135-137, 159
    sugar loaf 129-133
    taper 130, 132, 133
decanting 9, 17, 110, 112, 120, 126, 258, 259, 262, 263
    cradle 264
Delft, Holland 28, 71
delftware (see tin-glazed earthenware)
Delomosne & Son 9
Derby 70-72
Desvignes, Peter 198
dining habits 10, 11, 80, 104, 161, 214, 244
Dionysus (see Bacchus)
dipstick 8
Dorrell, Jane & May, Richard 183, 184
Dorrell, William, 184
Douro 7
Dowler 54
Dresser, Christopher 131, 132, 171, 172, 177
drinking glasses (see wine glasses)
Drinkwater, Sandilands 180, 181, 192
Dublin 46, 48, 129, 184, 201
Dudley, West Midlands 168
dumb waiter 10, 254, 255
Dumfries 189

E
Earle & Co 31
earthenware (see pottery)
Eastbourne 154
East India Company 189, 210
East, John 70
Eaton, William 192
ebony 54, 206, 215, 250, 260
Eclipse 65
Edinburgh 49, 112, 117, 119, 185, 190, 194, 227
Edington, James Charles 165
Edwards, B., Belfast 139
Edwards, John 203
Egyptian style 81, 102, 276
electroplate 80, 85, 86, 112, 167, 168, 186, 199, 200, 202, 203, 263, 264, 266, 267, 276
Eley, William 122
Elkington & Co 171, 203
Emanuel, Maurice & Michael 162
Emes, John 208
Emes, Rebecca & Barnard, Edward 121
enamelling 6, 146, 182
engraving 19, 21, 43, 68, 73, 80, 116, 117, 129, 133, 146, 168-171, 196, 198, 199, 220, 221, 225, 263
    diamond point 16, 23, 146, 224, 228, 232, 237
    stipple 24, 237
    wheel 126, 131, 134, 144, 146, 147, 158, 165, 166, 168, 169, 237
etching 146, 150, 168, 169, 244
etui 42
ewers 156, 162, 276, 279
Exeter 112, 116
exhibitions 8, 9

F
facetting 48, 236, 237, 241, 243
fakes and forgeries 270-278
Far East 7, 11
Farrell, Edward 186, 189
Farren, Thomas 78
Farrow & Jackson 28, 29, 32, 34, 37-39, 46, 54-56, 60, 151, 244, 246, 256, 258, 259, 268, 269
Favell, Rupert & Elliott, Henry 266
fermentation 14, 16
Fernell, Edward 187
Fiennes, Celia 76
Figg, John 161, 162, 221
filters and filtration 111-114, 117-121
flagons (see jugs)
flat-chasing 180, 181
Fogelberg, Andrew & Gilbert, Stephen 153
foil 266, 267
Fox, Charles 63, 118, 121
Fox, George 170
Fray, James 201
France and French forms 20, 45, 48, 64, 65, 76, 86, 102, 132, 177, 212, 228, 264, 266, 273, 276
funnels (see wine funnels)
furniture construction 92, 93, 96, 99, 104, 260, 261
Furniture History Society 279

G
Gamon, John 196
garde de vin (see wine coolers)
Garrard, R & S 162
Garrard, Robert 84, 162, 191
Garthorne, George 273
Gentleman's Cellar and Butler's Guide 266
George I 230
George III 199, 263
George V 150
German silver 58, 266
Germany 58, 65, 226, 265
Gieson, William van 59
Gilberd/Gilbert 67, 68
Gilbey 9
gilding 91, 92, 132, 172, 204, 205, 239
Giles, James 239, 240
Gillows 100-102
gin 186
ginger 29
Gladstone, William 26
Glasgow 194
glass
    cameo 83, 168, 175
    cased 143, 146, 147, 165, 169, 244
    coloured 146, 147, 165, 168, 169, 244 (see also decanters and jugs)
    cranberry 177
    cutting 87, 114, 129-133, 136-145, 148, 149, 151, 159, 161, 165, 166, 169, 176, 217, 244, 245, 265

glass (cont)
  enamelled 146, 177
  engraved 146
  etched 146
  flint 156, 228
  frosted 161, 164, 166, 175
  lead 7, 127, 156, 228, 229, 277
  blowing 14, 17, 20, 128, 132, 134, 150, 224, 240
  making 224, 228
  soda 228, 242, 277
  stained 146, 147
Glass Circle 279
glasses (see wine glasses)
goblets 6, 9, 222-243, 277 (see also cups)
  lidded 225
  silver 225-227
  silver gilt 152, 153, 224, 227
Goffe, John & Son, Birmingham 175
gold 11, 45, 47, 58, 75, 76, 80
Goldsmiths, Worshipful Company of/
Goldsmiths' Hall 9, 42, 69, 73, 117, 180, 181, 273, 279
gooseberry 29
gothic decoration 53, 54, 80, 95, 102, 105, 165, 186, 193, 200, 220
Gravelot, Hubert, François (Bourguignon) 79
grave, vin de 29 191
Great Fire of London 69
Grecian style 105, 107, 153, 168
Green & Co, London 164
Greene, John 228
Grinsell, John & Sons 267
Guild of Handicraft 177
Guinness 265
Gwin, James 182

H
hallmarks 11, 46, 47, 69, 73, 75, 116, 120, 154, 172, 177, 183, 185, 196, 202, 262, 263, 266, 273
Hamilton, Gavin 82
Hamilton, Sir William 82, 83
Hanover 263
harewood 97
Harvey, John 262
Harvey's Wine Museum 8
Hayne, Samuel & Cater, Dudley, 220
Heath & Middleton, 177, 267
Heely, James & Son 52, 54, 58
Heely, Neville 62
Heming, Thomas 183
Hennell, Robert 119, 198
Henshall, Revd Samuel 40, 42, 45, 48-50
Hepplewhite, George 96, 251
heraldry 14, 58, 76, 77, 81, 82, 111, 117-119, 126, 155-157, 167, 168, 184, 186-191, 196-201, 210, 215, 217-220, 225, 263, 272
hermitage 28, 188, 193
Hermitage Museum, 77
Hipkins, William 56
hock 10, 29, 35, 181, 185, 186, 188, 189, 244, 265
Hockley, Daniel 190
Hodson, John 90
Holland 226, 262, 278
hollands (gin) 132, 146, 184, 186, 240

hooks 29, 37, 38, 60, 97, 204, 218
Hope, Thomas 102, 105
Hukin & Heath 171, 172, 176, 177
Huguenot 75-77, 80, 196
Hull, Charles 59, 60
Hunt, John S 193
Hunt & Roskill 174
Hutton, William & Sons 175
Hyde, Thomas 184
hydrometer 8

I
ice 74, 83, 84, 87, 90, 93, 130, 133
ice pail 86, 87
ivory 49, 54, 63, 95, 157, 173, 192, 193, 216, 218, 271
imperial 25
India 189, 192, 193, 210, 211
inns (see taverns)
inscriptions 69, 79, 121, 155
Ipswich 67, 68
Ireland and Irish forms 10, 46-48, 70, 93, 103, 108, 109, 112, 139, 141, 156, 206, 255
Iron 135
  cast 64, 264
  wrought 264
Italy 65, 212

J
Jackson, Walter
Jacobites 232, 233, 234, 237
Japanning 54, 76, 79, 123, 258, 259
jardinière 90, 94
Jefferson, Thomas 271
Jennens & Bettridge 204, 261
Jerez 7, 155
Jernegan 75, 77, 79
jeroboam 25, 266
Johnson, Hugh 7,8
Jones, Robert & Son 49, 51, 55
jugs
  animal shapes 172, 173
  beer 156
  bird shapes 172, 173
  burgundy 164
  claret 148, 149, 152-177, 217, 276, 279
  coloured 160-162, 165, 169
  flask 167, 169
  hot water 153, 157
  with icing pocket 166
  indian club shape 159
  with metal mounts 161, 162, 164, 165, 168, 170-177
  silver 157, 166, 167
  water 166
  wine 152-177

K
Kandler, Charles 77
Kentwell Hall, Suffolk 35
kick 15, 17
knife 57, 266, 268

L
labels 132 (see also wine labels)
  bin 26-39, 96, 271
  makers' 207, 250

paper 26, 29, 186
lacquering 91, 123, 204, 216, 275
Langford, John & Sebille, John 197, 198
lead 26, 34, 49, 89, 90, 96
leather 93, 96, 99, 126, 135, 216, 258, 266, 267
Lee, J 158
Leman, W 22
Lestourgeon, William 197
lettering 26, 28-34, 39, 43
lighting 26, 130, 141
lignum vitae 200
Lisbon/lisbon 182, 184, 189
locks 94
Lund, Thomas 42, 56, 57
Lund, William, 56, 57, 266
Lysle, Anthony de 224

M
Mackay, J 119
Madeira/madeira 10, 28-30, 35, 182, 183, 185-189, 192, 193, 197, 252, 276
magnum 19, 23, 131, 133, 135, 139-142, 145, 148, 150, 151, 154, 174, 176, 196, 197, 200, 201, 206, 220, 254, 263
mahogany 54, 57, 76, 88-93, 95, 97, 98, 102-105, 109, 196, 198, 201, 206-209, 214, 215, 250-257, 260, 264
Makepiece, Robert 181
Malaga 155, 181, 182
Mallett & Son 176, 194
malmsey 30, 183
malvasia 183
Mansell, Sir Robert 224
manzanilla 192
marble 90, 91
Marie Antoinette 244, 245
Marie-Jeanne 25, 151
Marlborough, Earl/Duke of 75, 76, 80
Marquand, Frederick, New York 262
marriages 271, 272
marsala 30, 186, 192
Martin, George 226
marvering 15, 17
Marwood, Frederick T 64
Marx, Frederick & Louis 58
masonic emblems 22
Mauger, Thomas, Jersey 273
McConnell, Andy 130
McCrea, Frank Bradford 175
mead 183
Mein, James, Kelso 207
mell 148
Methuen Treaty 189
Methuselah 25
Metropolitan Museum, New York 79
mis-spellings 30, 33, 182, 183, 190
monteith 258, 262
Mordan, Sampson 173
Morel, Jean-Valentin & Co 85
Morel, Sèvres 276
Morrell, Anne & William 15
Morelli, Alessio 228
mother of pearl 148, 182, 184, 185, 261, 263
mountain 181, 182, 186
mugs 265
museums 8, 9

N
Nailsea 23, 142, 150
neck rings/string rings 16, 17, 19, 128-130,132-140, 142, 143, 150, 165
Nelson 30, 81, 102, 181, 260
neoclassical style 77, 81, 94, 95, 98, 105, 153, 156, 157, 180, 184, 196, 198, 210, 211, 227
Newcastle-upon-Tyne 112, 124, 142, 181, 190
Newton, Alfred 59
Nice/Neece 190
Nicholson, Peter & Angelo 105
nickel plating 55, 61, 62, 266, 267
Norman, Samuel 92
nutmeg 42, 43
nutmeg grater 43

O
oak 76, 90, 102, 105, 250
octagonal shape 19, 80, 91, 92, 96, 99, 157
old hock 189
ormolu 81, 87, 94, 115
Osler, F& J 147
ostrich egg 224
oyster bucket 93

P
paktong 210, 266
Pantin, Simon 196
papier mâché 204, 211, 212, 216, 261, 275
parcel gilding 92
parian ware 174
Paris 28, 32
Parker, Robert 11
patents 24, 25, 40, 45, 48, 49, 51, 52, 54, 56, 59, 60-62, 64, 65, 123, 265, 266
patina 15, 272, 275, 279
Pearson, John 189
Pearson Page 210, 275
Penrose, Waterford 139
Peppin, Robert 118
Pepys, Samuel 7, 14, 68
perfume bottles 45, 47, 48
pewter 70, 210, 211
Phipps, Thomas & Robinson, Edward 73, 187, 262
pine 102
pipe 35
pipe tampers 43
Piranesi 82
Pitts, William & Preedy, George 81
Plant, Stephen 61
planter (see jardinière)
plastic 271
plywood 206, 208
poison 69, 73, 240
pontil 17, 240, 243
porcelain 38, 258
port 9, 10, 26, 28, 29, 31, 32, 35, 135, 151, 181, 183-188, 190-192, 197, 208, 212, 213, 244, 252
    strainer (see wine funnels)
    tongs 268
Portland Vase 83
Portugal/Portuguese 189, 264
pottery 28, 76, 152, 154 (see also stoneware, creamware and tin-glazed earthenware)
Powell, Harry 150
Powell, James 150
Preston, Benjamin 217
prices 10, 11, 25, 279
privateers 22, 235, 237
punch 43, 258
punch bowl 262
punched decoration 69, 183
purpleheart 102

Q
quaich 69, 73
quillwork (see rolled paperwork)

R
Ramsden, Omar 203
Rathburne, Aaron 123
Ravenet, Simon Francis 182
Ravenshead Crystal 7
Ravenscroft, George 7, 124, 126, 127, 228
Rawlings, Charles & Summers, William 191-193
Read, Thomas 48
Redgrave, Richard 261
registration marks 168, 261
registration of designs 51, 173, 266
Reily, Charles & Storer, George 55, 56, 161, 162, 164, 165
Reily, John 190, 191
renaissance style 150, 154, 168, 191
reproduction 107, 270
restoration 97, 275
retailers 161, 164, 172, 174, 200, 201, 218, 265, 266
rhenish 181
Rhineland 154
rhinoceros horn 210, 211
Richards, George & Brown, Edward C 265
Richardson, Stourbridge 168
Ricketts, Henry 22, 24
Ridge, Joseph 265
Roberts, John & Co 199
rock crystal 150, 279
rococo style 43, 44, 77, 80, 92, 109, 177, 180, 184, 186, 193, 196-198, 200, 201, 206, 219, 221, 241, 261
Rodgers, Joseph 54
Rollos, Phillip 76, 77
roemer/römer 242
rolled paperwork 210, 211
rosewood 76, 200, 206
rum 132, 146, 183, 184, 186, 240, 242
rummer 242
Rundell Bridge & Rundell 81-83, 199, 200
Rundell, Philip, 83
rustic style 196, 197
Rysbrack, Michael 77

S
sack 7, 155, 228
salt glaze 154
St Petersburg 77
Santiago de Compostela 68
satinwood 92, 102, 203
sauterne 33, 188, 193
Saxony 132, 147
scallop 68, 70, 189
scent bottles (see perfume bottles)
Scotin, Gerard 79
Scotland and Scottish forms 22, 23, 49, 70, 73, 117, 148, 185, 186, 189, 194
Scott, Digby & Smith, Benjamin 82, 186, 188, 199, 200

scrimshaw 24
seals 14-24, 42, 43
Seaman, William 117
shagreen 47, 49
Sheffield 54, 138, 199, 265
Sheffield gilt 118, 195
Sheffield plate 76, 80, 81, 84, 86, 112, 180, 195, 199, 200, 216, 272
sherry 7, 10, 26, 28-31, 35, 183, 184, 186-189, 191, 192, 197, 244, 252
Shrapnel, Henry 56, 161
shrub 132, 184, 185
Sibley, Mary & Richard 201
sideboard 9, 74, 102, 103, 250, 256
silver 11, 43, 45, 49, 58, 63, 66, 69-71, 73, 76-85, 112, 116, 126, 133, 152, 156, 194, 196-203, 258, 262, 265 (see also hallmarks)
silver gilt 11, 55, 82, 83, 152-154, 162, 188, 190-192, 195, 199, 201, 216, 218, 219, 265
silver plate 143, 148, 266 (see also Sheffield plate)
Silver Society 279
Simon, André 7
Simson, George, 250
Singleton, Robert 46
Sissons, William & George 174
Sitges/Setjus 183
Slack, Benjamin 46
slate 34, 38, 39
Smith, Benjamin 188, 189, 191, 218
Smith, George 105
Smith, James 49
Sophia Augusta, Princess 263
South Staffordshire 182
Spain 155
spirits (see brandy, rum, hollands)
Spode 28, 32, 33
Stalker & Parker 79
Stevens & Williams, Stourbridge 168
stoneware 154
steel 47, 48, 55, 65, 128, 135, 264
stoppers, 126, 129, 130, 132, 133, 134, 136-139, 141-145, 148, 149, 151, 156, 157, 159, 165, 166, 169, 170, 177, 195, 214, 217, 218, 221, 263, 266-268, 274
Storr & Mortimer 161
Storr, Paul 82, 83, 120, 161, 174, 186, 190, 199, 200, 201
string rings (see neck rings)
Stuart, Stourbridge 150
Summers, William 193

T
tablecloth 9, 10, 89, 131, 132
tables
    dining 9, 194, 214
    horseshoe-shaped 9, 208, 251-253
    wine 254, 258
Tait, Benjamin 184
targs 112, 116-120
tapestries 76
tappit hen 25
tastevin (see wine tasters)
taverns 14, 15, 68, 242
terracotta 86
Thames 67, 70
thistle shape 121, 227
Thomason, Edward 51, 52, 54

Thompson, Charles Herbert 177
Thompson, William 47
Tiffany & Co, Paris 266
tiger ware 154, 168
Tillet, Gabriel 71
tin 33
tin-glazed earthenware 26, 28, 155, 262
toasts 9, 16, 222, 233
Todd Heatley 32
tôleware 86, 275
Tompion, Thomas 127
transfer printing 72, 182
tregnum 25
trolley (see decanter trolley)
tulipwood 93
Turner, Thomas & Co 265
Turton, William 184
Twigg, George 60, 61
Twyford, Robert 46

U
underglaze blue 70-72, 155
Unite, George 273
usquebaugh 69

V
Venice/Venetian 7, 126, 127, 138, 224, 226, 228, 229, 233
verre sur verre 177
Vertue, George 77
Verzelini, Giacomo 224
Victoria, Queen 263
Victoria & Albert Museum 9, 77, 79, 81
vintner 14, 26, 66, 68
Vintners, Worshipful Company of/Vintners' Hall 9, 42, 67, 68, 70, 126, 265

W
wagon (see decanter trolley)
Wakefield 252
waldglas 242
Wales and Welsh forms 70
Wales, Prince of/Prince Regent 24, 82, 158
walnut 54, 76, 90, 104
Wars of the Roses 66
Warwick Vase 82
Wastell, Samuel 70
Waterloo Co, Cork 139
Watson, Thomas 190
Watt, James 140
wax 13, 17, 42-44, 49
Webb, Thomas, Stourbridge 148, 168, 175
Wedgwood, 28, 32, 83, 212
West Indies 100
West Midlands 140, 161, 168
whisky 186
Whitefriars Glasshouse 150, 177
wicker 157, 259
Wier, Marshall 62
Willaume, David 80
Wilmot & Roberts 54
wine
    red 9, 128, 244
        white 9, 128, 142, 143, 155, 183, 244
wine bottles (see bottles)
wine cisterns 74, 76-79
wine coolers 29, 32, 74-107, 250, 256, 260, 272
    brass 210
    glass 86, 87
    hexagonal 91, 92, 96, 97, 99
    octagonal, 96, 99
    porcelain 86
    pottery 86
    sarcophagus form 102, 104, 105
    wood 88-107
wine drinking habits 9, 10, 11, 208, 214, 222, 242, 244, 251, 252, 254, 255, 269
wine fountains 76, 78, 265
wine funnels 9, 40, 110-123, 126, 129, 194, 262, 272 (see also tangs)
    electroplate 112
    enamel 112, 115
    glass 112, 114
    pewter 112, 116, 117
    pottery and porcelain 112, 114, 122
    Sheffield plate 112, 118
    silver 112, 116, 117
wine funnel stands 112, 117, 119, 122
wine glass coolers 258, 262
wine glasses 7-9, 114, 145, 161, 166, 222, 228-247, 254, 277, 278
    air twist stem 233-236
    Amen 232, 234, 237, 277
    baluster 7, 9, 229-231
    balustroid 229, 230
    coloured 240, 242, 244, 245
    colour twist stem 238, 277, 278
    deceptive 229, 230
    engraved 224, 230, 232, 233, 237, 241, 245
    etched 244, 245
    facet stem 9, 236, 237, 241, 243, 245
    firing 233, 236
    heavy baluster 228-230
    Jacobite 232-234, 277
    knops on 230, 231, 233, 235, 237
    latticino 228, 233
    Newcastle 231
    opaque twist stem 233, 235, 236, 239
    sets of 244-247
    Silesian stem 230, 231
    with gilding 239, 240
wine jugs (see jugs)
wine labels 8, 10, 40, 126, 128, 161, 164, 165, 178-193, 231, 262, 276
    bright cut 183, 184
    button 187
    cast 180, 181, 183, 186, 189, 190
    colonial 183
    crescent-shaped 180, 184, 185
    die-stamped 186, 190, 191, 192
    electroplated 186
    elephant 189
    enamel 182
    engraved and gilded 182
    escutcheons 180, 181
    flat-chased 180, 181
    foul anchor 185
    fretted 191
    gothic 186
    hallmarking 183
    heraldic 186, 187
    initial 186
    kidney-shaped 183
    letters 186, 191, 192
    made in China 184
    mother of pearl 182, 184, 185
    provincial 181, 182, 189, 190
    rectangular 180, 183, 185, 186, 190
    ring-form 186, 192
    Sheffield plate 181
    silver 178-193
    silver gilt 188-192
    tiger's claw 193
    vine leaf 186, 191, 192
wine merchants 8, 10, 11, 26, 31, 32, 35, 39, 66, 68, 69, 73, 150
wine shade 208
Wine Spectator 11
wine syphon
wine tasters 66-73
    glass 70
    pewter 70
    porcelain 70-72
    silver 67-71, 73
wine tray 261
Wolverhampton 61
Woolwich 154
Worcester 70, 71, 113, 239
wrigglework 180, 182, 210
Wright, James 63

Y
York 69, 112, 116
York, Duke of 77
York House Factory, Battersea

Z
zinc 33, 37, 38
Zouch, Sir Edward 224